Children's Bioethics

Children's Bioethics: The International Biopolitical Discourse on Harmful Traditional Practices and the Right of the Child to Cultural Identity

Maya Sabatello

MARTINUS
NIJHOFF
PUBLISHERS

2009

Library of Congress Cataloging-in-Publication Data

Sabatello, Maya.
Children's bioethics : the international biopolitical discourse on harmful traditional practices and the right of the child to cultural identity / Maya Sabatello.
p. cm.
Includes bibliographical references and index.
ISBN 978-90-04-17341-5
1. Children—Legal status, laws, etc. 2. Indigenous children—Legal status, laws, etc. 3. Children—Health and hygiene. 4. Medical ethics. I. Title.
K639.S23 2009
341.4'8572—dc22

2009000970

Koninklijke Brill NV incorporates the imprints Brill, Hotei Publishing, IDC Publishers, Martinus Nijhoff Publishers, and VSP.

PRINTED IN THE NETHERLANDS

In memory of my father, Eitan Franco Sabatello,

who entrenched in me the value of human rights.

TABLE OF CONTENTS

ACKNOWLEDGMENTS

I was about sixteen years old when a friend challenged me to watch the circumcision rite of a male newborn, a common, daily celebration among Jewish, Muslim, and other religious and cultural communities around the world. I won the bet, but the experience has profoundly changed my way of thinking. I became a vocal opponent of the practice, viewing it as barbaric. I took on the task of comprehensively examining the rite during my Ph.D. studies. After bouncing back and forth for some time about the legality of the practice, I eventually proved myself wrong: I cannot simply say, as perhaps I wanted to, that it was a human rights violation. That was the origin of this study. The journey was long, and I was lucky enough to have a number of people aiding and encouraging me throughout the process. At this point, I would like to express my gratitude and to thank them.

First, I would like to thank my mentor Dr. Alison Dundes Renteln for offering advice and for opening my mind to different ways of thinking. I would also like to express my appreciation to Professor Donald Miller and Dr. Janelle Wong for reading and for giving me constructive comments on my manuscript.

Secondly, I am indebted to the University of Southern California (USC), Los Angeles, for providing me with the most generous subsidies throughout the process as well as with a prolific intellectual environment. I would like to thank the Political Science Department and the Thematic Option Honors' Program for offering me the invaluable opportunity of combining teaching and research. Teaching "Law, Culture and Identity" with Dr. Renteln was particularly enriching and has been a great inspiration to my research and to my work since.

I am grateful to the USC Graduate School and Center for Religion and Civic Culture for awarding me fellowships and research grants. These awards were vital, and they enabled me to concentrate on my research and writing until its completion. In addition, I am incredibly appreciative to Dean Joan Metcalf Schaefer for granting me research awards. These awards were indispensable for the data collection, and they also made it possible for me to attend a session of the UN Committee on the Rights of the Child, Geneva, in May 2005, and to observe its work. I express my deep thanks to the Jesse M. Unruh Institute of Politics, USC: the special research award in the summer of 2003 that I received gave me the opportunity to experience, first hand, the interaction between international law, human rights, and politics at the United Nations, New York. This encounter has had a profound affect on both my professional and personal life. A special word of thanks also to Professor Sheldon Kamieniecki for brining me back in line when I started going in circles during my research and for his ongoing responsiveness and encouragement. Additionally, I thank the employees of the administrative staff of the Political Science Department for taking me under their wings and making my life so much easier.

During the writing process, I have been privileged to have a few other colleagues and friends who shared the experience with me. I am grateful to Dr. Vera Jelinek, Assistant Dean and Director of the Center for Global Affairs, NYU, MyKellann Ledden, and the rest of the staff there, for the tremendous opportunity they provided in allowing me to bring my research into practice and for the academic vibrancy of the center. I would also like to thank Dr. Howard S. Schiffman, founding director of the M.S. Program and clinical associate professor at the Center for Global Affairs for always believing in me and encouraging me to pursue my goals. I express my thanks to my close friends, Keren Shahar-Ben-Ami, Ady Schonmann, and Inbal Vanunu for sharing some of the toughest moments with me and for cheering me up. Special thanks also to Maxine Idakus, my editor, for her advice and for helping bring this book to conclusion.

I could not have completed this work without the support of the Sabatello family: my mother, Ilana, for her love and unwavering support; my brother Eilon, for always being proud of me and for going diving with me so I could take my mind off work; and my sister Ionit, for her assistance with the cover design. I am grateful to Orit for her encouragement and technical advice and to Yali who, even in the most stressful moments, always brought a smile to my face. I am particularly indebted to my brother Shai for his ceaseless support, friendship, and for giving me his time and great assistance in the editing of the book. The joining of the younger members of the family, Libi, and particularly my own son, Tomo, has also given me great pleasure and enabled me to further reflect on my work.

Finally, my partner, Daniel J. Chalfen, gave me the utmost freedom and inspiration to think, to develop, and to look at the world in a nonconformist way. Chalfen was patient during my never-endng working hours; he was the first source for brainstorming when I needed to sort out my thoughts, with a boundless breadth of knowledge that he was always enthusiastic to share, and with a great sense of humor to ease my stress.

Just as I was completing my writing, I realized how much I shared my late father's interests. His absence was deeply felt, as a father and a mentor, and I only wish that I could have shared this process with him in person. The final version is thus dedicated to his memory.

Maya Sabatello

February 2009

LIST OF ABBREVIATIONS AND ACRONYMS

Additional Protocol on Biomedical Research	Additional Protocol to the Convention on Human Rights and Biomedicine, concerning Biomedical Research
Additional Protocol on the Prohibition of Cloning	Additional Protocol to the Convention for the Protection of Human Rights and Dignity of the Human Being with regard to the Application of Biology and Medicine, on the Prohibition of Cloning Human Beings
Additional Protocol on Transplantation of Organs and Tissues	Additional Protocol to the Convention on Human Rights and Biomedicine, on Transplantation of Organs and Tissues of Human Origin
African [Banjul] Charter	African [Banjul] Charter on Human and Peoples' Rights
African Charter	African Charter on the Rights and Welfare of the Child
CEDAW	Convention on the Elimination of Discrimination against Women
Children's Committee	Monitoring Committee under the Children's Convention
Children's Convention	International Convention on the Rights of the Child
Conventions on Biomedicine	The set of the following conventions: the Convention on Human Rights and Biomedicine (or, the Oviedo Convention), the Additional Protocol on the Prohibition of Cloning, the Additional Protocol on Transplantation of Organs and Tissues, and the Additional Protocol on Biomedical Research
Convention on Human Rights and Biomedicine (or Oviedo Convention)	Convention for the Protection of Human Rights and Dignity of the Human Being with Regard to the Application of Biology and Medicine (the Oviedo Convention)
Declaration on Religious Freedom or Belief	Declaration on the Elimination of All Forms of Intolerance and of Discrimination Based on Religion or Belief

Disability Rights Convention	Convention on the Rights of Persons with Disabilities
EU	European Union
ECHR	European Court of Human Rights
ICCPR	International Covenant on Civil and Political Rights
ICERD	International Convention on the Elimination of All Forms of Racial Discrimination
ICESCR	International Covenant on Economic, Social and Cultural Rights
IVF	in vitro fertilization
NGOs	nongovernmental organizations
OAS	Organization of American States
OAU	Organization of African Unity
Oviedo Convention (or Convention on Human Rights and Biomedicine)	Convention for the Protection of Human Rights and Dignity of the Human Being with Regard to the Application of Biology and Medicine
UDHR	Universal Declaration of Human Rights
UNESCO	United Nations Educational, Scientific and Cultural Organization
UNICEF	United Nations Children's Fund
UNIFEM	United Nations Development Fund for Women
WHO	World Health Organization

INTRODUCTION

In contemporary discourse, bioethics has come to be synonymous with "the inquiry into the ethical implications of modern scientific and technological development in medicine."[1] It assumes the existence of physical pathology that can be objectively defined, and it aims at improving the understanding of the human body as a means of conquering it and providing solutions for its "dysfunctions."[2] The presumed universal acceptance of this secular system of scientific knowledge, however, may be somewhat unjustified.

Globalization has certainly introduced technological developments in medicine worldwide. Organ transplants, abortions, in vitro fertilization, and other medical procedures take place in remote communities around the world, which in the past would have been left outside the international trend. Scientific talk is increasingly used, putting into practice health programs, policies, and medical opportunities in various societies across the globe. Yet, even though many imagine that technological and scientific progress are glamorous, bodily and medical practices are still, for the most part, grounded in the daily life experiences of cultural and social groups. Furthermore, in spite of the secular appearance of contemporary bioethics, religious and cultural values still take the lead in health-related decision making around the world. These latter values are also integrated within one's cultural identity, touching upon a variety of definitions of personhood. Thus, the encounter between the universal notion of human rights and the existing medical pluralism may instigate a profound cultural clash. The categorization of medical/bodily practices as violent, torturous, or abusive acts may be extremely offensive. In some cases, international campaigns and national policies aimed at eradicating particular bodily practices may call into question fundamental convictions of cultures and cultural identities. Furthermore, biomedical practices are increasingly intertwined with the question on the meaning of citizenship in an era of globalization. In view of the conventional equation only between modern bioethics and a form of citizenship,[3] on the one hand, and the trend of Western countries to grant asylum on the grounds of persecution from harmful traditional practices in non-Western and developing countries,[4] on the other,

---

[1] Jessica H. Muller, "Anthropology, Bioethics and Medicine: A Provocative Trilogy," *Medical Anthropology Quarterly* 8, no. 4 (1994): 448.

[2] Deborah Lupton, *Medicine as Culture* (London: Sage Publications, 2003), 88.

[3] Victor V. Branford, "Science and Citizenship," *The American Journal of Sociology* 11, no. 6 (1906): 721–62; Emily Martin, "Toward an Anthropology of Immunology: the Body as the Nation State," *Medical Anthropology Quarterly* 4, no. 4 (1990): 410–26 (discussing the construction of the body as nation state).

[4] Granting asylum on the basis of women's fear from the practice of female genital

the reality of medical pluralism presses the question: what does it *really* mean to be a world citizen? How does it affect groups' boundaries and identities in a multicultural world? What is the interplay between these international biomedical practices, the international condemnation of some of the practices, and the discourse about active citizenship? These questions are particularly pertinent in the context of children. As those who are the first targets of both enculturation and harmful traditional practices, how is the child-citizen of the world configured into the diverse constructs of bioethics?

This book examines the international biopolitical discourse with respect to the child's right to cultural identity. It focuses on traditional bodily and medical practices that are performed on children for religio-cultural reasons.[5] It explores these practices as an essential ingredient of the construct of the group and of the child's cultural identity, and it places them in the broader political and legal discourses on human rights and bioethics in a multicultural world.

The study builds on the existence and the value of religious and cultural diversity. Following the well-established academic literature, the premise of the book is that human experience of health and illness is culturally shaped. Further, the rationales and the ethical principles that motivate the performance of traditional bodily practices are culturally and religiously grounded. Understanding such practices thus requires their contextualization within the appropriate religious, ethnic, and cultural community.

In light of this pluralism, the fact that the international human rights regime provides for only one set of standards requires scrutiny of their implementation.[6] This is particularly so considering the liberal Western orientation of the international human rights corpus and its underpinning tenets.[7] While the human rights regime presumably endorses the blessing of cultural diversity and its guarantor principle, tolerance,[8] religious, and cultural bodily practices occasionally evoke a great deal of anxiety. The antiquity of such practices seems to pose a major challenge to the so-called modern norms of society. The religious and cultural practices are viewed as driven by emotions rather than by objective rationality. In addition, they are based on communal

---

cutting has taken place in the United States, the United Kindom, and other countries. See Corinne A. Kratz," "Circumcision Debates and Asylum Cases: Intersecting Arenas, Contested Values and Tangled Webs," in *Engaging Cultural Difference: The Multicultural Challenge in Liberal Democracies,* ed. Richard A. Shweder, Martha Minow, and Hazel Rose Markus (New York: Russell Sage Foundation, 2002), 309–43.

[5] Hereafter biomedical practices, bodily practices, and religio-cultural bodily practices, used interchangeably.

[6] Makau Mutua, "The Complexity of Universalism in Human Rights," in *10th Annual Conference on "the Individual vs. the State" Central European University,* Budapest, June 14–16, 2002, 3, 5, http://www.ceu.hu/legal/ind_vs_state/Mutua_paper_2002.htm.

[7] Jack Donnelly, "Human Rights and Human Dignity: An Analytic Critique of Non-Western Conceptions of Human Rights," *American Political Science Review* 76 (1982): 312–15; Raimundo Panikkar, "Is the Notion of Human Rights a Western Concept?," *Diogenes* 120 (1982): 100; Mutua, 7.

[8] Rainer Baubock, "Cultural Minority Rights for Immigrants," *International Migration Review* 30, no. 1 (1996): 204; Alison D. Renteln, *The Cultural Defense* (Oxford: Oxford University Press, 2004), 211–12.

loyalty rather than individualism. Thus, even when religious and cultural bodily practices are minor in their pervasiveness, they are often perceived as a risk to a healthy society, or more so, to a healthy individual. Yet, if pluralism has any meaning, then bodily diversity, as a symbol of one's social order and his or her place in it,[9] is a prime feature. And, for liberal principles to be meaningful, there is an expectation that governments would tolerate "a great deal."[10] What is the interplay between the international legal and political discourses on traditional bodily practices and the right of the child to cultural identity? What are the acceptable norms of behavior, and what are the abusive ones in the context of bodily practices? Which religious or cultural biomedical practices are accepted in the mainstream? How are the acceptable and deplorable religious/cultural bodily practices constructed in the academic, legal, and political discourse? And where are the individual and the religious and cultural communities positioned in these discussions?

The study tackles these questions from the perspective of international law and policy. The growing appreciation in recent years of human rights concerns, including the theoretical recognition of religious and cultural diversity and the ongoing debates about groups' identities, yielded a substantial number of international documents. Thus, it provides a fertile ground for inquiry about the legal and social constructs of bodily practices, of groups' cultural identity, and of the formation of the self.

The study focuses on children as one of the most vulnerable subgroups in society. This concentration is justified on three grounds. First, the preoccupation of the Western legal discourse on bioethics with the doctrine of informed consent obscures the multiple and other nonindividualistic biomedical frameworks that exist. It also prevents many scholars from taking up cultural considerations relevant to the bioethical principles involved. As young children in both Western and non-Western communities are presumed to lack the capacity to make health-related decisions alone, concentrating on them as a group illuminates the need in a systematic and cross-cultural discussion about the suitable principles of bioethics for children.

Second, children's dependency on others for their survival places them in a special position of vulnerability. Despite the recognition of children as rights holders on their own in the twentieth century, their limited capacity to make health-related decisions, practically, precludes their full enjoyment of their granted rights.[11] This impediment is augmented considering their subordination to parental and/or communal authority as substitutive decision makers. Consequently, while children are the first to be exposed to religious

---

[9] Rhoda E. Howard, "Dignity, Community and Human Rights," in *Human Rights in Cross-Cultural Perspectives: A Quest for Consensus,* ed. Abdullahi Ahmed An-Na'im (Philadelphia: University of Pennsylvania Press, 1992), 89.

[10] Renteln, *The Cultural Defense,* 212.

[11] Martha Minow, "About Women, About Culture: About Them, About Us," in *Engaging Cultural Difference: The Multicultural Challenge in Liberal Democracies,* ed. Richard A. Shweder, Martha Minow, and Hazel Rose Markus (New York: Russell Sage Foundation, 2002), 262–63.

and cultural practices that may jeopardize their health, they are also the most invisible in the family/communal group, placing them in double and triple levels of vulnerability.

This peculiar status was one of the mobilizing forces leading to the almost universal adoption of the Convention on the Rights of the Child (Children's Convention or Convention).[12] Among its other provisions, Article 24(3) stipulates that states have an obligation "to abolish traditional practices [that are] prejudicial to the health of the child." However, the Convention remains silent as to *what* constitutes harmful practices, and the decision is left in the hands of the international bodies that monitor its implementation. How is the marginalization of religious and cultural practices constructed within the general international discussion? What role do the so-called internationally accepted standards play by including or excluding religious and cultural bodily practices from the conventional discourse? As the lack of definition runs the risk of eschewing fundamental religious and cultural practices that are off the dominant culture's agenda, a comprehensive analysis is needed.

Finally, observing the discourse on the relationship among children, culture, cultural identity, and traditional bodily practices is most challenging. There is no question that children are the prime targets of enculturation and socialization.[13] "Children stand at the heart of what cultural groups view as the most important of all: passing on their ways to the next generation,"[14] and "policies for cultural survival" often focus on children with the dual goal of "how to 'implant' the child in the culture and also the culture in the child."[15] Because children traditionally were perceived as property without rights, scholarly work focuses predominantly on the *parental* rights to entrench *their* cultural identity in their children, on the family's autonomy vis-à-vis the state, and on the respective communities as the site of enculturation.[16] Children, in contrast, were traditionally excluded from both the rights and the cultural talks.

The development of an international rights talk concerning children has shifted the analysis of their legal and political status. On the one hand, it led to the politicized discourse of gender inequalities and to the immense feminists' campaign against traditional practices that affect women and girls, such as female genital cutting. On the other hand, the recognition of children's rights, including rights to form and express their opinions, to freedom of religion, to self-determination, and the right to preserve both national and cultural identities[17] paved the way to a more serious examination of children's own voice

---

[12] Convention on the Rights of the Child, G.A. Res. 44/25, annex, 44th Sess., 61st plenary meeting. U.N. GAOR Supp. (No. 49), at 167, U.N. Doc. A/44/49 (1989), entered into force Sept. 2, 1990, reprinted in 28 I.L.M. 1448 (1989).

[13] Minow, "About Women, About Culture," 261.

[14] Ibid.

[15] Janet E. Halley, "Culture Constrains," in *Is Multiculturalism Bad for Women?*, ed. Susan M. Okin (Princeton, NJ: Princeton University Press, 1999), 103.

[16] Sharon Stephens, "Introduction: Children and the Politics of Culture in "late Capitalism," in *Children and the Politics of Culture*, ed. Sharon Stephens (Princeton, NJ: Princeton University Press, 1995), 10.

[17] Article 12 of the Children's Convention establishes the principle of "participa-

and interests. Recognizing children as rights holders with (at least) some breadth of autonomy thus necessitates also the inquiry about the legal status of children and their agency. Children can no longer be seen merely as passive vessels of a given culture but as subjects of it and its constructors. How do children, as powerful social agents of the construction of groups' culture, piece together particular bodily practices and their "self"? How does it play within the politics of the international system? How does the international discourse balance the child's right to cultural identity and religious freedom with states' responsibility to abolish traditional practices prejudicial to the child's health? How does it come to grips with the global patriarchal social structure (either gender, age, or West/East) without annihilating (physical) cultural diversity and instigating a "clash of civilizations"?[18] As no extensive comprehensive study exists on the subject of children's bioethics, this work offers the first consideration of these important questions.

The study takes an interdisciplinary approach to address the bioethics of children in light of their right to cultural identity. Cross-cultural anthropological and sociological accounts for the medical and bodily practices that involve children are provided, and content analysis is used to examine the issue of children's rights from legal, philosophical, and political outlooks. The practices were gathered from the work of the human rights bodies addressing the issue as they emerged from states' and nongovernmental organizations' (NGOs) reports that are submitted to them. As the decision whether the practices pose a health risk to the child (and should thus be prohibited) is in the hands of the international agents who monitor the Children's Convention's implementation, the way in which the religious and cultural practices are framed is of primary importance. It is my view that before one can determine which medical practice is accepted, and which should be rejected, one has to examine not only the physical aspects of the practice, but also the particular sociocultural context in which the child is raised. This is essential if one truly supports the child's rights, and, all the more so, acknowledges the role cultural identity plays in the child's exercise of these rights.

This study takes a cross-cultural examination of bodily and medical practices that are performed on children. Different from the traditional concentration on such practices when performed among minority groups, it takes on as a

---

tion," requiring states to assure children's right to express their views freely in all matters that affect them, in accordance with the age and maturity of the children. Article 14 of the Children's Convention refers to the child's right to freedom of thought, conscious, and religion; Articles 8 and 29(1)(3) of the Children's Convention refer to the right of children to preserve their cultural identity and to the right to be educated in a manner that would develop respect for their culture. Article 29(b) requires that children's education be "directed to the development of the respect for human rights and fundamental freedoms and for the principles enshrined in the Charter of the United Nations," which includes reference to the right to self-determination. Article 41 provides a protection clause, thus including also other international human rights treaties that referred to the right to self-determination and freedom of religion.

[18] The term was adopted from Samuel P. Huntington's contention on "The Clash of Civilizations."

premise that the performance of "exotic" bodily and medical treatment is universal and contingent on the viewer's perceptions. Thus, in order to study children's bioethics from an international and interdisciplinary perspective, the following working definitions are used.

The core legal working document is the Children's Convention. As a document that was almost immediately signed and ratified after its endorsement on November 20, 1989, by all but two UN member states,[19] it provides a universally acceptable standard for observation. Accordingly, following Article 1 of the Convention, a child will be defined as "every human being below the age of 18 years, unless under the law applicable to the child, maturity is attained earlier."[20]

The anthropological concept of culture as "a total way of life" follows the working definition that has been endorsed by the UN Educational, Scientific and Cultural Organization (UNESCO). Accordingly, "culture is a dynamic value system of learned elements, with assumptions, conventions, beliefs and rules permitting members of a group to relate to each other and to the world, to communicate and to develop their creative potential."[21] This definition is most appropriate because while it inherently includes the values, symbols, and set of practices that are endorsed and reproduced over time by any given group, it also leaves space for change and, hence, for agency.

An operational definition of medical culture is also necessary. Some scholars suggest a distinction between medical culture and medical system depending on the extent of theoretical coherency and on the patient-practitioner relationship.[22] Medical culture assumes "a looser and more general framework for understanding the health traditions of ethnic groups" and a somewhat eclectic healing practice that developed following contact with other medical cultures. It refers to "all things medical that go within a particular geographical area" or "composed of competing systems derived from distinct cultural groups."[23] Medical system, by contrast, is presumably built on "a consistent body of theory of medical ideas and practices" and on "the organization and power of its practitioners."[24] It includes (1) practitioners who adhere to a common body of knowledge and practice according to the logic that is derived from it, (2) patients who endorse the particular body of knowledge and recognize its practitioners, and (3) a theory that explains and guides the treatment of the illnesses in the society.

---

[19] The two states that did not ratify the Children's Convention are the United States and Somalia. Both countries, however, signed it (the United States on September 7, 2000, and Somalia on May 9, 2000).

[20] The debate whether fetuses fall within the scope of the Convention's protection is discussed further in Chapter 2 and particularly Chapter 7 in the context of genetic engineering.

[21] Canadian Commission for UNESCO, *A Working Definition of Culture for the Canadian Commission for UNESCO*, 1977, 6.

[22] Lisa L. Capps, "Change and Continuity in the Medical Culture of the Hmong in Kansas City," *Medical Anthropology Quarterly* 8 no. 2 (1994): 161–62.

[23] Ibid., 162.

[24] Ibid.

While theoretically such a distinction may be helpful, it is extremely difficult to apply on a practical level. All cultures include competing and sometimes contradicting elements, and the encounter between cultures inevitably affects all groups involved.[25] Furthermore, drawing the line of looseness that presumably distinguishes between the two can be done only in relation to other, presumably more cohesive, medical systems. Such a proposition, however, seems to imply comparing all medical cultures to the Western scientific one that is assumed to be the most developed and coherent one. Practically, then, it would only reinforce the hegemonic status of Western medical culture—an ethnocentrism that this study tries to avoid. Thus, both medical culture and medical system are referred to interchangeably.

Finally, for an inclusive definition of bioethics, this study redefines it to include all bodily or health-related practices that raise in-group and out-group moral considerations. This definition encompasses the array of bodily concepts or practices, both therapeutic and nontherapeutic, that are absorbed by or mandated for religious or cultural reasons. Such definition overcomes the difficulties associated with the distinction between religious and culturally motivated bodily practices,[26] and it is thus more equipped to enable a comprehensive cross cultural analysis of the various ethical contexts that are relevant to the study of the connection between body, medicine, culture, and identity. Accordingly, biomedical practices, bodily practices, and religio-cultural bodily practices are used to connote a similar meaning.

The outline for the book is as follows:

Chapter 1 begins with an overview of the inextricable relationship between biomedicine and human rights, the concept of medical cultures, and explains

---

[25] Western endorsement of acupuncture in recent years at formal medical institutions is one such example.

[26] The extent to which religious adherence differs from a cultural one and the relationship between the two concepts is controversial. Some view religion as only one aspect included within the general concept of culture, whereas others contend that it is the other way around, or, at least, that religion is a separate category. They insist that the roots, rationales, and motivations behind religious adherence merit a distinctive response. The issue was not resolved on the international level, despite ongoing efforts since the 1960s. For discussion on the relationship between religion and culture, see Yvonne M. Donders, *Towards a Right to Cultural Identity?* (Antwerp: Intersentia, 2002), 72; Philip Hefner, "The Spiritual Task of Religion in Culture: An Evolutionary Perspective," *Zygon* 33, no. 4 (1998): 540; Azizah Y. al-Hibri, "Is Western Patriarchal Feminism Good for Third World/Minority Women?" in *Is Multiculturalism Bad for women?* ed. Susan M. Okin (Princeton, NJ: Princeton University Press, 1999), 43; Daniel G. Scott, "Spirituality in Child and Youth Care: Considering Spiritual Development and 'Relational Consciousness,'" *Child & Youth Care Forum* 32, no. (2003): 117–31. See also Jeremy T. Gunn, "The Complexities of Religion and the Definition of 'Religion' in International Law," *Harvard Human Rights Journal* 16 (2003): 189–215 (distinguishing between three facets of religion: religion as belief, religion as identity, and religion as a way of life). For a comprehensive discussion on the international address of religious freedom, see Natan Lerner, *Religion, Beliefs, and International Human Rights* (Maryknoll, NY: Orbis Books, 2000); Bahiyyah G. Tahzib, *Freedom of Religion or Belief: Ensuring Effective International Legal Protection* (The Hague: Kluwer Law International, 1996). See also Chapter 6, Section E.2.

some of the difficulties associated with the pluralism of medical cultures. Next, the intersection between the body, society, and culture is examined in the context of children. Although children are often perceived merely as vulnerable members of society, particularly as far as bodily practices are concerned, they also wield significant power as the bearers of cultures and traditions. Developments in the understanding of children as active social agents are discussed, and some of the complexities with and questions about children's agency and bioethics are highlighted.

Chapter 2 outlines the drafting process of the Children's Convention. A thematic approach sheds light on the major debates that arose with regard to issues such as informed consent, experimentation, and harmful traditional bodily practice. In contrast to the common assumption, the chapter shows that the concerns about children's vulnerability in the biomedical sphere, including harmful traditional practices, were much broader than the well-known debate on female genital cutting. Achievements and failures of the drafting process are assessed with regard to issues pertinent to children's bioethics and beyond the Children's Convention, as has also been reflected in other subsequent international instruments.

Chapter 3 introduces four traditional bodily practices: male circumcision, tribal marking, extraction of a baby's milk teeth, and neck elongation. These practices were raised in the work of the international bodies, mainly the Committee on the Rights of the Child[27] and were discussed under the provision on harmful traditional practices. As the argument is advanced that contextualization is essential to the understanding of biomedical practices, this chapter examines the anthropological, sociological, and medical background of the selected practices.

Chapters 4 and 5 provide the political and human rights' legal frameworks for the analysis of children's bioethics. Chapter 4 considers the theoretical framework of the so-called politics of difference, the question of multiculturalism, and the difficulties with their application in the context of children. Efforts made on national and international levels to provide appropriate models for conflict resolution in the context of biomedicine and children are then evaluated. Chapter 5 provides an in-depth analysis and critique of the rights in question as far as children's bioethics is concerned. The chapter shows that neither of the rights falling within the scope of the protective approach nor within the participatory one is apt to properly advance the discourse on children's bioethics.

Both Chapters 6 and 7 call attention to the need to reconsider the framework for discussion on children's bioethical rights. In Chapter 6, a critique of the existing concepts of children's rights is provided, and an initial alternative framework for analysis is developed. The chapter argues that, for a suitable discussion, biomedical practices carried out on children should be evaluated within given medical and sociocultural contexts and in light of the child's right

[27] Hereafter the Children's Committee or the Committee.

to identity. How such a model could be implemented within the international human rights system is also considered. Chapter 7 raises the issue of "invented" traditional practices, specifically the practice of genetic manipulation in the context of disabilities. The alternative framework for a child-centered perspective is applied, and the conventional discourse on genetic selection is challenged.

The last chapter draws together the discussion on children's bioethics. The alternative model is further delineated, and various considerations that need to be taken into account are discussed. Finally, recalling the case selection, some biomedical conflicts that may arise are examined and suggestions are made for future paths of investigation.

CHAPTER 1
USING INTERNATIONAL HUMAN RIGHTS FRAMEWORK TO STUDY BIOETHICS

This chapter sets the framework for the discussion on children's bioethics. It begins with an explanation of the relationship between international human rights norms and bioethics, pinpoints the role globalization has played in this regard, and elaborates on the concept of medical cultures. Particular attention is paid to the Western, "principlism approach" of bioethics and to its critique. Next, how children are configured into these discussions is discussed. The connection between the body, society, culture, and cultural identity as reflected on the child, the power relations between the state, the child, and the parents as far as bodily/medical practices are concerned, and, finally, the issue of the child's agency while showing the complexities involved are examined.

A. INTERNATIONAL HUMAN RIGHTS AND BIOETHICS: AN INEXTRICABLE CONNECTION

Medical ethics and conduct are inseparable from the trend of international human rights. Political struggles against absolutism and the evolution of philosophical concepts of inalienable rights since the nineteenth century[1] were bolstered by scientific and intellectual accomplishments. When modern international human rights law developed in the post-World War II era, it did so simultaneously with the evolution of medical ethics. Indeed, both came into being as a response to the atrocities committed by the Nazis and their scientists and medical professionals during the war. The doctrine of informed consent altered the status of health professional as sole authority in health-related decision making and replaced the traditional paternalistic approach with one that is based on patients' rights. According to this concept, individuals' value, worth, and benefit were prioritized over the collective good. The expansion of medical practices and misconduct, which are categorized as human rights abuses, further strengthened the campaign for global justice.[2]

Globalization, immigration, and refugees have reinforced the connection between human rights and bioethics. International health policies aimed at improving the public health of people in third world countries afflicted with

[1] Henry J. Steiner and Philip Alston, *International Human Rights in Context: Law, Politics, Morals* (Oxford: Oxford University Press, 1996), 167–68.

[2] Corinne A. A. Packer, *Using Human Rights to Change Tradition: Traditional Practices Harmful to Women's Reproductive Health in Sub-Saharan Africa* (Oxford: Antwerpen Intersentia, 2002), 83.

diseases (such as HIV/AIDS)[3] also called attention to the economic and social disparities among nations. International research collaborations among different nations raised new ethical concerns regarding the bioethical standards that should be employed in various cultural contexts.[4] The introduction of scientific technology such as organ transplants and reproductive technology into remote societies opened new health opportunities to some but also illuminated others' vulnerability to exploitation, illegal international trade, and the reconstruction of the social caste of "haves" and "have-nots" onto both the national and international levels.[5] Finally, various systems of medical cultures, conventional (Western) medicine, and folk medicine increasingly coexist in many multicultural societies. Thus, the intersection between human rights and bioethics now encompasses not only such practices that have been historically considered as torture, and inhumane and degrading treatment, but it also touches upon notions of welfare, justice, and the determination of personhood.[6]

B. MEDICAL CULTURES

1. Historical Context

Cultural beliefs and practices relating to ill health are central in human society.[7] Societies have definitions of how the well person looks and feels,[8] what constitutes good health, and what causes illness. Societies dictate appropriate healing practices and specify who can provide them in order to cope with illness.[9]

Before the process of medicalization took root in the West, most societies were religiously based. They functioned on the basis of their sacred concepts and followed the ethics as delivered to them by spiritual leaders. Medicine and health were no different.[10] The definitions of health or illness as well as the causes for these physical states have often been tied to divine and supernatural explorations. Diseases were attributed to God's will and to the *moral* corruption

---

[3] Monica J. Casper and Barbara A. Koenig, "Reconfiguring Nature and Culture: Intersections of Medical Anthropology and Technoscience Studies," *Medical Anthropology Quarterly* 10, no. 4 (1996): 525; Veena Das, "Public Good, Ethics, and Everyday Life: Beyond the Boundaries of Bioethics," *Bioethics & Beyond (Daedalus)* 128, no. 4 (1999): 99–134.

[4] David P. Fidler, "'Geographical Morality' Revisited: International Relations, International Law, and the Controversy over Placebo-Controlled HIV Clinical Trials in Developing Countries," *Harvard International Law Journal* 42, no. 2 (2001): 312–23 (discussing theories in international relations about states' ethical obligations in the context of HIV therapies and placebo usage in researches conducted in developing countries).

[5] Lawrence Cohen, "The Other Kidney: Biopolitics Beyond Recognition," *Body & Society* 7, no. 2–3 (2001): 18; Nency Scheper-Hughes, "Commodity Fetishism in Organs Trafficking," *Body & Society* 7, no. 2–3 (2001): 32, 59.

[6] Jessica H. Muller, "Anthropology, Bioethics and Medicine: A Provocative Trilogy," *Medical Anthropology Quarterly* 8, no. 4 (1994): 450.

[7] A "society" generally consists of people who share a specific geographical area within which they interact together, guided by their culture. See Cecil G. Helman, *Culture, Health and Illness* (Oxford: Butterworth, 2000), 1, 5.

[8] Martha O. Loustaunau and Elisa J. Sobo, *The Cultural Context of Health, Illness and Medicine* (London: Bergin & Garvey, 1997), 91.

[9] Ibid., 74–78.

[10] Cynthia B. Cohen, Sondra E. Wheeler, and David A. Scott, "Walking on a Fine Line," *Hastings Center Report* 31, no. 5 (2001): 30–31.

of the individual ("sin").[11] Religious priests or shamen were the ones to allocate medical relief and deliver its ethical considerations as well.[12]

Secularization since the time of the Enlightenment, particularly in the nineteenth century, however, led to a shift. The search for an objective and universal science based on rational and neutrally visible facts[13] led to conflict between religious values and health.[14] Medicine replaced religion as the dominant moral ideology, transforming sin into sickness.[15] At first, its preoccupation was with the absolute authoritative role of "God's substitutes," the medical profession. After the horrendous medical misconduct during World War II, however, the shift toward contemporary notions of individual rights began to emerge.

2. The Principlism Approach and Its Critique

With the influence of Western (primarily Anglo American) philosophy and law, bioethics has come to be conceptualized as a field that prioritizes individuals and individuals' rights, self-determination, dignity, and privacy. It emphasizes rational logic and codified rules for a precise and objective thinking to guide human conduct and search for the good life.[16] Its focus is on perspective behavior, that is, how decisions *ought* to be made rather than how they *are* made.[17] Particularly, four leading principles of bioethics have taken roots.[18]

The first principle, *respect to autonomy*, refers to both the inherent integrity of human life and the personal autonomy of the particular subject. This concept is occasionally translated into the *doctrine of informed consent.* It requires that prior to any medical treatment, the patient is given sufficient information about the procedure to enable him or her to make a free and informed decision regarding consent. The emphasis is on the state of mind of the patient and constitutes a threshold to any medical intervention.

The principle of *nonmaleficence* is often regarded as the most basic oath of the medical profession and its obligation "to do no harm."[19] It is occasionally linked with its "mirrored principle" of beneficence, referring to the clinicians' duty to protect the patients' life and health during medical interventions, to minimize pain or discomfort, and to achieve results that benefit the individual or society. The principle of beneficence is a moral obligation (not necessarily

---

[11] Deborah Lupton, *Medicine as Culture* (London: Sage Publications, 2003), 86; Peter Conrad and Joseph W. Schneider, *Deviance and Medicalization: From Badness to Sickness* (St. Louis,: Mosby Publishing, 1980), 9.

[12] Conrad and Schneider, 9.

[13] Muller, 450.

[14] Lupton, 88; Peter Conrad, "Medicalization and Social Control," *Annual Review of Sociology* 18 (1992): 213.

[15] Conrad, 213.

[16] Muller, 450; Stephan E. Lemmes, "The Marginalization of Religious Voices in Bioethics," in *Religion and Medical Ethics,* ed. Allen Verhey (Cambridge: Wm. B. Eardman Publishing Company Michigan, 1996), 24, 35.

[17] Muller, 451.

[18] Tom L. Beauchamp and James F. Childress, *Principles of Biomedical Ethics* (New York: Oxford University Press, 2001).

[19] Ibid., 113.

an impartial one), and it has been traditionally construed as mercifulness, generosity, and compassion. It may, however, also include any act that is aimed at improving/promoting the interests of another.

Finally, the principle of *justice* is often derived from its inverse—*injustice.* It refers to a wrongful act or omission that prevents a benefit for one who is generally entitled to it or to a distribution of the burden that is done in a nonproportional manner.

The principlism approach rules on a normative standard that is presumed to transcend cultural diversity. Its premises are of a universal reason and of individuals who engage in similar processes of moral reasoning in order to reach one right solution in conflicted or ambiguous situations. It also assumes that all health professionals share a set of moral values that define the core of the appropriate medical practice.[20] Thus, the presumption is that medical practices can be critically observed and prohibited on a universal normative ground.[21]

In the late twentieth century, however, these assumptions have been challenged. First, the "medicalization shift" did not occur in many cultures around the world.[22] Numerous societies remained religiously oriented, and they maintained their previous systems of medical conduct and ethics. These are often linked to beliefs about the origin of a much wider range of misfortune, of which health is just one form. In some societies, the whole range of disasters is blamed on supernatural forces, divine retribution, or the malevolence of a witch or sorcerer.[23] In Hindu and Theravada Buddhist traditions, for example, illness is attributed to bad karma or demerits from a previous life. In Cambodia, sickness is accredited to dangerous house spirits and the failure to honor an ancestral spirit.[24]

In other societies, health and illness are understood more holistically. Physical pathologies are ascribed to imbalances in bodily, mental, and cosmic factors such as hot-cold, dryness-wetness, and humoral systems.[25] The healing methods attempt to balance various physical, psychological, ecological, and cultural factors[26] and to ensure that "one's social networks, with fellow human beings, with ancestors, and with deities are maintained in good working order."[27] In Latin American folk medicine, the hot-cold theory of disease holds that health is maintained or lost by the symbolic balance between the effect of

---

[20] Stuart F. Spicker, "Bioethic(s): One or Many?" *Journal of Medicine and Philosophy* 23, no. 4 (1998): 351–52

[21] Ibid., 350.

[22] Don G. Bates, "Why Not Call Modern Medicine "Alternative"?" *Perspective in Biology & Medicine* 43, no. 4 (2000): 512–17.

[23] Helman, 5.

[24] Maurice Eisenbruch and Lauren Handelman, "Cultural Consultation for Cancer: Astrocytoma in Cambodian Adolescent," *Social Science & Medicine* 31 (1990): 1296.

[25] Loustaunau and Sobo, 18.

[26] Ayala Lauterbach-Goren, "The Adaptability of Cancer Patients Who Turn to Complementary Medicnie in Addition to Conventional Medicine" (Ph.D. diss., Haifa University, Israel, 1998), 9, 17.

[27] In the literature, these methods are often termed "personalistic" models. Loustaunau and Sobo, 91, 98.

heat or cold on the body.[28] Preventive measures and recuperation from illness thus require maintaining or restoring (respectfully) the internal temperature of one's body by specific dietary practices and conciliation of the supernatural forces.[29] The pursuit of Chinese medical tradition after a harmony between the two contrasting cosmic principles of *yin*, described as dark, moist, watery, and female, and *yang*, described as hot, dry, fiery, and male[30] is another such example.

Perhaps not surprisingly, medical ethics varies among cultural groups as well. In contrast to Western preoccupation with the individual as the locus of decision making, in other cultures individuals are not expected to make health-related decisions themselves.[31] In some cultures, one's ill condition is believed to reflect a symptom of collective mischief.[32] As it is believed that the condition holds potential ramifications for the entire group, the community leaders, healers, or heads of families are the ones who are authorized to consent. Some cultures strike a different balance between individuals and the collective in the context of medical decision making. The Jewish religion, for instance, grants a power of medical decision making not only to the individual, but also to the community and to the family.[33] A similar concept exists in Asian cultures where the family and the community have greater weight than individuals. In Confucius ethics, for example, the family (rather than the individual) is the center of attention, and autonomy is collective rather than individualistic.[34] Likewise, the concept of kinship in traditional Vietnamese society expects that the family be involved in medical decisions of its members and that the decision is not left solely to the individual.[35]

Furthermore, the conceptualization of practices of medical ethics as "harmful," "beneficial," and "just" vary significantly.[36] Because the boundaries of acceptable and normative behaviors are socially and culturally constructed, practices that are viewed as benign or harmful to one culture may be viewed as damaging or compassionate, respectively, to others.[37] One such example is the different norms of disclosure of information on medical diagnosis that medical

[28] Helman, 19.

[29] Ibid.

[30] Ibid., 20.

[31] Leigh G. Turner, "Bioethics in a Pluralistic World: Truth Telling, Informed Consent, and Euthanasia" (Ph.D. diss., University of Southern California, 1996), 138; Shimon M. Galik, "An Unlimited Autonomy of the Individual—Is it A Question of Culture?," *A Letter to A Friend (Michtav LaChaver)* 59, no. 3 (1997): 14 (Heb.); Michael Cheng-tek Tai and Chung Seng Lin, "Developing A Culturally Bioethics for Asian People," *Journal of Medical Ethics* 27, no. 1. (2001): 51–52.

[32] Loustaunau and Sobo, 18.

[33] Galik, 14.

[34] Cheng-tek Tai and Seng Lin, 52.

[35] Maj Doung Nugen, "Cultural Shock—A Review of Vietnamese Culture and Its Concepts of Health and Disease," *Western Journal of Medicine* 142, no. 3 (1985): 410.

[36] Jill E. Korbin, "A Cross-Cultural Perspective on the Role of the Community in Child Abuse and Neglect," *Child Abuse & Neglect* 3 (1979): 10.

[37] Jill E. Korbin, "The Cross Cultural Context of Child Abuse and Neglect," in *The Battered Child*, 3rd ed., ed. Henry C. Kenpa and Ray Helfer (Chicago: University of Chicago Press, 1980), 23.

cultures have. In Western countries, the prevalent principle upholds the notion of disclosure of information and truth telling. Physicians are required to provide their patients with the necessary information that would enable them to make knowledgeable decisions about their medical treatment.[38] Other cultures, however, assume that the Western standard of disclosure holds a potential harm to the individuals. Some prefer indirect disclosure rather than the direct Western style. In Cambodia, for example, a disclosure is often made in the form of a religious ceremony or prayer.[39] Others prefer concealing medical information from the individual. In Taiwan, when a patient is diagnosed with a terminal disease, the first person to be notified is the head of the family (such as the father or the husband) who will confer with other family members about what course of treatment will be taken.[40]

Finally, those who are responsible for diagnosing and treating ill patients differ. In Western culture, the ability to diagnose poor health is granted to professionals educated in formal educational institutions[41] who are thought to be interpreting objective and scientific results. By contrast, in other cultures, healing methods are traditionally performed by local healers or family members who acquired their medical proficiency by observation of other healers, often older family members.[42] The South Asian practice of coining (*cao gio*) commonly used to free the body of "bad winds" that are presumably responsible for a range of ailments including headaches, backache, flu, and tension[43] is often performed by parents and perceived as an integral part of taking care of their child.[44] The treatment of *ceeb*, a "fright illness" that occurs, according to the Hmong people, as the result of an intense emotional experience, such as a frightening event or anger, requires immediate massage and prayer treatment by the community's

---

[38] While the principle of disclosure of information and truth-telling is the general rule in many Western countries, the extent of disclosure that is required may be different. The standard in the United States, for example, is of the material information that a "reasonable patient" would need to for the decision making. In Israel, the severity of the disease is taken into consideration. The lesser the necessity of the medical procedure, the more information is required to be disclosed. See Alysa Gordon, "Multiculturalism in Medical Decision-making: the Notion of Informed Waiver," *Fordham Urban Law Journal* 23, no. 3 (1995–96): 1329; Anna Karpman, "Informed Consent: Does the First Amendment Protect a Patients' Right to Choose Alternative Treatment," *New York Law School Journal Human Rights*16 (2000): 938; Ofra Golan, "The Requirement of "Informed Consent" as an Expression of Human Dignity," *Shaarei Mishpat* 2, no. 2 (2000): 177–78 (Heb.).

[39] Eisenbruch and Handelman, 1296.

[40] Cheng-tek Tai and Seng Lin, 52.

[41] Called also "professional" medicine, which is conducted by "biomedical practitioners." See Helman, 5.

[42] Lisa L. Capps, "Fright Illness in Hmong Children," *Pediatric/Nursing* 25, no. 4 (1999): 381.

[43] Robert E. Primosch and Stephen Kent Young, "Pseudobattering of Vietnamese Children (Cao Gio)," *Journal of American Dental Association* 101 (1980): 47; Nga Nguyen, Phuoc H. (Frank) Nguyen, and Loc H. Nguyen, "*Coin Treatment in Vietnamese Families: Traditional Medical Practices vs. Child Abuse,*" (Los Angeles: County of LA, Department of Children's Services, 1987), 3.

[44] Barbara A. Serrano, "Cultures Clash in Rearing Children—State Acts When Abuse Is Feared—Parents Follow Custom in Laotian Boy's Case," *Seattle Times*, August 30, 1991, A1.

healer who has often acquired his or her proficiency by observation.[45] Still, for others, healing ability is entrusted predominantly to God's gifted ones who received the power at birth.[46] Thus, even if professional healers, including medical school graduates or those who obtained their expertise by observation, are qualified, their authority and respect is only secondary.[47]

Thus, it is increasingly acknowledged that bioethics and medical conduct need to be observed in many voices.[48] While some principles may be generally accepted, their interpretation may vary significantly.[49] Principles of biomedical ethics, therefore, have to be understood and interpreted within one's cultural setting.[50] To what extent do the international monitoring bodies take this medical pluralism into account? How do they narrate the acceptability of medical diagnosis and its treatment? As medical practices are ingrained within one's entire system of knowledge and belief, these are important questions.

C. CHILDREN, BIOETHICS, AND MEDICAL CULTURE

Social science scholars have long observed the connection between the body and cultural identity. Anthropological and sociological discourses characterized the body as a central element of the society, and psychological scholars have gone to great lengths to explain the impact of the body on the construction of individual and group identities.

Emile Durkheim, one of the earliest sociologists observing the relationship between identity, rituals, and the body, discerned a few complementary levels in which the body plays a crucial medium between the individual and society.[51] First, the body is used as a source of the society. Observing sacred celebration and rites ceremonies in totemist societies, Durkheim viewed the bodily practices that joined the sacred rituals as "generators of social symbolism," evoking a collective energy and an emotional social solidarity that "creates a space for social life in which groups become conscious of themselves."[52] As a first site of "imagined community,"[53] Durkheim concluded that "without the body, there can be no life and society."[54] The body is also a site for social classification,

---

[45] Capps, "Fright Illness," 378, 381–82.

[46] Loudell F. Snow, "Folk Medical Beliefs and Their Implications for Care Patients: A Review Based on Studies Among Black Americans," *Annals of Internal Medicine* 81 (1974): 93.

[47] Ibid., 93–94.

[48] Spicker, 354.

[49] Godfrey B. Tangwa, "The Traditional African Perception of a Person: Some Implications for Bioethics," *Hastings Center Report* 30 no. 5 (2000): 40–41.

[50] Cheng-tek Tai and Chung, 53.

[51] Emile Durkheim, *The Elementary Forms of Religious Life,* trans. Josepf Ward Swain (New York: Free Press, 1965).

[52] Ibid., 465–66, 469–71, 385–92; Lauren Langman, "Culture, Identity and Hegemony: the Body in a Global Age," *Current Sociology* 51, no. 3–4 (2003): 225.

[53] "Imagined community" is built on Benedict Anderson's discussion on the cultural construction of a sense of a political community of the nation-state, whereby although "the members of even the smallest nation do not know most of their fellow-members, meet them or even hear of them, . . . in the minds of each lives the image of their communion." Benedict Anderson, *Imagined Communities,* rev. ed. (London: Verso, 1990), 6.

[54] Quoted in Chris Shilling, "Embodiment, Experience and Theory: In Defense of the

inducing a sense of collective order. The performance of bodily ritual practices (such as circumcision, scarification, tattooing, piercing) is associated with gender, birth, sexuality, and so forth, symbolizing the *social* value that is placed on individual identities.[55] Finally, the bodily experience and ceremonies create a *vital means by which individuals are attached to, and positioned within, their social milieu.*[56] Building on the connection between the body and the collective served energies, the physical congregation creates a *moral* commonality among the members of the group, allowing individuals to interact on the basis of shared understandings.[57] By providing individuals with this common morality and attachment, the rituals provide a space in which the social solidarity and reproduction are sustained.[58]

Modernization, or what Durkheim termed "the individual cult,"[59] did not and does not break apart the connection between the body, individual, and society. Individualization is viewed as representing the dominant culture of detachment, providing individuals with the tools to cope with economic and other struggles that are connected with modernity.[60] Yet the basic connections among body, society, and identity remained. Every society considers its social rituals sacred, whether religious or secular,[61] and every culture holds sacred its particular bodily images, norms of beauty, cleanliness, and other bodily images and practices that determine the particular way in which individuals interact with their societal environment.[62]

How does this connection between the body, society, and culture reflect on children?

1. Children, Body, and Culture

The connection between body, society, and culture is most apparent in the context of children. Children are the first site of enculturation, the process in which individuals absorb the cultural configuration of their community and identity as their own.[63] To a great extent, the process of enculturation is made on a subliminal level. It includes bodily expressions, systems of knowledge, and norms of behavior, as known to those who care for the child. Parental and others' bodily practices provide a model for children of how to relate to the world in the most basic forms—gestures, facial expressions, way of walking, postures,

Sociological Tradition," *Sociological Review* 49, no. 3 (2001): 332; See Durkheim 420–33 for his discussion on the tremendous importance of rites and ceremonies to society.

[55] Durkheim, 472–74, 492–93 ; Langman, 225.

[56] Durkheim, 420–28, 469–71.

[57] Ibid., 431–33, 445–49.

[58] Ibid., 432, 464, 474–75; Langman, 226.

[59] Durkheim, 472.

[60] Shilling, 336–37.

[61] T. K. Oommen, *Pluralism, Equality and Identity: Comparative Studies* (New Delhi: Oxford University Press, 2002), 23.

[62] Helman, 12.

[63] Alison D. Renteln, *The Cultural Defense* (Oxford: Oxford University Press, 2004), 12; Michael McDonalds, "Should Communities Have Rights? Reflections on Liberal Individualism," in *Human Rights in Cross-Cultural Perspectives: A Quest for Consensus,* ed. Abdullahi Ahmed An-Na'im (Philadelphia: University Pennsylvania Press, 1992), 151.

etc.—which children imitate and adopt as their own.[64] In times of illness and sickness alike, children acquire the reasoning and means of healing that are used by their care givers, as these are perceived as simple acts of survival.

Children's bodily enculturation is also intentional. Children are integrated into the community through bodily practices and rites.[65] Male circumcision, for example, is an obligatory religious rite in both Jewish and Islamic religions, and it is considered quintessential for full membership in the community.[66] The rite is also practiced by various tribes in Africa and among Australian Aboriginals as a symbol of the child's passage into manhood.[67] Full body tattoos are prevalent among various groups in the Pacific Islands. Among Maori warriors in New Zealand, it is believed to have both protective power and also reflects deep cultural and religious beliefs.[68] The practice of women's face tattooing in Papua New Guinea and in Samoan groups in New Zealand is carried out as a rite of passage to womanhood and symbolizes elements of struggle and resistance.[69]

These customs also subject children to a particular position of vulnerability. On the one hand, children's dependency on others for survival, the assumption (at least up to a certain age) of their incapacity, and the cultural conceptualization of child-adult relationships as power relations[70] rule them out as decision makers. Children are generally relegated to a lesser status in their familial and communal environment, and their preferences, if expressed, are often overlooked. Indeed, they are customarily situated at the bottom of all vertical and horizontal models of social stratification: social class, gender, ethnicity, nationality, and so on.[71] On the other hand, children hold significant power. Because failure to pass on the particular tradition would doom the culture to extinction, children are perceived as prime caretakers of the culture's future. For cultural survival, great efforts are thus made to ensure that children feel strongly committed to the culture. Just as children need to be incorporated into the culture, the culture needs to be absorbed by the children.[72]

---

[64] Katharine Young, "The Memory of the Flesh: The Family Body in Somatic Psychology," *Body & Society* 8, no. 3 (2002): 25.

[65] Durkheim, 54, 429.

[66] Abbie J. Chessler, "Justifying the Unjustifiable: Rite v. Wrong," *Buffalo Law Review* 45 (1997): 557, n. 1, http://www.cirp.org/library/legal/chessler; S. A. Aldeeb Abu-Sahlieh, "Muslims' Genitalia in the Hands of the Clergy: Religious Arguments about Male and Female Circumcision," in *Male and Female Circumcision—Medical, Legal and Ethical Considerations in Pediatric Practice,* ed. George C. Denniston, Frederick Mansfield Hodges, and Marilyn Fayre Milos (New York: Kluwer Academic/Plenum Publishers, 1999), 160.

[67] Godfrey B. Tangwa, "Circumcision—An African Point of View," in *Male and Female Circumcision—Medical, Legal and Ethical Considerations in Pediatric Practice,* ed. George C. Denniston, Frederick Mansfield Hodges, and Marilyn Fayre Milos (New York: Kluwer Academic/Plenum Publishers, 1999), 185.

[68] Helman, 16.

[69] Yvonne Underhill-Sem, "Marked Bodies in Marginalized Places: Understanding Rationalities in Global Discourses," *Society for International Development* 46, no. 2 (2003): 15–16.

[70] Jonathan Rutherford, "A Place Called Home: Identity and the Cultural Politics of Difference," in *Identity: Community, Culture, Difference,* ed. Jonathan Rutherford (London: Lawrence & Wishart, 1990), 10.

[71] Chris Jenks, "Many Childhoods?" *Childhood* 11, no. 1 (2004): 5.

[72] Janet E. Halley, "Culture Constrains," in *Is Multiculturalism Bad for Women?* ed. Susan

This mutual dependency is particularly critical in the context of health-related and bodily practices. While some healing and cultural bodily practices may be harmless and mainly symbolic, others may be injurious and detrimental to the children's health. Yet, as the youngest members of the community and its cultural proprietors, children may nevertheless be exposed to either without the ability to protect themselves and regardless of the potential injurious effects of the custom. How has children's vulnerability and power in the context of medical and bodily practices been addressed? To what extent can the principlism approach, which is essentially founded on these factors, be applied to children?

2. Children's Bioethics

In most cultures, children, unlike adults, are not viewed as capable of making choices.[73] Although variance exists across cultures on the definition of childhood and on the exact age of maturity,[74] as a group, children are generally assumed to lack the rationality and wisdom to know what is in their best interests. They are considered as those who need to be looked after and protected, even from themselves.[75]

The discussion on children and medical and health-related bodily practices reflects the unique status of children. The vast literature has concentrated on the question of substitute decision making and on who is the most suitable to make medical and bodily related decisions on a child's behalf. The analysis concerns the triangle between the child, the parents, and the state in an attempt to narrate what is in the child's best interest. Are the parents the most suitable decision makers on behalf of their child? What is the best balance when the interests of the parents and the child clash? When should states resort to their power as *parens patriae* and intervene in familial decision making on behalf of the child?

Traditionally, parents in Western societies are perceived as the best guardians of their child. As primary caretakers of the child, they are presumed to be most knowledgeable about what is in their child's best interest.[76] Assuming that parents have a shared (and similar) interest in their child, parents are given the benefit of the doubt that they will act in a manner that is in their child's best interest.[77] The perception of the family as "the most fundamental unit in society"[78] further consolidates the parents' power of decision making on

M. Okin (Princeton, NJ: Princeton University Press, 1999), 103.

[73] Martha Minow, "About Women, About Culture: About Them, About Us," in *Engaging Cultural Difference: The Multicultural Challenge in Liberal Democracies,* ed. Richard A. Shweder, Martha Minow, and Hazel Rose Markus (New York: Russell Sage Foundation, 2002), 261.

[74] Helman, 6.

[75] Jeremy Roche, "Children: Rights, Participation and Citizenship." *Childhood* 6, no. 4 (1999): 477.

[76] Lorrain Ireland and Immy Holloway, "Qualitative Health Research with Children," *Children & Society* 10 (1996): 159; Alexander M. Capron, "The Authority of Others to Decide About Biomedical Intervention With Incompetent," in *Who Speaks for the Child—the Problems of Proxy Consent,* eds. Willard Gaylin and Ruth Macklin (New York: Plenum Press, 1982), 66.

[77] Capron, 117.

[78] See the Preamble to the Convention on the Rights of the Child (hereafter Children's

behalf of their children. As the predominant guardians of the family unit, its safety and security, parents are assumed to have the entitlement and the duty to determine familial matters without external intervention.[79] Thus, states have shown reluctance to interfere with private family matters such as parent-child relationships, and they generally defer to parental decisions on behalf of their child.[80]

In the past few decades, however, parental decision making has been challenged, particularly in Western countries. Responding to doubts about the actual reliability of parents as suitable proxies of the child[81] and presumably also to a greater acceptance of an interventionist approach,[82] states increasingly invoke their power as *parens patriae* as protectors of the child. Under this power, when medical parental decisions do not seem to be in the best interests of the child, states can intervene and override the decision.[83]

For the most part, the question revolved around the legality of parental informed consent or its denial, questioning the rationality or the irrationality of parental health-related decisions. In this context, the literature distinguishes between three categories of medical and bodily negligence and abuse: general parental negligence, parental usage of folk medicine, and religio-culturally mandated practices. There is little controversy about a state's intervention when parents fail to provide medical treatment to their child for no substantial reason. In such cases, the negligence is assumed to be a symptom of general parental dysfunction, and states find it easier to justify intervention in family affairs.[84] The more contentious cases, however, are when state agencies intervene

---

Convention or Convention), G.A. Res. 44/25, annex, 44th Sess., 61st plenary meeting. U.N. GAOR Supp. (No. 49), at 167, U.N. Doc. A/44/49 (1989), entered into force September 2, 1990, reprinted in 28 I.L.M. 1448 (1989), which emphasizes the family, as "the fundamental group of society and the natural environment for the growth and well-being of all its members and particularly children" and the importance of the tradition and the cultural surrounding of the child.

[79] Patricia. A. King, "Treatment and Minors: Issues not Involving Lifesaving Treatment," *Journal of Family Law* 23 (1984–85): 254.

[80] See Gerlard Dworkin, "Consent, Representation and Proxy Consent," in *Who Speaks for the Child—The Problems of Proxy Consent,* ed. Willard Gaylin and Ruth Macklin (New York: Plenum Press, 1982), 104; Alison D. Renteln, "Is the Cultural Defense Detrimental to the Health of Children?" in *Law and Anthropology: International Yearbook for Legal Anthropology*, ed. René Kupper and Richard Potz (Dordrecht: Martinus Nijhoff, 1994), 27.

[81] Jane Lightfoot and Patricia Sloper, "Having a Say in Health: Involving Young People with a Chronic Illness of Physical Disability in Local Health Services Development," *Children & Society* 17 (2003): 277.

[82] Renteln, "Is the Cultural Defense Detrimental to the Health of Children," 27, 41.

[83] Ibid., 27.

[84] Cowen discusses the distinction between child neglect and child abuse and the difficulties in characterizing medical neglect. She refers to parental medical neglect as "a pattern of omission," when parents are unable, unwilling, unmotivated, or inconsistent in assessing the severity of an illness or accident and in seeking the necessary forms of preventive care (Perle Slavik Cowen, "Child Neglect: Injuries of Omission," *Pediatric Nursing* 25, no. 4 (1999): 403). Yet, although states increasingly formulate child neglect and abuse laws, including reporting and intervention policies, there are substantial cultural differences, among states in the same region, as to what constitutes child abuse and neglect. Thus, even if a justification

following the categorization of healing methods or religio-cultural mandated rites as neglect and abuse of the child.

A part of the controversy lies in the absence of universally accepted criteria to determine which behaviors and practices actually constitute medical neglect and abuse.[85] Groups and communities differ in their child-rearing practices and in their limits of acceptable behavior.[86] As Jill Korbin points out, "it is not the act itself that is the major criteria in defining child abuse in a culturally appropriate fashion, but the context in which the act occurs."[87] Thus, observation, analysis, and definition of child abuse require contextualizing the act.

Even death may have different significance in various cultural groups. The reliance of Christian Scientists exclusively on faith healing is often cited as an example. Deeming any Western medical intervention as detrimental to their religious adherence and beliefs, they refuse treatment even if death may occur and even if Western remedies could easily provide a cure.[88] In such cases, Western states have often taken the position that the child's best interest requires receiving the modern and scientifically based therapy.[89] The assumption is that religious conviction prevented the parents from properly considering the implications and risks associated with the biomedical treatments.[90] Hence, such a view cannot be "informed," and, therefore, it is essential that the state

---

of state intervention in some cases may be agreed upon, the practical interpretation and implementation of state intervention varies. Lau and Liu (1999), for example, discuss in this context the concept of child abuse and reporting patterns in Hong-Kong. They also briefly summarize studies conducted on the issue in Malaysia, Pakistan, Singapore, and India. (Joseph T. F. Lau and Joseph L. Y. Liu, "Conceptualization, Reporting and Underreporting of Child Abuse in Hong Kong," *Child Abuse & Neglect* 23, no. 11 (1999): 1160).

[85] Jill E. Korbin, "Child Maltreatment in Cross-Cultural Perspective: Vulnerable Children and Circumstances," in *Child Abuse and Neglect: Biosocial Dimensions,* ed. Richard J. Gelles and James B Lancester (New York: Aldin De Gruyter, 1987), 33–34 (discussing the definitional problem and the difficulties in reaching an operational cross-cultural definition of child abuse).

[86] See, for example, Lois Pierce, and Vivienne Bozalek, "Child Abuse in South Africa: An Examination of How Child Abuse and Neglect are Defined," *Child Abuse & Neglect* 28 (2004): 817–32 (discussing child abuse and neglect in South Africa); Ilgi O. Ertem and others, "Medical Neglect of A Child: Challenges for Pediatricians in Developing Countries," *Child Abuse & Neglect* 26 (2002): 751–61 (discussing the cultural barriers that lead to medical neglect of children in Turkey); Anne M. Ferrari, "The Impact of Culture Upon Child Rearing Practices and Definitions of Maltreatment," *Child Abuse & Neglect* 26 (2002): 793–813 (discussing parental child-rearing practices and definitions of child abuse and neglect in Hispanic, African American, and European Americans).

[87] Korbin, "A Cross-Cultural Perspective on the Role of the Community in Child Abuse and Neglect," 10.

[88] Renteln, "Is the Cultural Defense Detrimental to the Health of Children," 48.

[89] See for example, Lori G. Beaman, "Religion and Rights: the Illusion of Freedom and the Reality of Control," *Culture & Religion* 6, no. 1 (2005): 22–23.

[90] Les Haberfield, "Informed Consent and Infant Male Circumcision," *Australian Law Teachers Conference,* Sydney, New South Wales, Australia, October 3, 1997, Library of Circumcision Information and Resource Pages, http://www.cirp.org/library/legal/haberfield/; Christopher Price, "Male Circumcision: An Ethical and Legal Affront," *Bulletin of Medical Ethics* 128 (1997): 13–19.

intervene to protect its young citizens from harm.[91] Courts generally supported such reasoning on the basis of the child's particular vulnerability and the rebuff of arguments about parental rights and prerogatives when the child's physical health or safety is in serious danger.[92]

While this has been used as a justification for state intervention when children are in life-threatening situations,[93] it does not resolve much of the debate about other medical issues like folk healing or bodily practices. First, it is difficult to determine in advance the point at which a health condition will actually turn out to be a life-threatening situation. Furthermore, as one's illnesses and conditions normally occur within the private sphere and out of public view, the time gap for state agencies to act is, in effect, extremely limited[94] and may be too late for the child if death already occurred.

Theoretically, states' close monitoring of particular suspect cultural groups could alleviate the problem. As factors such as poverty, limited education, inadequate social resources, and parental immaturity are found to be correlated with levels of child abuse,[95] supervising such familial enclaves could help. However, such a proposition raises a few significant flaws. First, increased monitoring of "suspect cultural groups" contradicts the liberal notion of color-blind equality.[96] While poverty, limited education, and other susceptible factors for child abuse exist across all ethnic, religious, and cultural groups, there is an institutional bias against minority groups.[97] Aside from complicating the task of distinguishing between the effects of these factors and cultural practices,[98] it means that immigrants and members of minority groups would be the main

---

[91] There may be a distinction between allowing state intervention to provide medical care to the child and the response *post factum,* if death occurred. In the United States, for example, courts often issue an order for medical treatment when parents refuse to approve essential medical treatment to their child on the basis of their religious convictions. In the second scenario, in contrast, there is almost nationwide legislation that exempts Christian Scientist parents from child abuse and even from manslaughter if their refusal to accept Western medical treatment led to the child's death. Adam Lamparello, "Taking God Out of the Hospital: Requiring Parents to Seek Medical Care for Their Children Regardless of Religious Belief," *Texas Forum on Civil Liberties & Civil Rights* 6 (2001): 50; Elizabeth A. Lingle, "Treating Children by Faith Colliding Constitutional Issues," *Journal of Legal Medicine* 17 (1996): 306.

[92] See, for example, Beaman, note 59, discussing the Canadian Case of Bethany Hughes involving a sixteen-year-old cancer patient. She was a Jehovah's Witness member who refused a blood transfusion. The court dismissed her argument that she should not be forced to receive the treatment on the basis of her right to religious freedom. In the United States, see, for example, the case of *Jehovah's Witnesses v. King County Hospital* (278 F. Supp. 488 (W.D. Wash. 1967), *affd,* 390 U.S. 598 (1968)).

[93] Renteln, "Is the Cultural Defense Detrimental to the Health of Children," 55–56.

[94] Ibid., 55.

[95] Leon Eisenberg, "Cross-Cultural and Historical Perspectives on Child Abuse and Neglect," *Child Abuse & Neglect* 5 (1981): 305.

[96] Rhoda E. Howard, "Dignity, Community and Human Rights," in *Human Rights in Cross-Cultural Perspectives: A Quest for Consensus,* ed. Abdullahi Ahmed An-Na'im (Philadelphia: University Pennsylvania Press, 1992), 94–95.

[97] Leslie Berger, "Learning to Tell Custom from Abuse," *Los Angeles Times,* August 24, 1994, A16.

[98] Ibid.

targets of the welfare authorities' supervision, and these groups would be prone to excessive and unwarranted intervention in their family affairs. This is all the more so considering that at least, in the short run, immigrants are often more likely to experience some financial and social stress as they get accustomed to their new environment.[99] While protecting children's health and safety is clearly important and within states' legitimate interests, *a priori* determination of guilt would not be within the notions of equality and justice in liberal democracy.[100] At the same time, whereas the parental and communal decision making of children from minority groups would be held to a higher level of scrutiny, children who are not members of such cultural groups would not, although they may be exposed to harmful practices just as much. Hence, their health status and security are, in comparison, compromised.

Second, setting up a list of suspect cultural groups would be inherently arbitrary and even unrealistic. Medical cultures are not necessarily mutually exclusive even if some medical practices are rejected. The refusal of members of the Jehovah's Witnesses community to receive blood transfusions, for example, does not mean they reject other Western medical procedures.[101] Furthermore, various medical cultures increasingly mingle with and influence one another. Healing practices of Hmong immigrants in the United States, for instance, include, alongside their traditional medical culture, many Christian and Western practices.[102] Thus, drawing a list of "suspect cultural groups" is essentially left to the discretion of the states' law enforcement agencies and is more likely to be abused.

Finally, concerns arise in the context of what Richard Shweder has termed a natural and mutual "yuck response."[103] Although many medical folk practices do not necessarily pose any serious damage to the child's health and safety, they are nevertheless perceived as bizarre and harmful by mainstream society. While this has been particularly acute in the context of religio-culturally mandated bodily practices,[104] healing methods are not exempted from the cultural scrutiny. The Southern Asian practice of coining (see Section B.2) is one such example. Although the practice is not harmful, when immigrants in Western countries perform it, the lesions and red marks that it leaves often lead to its

---

[99] Maj Duong Nguyen, "Culture Shock: A Review of Vietnamese Culture and Its Concepts of Health and Disease," *Western Journal of Medicine* 142, no. 3 (1985): 411.

[100] Renteln, *The Cultural Defense*, 55.

[101] Furthermore, in an attempt to accommodate the particular medical needs of members of Jehovah's Witnesses community, efforts have been made to develop medical procedures including surgeries that do not require blood transfusion. See Valerie Reitman, "With Less Blood Shed," *Los Angeles Times*, Jan. 31, 2005, Health Section, F1 and F8; Kaaron Benson, "Management of the Jehovah's Witness Oncology Patient: Perspective of the Transfusion Service," *Cancer Control Journal* 2, no. 6 (1995), https://www.moffitt.usf.edu/pubs/ccj/v2n6/article13.html.

[102] Lisa L. Capps, "Change and Continuity in the Medical Culture of the Hmong in Kansas City," *Medical Anthropology Quarterly* 8, no. 2 (1994): 161–63.

[103] Richard Shweder, "'What About FGM?' and Why Understanding Culture Matters in the First Place?" in *Engaging Cultural Difference: The Multicultural Challenge in Liberal Democracies,* ed. Richard A. Shweder, Martha Minow, and Hazel Rose Markus (New York: Russell Sage Foundation, 2002), 222.

[104] Ibid., 216–22 (discussing the international campaign against female genital cutting).

misdiagnosis as child abuse.[105] Consequently, parents in the United States, for example, were falsely accused and faced prosecution and the temporary loss of their child's custody.[106] Therapeutic burns, practiced in Asian cultures, Near-Eastern countries, and Africa, have also been confused with child abuse due to the scarring they may leave.[107] The difficulty is how to overcome an initial yuck response in an unbiased manner so as to properly distinguish between injurious practices and others that are merely different.

These concerns are closely linked to the broader question of multiculturalism and tolerance, including the extent to which states are expected to accommodate various minority groups within their borders (see Chapter 4).[108] It is important to note that this question of multirculturalism and tolerance has been at the center of many debates on both the national and international levels. It has also been particularly politicized in the context of women's rights.[109] Many argue that accommodation is dangerous because it subjects women and girls in particular to additional levels of subordination and to traditional practices that are harmful to their health.[110] Although some customs may be cause for alarm, this excessive emphasis on gender-related practices has obscured the fact that it is not only women and girls who face potentially harmful traditional medical and bodily practices. Boys, too, are exposed to traditional practices such as circumcision, scarification, and the like.

Furthermore, focusing on bodily and medical practices of minority groups leads one to miss the point. Culture is a universal feature of humanity. Thus, traditional practices are performed not only by minority groups but also by majority groups. In communities where male circumcision is practiced by

---

[105] Gentry W. Yectman, "Cao Gio (Coin Rubbing): Vietnamese Attitudes Toward Health Care," *Journal of the American Medical Association* 244 no. 24 1980: 2749.

[106] In one reported case, a Vietnamese father who unsuccessfully used coining to heal his son committed suicide after being jailed and accused of child abuse. George K. Hong and Lawrence K. Hong, "Comparative Perspectives on Child Neglect and Abuse: Chinese Versus Hispanics and Whites," *Child Welfare* 70, no. 4 (1991): 474; Marie McCullough, "Medical Conditions Can Look Like Child Abuse," *Chicago Tribune*, May 30, 1995, Tempo, 3.

[107] Karen K. Hansen, "Folk Remedies and Child Abuse: A Review With Emphasis on Caida De Mollera and Its Relationship to Shaken Baby Syndrome," *Child Abuse & Neglect* 22, no. 2 (1997): 120; Samuel Forjuoh, "Pattern of Intentional Burns to Children in Ghana," *Child Neglect & Abuse* 19, no. 7 (1995): 837, 841.

[108] For a general discussion on multiculturalism, see Emy Gutman, ed., *Multiculturalism: Examining the Politics of Recognition* (Princeton, NJ: Princeton University Press, 1994); Bhikhu Parekh, *Rethinking Multiculturalism: Cultural Diversity and Political Theory* (Cambridge, MA: Harvard University Press, 2000); Ian Shapiro and Will Kymlicka, eds., *Ethnicity and Groups Rights* (New York: New York University Press, 1997); Martha Minow, "Putting Up and Putting Down: Tolerance Reconsidered," in *Comparative Constitutional Federalism: Europe and America*, ed. Mark Tushnet (New York: Greenwood Press, 1990).

[109] For discussion on women, health, and politics, see, the essays in Susan Sherwin, ed., *The Politics of Women's Health: Exploring Agency and Autonomy* (Philadelphia: Temple University Press, 1998); Rebecca J. Cook, "International Human Rights and Women's Reproductive Health," *Studies in Family Planning* 24, no. 2 (1993): 73–86; Ayelet Shachar, *Multicultural Jurisdiction: Cultural Differences and Women's Rights,* (Cambridge: Cambridge University Press, 2001) (discussing multicultural accommodation and women's rights).

[110] Minow, "About Women, About Culture," 252; Packer, 3–5; Cook, 73–75, 83.

adherent of religious faiths, such as Judaism and Islam in the Middle East, the rite is performed almost exclusively, in about 99 percent of the male population.[111] The ritual of tattooing for religious and cultural reasons is prevalent among men from the Shan tradition in various areas in Burma and Thailand,[112] and the elongation of women's necks is performed among the Padaung tribe of Myanmar and in some African societies.[113] Finally, Western corrective surgeries for disabilities, prenatal testing, and genetic engineering to overcome disease or disabilities are also medical/bodily cultural practices.[114] While some of them may be performed for therapeutic goals, others may reflect unjustified discriminatory attitudes toward specific groups of people. As some scholars have argued,[115] the increasing use of biomedical practices to attain a disability-free society often mirrors a perception of persons with disabilities as being in a subordinate position and from a cultural anxiety with physical and mental differences.[116] Thus, for a constructive international discussion on children's bioethics, Western and majoritarian traditional biomedical practices should be taken up as well.

D. CHILDREN'S BIOETHICS AND THE QUESTION OF AGENCY

1. Children and Social Agency

The discourse on children's agency is a relatively recent development. Although the relationships among individuals, cultures, and their role as social agents have been studied extensively in various disciplines of social sciences, prevailing notions of children have historically excluded them from the "agency talk." Similar to women, slaves, and other marginalized groups,[117] children were categorized mostly outside of the active social life. Their differentiation on the basis of biological maturity by adults, and in the case of the girl child, also gender distinction,[118] entrenched the presumption that children are only passive actors and *objects* of enculturation with little power, if at all, in its development.[119]

---

[111] Chessler, 557, n. 1; Abu-Sahlieh, 139; Packer, 7.

[112] Nicola Tannenbaum, "Tattoos: Invulnerability and Power in Shan Cosmology," *American Ethnologist* 14, no. 4 (1987): 695.

[113] Packer, 3.

[114] Sarah Franklin, "Science as Culture, Cultures of Science," *Annual Review of Anthropology* 24 (1995): 164; Muller, 458.

[115] Harlan Hahn, "The Political Implications of Disability: Definition and Data," in *The Psychological and Social Impact of Disability*, ed. Robert P. Marinelli and Arthur E. Dell Orto (New York: Springer Publishing, 1999), 8; David Pfeiffer, "Eugenics and Disability Discrimination," in *The Psychological and Social Impact of Disability*, ed. Robert P. Marinelli and Arthur E. Dell Orto (New York: Springer Publishing, 1999), 26; Adrienne Asch, Lawrence O. Gostin, and Diann M. Johnson, "Respecting Persons with Disabilities and Preventing Disabilities: Is There a Conflict?" in *The Human Rights of Persons with Intellectual Disabilities: Different but Equal*, ed. Stanley S. Herr, Lawrence O. Gostin, and Harold Hongju Koh (New York: Oxford University Press), 334–38.

[116] Hahn, 8; Tom Shakespear, "Cultural Representation of Disabled People: Dustbins for Disavowal?" *Disability & Society* 9, no. 3 (1994): 296–97.

[117] Ann Witz and Barbara L. Marshall, "The Quality of Manhood: Masculinity and Embodiment in the Sociological Tradition," *Sociological Review*, 51 (2003): 341.

[118] Ibid., 253.

[119] Pia Christensen and Alan Prout, "Working with Ethical Asymmetry in Social Research with Children," *Childhood* 9, no. 4 (2002): 480.

Modern social movements, the growth of consumer culture, and the influence of postmodernism and poststructuralists' theories,[120] however, reopened the discussion about the body, society, and agency. The feminist movement has been pivotal to this development, revolutionizing the understanding of power and subjectivity, and challenging the hegemonic concept of masculine agency.[121] Feminists called attention to the conceptualization of women as bodies without minds that marginalized them and to the need to reembody women as social agents.[122]

Shifts in the ways in which culture has been understood exacerbated the process. Perception of culture as dynamic and in an ongoing process of change substituted previous notions of culture as a fixed and nonchangeable factor.[123] Culture has increasingly come across as a site of internal and external contestation[124] and, furthermore, as both context and as something that can be chosen.[125] Indeed, the process of enculturation itself is now understood as providing a space for resistance toward the center (or the mainstream), allowing for diversity from within.[126] Although social and legal categorization such as child/adult, man/woman, etc., plays a significant role in organizing one's perception of the world,[127] the assumption is that challenges to culture and its practices are inherent to it, regardless of one's status within his or her social web.[128] The interaction and interdependency between individuals, social movements, and culture allow for different interpretations and negotiations—hence a place for social agency.[129] While the discourse on cultural deconstruction has been justly criticized for oversimplification and failure to grasp the enduring power of cultural practices over time,[130] it nevertheless established the setting needed for the development of a discourse on children's agency.

---

[120] Lupton, 23.

[121] Witz and Marshall, 341.

[122] Chris Rojek and Bryan Turner, "Decorative Sociology: Towards a Critique of the Cultural Turn," *Sociology Review* 48 no. 4 (2000): 635.

[123] Rodolfo Stavenhagen, "Cultural Rights: A Social Science Perspective," in *Cultural Rights and Wrongs*, ed. Halina Nieć (Paris: UNESCO Publishing, 1998), 5–6; Lyndel Prott, "Understanding One Another on Cultural Rights," in *Cultural Rights and Wrongs*, ed. Halina Nieć (Paris: UNESCO Publishing, 1998), 164.

[124] Sharon Stephens, "Introduction: Children and the Politics of Culture in "'Late Capitalism'" in *Children and the Politics of Culture*, ed. Sharon Stephens (Princeton, NJ: Princeton University Press, 1995), 22.

[125] Baubock, 207.

[126] Rutherford, 23.

[127] Martha Minow, *Not Only For Myself: Identity, Politics, and the Law* (New York: New Press, 1997), 64.

[128] Bonnie Honig, "My Culture Made Me Do It," in *Is Multiculturalism Bad for Women?* ed. Susan M. Okin (Princeton, NJ: Princeton University Press, 1999), 39.

[129] Rutherford, 26, 21. Scholars term the concept of social agency in various ways. Rutherford talks about "Structures of Feeling" (Rutherford, 22–23); Craig uses the term "action in context." (Anita P. Craig, "Cultural and the Individual," *Theory & Psychology* 13, no. 5 (2003): 641.)

[130] Renteln, *The Cultural Defense*, 11; Baubock, 4 (arguing that no absolute free decision about culture and identity can be assumed).

2. Children, Citizenship, and Participation

The discourse on children's agency is closely linked to notions of citizenship and participation. Under the political philosophy of governance as developed since the sixteenth century, people are expected to form and authorize the government (whichever type) by means of consent.[131] Traditionally, the focus has been on the formal institutional settings whose power and authority are contingent on the citizens' regular confirmation of consent.[132] As citizenship was essentially conceived in terms of one's participation (only) in the public domain,[133] it practically left children's participation out of the discourse.[134]

In the last decades, however, another model of participation has evolved. From the perspective of this new model,[135] citizenship and participation cannot have a rigid and fixed meaning.[136] Participation is contingent on one's capacity and connection with groups and/or ideas relative to the multiple interests and challenges one faces.[137] It is related more to an ongoing process of education that begins in childhood and continues until adulthood is traditionally reached.[138] Furthermore, citizenship and participation now embrace not only occasional voting and public activity, but also one's involvement in the private sphere.[139] Conceived as such, children's involvement in a web of social relations and interactions and their negotiation of their positions in various spaces (education, family, etc.) inherently qualifies as a form of citizenship.[140]

The array of articles in the Convention on the Rights of the Child (Children's

---

[131] Gillian Brown, *The Consent of the Governed: The Lockean Legacy in Early American Culture* (Cambridge, MA: Harvard University Press, 2001), 4.

[132] Ibid., 16.

[133] Jeff Spinner, *The Boundaries of Citizenship: Race, Ethnicity and Nationality in the Liberal State* (Baltimore: Johns Hopkins University Press, 1994), 46–47.

[134] The rivalry between the children's liberation movement, who call for granting children full equal rights as adults, and its opponents, who argue that such a proposal is unattainable, as well as on the arguably mid-way approach that has been taken in the Children's Convention is elaborated on in Chapters 2 and 6 of this book.

[135] In the literature, the new model is called "the life-world perspective," and it is distinguished from the previous "system perspective" model. See Marc Jans, "Children as Citizens: Towards A Contemporary Notion of Child Participation," *Childhood* 11, no. 1 (2004): 30–31.

[136] Ibid., 31.

[137] Ibid.

[138] Ibid., 31, 36; Brown, 16.

[139] Spinner, 46.

[140] Jans, 39. Jans distinguishes between four possible interpretations of citizenship: "a whole of rights," in which citizenship is exclusively linked to the entire bundle of rights that are granted to adults; "a whole of responsibilities," in which citizenship is tied up with the norms of behaviors and duties that adults are expected uphold; "citizenship as an identity," which connects individuals' identity with the sociocultural context, essentially the nation-state or geographical territory; and finally, "citizenship as a form of participation and involvement." In contrast to children's liberation advocates who call for the application of citizenship as a bundle of rights also to children (Martha Minow, "What Ever Happened to Children's Rights?" *Minnesota Law Review* 80, no. 1 (1995): 271, 277), Jans argues that notions of children as citizens can be attainable only if opting for the fourth option, as it is the only interpretation that takes into account all the particular factors of childhood, including rights, special need of protection, multiple groups of identification in an informal and local settings, and ongoing negotiation in their various spheres of life. See Jans, 38–39.

Convention or Convention)[141] indicates the endorsement of this approach as it explicitly grants children a right to participate in matters that are relevant to them. Article 5 provides that parental direction and guidance has to be "in a manner that is consistent with the evolving capacity of the child"; Article 13 guarantees the child's freedom of expression; Article 14 grants the child's right to freedom of conscience, thought, and religion. Most significantly, Article 12 of the Convention obligates "States Parties [to] assure [that] the child who is capable of forming his or her own views [has] the right to express those views freely in all matters affecting the child, the views of the child being given due weight in accordance with the age and maturity of the child." How does this form of citizenship translate into practice in the discourse on children's agency and participation? More specifically, the question whether children play a role as active social agents deserves consideration.

3. Children's Agency and Bioethics

Although the importance and scope of children's participation have been increasingly acknowledged in various contexts of decision making, such as public service and community development,[142] family relations,[143] education,[144] and others,[145] children's involvement in biomedical decision making has been rather limited. For the most part, it focused on medical treatment in formal medical institutions and on the question of informed consent.

Priscilla Alderson examined children's capacity to make informed decisions about nonemergency proposed medical treatment in her innovative book, *Children's Consent to Surgery*.[146] She conducted 120 interviews with children who faced surgery and underwent prolonged processes of rehabilitation between the ages of eight and fifteen. In her conclusion, she argues that given the right environment, including appropriate means of communication, consent by children who are encouraged to be involved in the process, at least from the age of eight, is not substantially different from that of adults.[147] "Competence to consent," she contends, "is not a fact" but a quality that develops through relationships, experience, and perceptions of childhood and its limits of behavior.[148] Other studies focused on children's participation in the evaluation of health service development,[149] in ethnographic research on children's

---

141 Convention on the Rights of the Child, G.A. Res. 44/25, annex, 44th Sess., 61st plenary meeting. U.N. GAOR Supp. (No. 49), at 167, U.N. Doc. A/44/49 (1989), entered into force September 2, 1990, reprinted in 28 I.L.M. 1448 (1989).

142 Lightfoot and Sloper, 277.

143 Elizabeth Such and Robert Walker, "Being Responsible and Responsible Beings: Children's Understanding of Responsibility," *Children & Society* 18 (2004): 231–42.

144 Priscilla Alderson and Christopher Goodey, "Research with Disabled Children: How Useful Is Child-Centred Ethics?" *Children & Society* 10 (1996): 106–16.

145 For example, anthropological research with children, see Lightfoot and Sloper, 277.

146 Priscilla Alderson, *Children's Consent to Surgery* (Buckingham, UK: Open University Press, 1993), 3.

147 Ibid., 190.

148 Ibid., 193.

149 Lightfoot and Sloper, 278, 287–89.

health and self-care,[150] and, recently, on children's perception of health and disabilities.[151] Still the discussion has been rather limited.

First, while children have been increasingly involved in research in Western societies, the overwhelming assumption has been that children's participation and agency in the context of biomedical issues can be remedied merely by extending the doctrine of informed consent to competent children. According to this view of "ethical asymmetry," as Pia Christensen and Alan Prout termed it,[152] no different methods or set of ethical considerations are required.[153] The problem with this approach is two-fold. First, as discussed earlier (see Section B), the doctrine of informed consent suffers from a significant Western bias, and it cannot necessarily be applied all around the globe. The second pitfall is grounded in the particular context of children. The presumption of the ethical asymmetry approach fails to take into account the fact that children's views and interests may be substantively different from adults' considerations and perceptions of the world.[154] Thus, for example, children with chronic illness or physical disability from the United Kingdom, who participated in a research study on the context of development of health services, ranked their communication with the medical staff (patronizing attitudes and withholding of information) as their primary concern.[155] Privacy, usually conceived as a cornerstone in adults' views on medical proceedings, was marked only as the sixth important factor, after recreation/entertainment facilities, "food equality," "hospital tuition," and flexibility of rules with regard to bedtime, visiting and going out, and before décor and timing of treatment.[156] To what extent are these differences taken into account from a cross-cultural and international perspective in the determination of the international bodies? As the international community is responsible for establishing standards for states' compliance with their obligations under the Children's Convention, including children as participatory subjects, these are important questions to explore.

Another limitation has to do with the concentration in the literature on formal health institutions, such as hospitals, children's welfare houses,

---

[150] Pia Handrup Christensen, "Children's Participation in Ethnographic Research: Issues of Power and Representation," *Children & Society* 18 (2004): 165–76.

[151] Such studies are discussed in Chapter 7. Kirsten Stalker and Clare Connors, "Children's Perceptions of Their Disabled Siblings: 'She's Different but it's Normal for Us'," *Children & Society* 18, no. 3 (2004): 218–30; Ireland and Holloway, 155–64; Alderson and Goodey, 106–16.

[152] Christensen and Prout, 482.

[153] Virginia Morrow and Martin Richards, "The Ethics of Social Research with Children: An Overview," *Children & Society* 10 (1996): 93–96; Christensen, 165; Ireland and Holloway, 158; Nigel Thomas and Claire O'Kane, "The Ethics of Participatory Research," *Children & Society* 12 (1998): 337. See also Morrow and Richards, 100–103, arguing that while similar ethical considerations that are applied in research with adults should apply also in research with children, researchers should also be wary of the issues of children's capacity and vulnerability and of the researcher's interpretation of the data.

[154] Stephens, 9; Lightfoot and Sloper, 278; Judith Cavet and Patricia Sloper, "Participation of Disabled Children in Individual Decisions about Their Lives and in Public Decisions about Service Development," *Children & Society* 18, no. 4 (2004): 284.

[155] Lightfoot and Sloper, 285. The study was conducted in the United Kingdom, with twenty-three children and young patients, aged thirteen to twenty. Ibid., 280.

[156] Ibid., 285.

etc., and on doctor-patient relationships. This, however, does not take into account many other health-related settings—the family and the community or the importance of social relations in this informal sphere. Even if the terms doctor and medical personnel are extended to include all practitioners who perform bodily procedures (e.g., private entities in various communities), the focus on the doctor-patient relationship ignores the reality by which a web of social relationships may be a better source for understanding the medical moral dilemma.[157] And yet bioethical research with children consistently shows that relationships and interdependency play a prominent role in the children's development and perceptions. In a study conducted in Scotland on the perception of siblings of children with disabilities aged seven to fifteen on disability, the researcher found that the most influential factor that constructed their perception of disability was the various roles they did or did not share with their disabled siblings (playmates, teachers' pet, annoying little brother, helper, etc.) and not a sense of personal tragedy or difference.[158] Thus, contextualizing the discussion of children's bioethics in a broader set of health-related institutions and relationships is in place.

Finally, the meaning of children's agency and children as citizens is, to a great extent, still obscure. Gerison Lansdown, in her study *Promoting Children's Participation in Democratic Decision-Making*, discusses the meaning of children's participation in view of the provisions in the Children's Convention and proposes three possible categories of involvement.[159] First is consultative participation. In this category, adults initiate a process to obtain information from children with the aim of improving legislation, policies, or services.[160] These processes follow the conventional structural power relationship between adults and children: they are adult led and managed, and children have no influence on the outcomes.[161] The second category, participative initiatives, aims at creating "opportunities for children to understand and apply democratic principles or [be] involved . . . in the development of services and policies that impact them."[162] This category of children's participation, while initiated by adults, nevertheless allows for sharing the power between adults and children through a collaborative partnership. It allows children to challenge or influence the outcomes and take a "self-directed action once the project is underway."[163] The third category is promoting self-advocacy. This category aims at "empower[ing] children to identify and fulfill their own goals and initiatives."[164] The issues of concern and the control over the process are in the hands of the children, and the adults' role is only to facilitate (but not to lead).[165]

While all three categories are relevant to advance children's rights, it appears

---

157 Muller, 452.

158 Stalker and Connors, 223–24, 228.

159 Gerison Lansdown, *Promoting Children's Participation in Democratic Decision-Making* (Florence, Italy: UNICEF & Innocenti Research Centre, 2001), 16.

160 Ibid.

161 Ibid. 17.

162 Ibid., 16.

163 Ibid., 21.

164 Ibid., 16.

165 Ibid., 27.

that only the second and third categories step away from the traditional binary opposite of adults-child, actually taking into account children as active agents. In view of the purpose of the Children's Convention to recognize children as rights holders and participatory citizens on one hand, and the silence of the Convention as to which form of involvement states are required to follow, on the other hand, the implementation of the Convention's intention to reconstruct notions of childhood, children, and citizenship may be at lost. To what extent do states listen to children's voices in bioethical dilemmas? To what extent does the Monitoring Committee under the Children's Convention, which monitors the implementation of the Convention, pay attention to children's role as active citizens within their national borders—and within its own work? The practical achievements of the Convention in this context have not been yet explored in a comprehensive and a cross-cultural manner. This book offers such examination.

E. CONCLUSION

Much has been said in the past few decades about the scientific revolution and its impact. Even more has been said, particularly following the experiences of World War II, about the need to prioritize the individual's benefit over the collective good. The principlism approach and its guiding doctrine of informed consent evolved on this background. They aimed at ensuring individual's autonomy, self-determination, and personal involvement in medical decision making. They also reflected the rise in the rights talk that took place since the mid-twentieth century. Indeed, the development of medical ethics has been intertwined with, and is perhaps even the springboard of, the entire international human rights regime as it is known today.

The perception of the principlism approach and the doctrine of informed consent as universal standards of medical ethics is misleading, however. Neither the process of secularization nor the medicalization shift has simultaneously taken root all across the world. Many societies remained religiously or, as some may view it, culturally primitive. Their construction of health, illness, the medical profession, and the medical ethics that are associated with it continue to be rooted in notions such as divine retribution, misfortune, witch's spell, or simply a different concept of the impact of one's entire cosmos on one's and the group's health. There is also great diversity with respect to questions such as how much individual involvement in medical decision making is needed, if at all, who are the ones responsible for diagnosing and treating ill patients, and what sort of medical interventions to follow in any case. There is thus an unavoidable medical pluralism, with many medical cultures coexisting at any given time. Processes of globalization, immigration, refugees, and others further exacerbated this phenomenon, as medical pluralism now exists not only when one looks at the world and its remote communities, but also within ostensibly every state.

The illusion of the universal application of the principlism approach is particularly evident in the context of children. Although children were recognized as rights holders, they are still often excluded from the biomedical discourse and decision making. While changes in the concept of participation have led to the acknowledgment of child's agency in an array of circumstances, the inclusion of children as social agents in the biomedical sphere has been lagging behind. There has been only limited scholarly work on children in this context, and the literature that exists has often focused on substitute decision making, on a possible extension of the doctrine of informed consent to children, and on children, particularly those belonging to minority groups, as mere victims of biomedical practices. This is so even though not only children belonging to minority groups are at risk and, furthermore, that children are not only potential victims of a given medical culture but those who hold the prime role and power of ensuring the culture's survival as may be reflected in the biomedical practices involved. Thus, for a proper examination of children's bioethics, a much further inclusive discussion about the intersection of children as rights holders, agency, and biomedical cultures is needed.

As the data in this study shows, such an approach is particularly appropriate with regard to children. As those who are most vulnerable to bodily practices, yet also hold power in the preservation of such customs and, hence, in the demarcation of one's membership in and in the survival of a given cultural community, whether the rites are religiously, culturally, or scientifically mandated may have only little difference to them. Ultimately, they are all inherently integral to their sense of belonging and identity. The examination, hence, has to bear in mind the child's social and cultural milieu.

Chapter 2 examines the extent to which issues pertinent to children's bioethics are incorporated into the final text of the Children's Convention, and beyond it. Understanding the controversies and the political forces that played a role in the drafting process of the Convention are important as they allow one to appreciate—and criticize—what has been achieved.

CHAPTER 2

CHILDREN'S BIOETHICS IN THE CONVENTION ON THE RIGHTS OF THE CHILD: HISTORICAL OVERVIEW OF THE DRAFTING PROCESS

Questions about children's health surfaced constantly during the drafting process of the Convention on the Rights of the Child (Children's Convention or Convention)[1] at the United Nations. Debates about the appropriate formulation to ensure a reduction in children's mortality, susceptibility to infectious diseases, and the necessity of basic health care services were integral to the negotiations. These discussions often took place under the traditional umbrella of children's special vulnerability and their need to be protected. References were made to parental responsibilities for taking care of the child and to states' duties to provide the infrastructure for appropriate development and the prevention of health-related harm. Specific proposals were also submitted on issues such as genetic engineering and experimentation with children. Moreover, the proposals were integral to the discussions on children as agents. The discussions included the child's role as a subject of medical treatment and experimentation, the relative benefits he or she should gain in view of the child's social and general environment, and proposals on the child as a targeted consumer of health and bodily related practices. Yet the final text of the Children's Convention contains no explicit reference to any of these latter biomedical practices. So, what went wrong?

This chapter offers an overview of the major debates that took place during the codification process on issues of children's bioethics.[2] As an international instrument that received almost universal support among state members of the United Nations, this discussion is important for two main reasons. First, it

[1] Convention on the Rights of the Child, G.A. Res. 44/25, annex, 44th Sess., 61st plenary meeting. U.N. GAOR Supp. (No. 49), at 167, U.N. Doc. A/44/49 (1989), entered into force September 2, 1990, reprinted in 28 I.L.M. 1448 (1989).

[2] The United Nations' official records regarding the drafting process of the Children's Convention are compiled in two books: United Nations Centre for Human Rights, ed., *Legislative History of the Convention on the Rights of the Child (1978–1989)*, U.N. Doc. HR/1996.Ser.1 (Geneva: United Nations, 1996); and Sharon Detrick, ed., *The United Nations Convention on the Rights of the Child: A Guide to the "Travaux Preparatoires"* (Dordrecht: Martinus Nijhoff, 1992)). Throughout the chapter, these documents are referred to as cited in their formal form and according to their title and citation at the United Nations. At the end of each citation, a reference is added to these two books, as appropriate. Because each chapter of the book *Legislative History* discusses an article of the Children's Convention and is paginated separately, this chapter's citations are to articles, followed by the page number in the particular chapter.

assists in the evaluation of states' compliance with their commitments under the Children's Convention. This is particularly interesting in the context of the Convention, as the *travaux preparatoires* contain not only a summary of the discussions, but also specific comments and statements that were purposefully inserted by state delegations for future guidance on the interpretation of the provisions and their implementation thereof.[3] Second, the legislative history of the drafting process sheds light on the scope and content of a general theory on children's bioethics. What were the arguments raised in the context of children's bioethics? Which positions were endorsed and why? How did the intersections among children's religious freedom, bodily integrity, health, and identity evolve? And what are the implications of these relationships on children's bioethics?

To answer these questions, an innovative approach to the description of the drafting process is taken. Instead of the conventional method of article-by-article discussion, a thematic analysis is provided. The drafting process is examined through the lens of children's bioethics, pointing to the relevant elements of the issues that were raised. General procedures used at the United Nations between 1978 and the adoption of the Children's Convention in 1989 are explained. This will facilitate an understanding of the international forces involved and will provide some explanation for the failures and achievements of the process. The formulation process is examined, touching briefly on a few of its most significant provisions and providing an in-depth analysis of the discussions that revolved around the issue of children's bioethics. Observing the process in its entirety, the extent to which the issue of children's bioethics and its contentious dilemmas are eventually integrated into the Convention is reviewed. Which bioethical concerns were explicitly addressed? What are the achievements and failures? And how can they be explained?

As will be shown, the absence of clear and definite provisions that are pertinent to children's bioethics in the Children's Convention indicates the controversial nature of the subject rather than a lack of care or attention. Moreover, examination of the *travaus preparatoires* suggests that the omission of these proposals was, in fact, a Western triumph in maneuvering the politics of drafting. Still, the Conventon's address of bioethical concerns should be evaluated beyond the Convention's explicit wording and in light of its other key features, including its holistic approach, its fundamental creeds, and others. The impact the Convention and its text have had on the development of other

---

[3] Under Article 32 of the Vienna Convention on the Law of Treaties (1155 U.N.T.S. 331, 8 I.L.M. 679, entered into force January 27, 1980), the *travaux preparatoires* of a treaty can provide "supplementary means of interpretation" in cases of unclear provisions. The requests of a few states parties to insert comments to clarify their understanding of commitment under the Children's Convention were unusual for the drafting process of an international treaty. However, while the legal counsel advising on the issue pointed out that, "it is strange . . . and uneasy to assess what conclusions States may later draw from the inclusion of such statements," he found no prohibition in law or practices for such a practice, and the statements were inserted as a part of the *travaux preparatoires*' compilation. See U.N. Economic and Social Council, *Report of the 1989 Working Group on a Draft Convention on the Rights of the Child*, 45th Sess., Agenda Item 13, paragraph 731, U.N. Doc. E/CN.4/1989/48 (March 2, 1989).

international instruments pertaining to children's bioethics is important as well. These issues are considered, drawing attention to remaining lacunae and suggesting directions for future research.

A. DRAFTING THE CHILDREN'S CONVENTION

The adoption of the Children's Convention on November 20, 1989, was the conclusion of ten years of work by the UN working group. It marked a peak in the efforts to entrench the notion of children and children's rights as it evolved during the 1960s and the 1970s, particularly in the Western world. The endorsement of the Convention also coincided with the growing body of international human rights.[4] The simultaneous drafting of the International Convention against Torture and Other Cruel, Inhuman or Degrading Treatment or Punishment[5] generated additional political pressure and created an incentive for states to take the question on children's rights seriously if they wished to stay in tune with international politics.[6] While Poland's initial proposal in 1978 for a convention on children's rights was discarded with a lack of support,[7] once the working group was established in 1979,[8] the drafting process started to develop momentum. This was exacerbated especially during the last few years of the process, with growing pressure to finalize the text before the tenth anniversary of the United Nation's 1979 International Year for Children.[9]

The drafting process was considered an inclusive open-ended one. Not only were all forty-three states that were members of the Commission on Human Rights allowed to take part, but other states' delegates, who had the status of observers, could participate and make interventions on the floor.[10] Furthermore, the participation of nongovernmental organizations (NGOs) in the process was considered a hallmark in the work of the working group. Theoretically these organizations did not have a right to speak. In practice,

---

[4] Detrick, *The Children's Convention "Travaux Preparatoires,"* 20, 22.

[5] Convention against Torture and Other Cruel, Inhuman or Degrading Treatment or Punishment, G.A. Res. 39/46, annex, 39 U.N. GAOR Supp. (No. 51), at 197, U.N. Doc. A/39/51 (1984), entered into force June 26, 1987.

[6] Detrick, *The Children's Convention "Travaux Preparatoires,"* 23.

[7] Ibid., 21. Poland expressed its support for a convention on the rights of the child in 1959, when the Declaration on the Rights of the Child was drafted. The issue, however, was not discussed substantially, and, despite the various references to children and their need for special protection over the years, it remained dormant until January 1978 (ibid., 20–21).

[8] The Commission on Human Rights decided to establish an informal open-ended working group in 1979 that would convene for one week during the session of the Commission to consider the question of a draft convention on the rights of the child. The working group met again in 1980 and was authorized in 1981 and each year thereafter to meet prior to the Commission session. The working group met for two weeks in 1988 to complete the first reading of the draft convention. The second reading of the draft was conducted from November 28 to December 9, 1988, and adopted its report from February 21 to 23, 1989 (*Legislative History* on Article 1 (Definition), 10; Cynthia P. Cohen, "The United Nations Convention on the Rights of the Child: Involvement of NGOs," in *The Legitimacy of the United Nations: Towards an Enhanced Legal Status of Non-State Actors,*" (Theo C. van Boven, Cees Flinterman, Fred Grunfeld, and Rita Hut eds., Utrecht, the Netherlands: SIM Special 19, 1997): 169, *available at* http://www.uu.nl/content/14Price.pdf).

[9] Detrick, *The Children's Convention "Travaux Preparatoires,"* 21–22.

[10] Ibid.

their influence was significant and, when requested, they were only rarely denied the opportunity to take the floor.[11] They worked behind the scenes, interacting with state delegates, lobbying for feasible and alternative proposals, and playing a neutral mitigating force to bridge East-West tensions: this turned out to have a great impact.[12]

The working group operated on the basis of consensus, and no proposal, including the final adoption of the Children's Convention's text, was taken to a vote.[13] This procedure surely facilitated the passage of the Convention through the UN bodies and made it easier to obtain states' signatures and ratifications of the Convention later. As scholars point out, however, it also came with a price. Aside from the length of time that was required to reach the consensual text for the Convention, the more profound consequence was that when consensus could not be reached, proposals were simply abandoned, even if there was clear majority support.[14] One of the most relevant proposals in the context of the present study was the proposal to include an explicit provision limiting medical experimentation on children, which was eventually deleted by the ruling of the chairman, Professor Adam Lopatka from Poland, despite the proposal's overall support.[15] Other deletions included a provision on state responsibility "[to] ensure that no child is subject to coercion which would impair his freedom to have or to adopt a religion or belief of his choice,"[16] a reference to a specific list of prohibited harmful traditional practices under Article 24(3) of the final text,[17] and a provision on mass media and marketing of breast-feeding substitutes.[18]

Despite the extensive participation of state members of the Commission on Human Rights, other state delegations and NGOs, as well as the consensual rule of procedure, the final text was criticized. Complaints were made about the small number of delegates from Africa, Asia Pacific, the Middle East, and Latin America, and, consequently, on the Western bias in the content of the Children's Convention.[19] Others, in contrast, suggested that, ultimately, the floor in which the discussions took place did reflect and integrate non-Western views.

---

[11] Cohen, 171–72, 176; Sonia Harris-Short, "Listening to 'the Other'? The Convention on the Rights of the Child," *Melbourne Journal of International Law* 2 (2001): 316; Detrick, *The Children's Convention "Travaux Preparatoires,"* 22.

[12] Cohen, 177–79.

[13] Ibid., 171.

[14] Detrick, *The Children's Convention "Travaux Preparatoires,"* 22; Cohen, RSS 171.

[15] Detrick, *The Children's Convention "Travaux Preparatoires,"* 23; *Legislative History* on Article 24 (Health), 38.

[16] Detrick, *The Children's Convention "Travaux Preparatoires,"* 240–41. This decision ensued during the discussion on Article 7 bis on Freedom of Thought, Conscience and Religion (Article 14 in the final text).

[17] *Legislative History* on Article 24 (Health), 38.

[18] Detrick, *The Children's Convention "Travaux Preparatoires,"* 278–79; *Legislative History* on Article 24 (Health), 11–12.

[19] Harris-Short, 321–22; Jenny Kuper, "Reservations, Declarations and Objections to the 1989 Convention on the Rights of the Child," in *Human Rights as General Norms and a States' Right to Opt Out: Reservations and Objections to Human Rights Conventions,* ed. J. P. Gardner (London: B.I.I.C.C. Publishing, 1997), 105.

As Philip Alston points out, "while by no means perfect, [the Convention] is [nevertheless] probably more sensitive to different approaches and perspectives than most of the principal human rights treaties adopted earlier."[20] Either way, the overall product established a legally binding instrument that articulates a worldwide moral and legal standard for the treatment of children.

The bare facts on the rapid universal endorsement of the Children's Convention are significant as they reflect the wide support for this new global order. The Commission on Human Rights adopted the finalized draft of the working group shortly after it was completed in the fall of 1988.[21] The General Assembly adopted the Convention unanimously, and it was opened for signatures on November 20, 1989. Fifty-eight countries signed the Convention at the formal signing ceremony on January 26, 1990.[22] The Convention came into force more quickly than any other human rights treaty, just about six months later, on September 2, 1990.[23] Four years after its adoption, 155 states were already parties to it.[24] As of March 1995, 170 states had ratified or acceded to the Convention.[25] By 2001, all 191 states, with the exception of the United States and Somalia, signed and ratified the Convention.[26] Yet there is also no other human rights treaty that has as many states' reservations, declarations, and objections as the Convention. Fifty-six states made declarations or reservations to substantive provisions of the Convention by 1997. Twenty-five of them were European or developed countries, and nine states parties made general reservations.[27] Thus, the discussion on a universal theory of children's biomedical (and other) rights is particularly engaging.

B. THE INNOVATIVE CREED OF THE CHILDREN'S CONVENTION

Although the Children's Convention was not the first international instrument dealing with children, its approach created significant legislative reform. Aside from the legally binding nature of the Convention, which was to replace the previous toothless declarations on the rights of children,[28] it

[20] Philip Alston, "The Best Interests Principle: Towards a Reconciliation of Culture and Human Rights," in *The Best Interests of the Child: Reconciliation of Culture and Human Rights*, ed. Philip Alston (New York: Oxford University Press, 1994), 7.

[21] Cynthia P. Cohen and Susan Kilbourne, "The Jurisprudence of the Committee on the Rights of the Child: A Guide for Research and Analysis," *Michigan Journal of International Law* 19, no. 3 (1998): 638. Although the second reading of the draft convention took place in November to December 1988, it was technically under the auspices of the 1989 session of the Human Rights Commission. (Cohen and Kilboume, ibid., n. 34)

[22] Cohen and Kilbourne, 634, n. 8.

[23] Ibid., n. 9.

[24] Alston, 2.

[25] Kuper, 104.

[26] Harris-Short, 305.

[27] William A. Schabas, "Reservations to the Convention on the Elimination of All Forms of Discrimination Against Women and the Convention on the Rights of the Child," *William and Mary Journal of Women and Law* 3 (1997): 86; Kuper, 106–09.

[28] Previous international declarations on the rights of children are: the Geneva Declaration on the Rights of the Child of 1924, adopted September 26, 1924, League of Nations O.J. Spec. Supp. 21, 43 (1924) and the United Nations' 1959 Declaration on the Rights of the Child, G.A. Res. 1386 (XIV), 14 U.N. GAOR Supp. (No. 16), at 19, U.N. Doc. A/4354 (No-

offered a new outlook to observe children and children's rights. While the 1959 Declaration on the Rights of the Child already recognized two rights for children, the right to a name and the right to a nationality,[29] the Convention was the first to address the question of children's rights in a substantial manner. In addition to the customary paradigm of care and protection for children, the Convention also intended to build a model that grants the child his or her "individual personality rights"[30] in the most comprehensive manner. It was also the first international convention to follow the UN Declaration of Human Rights (UDHR), including within its scope civil, political, economic, social, cultural, and humanitarian rights. Furthermore, the Convention also expanded on the UDHR, integrating developments that occurred in the field of human rights.[31]

Thus, for example, while the principle of nondiscrimination enshrined in Article 2 of the Children's Convention follows the wording in parallel provisions in the Bill of Rights,[32] it also supplements the rights by adding, as prohibited grounds for discrimination, "ethnic or social origin," "disability," and "discrimination and punishment on the basis of the status, activities, expressed opinions, or beliefs of the child's parents, legal guardians, or family members."[33] In the context the child's right to life, the drafters endorsed the

---

vember 20, 1959). The latter declaration was considered the springboard for the drafting of the Children's Convention. See Detrick, *The Children's Convention "Travaux Preparatoires,"* 19.

[29] Principle 3 of the 1959 Declaration on the Rights of the Child.

[30] Cohen and Kilbourne, 637–38. A commonly used terminology for the combination of the triple dimensions towards children in the Children's Convention is the "3Ps approach," standing for "provision, protection, participation" (Marie-Francoise Lucker-Babel, "The Right of the Child to Express Views and to Be Heard: An Attempt to Interpret Article 12 of the UN Convention on the Rights of the Child," *International Journal of Children's Rights* 3 (1995): 391). Kuper divides the rights enshrined in the Children's Convention into the three categories of the "3Ps' approach": "the provision to children of adequate nutrition, shelter, family contact, education, health care and recreation; the protection from abuse and exploitation, which includes the concept of prevention, and finally—the participation of children in decisions made about themselves and in social, economic, religious and political life" (Kuper, 104).).

[31] Alston, 1.

[32] Article 2(1) of the Universal Declaration of Human Rights, adopted and proclaimed by G.A. Res. 217 A (III), U.N. Doc. A/810, at 71 (1948); Article 2(1) of the International Covenant on Civil and Political Rights, opened for signature December 16, 1966, G.A. Res. 2200A (XXI), 21st Sess., U.N. GAOR Supp. (No. 16), at 52, U.N. Doc. A/6316 (1966), reprinted in 999 U.N.T.S. 171, entered into force March 23, 1976. The principle of nondiscrimination is stipulated in an array of other international treaties as well, including Article 2 of International Covenant on Economic, Social and Cultural Rights, adopted Dec. 16, 1966, G.A. Res. 2200A (XXI), 21 Sess., U.N. GAOR Supp. (No. 16), at 49, U.N. Doc. A/6316 (1966), reprinted in 993 U.N.T.S. 3, entered into force January 3, 1976; Article 1 of the European Convention for the Protection of Human Rights and Fundamental Freedoms, 213 U.N.T.S. 222, entered into force September 3, 1953, as amended by Protocols Nos. 3, 5, 8, and 11, which entered into force on September 21, 1970, December 20, 1971, January 1, 1990, and November 1, 1998, respectively; Article 2 of the African [Banjul] Charter on Human and Peoples' Rights, adopted June 27, 1981, OAU Doc. CAB/LEG/67/3 rev. 5, reprinted in 21 I.L.M. 58 (1982), entered into force October 21, 1986, and others (hereafter UDHR; ICCPR; ICESCR; and African [Banjul] Charter, respectively).

[33] See, however, that proposals to add an explicit prohibition for discrimination of chil-

Indian proposal to add a state's obligation "to ensure to the maximum extent possible the survival and development of the child."[34] Building on the positive spirit of the Convention and on the special meaning the terms have acquired in the work of international organizations, the drafters were persuaded that the reference to "survival and development" is complementary to the child's right to life and justifies placing a greater responsibility on states to ensure "the full development [of the child's] personality, both from the material and spiritual points of view."[35]

Finally, featuring development in the conceptualization of children as rights holders and as social agents, the drafters incorporated provisions giving voice to the children. The main anchor for this development is spelled out in Article 12 of the Children's Convention dealing with "respect to the child's views." It requires states to ensure that a child "who is capable of forming his or her own views" has the right to express freely these views—and to have them taken seriously[36]—in all matters that affect the child "in accordance with their age and maturity." However, as an overreaching principle of the Convention, Article 12 is explicitly and implicitly integrated throughout the Convention. Article 12 is particularly linked with the concept of the child's evolving capacity, established in Article 5 of the Convention, to ensure the gradual realization of the child's exercise of rights and taking into account the rights and duties of those who raise, guide, and take primary responsibility for the child.[37] The overall principle of respect to the child's views thus introduces a key and profound challenge to the traditional approach to children as passive observers and recipients of adults' values, influences, and protections.[38]

In addition to the legal discourse, the Children's Convention offers a social and cultural lens to address children's rights. Just as it promotes the legal philosophy of the indivisibility of civil, political, economic, social, cultural, and humanitarian rights, on the social level, it emphasizes the interdependency between children and their environment, particularly the family and the community. Instead of separate autonomous individuals who are active vis-à-vis

---

dren who are born out of wedlock (submitted, for example, by China) were not incorporated in the provision due to disagreements among the state delegations. Some delegates as well as the Committee on the Children's Convention nevertheless argue that this ground for discrimination is included within the provision, under the auspices of "other status." Sharon Detrick, *A Commentary on the United Nations Convention on the Rights of the Child* (Dordrecht: Martinus Nijhoff, 1999), 76; Committee on the Rights of the Child, *General Guidelines Regarding the Form and Contents of Periodic Reports to be Submitted by States Parties under Article 44, paragraph 1(b) of the Convention,* paragraphs 27, 10, U.N. Doc. CRC/C/58 (November 20, 1996) (hereafter General Guidelines). These guidelines are elaborated on later on in Section E.3.

[34] Article 6 of the Children's Convention.

[35] *Report of the 1989 Working Group on a Draft Convention on the Rights of the Child,* paragraphs 87–90 (*Legislative History* on Article 6 (Life, Survival and Development), 8–9).

[36] Lucker-Babel, 394.

[37] U.N. Economic and Social Council, *Report of the 1987 Working Group on a Draft Convention on the Rights of the Child,* 43rd Sess., Agenda Item 13, paragraph 106, U.N. Doc. E/CN.4/1987/25 (March 3, 1987); Detrick, *A Commentary on the Children's Convention,* 117.

[38] Gerison Lansdown, *Promoting Children's Participation in Democratic Decision-Making* (Florence, Italy: UNICEF & Innocenti Research Centre, 2001), 1–2.

the state, it fosters a complex web of relationships between and among the family, community, and the state as a predominant determinative element of bestowing and facilitating rights. In this sense, it follows the interrelational approach that has often characterized much of the feminist discourse and sets the tone for what scholars argue should be the starting point for children's rights: "a recognition of the relationships children have with parents and with the state, and the relations also arising between parents themselves and the state."[39]

Indeed, it is perhaps as a result of the cultural encounter between relatively strong non-Western states and their Western counterparts in the process, the input of a high level of participation of women and NGOs supporting women's issues,[40] or a combination of the two, that the Children's Convention pays particular attention to the relationships of the child with his or her close milieu. It emphasizes the family as the most natural environment for the growth and development of the child. Various provisions stipulate the right of the child to know, to be cared for, and to establish relationship with his or her parents.'[41] The parents and others who care for the child are given priority in the direction, guidance, and general upbringing of the child, including in the context of religion.[42] Furthermore, the child, including a child belonging to a minority group, is granted the right to preserve his or her identity and to enjoy, profess and practice, and use his or her culture, religion, and language, respectively.[43]

At the same time, the Children's Convention places some special responsibilities and limitations on the child's rights and interests. The child is expected to develop a respect for his or her parents, cultural identity, language, and natural environment.[44] In the context of the child's best interests, the drafters intentionally opted for the more limiting wording. They required that in all actions concerning children, the child's best interests should be given "a" (and not "the") paramount consideration. They rationalized that there are cases in which the competing interests of other individuals, justice, and the society at large should have at least equal, if not greater, importance than the interests of the child.[45] Thus,

---

[39] See Chapter 6. Martha Minow, "Rights for the Next Generation: A Feminist Approach to Children's Rights," *Women's Law Journal* 9 (1986): 3; Anne McGillivray, "Why Children Have Equal Rights: in Reply to Laura Purdy," *International Journal of Children's Rights* 2 (1994): 255.

[40] Harris-Short, 317–18.

[41] Articles 7, 9(3), 10(2), 27(2), and 27(4) of the Children's Convention.

[42] Articles 5, 18 and 14(2) of the Children's Convention, respectively. The parental right to guide and direct the child is mitigated by the principle of "evolving capacities."

[43] The child's right to preserve his or her identity is discussed further in Section E.2.c. See Articles 8 and 30 of the Children's Convention.

[44] Article 29(c), 29(e), 13(2), 14(3) and 15(2) of the Children's Convention. Additionally, as is common in other international human rights treaties, the child's freedom of expression, manifestation of religion or belief, and freedom of association may be limited to protect interests such as the public safety, health morals, or fundamental rights and freedoms of others.

[45] U.N. Commission on Human Rights, *Report of the 1981 Working Group on a Draft Convention on the Rights of the Child,* paragraph 30, 38th Sess., U.N. Doc. E/CN.4/L.1575 (February 17, 1981) (*Legislative History* on Article 3 (Best Interests), 11); *Report of the 1989 Working Group on a Draft Convention on the Rights of the Child,* paragraphs 17–24 (*Legislative History* on Article 3 (Best Interests), 20–21).

consideration of the child's best interests is intertwined and dependent on the child's other settings.[46]

To what extent is this holistic approach of human rights reflected in issues that are pertinent to children's bioethics? What were the political forces that played a role during the drafting process in this regard and determined the international standards of children's bioethics?

C. DRAFTING CHILDREN'S BIOETHICS INTO THE CHILDREN'S CONVENTION

The working group grappled with a number of biomedical practices during the drafting process of the Children's Convention: informed consent, traditional practices, experimentation, and drugs/medicalization. Each of these categories is discussed separately. Before doing so, a few comments on the scope of the study and the process of categorization are in order.

1. Scope of this Study

A substantial part of the working group's deliberations in the context of children's health revolved around measures of prevention. The main provision on the issue, Article 24 of the Children's Convention, addresses states' obligations to take measures to reduce morbidity, mortality, malnutrition, and other harmful environmental hazards. It requires them to provide appropriate immunization, clean water, and a hygienic environment. Ample literature has developed concerning the interpretation of these provisions along with national and international programs targeting various aspects of disease prevention (such as HIV, hunger, and malnutrition, etc.). The importance and value of these programs is clear, notwithstanding the criticism justly raised about their inattentiveness to the cultural considerations of the targeted groups of protection.[47] However, the discussion about such programs and other measures taken to improve children's health around the world is beyond the scope of this study. While the Convention provides the international legal framework for this analysis of children's bioethics, this study aims at proposing the philosophical, social, and cultural dimensions of the subject matter that needs to be taken into account. Furthermore, this study does not intend to examine the issue of children's health per se, but rather it intends to explore the cultural construction of biomedical practices in view of the child's right to preserve his or her identity.

2. Difficulties with the Process of Categorization

The various categories of biomedical practices are inextricably intertwined with one another, and there is an unavoidable overlap between them. While informed consent is often raised in the context of medical treatment, it is equally

---

[46] Alston, 4. Traditionally, the principle of the child's best interests was applied in international instruments mostly in the contexts of divorce and custody. The formulation of the principle in the Children's Convention aimed at including other contexts as well, although not giving it paramount weight.

[47] Collins O. Airhihenbuwa, *Health and Culture: Beyond the Western Paradigm* (Thousand Oaks, CA: Sage Publications, 1995), x.

relevant in the context of traditional practices, whichever practices they may be. The debate whether one can consent to mutilation of parts from his or her body raises similar philosophical questions of autonomy, self-determination, and identity, be the reason healing, religious observance, or cultural beliefs. Similarly, although the concept of traditional practices has come to be synonymous with nonconventional and backwards practices, what falls within the scope of the term is dynamic. Some practices may opt out from the category over time, whereas others may be simultaneously and continuously invented. The Asian healing practice of acupuncture, for instance, was previously considered as abusive and harmful in many Western states, but it is now often recommended within mainstream medical institutions. Medicalization, commonly assumed to be for healing, may also connote excessive reliance on scientific developments and unnecessary provision of medication to children for social reasons, such as the provision of growth hormones and other drugs aimed at enhancing the child's capacities. Furthermore, genetic modification *as* biomedical cultural practice theoretically could be grouped under the same umbrella as elongated neck or scarification. Indeed, as is shown in Chapter 7, all these biomedical practices are ultimately carried out in order to mark one's cultural membership in the respective communities. Thus, the division of biomedical practices into definitive categories is inherently arbitrary.

A particular note has to be made about the relationship between experimentation with children and the doctrine of informed consent. Because the doctrine was significantly advanced within the discourse on human rights only after the horrendous experimentations on human subjects during World War II, it is almost impossible to separate the discussions between the two categories. However, the two issues were approached differently during the drafting process, hence meriting the separate discussion. One difference was that while informed consent was essentially raised in the context of empowerment and participation of children, the discussion on experimentation revolved around questions of protection, albeit references to informed consent. Thus, although the two issues may sometimes intersect, in other times they are only complementary to one another in terms of the approach taken with children under the Children's Convention.

The other difference in the manner in which these two categories were approached was the question of who is the subject of empowerment and of protection. The discussion on informed consent revolved around the initial empowerment of children as decision makers, taking into account their evolving capacities, situations of children's incapacity, and the possible need for substitute decision makers. The subject of protection in the context of experimentation, in contrast, potentially includes a broader range of ages up to adulthood. While it surely includes all born children who are able to form their own views, it also raised a question about the status of fetuses under the Children's Convention and the measures needed for fetal protection in view of new scientific developments. Whether the fetus is included within the definition of the child and the derivative debate between the pro-life and pro-abortion activists are beyond the scope of this study. It is important to note, however, that the issue was a great source of tension during the discussions of the working group. It was raised in various provisions[48] and was never fully resolved but with the agreement that the Convention should be phrased in the most neutral way, so as to facilitate the adoption of national policies both to legalize or to outlaw abortions.[49] According to the compromise reached, references to the fetus as a separate subject were omitted from the operative part of the Convention, and the explicit reference to the child "before and after birth"' remained only in the Preamble.[50] While scholars still debate the legal implications of this settlement in terms of the fetus's status, provisions on the need to provide appropriate prenatal health care for women and to develop family planning services, for example, were nevertheless included in the final text.[51] Moreover, as discussed in the context of genetic manipulation (Chapter 7), the entry into force of the European Convention on Human Rights and Biomedicine (the Oviedo Convention) in 1999 and its additional protocols may also have further implications on the status of the fetus under international law.[52] Thus, the fetus question, as far as the discussion on the issue of children's bioethics is concerned, remains very much a vivid and relevant component in the entire picture and merits separate discussion.

---

[48] Including the Preamble, the definition of the child, the right to life, survival, and development, and others.

[49] U.N. Economic and Social Council, *Report of the 1980 Working Group to the Commission on Human Rights,* paragraphs 28–36, U.N. Doc. E/CN.4/L.1542 (1980); U.N. Economic and Social Council, *Report of the 1989 Working Group on a Draft Convention on the Rights of the Child,* paragraphs 75–90 (*Legislative History* on Article 1 (Definition), 11–12, 16–18, 19–21, respectively). See also U.N. Economic and Social Council, *Report of the 1980 Working Group to the Commission on Human Rights,* paragraphs 4–14, U.N. Doc. E/CN.4/L.1542, reproduced in paragraph 277 of the 1980 U.N. Economic and Social Council, *Report of the Working Group to the Commission on Human Rights,* U.N. Doc. E/CN.4/1408 (1980); *Report of the 1989 Working Group on a Draft Convention on the Rights of the Child,* paragraphs 87–90 (*Legislative History* on the Preamble, paragraphs 16–17, 30–33, respectively).

[50] Paragraph 9 of the Preamble reads:

> *Bearing in mind* that, as indicated in the Declaration of the Rights of the Child, adopted by the General Assembly of the United Nations on 20 November 1959, "the child, by reason of his physical and mental immaturity, needs special safeguards and care, including appropriate legal protection, *before as well as after birth* [emphasis added].

[51] Articles 24(2)(d) and 24(2)(e) of the Children's Convention.

[52] Convention for the Protection of Human Rights and Dignity of the Human Being with Regard to the Application of Biology and Medicine: Convention on Human Rights and Biomedicine (the Oviedo Convention) (ETS No. 164), entered into force December 1, 1999; Additional Protocol to the Convention for the Protection of Human Rights and Dignity of the Human Being with regard to the Application of Biology and Medicine, on the Prohibition of Cloning Human Beings (ETS No. 168), opened for signature on January 1, 1998, entered into force March 1, 2001; Additional Protocol to the Convention on Human Rights and Biomedicine, on Transplantation of Organs and Tissues of Human Origin (ETS No. 186), opened for signature on January 24, 2002, entered into force May 1, 2006; Additional Protocol to the Convention on Human Rights and Biomedicine, concerning Biomedical Research (ETS No. 195), entered into force September 1, 2007 (hereafter the Convention on Human Rights and Biomedicine or the Oviedo Convention, interchangeably; Additional Protocol on the Prohibition of Cloning, the Additional Protocol on Transplantation of Organs and Tissues; and Additional Protocol on Biomedical Research, respectively. The term "Conventions on Biomedicine" will be used to refer to this set of conventions together).

Deliberations about the different categories of biomedical practices were raised in various contexts and stages of the working group's discussion. Some were not included in the original Polish proposal (see Section A) but were incorporated later on.[53] Others may have roots in one context but then took on lives of their own. Following the process in its entirety, a comprehensive account of the discussions that took place on the issue of children's bioethics will be provided (see Section D). This includes not only the politicized and well-known discussion on female genital cutting, but also the concealed and less-known cases that did not receive the forestage.[54]

The discussion now turns to the four categories of biomedical practices that were raised during the drafting process of the Children's Convention: informed consent, traditional practices, experimentation, and drugs/medicalization.

D. CATEGORIES OF BIOMEDICAL PRACTICES

1. Informed Consent

Whether a child has or should have the right to give informed consent was one of the key issues in the working group's consideration of bioethical concerns. This attention clearly reflected the Western spirit and its emphasis on autonomy and individualized rights.[55] As scholars have suggested, there is an "ethical symmetry" between children and adults, and, thus, in medical dilemmas with children, efforts should be made to apply the same ethical standards that are applied to adults.[56] The question was raised mainly in the discussions on respect to the views of the child and on the child's right to health by both state delegations and NGOs.

a. Respect for Children's Views on Medical Treatment

Neither the original Polish draft convention nor the views submitted on it addressed children's informed consent. It was raised shortly afterwards, however, indirectly, in the revised version that the representative of Poland submitted in October 1979.[57] The proposal, originally submitted with the unofficial heading of "the child's right to express opinions," explicitly gave children the right to express their views in matters concerning their medical treatment.[58] The 1980

---

[53] Poland submitted to the UN Commission on Human Rights a first draft proposal in early 1978. This initial proposal followed to a great extent the 1959 Declaration on the Rights of the Child. The scope of rights that it granted children was limited, the language of the proposal was relatively vague, and it also lacked provisions about implementation. This proposal was thus rejected shortly after. When the working group had its first meeting in 1980, Poland presented a revised proposal that contained more substantial text and was used as a basic working document. Detrick, *The Children's Convention "Travaux Preparatoires,"* 20–22.

[54] For the sake of convenience, unless stated otherwise, articles are discussed according to their number in the final text of the Convention.

[55] See the critique of the doctrine of informed consent in Chapter 1, Section B.2.

[56] Pia Christensen and Alan Prout, "Working with Ethical Asymmetry in Social Research with Children," *Childhood* 9, no. 4 (2002): 484.

[57] Hereafter the revised Polish draft.

[58] Article 12 of the Children's Convention that the Committee on the Children's Convention refers to as "respect to the views of the child"; this article is referred to as Article 7 throughout the first and second readings.

working group adopted the proposal as a basic working text,[59] which read "The States Parties to the present Convention shall enable the child who is capable of forming his own views the right to express his opinion in matters concerning his own person, and, *in particular,* marriage, choice of occupation, *medical treatment,* education and recreation [emphasis added]."[60]

In the discussions of the working group in 1981, some debate ensued about the extent of respect for the child's views and about the nature of state obligations. The Australian delegation suggested refocusing the provision on state responsibility "to assure to the child the right to express his opinion" taking into account his age and maturity.[61] The representative of Denmark expressed the view that granting the child the right to express his or her opinion may not be sufficient; the child should also have actual influence in such matters. He reformulated the provision, giving "the parents or other guardians the right and duty to decide in matters concerning the person of the child."[62] He did not specify the list of matters, yet he added that "the child shall, as soon as possible, have an influence in such matters" with greater responsibility as he gets older and "with the aim of preparing him for the life of a grown up."[63] In a response, the American representative put forward for consideration a revised version that referred to the child's rights to express his or her opinion "effectively and non-violently." It also referenced other life spheres allowing for the child's views to be heard by adding to the list in the provision "religion, political and social beliefs, matters of conscience, cultural and artistic matters, travel, [and] place of residence."[64]

Following the proposal, a discussion was held on, *inter alia,* the extent of state responsibility to ensure the child's right to express his or her opinion. The appropriateness of the word effectively as a qualifying term for the child's input in expressing these views was also on the table. No substantial disagreement is described about the principle of the child's right to express his or her view in matters of medical treatment. One speaker simply compared the rights of the child to all other individuals under the law, remarking that the "State is under no obligation, as a matter of law, towards children: the child should have a degree of freedom comparable to that enjoyed by an individual under

[59] Detrick, *The Children's Convention "Travaux Preparatoires,"* 224.

[60] *Legislative History* on Article 12 (Participation), 4.

[61] *Report of the 1981 Working Group on a Draft Convention on the Rights of the Child,* paragraphs 74 (*Legislative History* on Article 12 (Participation), 8); Detrick, *The Children's Convention "Travaux Preparatoires,"* 224–25.

[62] Ibid.

[63] Ibid.

[64] The proposal read,

> The States parties to the present Convention shall enable the child who is capable of forming his own views the right to express his opinion effectively and non-violently in matters concerning his own person, and *in particular,* religion, political and social beliefs, matters of conscience, cultural and artistic matters, marriage, choice of occupation, *medical treatment,* education, travel, place of residence, and recreation [emphasis added].

Report of the 1981 Working Group on a Draft Convention on the Rights of the Child, paragraph 76 (*Legislative History* on Article 12 (Participation), 8).

the Covenants and comparable instruments of law."[65] Nevertheless, the explicit reference to children's rights to express their opinions in matters concerning their medical treatment was eventually omitted. In the *travaux preparatoires* on the article, it states that "most delegations felt that the matters concerning the child in which the States Parties to the Convention would enable him to express his opinion should not be subjected to the limits of a list, and therefore the list ought to be deleted."[66] The list was subsequently deleted along with the state representatives' endorsements of the American proposal to add "all" before the word "matters" so as to ensure the greater scope of issues in which the child's views should be heard.[67]

Considerations of the provision continued with significant modifications after the 1981 session of the working group. However, the explicit reference to children's rights to express their views in the context of medical treatment was not revisited. At the same time, proposals phrased in a manner that appeared to restrict the child's right to express his or her views were also generally rebuffed. For example, the working group rejected the Japanese proposal (supported by Italy, Kuwait, and the USSR) to restrict the child's right only to those matters "affecting the rights of the child." Faithful to the rationale expressed when deleting the list, the working group opted for the more expanded version that refers to "all matters *affecting the child* [emphasis added],"[68] which allows for a broader scope of matters for the child's views to be heard.

b. Informed Consent, Medical Treatment, and Experimentation

The second round of discussions about the issue of children's informed consent took place under the working group's consideration of Article 24 on health.[69] This was to be expected considering that the protection of human subjects in medical treatment and experimentation through the guarantee of their informed consent has been a cornerstone in (Western) bioethical discourse since the emergence of modern international human rights standards after WWII.[70] Less expected, however, was the time and circumstances in which

[65] *Report of the 1981 Working Group on a Draft Convention on the Rights of the Child,* paragraph 77 (*Legislative History* on Article 12 (Participation), 8); Detrick, *The Children's Convention "Travaux Preparatoires,"* 225.

[66] *Report of the 1981 Working Group on a Draft Convention on the Rights of the Child,* paragraph 78 (*Legislative History* on Article 12 (Participation), 8).

[67] The new paragraph read, "The States parties to the present Convention shall assure to the child who is capable of forming his own views the right to express his opinion freely in all matters, the wishes of the child being given due weight in accordance with his age and maturity." See *Report of the 1981 Working Group on a Draft Convention on the Rights of the Child,* paragraph 80 (*Legislative History* on Article 12 (Participation), 9).

[68] *Report of the 1989 Working Group on a Draft Convention on the Rights of the Child,* paragraph 235 (*Legislative History* on Article 12 (Participation), 12–13).

[69] Article 24 of the final text convention was based on Article 13 of the revised Polish draft. It was discussed and adopted by the working group in 1985, 1987, and 1988 as Article 12 bis throughout the first and second readings (see *Legislative History* on Article 24 (Health), 9).

[70] It is interesting in this context to follow the drafting process of Article 7 of the ICCPR and the rationales that were raised for adding a reference also to the prohibition of medical or scientific experimentation without the subject's free consent. See Marc J. Bossuyt, *Guide to*

the issue was raised in the context of children. First, although the proposed provision on health and health services was integrated into the Polish revised draft of 1978, it was not until 1987 that the issue of the child's informed consent was explicitly brought up. More peculiar was the fact that when it was eventually raised, it came about as an almost casual remark by the Italian representative, expressing concern that "female circumcision was practiced on children without their consent."[71]

No further discussion on the issue was developed following this note during the session of 1987. However, it was raised again in 1988 in an explicit and comprehensive written proposal submitted by the NGO group. The proposal read as follows:

> 4. The States Parties to the present Convention shall ensure that no child be subject to any medical or scientific investigation, experimentation or treatment unless it is necessary for the physical and psychological health of the child. The free and fully-informed consent of the child shall be obtained or, when this is inappropriate, that of the parents.[72]

Perhaps because of the relative late submission of the proposal, only shortly before the working group adopted the textual draft on health and health services in its first reading, it was not followed by any substantial consideration. It was reintroduced with renewed force when the representatives of the Philippines and Venezuela championed the NGOs' initiative during the discussions at the second reading towards the end of 1988. Paragraph 4 of the Venezuelan proposal, used as the basis for negotiations of the draft convention, read as follows:

> 4. States Parties shall ensure that a child shall not be subject to any medical or scientific experimentation or treatment unless it is with the free and informed consent of the child or where appropriate that of the child's parents. In any case, such experimentation or treatment shall not be adverse for the child and shall not affect his health in the future.[73]

In an attempt to expedite the agreement on the article, the chairman appointed a drafting group (composed of representatives of Australia, Mexico, the Philippines, and Venezuela) to create a consolidated text.[74] The drafting group subsequently submitted its proposal to the working group, which was similar to the proposed paragraph above, but with a modification of the second sentence of the paragraph. The words "and shall not affect his health in the future" were replaced with a state's positive duty, reading "and shall be in the

the "Travaux Preparatoires" of the International Covenant on Civil and Political Rights (Dordrecht: Martinus Nijhoff, 1987), 147–58.

[71] *Report of the 1987 Working Group on a Draft Convention on the Rights of the Child,* paragraph 34 (*Legislative History* on Article 24 (Health), 24).

[72] *Legislative History* on Article 24 (Health), 26.

[73] *Report of the 1989 Working Group on a Draft Convention on the Rights of the Child,* paragraph 410 (*Legislative History* on Article 24 (Health), 34).

[74] *Report of the 1989 Working Group on a Draft Convention on the Rights of the Child,* paragraph 411 (*Legislative History* on Article 24 (Health), 34).

furtherance of child health."[75] However, the discussion that ensued revealed four main points of disagreement among state delegates, and the proposal was eventually omitted.

The first point was the question of what sort of medical interventions would require informed consent. The draft proposal referred to "any medical or scientific experimentation or treatment," but no consensus on the scope could be reached. The observer for the Netherlands suggested the deletion of the words "or treatment" entirely; and the Sweden delegate proposed, instead, to retain the original draft proposal but to specify it further. Accordingly, he suggested adding after the word "treatment" the words "of an experimentation nature," so it reads "any medical or scientific experimentation or treatment *of an experimental nature* [emphasis added]."[76]

The second and third questions were interlinked, querying who are the subjects authorized to give informed consent and, among them, who is to be the prime consenter.[77] The consolidated proposal empowered the child and gives only a secondary role, "where appropriate," to the parents. Yet neither the circumstances in which "where appropriate" would apply nor the mere reference to parents as substitute consenters was agreed upon. Portugal, supported by several other speakers, suggested adding "legal guardians" as an alternative to parental consenters. Other delegations, by contrast, continued referencing only the child's parents. The representative of the USSR argued that "there should be no alternative as to whose consent was needed for the child to be subjected to medical or scientific experimentation." He proposed, instead, that the consent of *both* the child and his or her parents was to be sought.[78] The observer for Canada further stepped back, suggesting switching the order of alternative consenters altogether. He proposed that parental consent should be sought first and only then, when appropriate, that of the child.[79] The observer explained his proposals by the fact that "in emergency cases the consent cannot be obtained immediately," referring also to circumstances in which "[it] may not be obtained for religious or similar reasons."[80]

The last contentious point revolved around the requirement that "such experimentation or treatment shall not be adverse for the child and shall not affect his health in the future."[81] The delegates debated the appropriate wording

---

[75] *Report of the 1989 Working Group on a Draft Convention on the Rights of the Child,* paragraph 411 (*Legislative History* on Article 24 (Health), 35–36). This replacement followed the Philippines' proposal, which was submitted to the working group at the second reading (*Legislative History* on Article 24 (Health), 33).

[76] *Report of the 1989 Working Group on a Draft Convention on the Rights of the Child,* paragraphs 416–420 (*Legislative History* on Article 24 (Health), 37).

[77] *Report of the 1989 Working Group on a Draft Convention on the Rights of the Child,* paragraph 422 (*Legislative History* on Article 24 (Health), 37).

[78] *Report of the 1989 Working Group on a Draft Convention on the Rights of the Child,* paragraph 423 (*Legislative History* on Article 24 (Health), 37).

[79] *Report of the 1989 Working Group on a Draft Convention on the Rights of the Child,* paragraph 424 (*Legislative History* on Article 24 (Health), 37).

[80] Ibid.

[81] As Venezuela proposed. See *Report of the 1989 Working Group on a Draft Convention on*

to capture the degree of harm that shall be prohibited and who benefits from the protection. The representative of the United States proposed replacing the word "adverse" by the word "harmful" or "injurious."[82] This amendment adds elements of deliberate infliction of harm and of the likelihood of actually causing harm into the considerations[83] that were not generally disputed. However, the deliberations about whether the requirement that the experimentation or treatment would be "in the furtherance of child health" should remain was apparently the final strike for the proposal. The observer for the Netherlands proposed its deletion. Others suggested replacing it with furtherance of "public health" or with "medical knowledge" (the United Kingdom). These were immediately followed by the Australian proposal to revise the paragraph so it would read "in the furtherance of the health of children and in accordance with any relevant ethical guidelines and rules" and by a note submitted by Portugal, stressing that the requirement needs "to underline that the medical or scientific experimentation should be a need and benefit for the child who is going to suffer, and not only to promote the health of children world-wide."[84]

As the questions continued, the Venezuelan representative voiced concern that the provision as it currently stands "opens a door to abuse" and suggested discontinuing the negotiations on this matter until further consultation with experts from the World Health Organization (WHO).[85] This position was seconded by the Polish delegation.[86] Finally, in the absence of its government's instructions on the matter, the French representative refused to make a definite decision at this point.[87] With no consensus, the chairman decided to delete the provision from the article. Although various delegations expressed support in favor of the paragraph and expressed willingness to continue the discussion on the proposal, his ruling remained in place.[88]

2. Harmful Traditional Practices

In what seems to be a response to one of the most controversial issues associated with the Children's Convention, a vast literature on harmful

---

the Rights of the Child, paragraph 410 (*Legislative History* on Article 24 (Health), 34).

[82] *Report of the 1989 Working Group on a Draft Convention on the Rights of the Child,* paragraph 416 (*Legislative History* on Article 24 (Health), 37).

[83] Both "harmful" and "injurious" are defined in Oxford dictionary as "causing or likely to cause" harm or injury, especially that which involves deliberate inflicted of harm or "maliciousness." Although "adverse" is defined as equated with "harmful," it seems to connote weaker detrimental implications with no malevolent intents, as it is equated also with "unfavorable." See *The Concise Oxford Dictionary,* 10th ed., s.v. "harmful" and "injurious."

[84] *Report of the 1989 Working Group on a Draft Convention on the Rights of the Child,* paragraphs 419, 421, 422 (*Legislative History* on Article 24 (Health), 37).

[85] *Report of the 1989 Working Group on a Draft Convention on the Rights of the Child,* paragraph 425 (*Legislative History* on Article 24 (Health), 37–38).

[86] *Report of the 1989 Working Group on a Draft Convention on the Rights of the Child,* paragraph 426 (*Legislative History* on Article 24 (Health), 38).

[87] *Report of the 1989 Working Group on a Draft Convention on the Rights of the Child,* paragraph 427 (*Legislative History* on Article 24 (Health), 38).

[88] The representative of Norway also stated that "his delegation strongly objected" to the chairman's ruling. *Report of the 1989 Working Group on a Draft Convention on the Rights of the Child,* paragraphs 428–430 (*Legislative History* on Article 24 (Health), 38).

traditional practices has developed in recent years. The custom of female circumcision received particular attention as the focus of heated debates during the drafting process of the Convention. Arguments for and against singling out the practice are often pointed out. The adamant U.S.-led Western bloc demanding that states parties eliminate the practice has been almost legendary. Senegal's call for the protection of cultural diversity also in the context of female circumcision is considered nearly common knowledge within the international human rights discourse on cultural relativism. Although some argue that the compromise reached "was a significant concession to Third World states,"[89] with the endorsement of Article 24(3) of the Convention, all sides seemed to claim victory. For Western states and activists, the provision was marked as one of the most significant steps toward the advancement of women and children's rights.[90] The absence of a specific reference to female circumcision in the final text was hailed as a non-Western victory, resisting Western states' cultural imperialism. Finally, the provision was celebrated by the NGO group as a prime accomplishment during the process.[91]

Yet the almost exclusive international focus on female circumcision overlooks other harmful traditional practices whose eradication was similarly requested. As a consequence, commentary on the drafting process of Article 24(3) of the Children's Convention has been partial and incomplete. This section offers an overview of the bigger picture. In addition to the examination of the debates that occurred with regard to female circumcision, other harmful traditional practices that were submitted for consideration to the working group, specifically excessive medical treatment, experimentation and genetic engineering, and drugs and medicalization are discussed. The need to protect children from modern and Western health and medical practices, as well, did not escape the drafters' eyes. In fact, the discussion on these modern biomedical practices preceded the debate on female circumcision, and it was these practices to which the phrase "detrimental to the child's physical and psychological development" originally referred. The connotation between harmful traditional practices and female circumcision is thus merely a success of the Western states' politics of drafting.

a. Female Circumcision

Proposals concerning the need to protect children from harmful practices that may affect their health were raised early on in the discussions of the working group. Sweden called attention to the importance of preventing "children from being subjected to practices which involve physical abuse and affect their present and future health or well-being" in the first round of comments on the original Polish draft proposal.[92] The Swedish view, however, was not integrated

[89] Lawrence J. LeBlanc, *The Convention on the Rights of the Child: United Nations Lawmaking on Human Rights* (London: University of Nebraska Press, 1995), 88–89, quoted in Harris-Short, 327.

[90] Harris-Short, 327.

[91] Cohen, 183.

[92] It read: "4. The States Parties . . . shall undertake to protect children from any medical investigation or treatment detrimental to their physical or psychological development." See

into the revised Polish draft of 1979 or into the modified proposal of 1982.

In 1984, the NGO group took the lead on the issue. At this point, two proposals were in front of the working group, both submitted by NGOs. The first, submitted by the solitary voice of the International Federation of Women in Legal Careers, made the first explicit reference to harmful traditional practices. In its proposal "concerning sources of serious damage to children's health other than disease and malnutrition, namely: domestic abuse; use of drugs of whatever kind; harmful labor; traditional practices affecting health," paragraph 4 required states parties to undertake the responsibility "to adopt clearly defined national policies for the abolition of the sexual mutilation of female babies and children."[93]

The second proposal was made on behalf of the entire NGO group. Interestingly, although it clearly aimed at targeting harmful bodily practices that are detrimental to children's health, the proposal did not refer to "traditional practices" but to states' protection of children from "medical investigation or treatment." Only later, in its supplemental text submitted to the working group in 1985, did the NGO group amend its proposal by adding an explicit reference to protecting children from "being subjected to traditional practices harmful to their health."[94]

Neither of the proposals was discussed during the sessions of the working group in 1985 and in 1986. The resubmission of the NGO group proposal during the discussion in 1985 was turned down as being premature considering the subject matter of the proposal,[95] whereas the discussion on a much more Western and conservative proposal that was submitted in 1986 was postponed. Finally, by the time the working group tackled the issue of traditional practices in its session in 1987, the original NGO proposal was utterly changed. The new proposal, submitted by Radda Barnen International on behalf of the NGO group, no longer contained the specific reference to "any medical investigation or treatment" but only mentioned "traditional practices." It read "States' Parties . . . shall seek to eradicate traditional practices harmful to the health of children and shall take all appropriate action including necessary legislative, administrative, social and educational measures to ensure that children are not subjected to such practices."[96]

Legislative History on Article 24 (Health), 8.

[93] *Legislative History* on Article 24 (Health), 13–14. The proposal called for abolishing such practices by "[intensifying] health education programmes for all levels of the population and for practitioners of traditional medicine so as to inform public and practitioners alike of the multiple dangers of such practices for the children's physical and mental health."

[94] The amended proposal read: "5. The States Parties . . . shall undertake to protect children from any medical investigation or treatment detrimental to their physical or psychological development, and to take all appropriate and necessary measures to prevent children being subjected to traditional practices harmful to their health." The underlined sentence was the addition proposed in 1985. See, *Legislative History* on Article 24 (Health), 15.

[95] U.N. Economic and Social Council, *Report of the 1985 Working Group on a Draft Convention on the Rights of the Child*, 41st Sess., Agenda Item 13, paragraph 40, U.N. Doc. E/CN.4/1985/64 (April 3, 1985) (*Legislative History* on Article 24 (Health), 21).

[96] U.N. Economic and Social Council, *Report of the 1986 Working Group on a Draft Con-*

Subsequently, the overall spirit of the discussion turned to non-Western practices. The representative of the United Kingdom questioned whether "the reference to 'traditional practices harmful to the health of children' meant female circumcision" and requested clarifications of the wording "traditional practices," as "[it] might possibly be interpreted more widely than the authors intended."[97] Representatives from Canada, Australia, the United Kingdom, the United States, and the Netherlands requested that specific reference to female circumcision be made.[98] The Italian representative expressed the opinion that while cultural pluralism is important, there is a need "for changes in attitudes which would eliminate this [female circumcision] problem."[99] The observer for Canada rationalized it as a way "to give some clear content to the draft article," and the representative of the United States explained that the explicit reference would "address the traditional practice of greatest concern," "would give greater content to the phrase "traditional practice," and "would demonstrate that the practices to be abolished were those of a serious nature."[100]

The representative of Senegal, in contrast, argued for "prudence when dealing with issues that entailed differences in cultural values" and "the dangers of forcing practices into clandestinely if they were prohibited by State legislation."[101] While his arguments for cultural tolerance were rejected, his adamant opposition to the specific reference and his submission of the only-slightly-changed alternate proposals succeeded.[102] Not only did the provision fail to single out female circumcision as a custom targeted by the provision, but other Western repeated attempts to strengthen state responsibility in eradicating such harmful traditional practices failed as well. In view of the Senegalese strong objection and following the expressed understanding of the delegations for Canada, Japan, Sweden, Venezuela, and Finland that the term "traditional practices" included all those practices outlined in the *1986 Report of the Working Group on Traditional Practices Affecting the Health of Women and Children,*[103] the Senegalese proposal slowly gained support. It read "The

vention on the Rights of the Child, 42nd Sess., Agenda Item 13, paragraph 50, U.N. Doc. E/CN.4/1986/39 (March 13, 1986) (*Legislative History* on Article 24 (Health), 22).

[97] *Report of the 1987 Working Group on a Draft Convention on the Rights of the Child,* paragraph 29 (*Legislative History* on Article 24 (Health), 23).

[98] *Report of the 1987 Working Group on a Draft Convention on the Rights of the Child,* paragraphs 30–35, 38 (*Legislative History* on Article 24 (Health), 23–25).

[99] *Report of the 1987 Working Group on a Draft Convention on the Rights of the Child,* paragraphs 29, 31, 34, 37–39 (*Legislative History* on Article 24 (Health), 23–24).

[100] *Report of the 1987 Working Group on a Draft Convention on the Rights of the Child,* paragraphs 30, 35 (*Legislative History* on Article 24 (Health), 23–24).

[101] R*eport of the 1987 Working Group on a Draft Convention on the Rights of the Child,* paragraphs 29 (*Legislative History* on Article 24 (Health), 23).

[102] The two changes in the Senegalese first and final proposals were: (1) the omission of the words "as far as possible," which were inserted between the words "seek" and "to take" and (2) the replacement of the words "to combat traditional practices" with the words "with a view to abolishing traditional practices." See R*eport of the 1987 Working Group on a Draft Convention on the Rights of the Child,* paragraphs 31, 37–39 (*Legislative History* on Article 24 (Health), 25).

[103] The report focuses mainly on female circumcision, traditional birth practices, and preferential treatment for male children. *Report of the Working Group on Traditional Practices Affecting the Health of Women and Children,* U.N. Commission on Human Rights, 42nd Sess.,

States Parties to the present Convention shall seek to take all effective and appropriate measures with a view to abolishing traditional practices that affect the health of children."[104]

Aside from the omission of the words "seek to," as proposed by the Venezuelan delegation, the provision remained the same in the final text.[105]

b. Experimentation, Scientific Developments, and Genetic Manipulation

Efforts to protect children from experimentation and other scientific developments harmful to their health also continued after the failure to incorporate it within the provision on harmful traditional practices in Article 24(3). In particular, three additional interesting proposals brought to the working group deserve attention. The first proposal was in the form of a comment made during the technical review of the draft convention in 1988. Drawing on the work of the UN Working Group on Slavery, it was suggested that both the concept of mutilation and the use of children for medical experimentation should be specifically forbidden.[106] There are no recorded reactions to this proposal.

Another proposal was submitted by an NGO, the World Association of Children's Friends, during the second reading of the article on the definition of the child in 1988. The proposal suggested inserting a new article specifically targeting the issue of genetic experimentation and manipulation, and it included a minimum list of practices that would be prohibited. Among the practices mentioned were cloning, xenotransplantation (implementation and fusion of human tissues or genes with other species), sex selection by genetic manipulation, and research and experimentation on living embryos.[107]

Item 19, U.N. Doc. E/CN.4/1986/42 (February 4, 1986) (hereafter *1986 Report on Harmful Traditional Practices*).

[104] *Report of the 1986 Working Group on a Draft Convention on the Rights of the Child*, paragraphs 29, 31, 34, 37–39 (*Legislative History* on Article 24 (Health), 23–25). Proposals to strengthen state obligations included adding "by all appropriate means" after "seek" (Canada); referring to the obligations states undertake under the provision, the observer for the Netherlands argued that the wording is "too weak" and that "'seek' ought to be replaced by a more forceful language" (*Report of the 1987 Working Group on a Draft Convention on the Rights of the Child*, paragraphs 30, 32). The WHO proposed deleting the word "to seek" as well, arguing that it is a "highly unusual [verb] in human rights treaties since it further dilutes the nature of an already qualified obligation." See U.N. Commission on Human Rights, *Technical Review of the Text of the Draft Convention on the Rights of the Child*, 45th Sess., Article 12 bis (page 32), U.N. Doc. E/CN.4/1989/WG.1/CRP.1 (October 15, 1988).

[105] This Venezuelan proposal was raised during the discussion and was adopted at the working group at the second reading. See *Report of the 1989 Working Group on a Draft Convention on the Rights of the Child*, paragraph 410 (*Legislative History* on Article 24 (Health), 35).

[106] These comments were submitted to the consideration of the working group by the United Nation's Working Group on Slavery (Subcommission on Prevention of Discrimination and Protection of Minorities) in 1988. *Technical Review of the Text of the Draft Convention on the Rights of the Child*, 10 (*Legislative History* on Article 24 (Health), 32).

[107] Other prohibited practices on the list were the creation of embryos using sperm from other individuals, ectogenesis, fusion of embryos, or any other operation likely to result in the mostrous/abnormal creation of children from persons of the same sex, creation of identical twins, experimentation on living embryos whether viable or not. See *Legislative History* on Article 1 (Definition), 18.

The proposal, however, was not formally discussed at the working group. While a late submission may partially account for the lack of address, it is more likely that its content was the reason. The close link between the proposal and the question of the status of the fetus may have intensified the fear of state delegates that it would reopen the controversy about abortions, which had been previously concluded with the nonsolution compromise.[108] In addition, the lack of agreement on the matter among the members of the NGO group left it with insufficient lobbying support.[109] Finally, the submission of another (third) proposal, formulated broadly enough to prohibit genetic engineering and use of other scientific practices on children, seemed to receive wider support. It was thus assumed that the discussion on the more contentious proposal was not needed.

This third proposal was submitted by the NGO group in 1988, shortly after the first round of discussion on traditional practices and even before its adoption at the first reading of the draft convention. In what appears to be an attempt to rectify the omission of experimentation and excessive treatment,[110] the proposal suggested adding to Article 24 on health two new paragraphs consecutively with paragraph 24(3) on traditional practices. The new paragraphs reintroduced and elaborated its proposal from 1985 to protect children from (Western-oriented) biomedical practices. The first paragraph required states parties to prohibit children from "medical or scientific investigation, experimentation or treatment unless it is necessary for the physical and psychological health of the child." It also required that "the free and fully-informed consent of the child shall be obtained or, when this is inappropriate, that of the parents."[111] The second new paragraph revisited the issue of children's excessive consumption of medication and substances that was presumably already taken care of under Article 33 dealing with drugs.[112] The paragraph proposed to "prohibit the marketing and distribution of chemical, pharmaceutical, nutritional and other substances and products which are likely to be consumed or used by children and which are harmful to their health."[113]

[108] See the discussion on the compromise with regards to the fetus in Section C.2. The proposal also included an amendment to Article 1 of the draft, extending the Children's Convention's protection "to the conceived, unborn child from genetic experimentation and manipulation injurious to his physical, moral or mental integrity or to his health." See, *Legislative History* on Article 1 (Definition), 18.

[109] Cohen, 176. It is interesting in this context to compare the proposal on genetic engineering with Article 24(3) on traditional practices as a reflection of international and internal politics. Both proposals were NGO led, and, furthermore, both were originally submitted by a solitary NGO voice and not on behalf of the entire NGO group. However, while the proposal on traditional practices was picked up by the NGO group and eventually also by state delegates, the second was not. And while the option of including a list of experimental practices was not discussed at all, the option of singling out female circumcision was a highly controversial and, at least at first, it appeared as a rather plausible option.

[110] See discussion on informed consent in Section D.1.b.

[111] *Legislative History* on Article 24 (Health), 26.

[112] The drafting of Article 33 of the Children's Convention is discussed in Section D.2.c.

[113] *Legislative History* on Article 24 (Health), 26.

However, the latter paragraph was not formally discussed, and by the time the representatives of Venezuela and the Philippines took on the initiative with regard to the first paragraph in the 1988–89 session of the working group, the discussion refocused the attention on the question of informed consent. Instead of a requirement that, as a general rule, such practices would be prohibited unless they are necessary for the health of the child, informed consent could now sanction the practices.[114] It read "States Parties shall ensure that a child shall not be subject to any medical or scientific experimentation or treatment *unless it is with the free and informed consent of the child or where appropriate that of the child's parents* [emphasis added]."[115]

Furthermore, as mentioned in Section D.1, the goal of protecting children from excessive and unnecessary treatment was undermined by a Western-led initiative. The proposals of the observer for the Netherlands and the Swedish delegation to limit the provision only to experimentation with children and to exclude medical treatment, the debate about the order of the child and the parents as consenters, and the astonishing backing of the observer for the Netherlands, the United Kingdom, and others to omit the child as the primary beneficiary of the experimentation for the public's good or for general medical knowledge all contributed to the chairman's decision to delete the provision from the final text.

c. *Medicalization, Drugs, and Children*

The final text of Article 33 of the Children's Convention, entitled "Drug Abuse" was, so it seems, a somewhat unexpected yet rapid development of the drafting process. Neither the original Polish draft proposal nor the comments received on it addressed the issue of children's medicalization.[116] It emerged during the discussions of the working group in the context of health and health services, and the repetition of proposals on the subject matter by both state delegations and NGOs seems to have had its impact. Subsequently, the content of the article was adopted in its final form in 1986, even before the first reading of the Convention was completed.[117]

It was the Spanish delegation that first brought the issue of drug usage and its possible harm to children's health to the attention of the working group in 1978. In a comment Spain submitted regarding the first Polish draft proposal in the context of the principle of the child's best interests, it proposed that "[enabling] the child to develop physically, morally, spiritually and socially in a healthy and normal manner" would be also by explicit reference to "avoiding anything that damages or may impair his physical or mental health, especially

---

[114] The amended proposal at first reading only required that it would not "be adverse" for the child's present and future health (see Section D.1).

[115] *Report of the 1989 Working Group on a Draft Convention on the Rights of the Child*, paragraph 410. (The Venezuelan proposal was submitted to the working group at the second reading. See *Legislative History* on Article 24 (Health), 34.)

[116] *Legislative History* on Article 33 (Drug Abuse), 3.

[117] Article 33 was referred to as Article 18 bis throughout the first and second readings. See *Legislative History* on Article 33 (Drug Abuse), 4.

drugs in any of their forms."[118] Poland did not integrate Spain's view in its revised draft, and no particular note was taken on it during the discussions held on this article at the first reading.

In 1982, the representative of China took the lead in pursuing the prohibition of drug usage, initially under the umbrella of health and health services. In a proposal submitted to the consideration of the working group, the representative of China proposed inserting a subparagraph to the Polish revised draft requiring that "[in particular], States Parties shall undertake measures with a view to: . . . (d) Preventing and prohibiting the child from using drugs."[119] The proposal was not discussed because of a lack of time.[120] In 1984, another proposal to include reference to drugs within the protective measures for ensuring the child's health was submitted by the International Federation of Women in Legal Careers. Emphasizing the concern that "[*inter alia*], the use of drugs of whatever kind" is a potential source of "serious damage to children's health," it proposed a new paragraph by which "States Parties . . . undertake: . . . (3) To take all necessary scientific, technical, educational and remedial measures for the national and international combating of drug abuse and, in particular, the use by children of *drugs of whatever kind* [emphasis added]."[121]

Although neither of the proposals at this point was taken up at the session of the working group, by 1985 the representative of China raised the idea of drafting a separate provision on drug usage. Slightly amending his previous proposal, the new article required states "to . . . take measures to prevent and prohibit children from *taking* drugs [emphasis added]."[122] Also this proposal was not considered, and the records do not provide any particular reason.

However, when the representative of China resubmitted a proposal in 1986 narrowly circumscribing its scope to notions of drug abuse and criminal responsibility, the proposal did make it to the floor.[123] The new provision limited the scope of prohibited drugs to "narcotic drugs as defined in the relevant international conventions," and made an explicit reference to state responsibility in this context "to prevent and prohibit trafficking in narcotic drugs by a child."[124] Other amendment proposals led by the observer for the Netherlands and the representative of the German Democratic Republic refined these two aspects of the new provision, essentially endorsing the position lobbied since 1986 by the NGO group.[125] With the consolidated proposal that was finally

---

[118] *Legislative History* on Article 3 (Best Interests), 6.

[119] *Legislative History* on Article 33 (Drug Abuse), 4.

[120] *Legislative History* on Article 33 (Drug Abuse), 4; Detrick, *The Children's Convention "Travaux Preparatoires,"* 344.

[121] *Legislative History* on Article 33 (Drug Abuse), 5.

[122] *Report of the 1985 Working Group on a Draft Convention on the Rights of the Child*, annex II (*Legislative History* on Article 33 (Drug Abuse), 5).

[123] Detrick, *The Children's Convention "Travaux Preparatoires,"* 427; *Legislative History* on Article 33 (Drug Abuse), 6.

[124] *Report of the 1986 Working Group on a Draft Convention on the Rights of the Child*, paragraph 77 (*Legislative History* on Article 33 (Drug Abuse), 6).

[125] Ibid.

submitted by an informal drafting group,[126] the provision was adopted at the first reading of the working group by consensus. The new provision read as follows:

> The States Parties to the present Convention shall take all appropriate measures, including legislative, social and educational measures, to protect children from the illegal use of narcotic and psychotropic substances as defined in the relevant international treaties, and to prevent the use of children in the illegal production and trafficking of such substances.[127]

For the most part, the article remained in its present form after the second reading. In the discussions held in the 1988–89 session, the working group endorsed a few minor changes.[128] It refrained, however, from giving any formal consideration to the other relevant proposal that was submitted for its consideration under Article 24 on health, obligating states "to prohibit the marketing and distribution of [harmful] chemical, pharmaceutical, nutritional and other substances and products."[129] Thus, with no specified reason for the neglect, the paragraph was eventually not incorporated in either the article on health or the article on drugs.

E. WHO WON, WHO LOST?

The Children's Convention's handling of the various aspects of children's biomedical practices is clearly disappointing. There is no explicit reference to the child's right to give informed consent, and the omission of qualifying words to explicate the input of the child in medical matters ("shall have an influence," "effectively,") casts doubts on the extent to which the child's right to have his or her views respected actually extends to the point of decision making. In contrast to the obvious intention of the sponsors of Article 24(3), the provision contains no list of harmful traditional practices, and the concentration on female circumcision distracted delegations from the original intention. The unmistakable objectives of formulating a parallel provision tackling experimentation with children, excessive medical consumption, and medicalization of children were dropped. Different from the original Chinese proposal or successive proposals that aimed at targeting *all kinds* of drugs under Article 33 of the Convention, only abusive and criminally oriented drug usage

[126] The informal drafting group consisted of delegations from China, Canada, the German Democratic Republic, the Netherlands, and the United Kingdom.

[127] *Report of the 1986 Working Group on a Draft Convention on the Rights of the Child*, paragraphs 82–83 (*Legislative History* on Article 33 (Drug Abuse), 6–7).

[128] The working group added the word "administrative" between the words "legislative" and "social," and replaced the word "illegal" with "illicit" for harmonization purposes with the terminology used in the "relevant international treaties." The replacement was made following the comments made by the Narcotic Drugs Division and the WHO, referring to the Single Convention of Narcotic Drugs (1961) and the Convention of Psychotropic Substances (1971). The working group endorsed also the proposal to delete the words "to the present Convention." *Technical Review of the Text of the Draft Convention on the Rights of the Child*, 38. See also *Legislative History* on Article 33 (Drug Abuse), 8.

[129] *Legislative History* on Article 24 (Health), 26.

was banned, and the rushed submission of the alternative proposal of handling the marketing and distribution of the harmful substances and products was not even formally discussed. Certainly, not all proposals in such a process hold equal weight, merit, or in-depth consideration, if they did not get sufficient support. Yet when assessed in view of the numerous drafters' attempts to embark upon the eradication of all the health-related practices harmful to children, the disappointment is understandable.

This malaise is clear given the promising prospect for the provision on experimentation with children. The original sponsors of the proposal, the NGO group, faulted the ruling because it was "too little too late." Insufficient expertise, belated and lack of a timely response from the legal office of the WHO, and eventually, a shortage of time, were the main reasons raised for the failure.[130] By the time an appropriate alternative draft was prepared, the working group had already entered its second reading, and despite its endorsement by the Indian delegation, the submission of new provisions at this stage was barred. On the other hand, it was argued that the remaining time was insufficient for additional negotiations on the inclusion of the paragraph within the scope of the article on health.[131]

The examination of the discussions up to the chairman's decision to delete the provision, however, only deepened the frustration. In fact, although his ruling can be theoretically explained given the working group's consensus rule of procedures, one is nevertheless left with a sense that this result was almost purposeful. The refocus on the question of informed consent, on the type and form of included treatments, and on the collective's benefit rather than on the potentially harmful consequences of the experimentation to the individual child, generates the impression that the termination of the discussion may have more to do with the uneasiness Western states felt with such a reference that might also include their traditional practices. This is especially true considering that the most fundamental Western bioethical standard since WWII presumably upholds the individual's safety over general medical knowledge. The fact that the proposal was put forward particularly by developing states (the Philippines, Venezuela, India, Mexico)[132] further strengthens this sense. Thus, even with the regret expressed by representatives of a few Western states,[133] this failure seems to be a direct victim of power imbalance and international politics.

The omissions also reflect shifts in the approach and in the subjects who are the targets of the evolving international human rights regime. A comparison of the legislative process of Article V(5) of the Declaration on the Elimination of All Forms of Intolerance and of Discrimination Based on Religion or Belief (Declaration on Religious Freedom or Belief) is instructive. The declaration, adopted by the General Assembly in 1981, stipulates that "the practices of a

[130] Cohen, 183.

[131] Ibid.

[132] Australia was the only "Western" state on the ad hoc informal drafting group of the article.

[133] The representatives of Ireland, Venezuela, the Philippines, the United States and Norway expressed their support in the paragraph and their regret to its deletion.

religion or belief in which a child is brought up must not be injurious to his physical or mental health or to his full development, taking into account article I, paragraph 3 [acceptable limitations on one's freedom of manifestation of religion or belief]."[134]

Despite the similarity in wording with Article 24(3), the rationales for its formulation differ significantly. In the case of the Declaration on Religious Freedom or Belief, supporters of the Argentinean proposal to address the issue[135] as "certain practices could cause physical, psychological, moral or mental harm to the child," specifically referenced only "the refusal of any blood transfusion and the refusal to send children to school advocated by certain religious sects."[136] Aside from the fact that these practices do not contain any particular mention of gender indication, they also seem to reflect concerns with regard to minority groups rather than with traditional practices that are performed nationally, by a majority of the relevant population in a given state (as has been the case, for example, with female circumcision). Furthermore, in contrast to the obvious ramification of female circumcision and other non-Western traditional practices as was evidenced during the legislation of Article 24(3) of the Children's Convention, the drafters of the 1981 Declaration were clearly reluctant to take a particular moral stance. Raising concerns that the wording of the Argentinean proposal might open the door to improper state intervention in the upbringing of children and in the determination of what is moral and what is not, the drafters thus opted for the proposal of the United Kingdom to replace the word "moral" with "mental" in order to avoid the judgment.[137]

Interestingly, the Declaration on Religious Freedom or Belief was not mentioned at all during the drafting of the Children's Convention. Although its nonlegally binding character compared to a treaty may account partly for this,[138] its neglect is odd considering that at the time of the drafting of the

---

[134] Declaration on the Elimination of All Forms of Intolerance and of Discrimination Based on Religion or Belief, G.A. Res. 36/55, 36 U.N. GAOR Supp. (No. 51), at 171, U.N. Doc. A/36/684 (1981).

[135] Argentina's proposal read: "the decision concerning the religion or belief in which a child should be brought up must not be injurious to his health, and must not do him physical or moral harm." See U.N. Economic and Social Council, *Report of the 1980 Working Group on the Draft Declaration on the Elimination of All Forms of Intolerance and of Discrimination based on Religion or Belief*, 36th Sess., Supp. no. 3, paragraph 31, 114, U.N. Doc. E/1980/ 13, E/CN.4.1408 (February 4–March 14, 1980).

[136] U.N. Economic and Social Council, *Report of the 1981 Working Group on the Draft Declaration on the Elimination of All Forms of Intolerance and of Discrimination based on Religion or Belief*, 36th Sess., Supp. no. 3, paragraph 31,. 141, U.N. Doc. E/1982/25; E/CN.4/1475 (February 2–March 13, 1981).

[137] Other proposals that were endorsed are the Philippines' proposal to have a specific reference to the child's "full development" and France's addition at the end of the sentence, reading "taking into account Article I, paragraph 3," referring to the limitation clause of the declaration. *Report of the 1981 Working Group on the Draft Declaration on the Elimination of All Forms of Intolerance and of Discrimination based on Religion or Belief*, paragraphs 26–33, 141–142.

[138] Yet some argue that as a normative document, the declaration or at least some of its provisions have become a part of customary international law. See Natan Lerner, *Religion, Beliefs, and International Human Rights* (Maryknoll, NY: Orbis Books, 2000), 89; Bahiyyah G.

Children's Convention, it was the only other international document containing a similar provision. It thus reinforces the sense that political maneuverings are what shape human rights standards.

Despite the omissions, for at least four reasons the issue of children's bioethics cannot be viewed as excluded from the final text or from the international discourse. The Children's Convention's holistic approach and the inseparable link and overlap between and among the various provisions in both content, spirit, and scope; the innovative principles that laid the groundwork for further discourse on children's rights; the Convention as a living document that is in an ongoing process of evolvement, particularly as developed by the Monitoring Committee under the Children's Convention (Children's Committee or Committee); and, finally, the Convention's impact on the endorsement of other international human rights conventions that are pertinent to the issue of children's bioethics are all important for the discussion. These are all elaborated on below, pinpointing the complexities involved and the more acute questions for the particular discourse on children's bioethics.

1. Children's Bioethics in View of the Children's Convention's Holistic Approach

Although the most direct concern for children's health and for the need to protect them from familial, communal, environmental, and other hazardous practices is articulated in Article 24 on health, other provisions are linked with it and may raise, even if less directly, the accompanying biomedical and bioethical considerations.[139]

One article that is closely linked with biomedical practices and its dilemmas is Article 14 of the Children's Convention on the child's freedom of religion or belief. In addition to state obligations to respect children's rights to freedom of thought, conscience, and religion, the article also includes two potentially clashing rights. On the one hand, it requires states "[to] respect the rights and duties of the parents and, where applicable, the legal guardians, to provide direction to the child in the exercise of his or her [religious] right, in a manner consistent with [the child's] evolving capacities." On the other hand, it contains a limitation clause on one's freedom to manifest his or her religion or belief, if

---

Tahzib, *Freedom of Religion or Belief: Ensuring Effective International Legal Protection* (The Hague: Kluwer Law International, 1996), 187.

[139] It is interesting to observe in this context the differences between Article 7 of the ICCPR and Article 37 of the Children's Convention. While both contain a prohibition of torture or other cruel, inhuman, and degrading treatment, the first includes an explicit reference to the prohibition of subjecting one to medical and scientific experimentation without his or her informed consent, which is of course linked with bioethical considerations. Although Article 37 of the Children's Convention was inspired by its counterpart in the ICCPR and follows its wording with regard to the prohibition of torture etc., it does not contain a similar reference to experimentation but deals strictly with the traditional concept of standards applied in circumstances of deprivation of liberty and administration of (juvenile) justice. Furthermore, the question of experimentation with children was not raised during the discussions in the context of torture, inhuman, and degrading treatment at all. See *Legislative History* on Articles 37 and 40 (Children Deprived of their Liberty and Administration of Juvenile Justice, respectively).

prescribed by law and "[is] necessary to protect public safety, order, health or morals, or fundamental rights and freedoms of others."[140]

In the context of biomedical practices, however, striking the balance between these factors is particularly complicated. Some bodily practices are religiously or culturally mandated and are considered fundamental to the group's and the child's identity. Bearing in mind that abstention from performing the practices may have significant ramifications on the group in its entirety, the observance of the practices may be completely integral to and inseparable from the parental "rights and duties" to provide religious direction to their child. Theoretically, the principle of the child's evolving capacities strikes a balance. Yet the importance of such practices, regardless of outsiders' perceptions that the practices are harmful and the variation of the mandated time for the practices' performance (ranging from the time of birth, at a very young age, adolescence, or alternatively, even still in the uterus) may create a direct clash between direction and guidance, the limitation clause, and biomedical practices. Furthermore, the working group did not endorse the American proposal to stipulate a specific prohibition subjecting the child "to coercion that would impair his freedom to have or to adopt a religion or belief of his choice."[141] Even if it was adopted, children's objective inabilities to participate in the decision making at a very young age may still subject them to the control of the family and the community, and impede their granted right to freedom of religion or belief or their ability to opt out of a religion or belief.

Article 19 of the Children's Convention is another important provision in this context. The article, innovative in its expressed protection of children against intrafamilial abuse and neglect within the international human rights discourse,[142] obligates states to protect children from a broad range of acts committed by "parent(s) or any other person who has the care for the child." It contains a nonexhaustive list of prohibited acts, "including physical and mental violence, injury or abuse, neglect or negligent treatment and maltreatment or exploitation." Although the drafters did not make any explicit connection between abuse and neglect and biomedical practices, linguistically and content wise, there is no doubt that the list of acts may extend to include biomedical practices such as parental refusal of medical treatment "for religious or similar reasons," as the observer for Canada noted during the discussions on health and informed consent,[143] or, alternatively, intrusive medical procedures.

Finally, a note has to be made with regard to Articles 35 and 36 of the Children's Convention dealing with the protection of children from "sale,

140 Article 14(2) and 14(3) of the Children's Convention, respectively. The limitation clause stipulated in Article 14(3) follows its counterpart in Article 18 of the ICCPR.

141 *Legislative History* on Article 14 (Religious Freedom), 4, 9. See also in this context that, due to the objection of representatives from mainly Islamic states, the drafters rejected the insertion of a subparagraph explicitly granting the child the right to adopt or change his or her religion or belief by choice. See *Legislative History* on Article 14 (Religious Freedom), 11, 17–20.

142 Cohen, 319.

143 *Report of the 1989 Working Group on a Draft Convention on the Rights of the Child*, paragraph 424 (*Legislative History* on Article 24 (Health), 37).

trafficking and abduction" and from "other forms of exploitation," respectively. The essence of the two articles originated during the discussion on children's abuse and neglect yet was separated from it later on. Throughout the discussions, the drafters were persuaded that properly tackling the need to secure children's protection from various forms of abuse, neglect, and exploitation merits address in separate provisions. Consequently, familial maltreatment was separated from extrafamilial abuse, neglect, and exploitation, and in a compromised decision of the working group following the discussion in 1987, the provision on children's extrafamilial exploitation was split into four themes: economic; sexual; sale, trafficking, and abduction; and "other forms of exploitation."[144] While the final text contains no reference to the possible exploitation of children as organ donors, comments and proposals did link between children's exploitation and their bodies. Thus, for example, in 1984 the International Federation of Women in Legal Careers and the International Abolitionist Federation submitted to the working group a proposal "to sanction all such practices as exploitation by prostitution, the sale of children for purposes of . . . slavery, . . . mutilation or the administration of drugs and toxic substances."[145] The NGO group submitted a proposal dealing with extrafamilial treatment and exploitation of children, requiring states to "undertake to protect the child against all forms of neglect, abuse, social and economic exploitation, degradation and all acts violating the moral, spiritual or physical integrity of the child."[146] Another proposal that states "enact laws to prevent the abduction, sale or trafficking of children *in any form from the time of conception up to the age of 18 and/ or of human organs* [emphasis added]" was circulated following the request of the Argentinean delegation.[147] Although neither of these proposals was discussed, they do provide a sense of scope of protection intended under the Convention.

This is particularly so in view of the discussion that ensued on what was eventually adopted as Article 36, protecting children from other forms of exploitation. The original proposal of an informal drafting group comprised of delegations from Brazil, France, the Netherlands, the United States, and Venezuela included protection against "all acts prejudicial to the moral, spiritual, mental or physical integrity of the child."[148] Following the objection raised by delegations from Finland, the United States, and others, the word "integrity" was replaced by the word "welfare," and the list of various aspects of

[144] Articles 19, 32, 34, 35, and 36 of the Children's Convention, respectively. *Report of the 1987 Working Group on a Draft Convention on the Rights of the Child*, paragraph 78–79 (*Legislative History* on Articles 34–36).

[145] *Legislative History* on Article 34 (Sexual Exploitation and Abuse), *Legislative History* on Article 35 (Sale, Trafficking and Abduction), and *Legislative History* on Article 36 (Other Forms of Exploitation).

[146] *Legislative History* on Article 34 (Sexual Exploitation and Abuse), *Legislative History* on Article 35 (Sale, Trafficking, and Abduction), and *Legislative History* on Article 36 (Other Forms of Exploitation).

[147] *Legislative History* on Article 35 (Sale, Trafficking, and Abduction), 14. The request followed the report and recommendation of the Latin American NGOs meeting in 1988 on the Children's Convention.

[148] *Report of the 1987 Working Group on a Draft Convention on the Rights of the Child*, paragraphs 90–95. (*Legislative History* on Article 36, 10–11).

the child's interests was eventually omitted. However, this omission was made simultaneously with the adoption of the broad reference to "all other forms of exploitation," based on a consensus that there is a need to ensure that children receive full protection from exploitation. As the representative of the USSR pointed out,

> the selection of terms such as moral, spiritual, mental or physical [exploitation] did not cover all aspects of the interests of the child which needed to be protected from exploitation. The child was brought up in a society; being an active member of the society, he had a wide range of social interests that needed to be promoted.[149]

Given this legislative intention, these articles may be interpreted to include substantial bioethical concerns. This is particularly so considering the possible usage of children as organ donors, including the developments of reproduction techniques allowing parents to choose the genetic combination of their child for healing purposes of the child's other family members, in order to fulfill their own religious duties or as a means to preserve their own cultural identity.[150]

Thus, the array of articles revolving around children's physical, mental, moral, and other health and bodily related aspects that require special attention, whether brought up in the original Polish proposal, developed as progeny thereof, or evolved as separate articles throughout the process, broadens significantly the scope of the discussion.

2. Children's Bioethics in View of the Children's Convention's Innovative Creed: Children's Development, Agency, and Right to Identity

The Children's Convention stipulates at least three significant and innovative provisions to advance children's rights that are particularly relevant to the discussion on children's bioethics: children's right to life, survival, and development; children's agency; and children's rights to preserve their identity. As biomedical and religio-cultural practices cut across an array of other aspects of a child's life and rights, they necessarily relate not only to health concerns, but also to all other pieces that play a role in the development and formation, both physical and moral, of the person he or she is. Moreover, because the child's right to identity is often regarded as epitomizing human's dignity, agency, and his or her entire being,[151] it necessarily relates to and embodies within it the discourse on such practices.The first two provisions are discussed earlier (see Section B), and they will be briefly discussed here in order to explicate the bioethical dilemmas that may arise under their scope. A more extensive discussion on the child's right to preserve his or her identity will be provided as it is inextricably linked with debates on children's bioethics.

---

[149] *Report of the 1987 Working Group on a Draft Convention on the Rights of the Child*, paragraphs 90–95 (*Legislative History* on Article 36, 11–12).

[150] This latter example is discussed further in Chapter 7 on genetic manipulation.

[151] Ya'ir Ronen, "The Child's Right to Identity as a Right to Belong," *Tel Aviv University Law Review* 26, no. 3 (2003): 943, 947.

a. Right to Life, Survival, and Development

Article 6 of the Children's Convention reiterates the child's fundamental right to life as is also guaranteed in an array of other international treaties.[152] However, the principle as enshrined in the Convention goes beyond its traditional scope of merely protecting against intentional or arbitrary deprivation of life.[153] The addition of "survival and development," it has been argued, may require states to take positive measures to ensure that they provide an optimal environment for childhood and for the child's physical, mental, spiritual, moral, psychological, and social growth.[154] As Douglas Hodgson remarks, "it does not seem logical or reasonable to distinguish between loss of life through summary execution, torture or disappearance and that [loss of life] incurred through malnutrition or epidemic that could have been readily avoided."[155] This, however, raises several questions: What sort of physical, mental, spiritual, moral, and other harm merits state intervention? What is the balance between the various components of the child's health or well-being? It further brings back into the equation the fetus question and the possibility of genetic engineering and experimentation with children. To what extent is the medicalization of children justified as a means to bring them in line with the common scale of normal growth or to enhance their natural development? Do disabilities erect a barrier to the optimal environment for the child's development and growth? Which disabilities count?

b. Children's Agency

As discussed earlier (see Sections B and D.1), one of the chief achievements of the Children's Convention is its innovative integration of the concept of children's agency. This concept is embodied in the articulation of "respect to the child's views" under Article 12, which was argued to grant children a substantive right to be actors in their own lives and also a procedural right to challenge, promote, and protect their rights.[156] The article is further regarded as a precondition to the implementation of the Convention in its entirety, and, contrary to many other provisions in the Convention, it has been argued to be detailed and clear enough for immediate implementation.[157] Basically, and as emanates also from the *travaux preparatoires*, however, children's agency is

---

[152] The right to life is protected, among others, in Article 3 of the UDHR; Article 6 of the ICCPR; Article II of the Convention on the Prevention and Punishment of the Crime of Genocide, 78 U.N.T.S. 277, entered into force January 12, 1951; Article II of the International Convention on the Suppression and Punishment of the Crime of Apartheid, adopted and opened for signature, ratification by G.A. Res. 3068 (XXVIII), November 30, 1973, entered into force July 18, 1976, in accordance with Article XV, 1015 U.N.T.S. 243; the Geneva Conventions of 1949; and in other regional treaties.

[153] Paragraph 3 of Human Rights Committee, *The Right to Life (General Comment No. 6)*, 6th Sess. (1982), Compilation of General Comments and General Recommendations Adopted by Human Rights Treaty Bodies, U.N. Doc. HRI\GEN\1\Rev.1, at 6 (1994).

[154] Rachel Hodgkin and Peter Newell, *Implementation Handbook for the Convention on the Rights of the Child* (New York: UNICEF, 1998), 103.

[155] Douglas Hodgson, "The Child's Right to Life, Survival and Development," *International Journal of Children's Rights* 2, no. 2 (1994): 381.

[156] Lansdown, 2.

[157] Lucker-Babel, 395.

inextricably linked with biomedical concerns. The drafters' reference to it with regard to health-related settings was explicit. The deletion of the unequivocal reference to the child's right to express his or her views in medical matters did not arise from a disagreement, but rather from the drafters' intent not to limit the right only to a particular list of settings.[158] Thus, although no specific references on the child's agency role in medical matters were endorsed in the final text, the overall spirit stemming from this article has not only taken a step ahead with the entrenchment of children's rights, but it has actually established an overreaching framework from which all children's rights, including children's bioethics, need to be approached. How is the child's right to respect his or her views in matters of medical procedures interpreted? To what extent does the provision translate, in practice, to mean more than informed consent? And who are the consenters?

c. *The Child's Right to Identity*

Although the concept of the child's right to identity was introduced to the working group relatively late in the drafting process, the eventual inclusion of the article is considered to be one of the key innovations of the Children's Convention. No other international human rights treaty has previously protected this right, and in view of other provisions that were under discussion (particularly, name and nationality; separation from parents and parental responsibility), the explicit reference to the child's identity, per se, appeared to some as unnecessarily abundant. However, the drafters' were eventually convinced that the child's right to identity is unique among other rights and merits the special protection. Stipulated in Article 8 of the Convention, the provision obligates states "to respect the right of the child to preserve his or her identity" and to provide appropriate assistance and protection to "reestablish [it] speedily" if the child is illegally deprived of some or all elements of this identity.[159] While debates on the scope and implications of the right continue, there can be no doubt that this recognition has opened a new avenue for the consideration of children's rights. This latter point is elaborated on in Chapter 6, where the argument is made that the child's identity is of great importance if one seriously considers the child's exercise of his or her human rights. In line with the goal of the present chapter, however, the following discussion sheds light on the drafting process of the child's right to preserve his or her identity and briefly ties it to the general discourse on children's bioethics.

Article 8 of the Children's Convention originated in 1985 with the Argentinean proposal of an article aimed at guaranteeing children's right to recover their familial and biological identity if they are forced to grow up in a familial environment different from their natural one.[160] It stated the child's

---

[158] *Report of the 1981 Working Group on a Draft Convention on the Rights of the Child,* paragraph 78 *(Legislative History* on Article 12 (Participation), 8).

[159] Article 8 of the Children's Convention.

[160] The proposal was submitted in view of the growing phenomena of "children's disappearance" and of the abduction of children and of pregnant women from their families and under the military junta in the 1970s. George A. Stewart, "Interpreting the Child's Right to

"inalienable right to retain his true and genuine personal, legal and family identity" and required states parties "to give special protection and assistance with a view to reestablish the child's true and genuine identity as soon as possible" when a child has been "fraudulently deprived of some or all of the elements of his identity." The proposal further specifically referenced the child's "blood relations" as a primary source of identity to be restored.[161]

Characteristic of the dynamic drafting process, by the time the proposal was brought to the discussion in 1986[162] and particularly until its endorsement in its present form in 1988, the original proposal was significantly changed. However, a few points that were raised during the discussions merit attention. First, the sponsors of the proposal, led by Argentina, Poland, Brazil, and the NGO group made it a point that there is a distinction between the child's legal identity and his or her "true and genuine" one.[163] The first refers to institutionalized elements of identity addressed in other provisions of the Children's Convention, particularly, registration and nationality (Article 7) and legally recognized familial placements of the child, either biological or replacement (Articles 9 and 18). The child's "true and genuine identity," by contrast, refers to a much broader concept of identity. The assumption is that unlike legal identity that is subscribed in law and can be violated or replaced, the latter also includes the child's general cultural background. As such, it is inalienable to the child and cannot be deprived of, legally or illegally.[164] The representative of Egypt was further explicit in this point, proposing a formulation of "the child's right to respect for his or her human, racial, national and cultural identity and dignity."[165] The wording of "including" that the drafters settled on thus appears as indicative of the drafters' endorsement of the distinction.

Secondly, the examination of the *travaux preparatoires* shows that the drafters' notions of identity intended to target, in particular, biological and

---

Identity in the UN Convention on the Rights of the Child," *Family Law Quarterly* 26, no. 3 (1992): 221.

[161] *Report of the 1985 Working Group on a Draft Convention on the Rights of the Child*, paragraph 9 and annex II (*Legislative History* on Article 8 (Identity), 4; Detrick, *A Commentary on the Children's Convention*, 160).

[162] During the discussions in 1986, two additional proposals on the issue were already submitted to the consideration of the working group. The first was a Polish proposal, in which the word "retain" replaced the word "preserve" before "his true and genuine identity" and deleted the reference to the child's blood relations. The second proposal submitted by the NGO group required states parties "to take all appropriate measures to enable the child to exercise his or her inalienable right to know and to retain his or her true and genuine personal, legal and family identity." See *Report of the 1986 Working Group on a Draft Convention on the Rights of the Child*, paragraph 33 (*Legislative History* on Article 8 (Identity), 5).

[163] *Report of the 1986 Working Group on a Draft Convention on the Rights of the Child*, paragraph 35 (*Legislative History* on Article 8 (Identity), 6).

[164] *Technical Review of the Text of the Draft Convention on the Rights of the Child*, paragraph 22–23 (*Legislative History* on Article 8 (Identity), 9). It is interesting to note in this context that the only right that has been explicitly qualified under the existing international human rights framework as an "inalienable" right is the right to life. Detrick, *A Commentary on the Children's Convention*, 127.

[165] *Report of the 1989 Working Group on a Draft Convention on the Rights of the Child*, paragraph 92 (Detrick, *The Children's Convention "Travaux Preparatoires,"* 127).

familial sources of identification. Argentina's proposal originally referenced to "blood relations" and to "family identity," the latter term supported in the proposals submitted by the Polish delegation and the NGO group.[166] The notion of "family identity" remained in the draft throughout most of the discussions, including in the consolidated proposal of the informal drafting group composed of delegations from Argentina, the Netherlands, Norway, Poland, and the International Commission of Jurists.[167] Also when the working group was about to adopt the text at the second reading in 1988, Mexico still made an effort to include "biological elements of [the child's] identity."[168] This limitation, however, was not included in the final draft.

Thus, the article as it currently stands does not simply grant the child a right to identity, per se, nor does it contain a limitation only to the legally recognized aspects of the child's identity or to his or her biological ties. Drawing on this background, scholars argue that the list of sources of identification enumerated in the provision is nonexhaustive and that it also encompasses ethnic, religious, linguistic, sexual, and racial identities.[169] As demonstrated in Chapter 1, however, these sources of identification inherently also include biomedical practices. As health is social construct and as religio-cultural bodily practices are part of the child's enculturation into the community, the child's development is necessarily both constrained and liberated by them. Thus, although the Children's Committee does not provide formal clarification on the components of the child's identity or on state responsibility in this regard,[170] the various principles of the Children's Convention open a door for additional biomedical sources of identification. This includes the child's identity arising from artificial reproductive technology, genetic engineering, and, increasingly, disability-related identity.[171] As such, it is particularly relevant to the analysis and the development of a comprehensive theory of children's bioethics.

3. Children's Bioethics in View of the Children's Committee's Jurisprudence

Although the Children's Convention's text is a *fait accompli* at this point, the issue of children's rights, including children's bioethics, is a developing field of inquiry. Terminology can be interpreted differently over time, giving life to new

---

166 *Report of the 1985 Working Group on a Draft Convention on the Rights of the Child,* paragraph 9 and annex II; *Report of the 1986 Working Group on a Draft Convention on the Rights of the Child,* paragraph 33 (*Legislative History* on Article 8 (Identity), 5–6).

167 *Report of the 1986 Working Group on a Draft Convention on the Rights of the Child,* paragraph 40 (*Legislative History* on Article 8 (Identity), 6).

168 *Report of the 1989 Working Group on a Draft Convention on the Rights of the Child,* paragraph 336 (*Legislative History* on Article 8 (Identity), 10).

169 The right to ethnic, linguistic, and religious identity of children members of minority groups is stipulated in Article 30 of the Convention and follows its counterpart in Article 27 of the ICCPR. See also Detrick, *A Commentary on the Children's Convention,* 162–63.

170 Part IV(B), paragraph 54 of the General Guidelines.

171 Stewart, 224; Anna Kirkland, "Identity and the Properly Functioning Individual: Imagining the Confluence of Fat Rights and Disability Law," USC Center for Law, History and Culture Workshop (2004): 35–37, 43–47, http://law.usc.edu/academics/centers/clhc/archives/workshops/documents/kirkland_000.pdf (discussing the relationship between personhood, disabled identity, and law in the context of the Americans with Disabilities Act).

or renewed issues of interest and adapting to various developments that occur in the field. The Children's Committee's jurisprudence on the matter plays an important role in this context. This is especially so considering its various sources of influence, including jurisprudence of other treaty bodies, scholastic work on children's development, personal expertise of the Committee members, and the information provided to them by NGOs and other UN bodies, such as the WHO and the United Nations Children's Fund (UNICEF).[172] The determination of the scope and breadth of children's bioethics, as with all other issues under the Convention, is thus, to a great extent, still a work in progress. What sort of guidelines does it envision in the context of children's bioethics? To what extent has it incorporated and advanced the creed of the Convention in the context of children's bioethics?

The Children's Committee has clearly taken an active approach to reply to some of the issues raised. In addition to a few general comments that it issued,[173] it promulgated reporting procedures and General Guidelines Regarding the Form and Content of Periodic Reports to be submitted by states parties (1996).[174] The General Guidelines cluster the articles into sectors according to topic, reflecting "the Convention's holistic perspective of children's rights: that they are indivisible and interlaced and that equal importance should be attached to each and every right recognized therein."[175] They have also clearly taken into account (at least some) of the word and spirit of the discussions held during the drafting process in its evaluation of state compliance with the Children's Convention. Such an approach can be observed, for example, in the context of respect for children's views in medical matters,[176] in its paramount attention to traditional practices affecting girls and its specific reference to female circumcision,[177] and with regard to illicit consumption of substances

---

[172] Article 45 of the Children's Convention allows the Committee to obtain information from various UN bodies, NGOs, and scholars. (For a discussion on the factors influencing the Committee's jurisprudence, see Cohen and Kilbourne, 649.) UNICEF is the acronym for "United Nations International Children's Emergency Fund," the original name of the organization. Its name was shortened in 1953, but the acronym remained.

[173] So far the Children's Committee has issued only a few general comments that will be elaborated on, where relevant, in Chapters 5 and 6.

[174] See Committee on the Rights of the Child, General Guidelines; Overview of the Reporting Procedures, 7th Sess., paragraphs 5, 2, U.N. Doc. CRC/C/33 (October 24, 1994).

[175] Paragraph 9 of the General Guidelines.

[176] Part VI(B), paragraph 93 of the General Guidelines.

[177] Part IV(B), paragraph 97 of the General Guidelines. The Canadian delegation expressed during the drafting process the view, supported by the representatives of Japan, Sweden, and Venezuela, that the term "harmful traditional practices" be interpreted as including all those practices discussed in the *1986 Report on Harmful Traditional Practices.* The only reference in the report to non-Western states is in paragraph 167, pointing to the historical preference for men and boys in Europe in the second half of the 19th century and the consequences it had on women and girl's health. The male preference is attributed to social and economic disadvantages of women and girls. The report discussed three main practices: female circumcision, traditional birth practices, and preferential treatment for male children, along with brief discussions on forced feeding of women, early marriage, the various taboos or practices that prevent women from controlling their own fertility, and nutritional taboos. In contrast, the only reference to boys is in the general and nonexclusive mentioning of

by children.[178] Furthermore, the Committee seems to have made its overseeing of the issues that are pertinent to the various aspects of children's rights rather clear. Thus, for example, the Committee made efforts to incorporate proposals that were not discussed (such as the proposal on the marketing and distribution of substances).[179] Influenced by external sources such as NGOs reports, scholastic literature, and jurisprudence of other treaty-based bodies, the Committee even inserted specific references on other relevant issues that were not at all dealt with during the drafting process yet developed a political momentum later on.[180]

In contrast to this proactive approach, however, the Children's Committee remained completely silent on other issues. Most visibly is the lack of reference in its General Guidelines to any of the Western-oriented biomedical practices, including scientific developments, experimentation with children, and medical treatment of children—despite the arguable majority's support for the inclusion of such a provision that was expressed during the drafting process.[181] Some argue that the Committee's refusal to deal with experimentation and genetic engineering may be rooted in the drafters' compromise with regards to the status of the fetus under the Children's Convention and the question of abortion.[182] This assumption is strengthened considering that it did provide some protective measures to regulate experimentation with children in the context of the HIV/AIDS epidemic and following the reports of abuse and exploitation of the target group of experimentation.[183] However, considering the immense impact these practices have on children's rights and on children's

"other forms of mutilation (facial scarification)" without any further elaboration. See *Report of the 1987 Working Group on a Draft Convention on the Rights of the Child*, paragraph 37 (*Legislative History* on Article 24 (Health), 25).

[178] In paragraph 155, it requests that states indicate all appropriate measures adopted to protect children from the illicit use of narcotic drugs and psychotropic substances. In paragraph 156, it requests additional information on issues such as the relevant international treaties to which the state is a party, awareness-raising programs, and measures of assistance undertaken to ensure the physical and psychological recovery and the social integration of the child.

[179] Paragraph 157 of the General Guidelines. This guideline coincides with the content of the two other proposals that were in front of the working group, yet never discussed. One is a suggestion of the representative of the United States that the article "should include a reference to other drugs, such as alcohol." (See *Report of the 1986 Working Group on a Draft Convention on the Rights of the Child*, paragraph 81). The second is the NGO group's proposal on the prohibition of marketing and distribution of substances harmful to the children's health discussed in Section D.2.a (*Legislative History* on Article 24 (Health), 26).

[180] One example is the Children's Committee's addressing corporeal punishment as a disciplinary method in schools. Although the working group did not discuss the issue per se, the Committee incorporated the issue in its Concluding Observations based on the interpretation given to the practice by the Human Rights Committee and the Human Rights Court of the Council of Europe as falling within the scope of prohibited cruel and degrading treatment. Cohen and Kilbourne, 649–50.

[181] Detrick, *The Children's Convention "Travaux Preparatoires,"* 23.

[182] Cohen and Kilbourne, 650; Cohen, 174.

[183] Committee on the Rights of the Child, *HIV/AIDS and the Rights of the Child (General Comment No. 3)*, U.N. Doc. CRC/GC/2003/3 (2003) (hereafter *General Comment No. 3 (HIV/AIDS)*).

lives, the Committee may soon be required to address them. This is especially so in view of the increasing usage of scientific developments and their internalization within one's identity as an individual and as a member of a group. Thus, despite the limited number of general comments the Committee issued so far, the argued persisting uncertainty in the Committee's interpretation of the articles,[184] and the omission of reference to children and scientific development, the Committee's work nevertheless provides a continually developing basis for observation. Indeed, just as the Committee incorporated biomedical concerns that were raised during the drafting process into its work, so too it allows other biomedical practices, both traditional and invented, to come under its wings—if it so chooses.

4. Other International Instruments Addressing Children's Bioethics

Aside from the clear significance of the Children's Convention itself in the promotion of children's rights, another result was its impact on other international and regional bodies. In addition to scholastic, legal, and advocacy work conducted directly in view of the Convention, it also inspired other national and international initiatives to codify children's rights, establishing new standards for tackling issues concerning children's rights. Both the Council of Europe and the Organization of African Unity (OAU) adopted children's rights treaties and other international bodies such as UNICEF, the UN High Commissioner for Refugees, the United Nations Educational, Scientific and Cultural Organization (UNESCO), and others have modified their policies in the Convention's spirit.[185]

Naturally, not all instruments include provisions that are pertinent to the discussion on children's bioethics.[186] However, as the body of human rights treaties pertaining to children' rights develops, it allows breaking away from the traditional construction of children as only passive vessels who need protection. As such, they supplement the Children's Convention and entrench the realization of children as rights holders.[187]

In Europe, the most pertinent progress has been the adoption of the European Conventions on Biomedicine, which specifically encompasses children.

---

[184] Cohen and Kilbourne, 642.

[185] Ibid., 653.

[186] The two most recent conventions adopted in the context of children are the European Convention on the Exercise of Children's Rights (ETS No. 160), entered into force January 7, 2000, and the European Convention on Contact Concerning Children (ETS No. 192) entered into force September 1, 2005. The first aims at guaranteeing the child's rights by "improving and accelerating general court procedures where the interests of the child are at stake, hearing the child and the proper representation of the child [in family matters]." The second deals with the importance of family relations, taking into account the "internationalisation of family relationships" in Europe and transatlantic custody conflicts. See paragraph 3 of the Explanatory Report on the Convention on the Exercise of Children's Rights, http://conventions.coe.int/Treaty/en/Reports/Html/160.htm and paragraph 1 of the Explanatory Report on the Convention on Contact Concerning Children, http://conventions.coe.int/Treaty/en/Reports/Html/192.htm.

[187] The Convention on Contact Concerning Children explicitly stipulates its intention to supplement the Children's Convention.

These include the Convention for the Protection of Human Rights and Dignity of the Human Being with regard to the Application of Biology and Medicine (the Oviedo Convention) (1997), the Additional Protocol on Transplantation of Organs and Tissues of Human Origin (2002), the Additional Protocol on the Prohibition of Cloning Human Beings (1998), and the Additional Protocol concerning Biomedical Research (2005).[188] For the most part, these conventions take the traditional approach to children as individuals who lack the capacity to consent to the various medical interventions and whose proxy consent would suffice.[189] However, the archetype Convention on Human Rights and Biomedicine (the Oviedo Convention) takes a step forward as far as the doctrine of informed consent is concerned. As a general principle, it states that "the opinion of the minor shall be taken into consideration as an increasingly determining factor in proportion to his or her age and degree of maturity."[190] It thus specifically follows the concept of agency as has been negotiated and ultimately adopted, albeit without particular reference to biomedical contexts, in Article 12 of the Children's Convention.

Significant developments also occurred within the African region. In 1990, the OAU adopted the African Charter on the Rights and Welfare of the Child (African Charter), which entered into force in 1999.[191] The African Charter contains not only reiteration of the cornerstone principles of the Children's Convention, but some articles even appear to expand on it. Following Article 3 of the Children's Convention, for example, the African Charter establishes the principle of the child's best interests, yet requires that it is "the" (rather than "a") primary consideration. Similarly, endorsing the principle of respect to the child's views, the African Charter endorses the broader terminology of "a child who is capable of *communicating* his/her own views," which seems to follow UNICEF's comment during the drafting of the Children's Convention.[192] It also explicitly requires in Article 4 that "[these] views shall be taken into consideration by the relevant authority in accordance with the provisions of appropriate law." Furthermore, Article 21 of the African Charter is explicitly dedicated to children's "protection against harmful social and cultural practices." It requires states to take

---

[188] See note 52.

[189] See Article 6 of the Convention on Human Rights and Biomedicine; Article 20 of the Additional Protocol on Transplantation of Organs and Tissues; Article 15 of the Additional Protocol on Biomedical Research;

[190] Article 6(2) of the Convention on Human Rights and Biomedicine.

[191] African Charter on the Rights and Welfare of the Child, OAU Doc. CAB/LEG/24.9/49 (1990), entered into force November 29, 1999 (hereafter African Charter). As of February 2004, thirty-seven African states have ratified the African Charter, among them Angola, Benin, Botswana, Burkina Faso, Cameroon, Cape Verde, Chad, Egypt, Equatorial Guinea, Gambia, Guinea, Kenya, Libya and Lesotho. Central African Republic, Congo, Djibouti, Gabon, and others signed it but did not ratify it. See Web site of the African Committee of Experts on the Rights and Welfare of the Child, http://www.africa-union.org/child/home.htm#.

[192] *Technical Review of the Text of the Draft Convention on the Rights of the Child*, 21–22 (*Legislative History* on Article 12 (Participation), 10).

> all appropriate measures to eliminate harmful social and cultural practices affecting the welfare, dignity, normal growth and development of the child and in particular: (a) those customs and practices prejudicial to the health or life of the child; and (b) those customs and practices discriminatory to the child on the grounds of sex or other status.

Subparagraph 2 makes particular reference to the prohibition of child marriage and the betrothal of girls and boys (defined as persons under the age of eighteen).

Finally, on May 3, 2008, the Convention on the Rights of Persons with Disabilities (Disability Rights Convention) entered into force.[193] The Disability Rights Convention follows the holistic and comprehensive approach of the Children's Convention and contains a few important provisions for this discussion. Aside from a saving clause that requires states to ensure that children with disabilities enjoy the full scope of human rights, on an equal basis with others, it also reiterates the Children's Convention's principles of evolving capacities, agency, best interests, and informed consent in the provision of health care.[194] It also follows the requirement that states abolish "harmful practices relating to persons with disabilities, including those based on sex and age, in all areas of life" (albeit under the provision dealing with awareness-raising rather than health, as under the Children's Convention).[195] Finally, in addition to the child's legal measures of identity (name, nationality, and the right to know and to be cared for by one's parents), Article 3(h) of the Disability Rights Convention stipulates, among its general principles, "respect for the right of children with disabilities to preserve their identities." While, by definition, children with disabilities are included also within the Children's Convention, the Disability Rights Convention reinforces these important principles.

Although the European Convention on Human Rights and Biomedicine, its additional protocols, the African Charter, and the Disability Rights Convention are all already in force, it is only a rather recent development.[196] Thus, they have not yet created a comprehensive jurisprudence on children's rights.[197]

[193] The Convention on the Rights of Persons with Disabilities was adopted by the UN General Assembly by consensus on December 13, 2006 (G.A. Res. A/61/611 (2006)). It is the eighth core human rights treaty on the international level and includes an optional protocol, which was adopted by the General Assembly on the same day. Both the convention and its protocol were opened for state signature and ratification in March 2007, and entered into force on May 3, 2008. As of January 2009, 138 states signed the convention, and forty-six states ratified it; seventy-one states signed the optional protocol and twenty-seven ratified it. Convention on the Protection and Promotion of the Rights and Dignity of Persons with Disabilities, G.A. Res. A/61/611 (2006), entered into force May 3, 2008 (hereafter Disability Rights Convention). The text of the convention is available at http://www.un.org/disabilities/convention/conventionfull.shtml. For more information on the Disability Rights Convention, see http://www.un.org/disabilities/convention/signature.shtml.

[194] Articles 3(h), 7, and 25(d) of the Disability Rights Convention.

[195] Article 8(b) of the Disability Rights Convention.

[196] See notes 52, 191, and 193.

[197] The first conference of the states parties to the Disability Rights Convention to elect twelve members of the committee took place in New York on November 3, 2008.

Furthermore, and particularly in the context of the African region, conflicts between the international Children's Convention and the African Charter are likely to occur. Indeed, the African Charter may even be interpreted as narrowing children's rights, despite its provision reserving all rights under the Children's Convention. For example, taking into account the child's views "in accordance with the provisions of appropriate law" may include not only national legislation that will have to be adapted to the international standards, but also local and customary law that may not respect the child's views. Similarly, the references throughout the African Charter to the child's cultural values and in particular to his or her "responsibilities towards his family and society, the State and other legally recognized communities and the international community" to, among others, "respect his parents, superiors and elders at all times" and "to preserve and strengthen African cultural values in his relations with other members of the society," may erect a barrier to the child's right to freely express and genuinely have his or her views respected.[198] However, they clearly reflect the developing trend of recognizing children as rights holders and the efforts made to strengthen children's agency, notwithstanding the potential conflict with the child's cultural background and social values. These instruments and the work of the committees that will monitor their implementation[199] thus provide an additional relevant and significant basis for future developments. To what extent do these recent instruments advance the concept of children as agents in the context of biomedical practices? How are the various biomedical practices tied with the question of children's development and identity? These are important questions in view of the increased scientific and medical developments.

F. CONCLUSION

In contrast to the conventional assumption that female circumcision was almost the sole or the predominant concern of the drafters in the context of harmful traditional practices, the examination of the *travaux preparatoires* clearly shows that this was not the case. An array of other pertinent issues was discussed under the same umbrella, including informed consent, experimentation with children, scientific developments, and excessive medicalization of children. Despite recurring efforts to address explicitly these other issues, the final text contains only relics of them. As often is the case in such global-scale processes, international politics, political imbalance, and inevitable compromises are the prime causes.

[198] Article 31 of the African Charter. See the discussion in Corinne A. A. Packer, *Using Human Rights to Change Tradition: Traditional Practices Harmful to Women's Reproductive Health in Sub-Saharan Africa* (Oxford: Antwerpen Intersentia, 2002), 115–23 explaining why the references to culture and to the duty language within the international instruments of the African region do not necessitate such a conflict.

[199] According to Articles 32–45 of the African Charter, a committee is expected to be established to monitor the implementation of the charter. The committee has not yet created substantial jurisprudence. The European Court of Human Rights delivered a few pertinent cases (see Chapter 7).

This result does not obstruct the relevance of the Children's Convention to the discussion on children's bioethics. On the contrary, the holistic approach of the Convention demands that the issue be examined not only if explicitly mentioned, but also in view of other rights that are intrinsically tied to biomedical practices. This includes the child's right to religious freedom and the child's protection from abuse and exploitation. Moreover, the overreaching innovative creeds of the Convention are valuable sources for guidance. Except for the the notion of child's agency and the child's right to life, survival, and development, the explicit reference to the child's right to preserve his or her identity is a key consideration. It was not only unequivocally connected with one's biological and familial characteristics during the drafting process, but also with the much broader context of the child's social and cultural milieu. This connection is not in vein; it is in fact the only way to fully endorse the child as an agent who can exercise his or her rights. Besides, if the *travaux preparatoires* have any meaning, then one needs to give these aspects due consideration.

Indeed, within its authority, the Children's Committee has clearly taken an active approach to reincorporate bioethical concerns that were raised during the drafting process but did not prevail in the final text. Although its issuance of general comments has been so far limited, its formulation of the General Guidelines nevertheless reinstalled specific measures to assess state compliance with the treaty following the word and spirit of the discussions held during the drafting process. However, it did so only selectively. While the issue of female circumcision received a great deal of attention, Western-oriented biomedical practices remained for the most part off the Committee's radar. Considering scientific progress and developments in international human rights law, particularly, the entry into force of the European Convention on Human Rights and Biomedicine, its additional protocols, the African Charter, and the Disability Rights Convention, it would be difficult for these practices to remain off the agenda for long. For the time being, however, ambiguity and lacunae remain, drawing attention to the practical aspects of the Children's Convention—yet also opening the door for the expansion of the scope of biomedical dilemmas concerning children that are to be considered under it.

The next chapter examines an array of traditional practices performed for medi-cultural (including religious) rationales. All the practices under consideration were raised within the work of the international bodies, and they are integral to and play a significant role in the constitution of the child's identity. Among them are male circumcision, scarification, and elongation of the neck. This examination and the legal analysis that follows it (Chapters 4 and 5) will enable inferring some conclusions on the construction of harmful traditional practices stipulated in Article 24(3) of the Children's Convention. Pointing to the flaws in the existing method of analysis of such practices, Chapter 6 suggests an alternative method that is based on the child's identity, and applies it in Chapters 7 and 8 to the traditional practices—and to the "recently developed" traditional biomedical practice of genetic manipulation.

CHAPTER 3

TRADITIONAL BODILY PRACTICES: CASE STUDIES

Chapter 2 examined the drafting process of the Convention on the Rights of the Child (Children's Convention or Convention)[1] with regards to bioethical concerns. Although the final text does not include the array of biomedical practices that were considered in this context, the drafters' intention to include them was clear. The only explicit provision that ultimately remained is Article 24(3), concerning state obligation to eradicate harmful traditional practices. Despite the heated debates about what would be included within the scope of this article, the drafters ultimately left it to the determination of the Monitoring Committee under the Children's Convention (Children's Committee or Committee).

This chapter focuses on four controversial traditional bodily practices that are performed on children. The practices are male circumcision, tribal marking, extraction of baby milk teeth, and neck elongation, all of which have been discussed in the work of the international human rights bodies as falling within the scope of harmful traditional practices. The chapter explains the justification for the case selection and then discusses each practice in view of its social and cultural meaning. Medical implications that have been associated with the customs as well as the other incentives that play a role in their preservation are explored. The chapter aims at establishing the historical, cultural, and medical aspects of these traditional bodily practices in order to demonstrate the contingent nature of biomedical procedures. As human rights and children's rights in particular cannot be discussed separately from the environment in which they apply, this contextualization is essential for the legal and policy analysis of children's bioethics in subsequent chapters.

A. CASE SELECTION

The cases selected for this study involve biomedical practices that are culturally empowering or are at least perceived as such by their respective communities. Bodily practices that are motivated by hate, revenge, or by reason of punishment (such as the vendetta practice in Albania or corporeal punishment) are excluded, despite their clear impact on health. For similar reasons, practices that aim at the destruction rather than modification of the body or at the exploitation (sexual or other) of another person are not

[1] Convention on the Rights of the Child, G.A. Res. 44/25, annex, 44th Sess., 61st plenary meeting. U.N. GAOR Supp. (No. 49), at 167, U.N. Doc. A/44/49 (1989), entered into force September 2, 1990, reprinted in 28 I.L.M. 1448 (1989).

analyzed. Examples of such practices are the widowhood practice of *Sati* in India, the practice of having sex with a virgin as a healing method for HIV/AIDS as documented in South Africa and other African states,[2] and slavery practices such as the Troksi in Ghana.[3]

Additionally, traditional practices that are associated with reproduction, such as childbirth practices, nutritional taboos during pregnancy, and female circumcision are not part of this study. One reason is that the discourse about reproduction is inextricably preoccupied with issues of discrimination and gender relations. While this discussion is significant for the analysis of women and girl's rights, it often leads one to overlook other considerations. By excluding these customs, this chapter attempts to avoid the "gender trap" and concentrate on children and agency in the context of bioethics.

Another reason is that reproductive practices raise a unique complexity in the delineation of childhood versus adulthood, which applies only to girls. In various cultures, a girl's age of maturity is determined by her reproductive development (usually, earlier than a boy), after which she may be qualified to marry and reproduce.[4] Although within the international discourse she may still be regarded as a child, not yet having reached the fixed ideal age of majority, in her particular cultural community she may be already excluded from the children's group. Still, it is in this period when she may also be exposed to the various reproductive practices that boys, naturally, are not. Notwithstanding the international criticism about the inappropriateness of such determinations of majority by physical measures alone, it seems almost impossible (and sociologically perhaps also improper) to separate the discussion on girls-as-women and girls. The exclusion of traditional practices that surround girls' reproductive health thus avoids confusion.

Some scholars warned that grouping men and women under one category, if both also suffer from discrimination, would create a false "neutral equality discourse" and hence should be avoided.[5] Women and girls' experiences differ from men and boys,' and there is no doubt that the existence of discriminatory practices further accentuates these differences. Son preference practices such as greater abuse, avoidance of medical treatment, and general neglect of girls are particularly notorious for having direct and indirect effects on women and girls' health and development. Although these arguments are not in dispute,

---

[2] Farhana Zuberi, *Assessment of Violence Against Children in the Eastern and Southern Africa Region—Results of an Initial Desk Review for the UN Secretary General's Study on Violence against Children* (UNICEF, 2005), 158, http://www.unicef.org/southafrica/SAF_resources_vac_es-arassessment.doc.

[3] Although slavery practices may have health implications, they are not carried out for medico-cultural rationales in the sense that is being examined in this work.

[4] In Albania, for instance, while childhood extends up to the age of eighteen, boys and girls who marry before this age acquire full capacity to act. This majority status remains even if the marriage is declared invalid or is dissolved before reaching the age of eighteen. Committee on the Rights of the Child, *Initial State Report: Albania,* paragraph 46 U.N. Doc. CRC/C/11/Add.27 (July 5, 2004).

[5] This argument was raised in the context of cosmetic surgeries. Kathy Davis, "A Dubious Equality: Men, Women and Cosmetic Surgery," *Body & Society* 8, no. 1 (2002): 50–51.

the fact that both girls and boys lack the legal capacity to give an informed consent to medical treatment and that they both depend on their care givers for their survival, establishes a unique shared basis between the genders that is essential in the discussion on biomedical practices. This distinguishes them as a subgroup from adults. Excluding reproductive-related traditional practices thus allows grouping boys and girls on the basis of biomedical cultures rather than gender relations. It sets aside the contentious key distinction between the genders, while still maintaining the pluralism that ethnic, economic status, and other aspects, which impact one's experiences and identity, creates.

The third reason for the exclusion of these practices associated with reproduction has to do with redundancy. Under the umbrella of the women's rights movement, traditional practices affecting women's reproductive health have been thoroughly discussed by the international community, as well as by regional committees, individual national states, the medical profession, scholars, and human rights activists.[6] These include the practices of female circumcision, son preference, early marriage and dowry, early pregnancies, food taboos during pregnancies and damaging childbirth practices, and violence against women. Particular attention has also been given to girls as the coining of the term "girl-child" exemplifies. Considering the universality of bodily practices, however, logically, there is also a universal potential of harm that transcends the power relationships between the genders. Biomedical practices and religio-cultural divides inevitably encompass also boys as a vulnerable group, yet no similar concept of the boy-child has been developed. The selection of cases thus aims not only at avoiding unnecessary repetition, but also revisits boys in the context of biomedical practices who have been overlooked for the most part.

The selection of the four traditional biomedical practices was made on the basis of their shared characteristics. They are all often connoted with a sense of antiquity and follow the commonly used definition of traditional practices as "long standing, resistant to change and embedded within the cultural fabric of a community."[7] They are carried out on the body of the subject and may involve health implications. They are customarily sanctioned (or at least required) by parental or others' consent, presumably as a part of their prerogative as those who are responsible to care for their child. Furthermore, the performance of the practice is often initiated by others rather than by the child himself or herself on

[6] Among the international bodies dealing with the issue are the United Nations Development Fund for Women (UNIFEM), the United Nations Children's Fund (UNICEF), the Children's Committee, and the committee under the Convention on the Elimination of Discrimination against Women, G.A. Res. 34/180, 34 U.N. GAOR Supp. (No. 46), at 193, U.N. Doc. A/34/46, entered into force September 3, 1981 (hereafter CEDAW); regional committees include such agencies as the Organization of African Unity (OAU) and the Inter-African Committee on Traditional Practices Affecting the Health of Women and Children (IAC). The World Health Organization (WHO) has also taken a stance on the issue. These categories were formally formulated in 1995. See U.N. Office of the High Commissioner for Human Rights, *Fact Sheet No. 23: Harmful Traditional Practices Affecting the Health of Women and Girls,* Part I, http://www.unhchr.ch/html/menu6/2/fs23.htm.

[7] Corinne A. A. Packer, *Using Human Rights to Change Tradition: Traditional Practices Harmful to Women's Reproductive Health in Sub-Saharan Africa* (Oxford: Antwerpen Intersentia, 2002), 3.

the basis of the guardians' cultural beliefs. Finally, all the practices are rooted in religio-cultural beliefs, which are believed to be among the most powerful sources of one's identification. As such, while children may be expected to fulfill their respective obligations by following the cultural traditions, they also have room for agency. The practices exhibit variance, however, with regards to the sources of their beliefs. Specifically, the cases can be discerned on two dimensions. The first one is whether the practice is religiously mandated (male circumcision, for instance) or culturally constructed.[8] The latter includes also biomedical practices that may be common in a particular religion yet not required by it (as is often the case with tattooing, for example). The second dimension reflects a distinction between traditional medicine (tooth extraction, for example) and Western (scientific) medicine (male circumcision). Thus, overall, the case selection shows a range of "imagined communities" of biomedical cultures and questions the extent to which the new world order of children as rights holders empowers them in biomedical circumstances.

B. TRADITIONAL BODILY PRACTICES: BACKGROUND AND CONTEXT

1. Male Circumcision

It is estimated that one-fifth of the world's male population is circumcised, though the rate varies greatly by geographic location, by religious affiliation, and, to some extent, by socioeconomic classification.[9] Circumcision is uncommon in Asia, South America, Central America, and most of Europe (less than 20 percent).[10] In Canada, approximately 48 percent of males are circumcised, and in the United States most (about 60 percent) of its newborn males are circumcised for nonreligious reasons. In communities where circumcision is practiced by religious faiths, such as Judaism and Islam, or for cultural beliefs, such as in African tribes, male circumcision is more common (almost exclusively).[11]

The practice essentially entails the removal of the entire foreskin, which consists of two layers of tissue covering the entire gland.[12] The methods used to

---

[8] The division between the two is somewhat arbitrary. There is often an assumption that religious customs are mandatory, whereas cultural practices are optional. The relationship between religion and culture, however, is complex, and delineating the line between them is difficult. This complexity and the definition of religion are elaborated on in Chapter 5, Section E, note 117 and Section E.2.

[9] Carole M. Lannon and others, "Circumcision Policy Statement," *Pediatrics* 103, no. 3 (1999): 686.

[10] Among the countries in which the rates of male circumcision are below 20 percent are Cambodia, China, Mongolia, Myanmar, Nepal, Papua New Guinea, India, Lau, and others. Daniel T. Halperin and Robert C. Bailey, "Male Circumcision and HIV Infection: 10 Years and Counting," *Lancet* 354, no. 9191, (1999): 1814.

[11] Abbie J. Chessler, "Justifying the Unjustifiable: Rite v. Wrong," *Buffalo Law Review* 45 (1997): 557, n. 1, http://www.cirp.org/library/legal/chessler; S. A. Aldeeb Abu-Sahlieh, "Muslims' Genitalia in the Hands of the Clergy Religious Arguments about Male and Female Circumcision," in *Male and Female Circumcision—Medical, Legal and Ethical Considerations in Pediatric Practice,* ed. George C. Denniston, Frederick Mansfield Hodges, and Marilyn Fayre Milos (New York: Kluwer Academic/Plenum Publishers, 1999), 139.

[12] Chessler, 565.

perform the practice and the people who are authorized to do so vary, though a general distinction between traditional methods versus (Western) medical ones can be made. These are commonly contingent on the religio-cultural context in which the practice takes place, though either way, no anesthesia is used.

The practice of male circumcision is grounded in both religious and cultural justifications. It is religiously mandatory within Jewish and Islam religions and represents a powerful symbol of membership and identity. For Jews, the practice is explicitly mentioned in the Hebrew Bible as a monologue where God commands Abraham to circumcise himself and his offspring.[13] The practice, *Brit Milah*, is considered a quintessential Jewish act, a symbol of an everlasting covenant between God and the Jewish people, and a primary emblem of Jewish identity. The *Brit* is performed on the eighth day of life of a newborn son,[14] accompanied with a blessing and a naming ceremony. The ceremony symbolizes the acceptance of the newborn male into the Jewish community, a commitment that he is expected to adopt on his own when he reaches the age of thirteen, in his *Bar Mitzvah*. As an uncircumcised male may be expelled from the Jewish people, the tradition has great social significance, and most Jews, religious or secular, are likely to follow it.

There is no equivalent explicit obligation for the circumcision of Muslim male children. The Islamic Quo'ran, the only holy book for Muslims,[15] has no reference to the custom. However, the rite originated with the belief that the Prophet Muhammad, an exemplary figure to follow, was circumcised. Later on, it received an independent power through the *sunnah* (the sayings and the practices of the Prophet).[16] There is variation as to the age at which the circumcision ceremony occurs. Most Muslims typically do so between the ages of four and thirteen,[17] though among various communities in Kenya, the circumcision is performed as a rite of passage, sometime between the ages of twelve and twenty.[18] If a Muslim remains uncircumcised until adulthood,

---

[13] Genesis 17:4–14:

> I will establish my covenant between me and you, and your offspring after you throughout their generations, for an everlasting covenant, . . . And I will give you, and to your offspring after you, the land where you are not an alien, all the land of Cannan, for a perpetual holding, and I will be their god. . . . This is my covenant, which you shall keep between you and me and you and your offspring after you: Every male among you shall be circumcised. You shall circumcise the flesh of your foreskin; and it shall be a sign of the covenant between me and you. Throughout your generations every male among you shall be circumcised when he is eight years old, . . . Any uncircumcised male who is not circumcised in the flesh of his foreskin shall be cut off from his people; he has broken my covenant.

[14] The *Brit* would be performed on the eighth day even if it falls on the Sabbath or Yom Kippur, the Day of Atonement, though it would be delayed for health reasons. Chessler, 584.

[15] Abu-Sahlieh, 132.

[16] Ibid., 133–51.

[17] Ibid., 132.

[18] Alice Akunga and others, *The Impact of HIV/ AIDS on Education in Kenya and the Potential for Using Education to the Widest Sense for the Prevention and Control of HIV/ AIDS: Final Report* (Government of Kenya & UNICEF Kenya Country Office publication, 2000), 22, http://www.kanco.org/ktmlstandard/files/uploads/HIVaids%20and%20education%20in%20Kenya.pdf.

circumcision becomes obligatory, "except for those who are foolish or cannot undergo the procedure for health reasons."[19]

In both non-Western and Western societies, many perform the practice of male circumcision for cultural reasons. In Nigeria, for example, where it is estimated that more than 80 percent of the male population is circumcised, the most prevalent rationales given for the practice are cultural rather than biblical reasons.[20] The justifications are grounded in the general adherence to "tradition," aesthetic belief that the practice enhances fertility or sexual pleasure, and for other health reasons.[21] Among various Christian groups in Africa, male circumcision is performed and promoted as a traditional custom and as a link to the past, although the rite has no religious significance within Christianity.[22] In various African and Australian aboriginal communities, such as the western African animist group, the Dogon people of Mali, and the Tanzanian Mackonde group, the rite is still performed as a puberty or premarital rite.[23] Among the Nso' of the grassy highlands of Bamenda in Cameroon, for example, circumcision is performed when the male child reaches adolescence. The adolescent is separated from his parents a few days before the circumcision, for rest, and is returned to his home seven days after the procedure is performed. The rite is primarily an initiation ritual, a purely secular ritual of passage into adulthood holding a great significance.[24] Among Tanzanian Chagga tribe and the Maasai tribe in eastern Africa, uncircumcised men are perceived as timid and immature adolescents who do not yet have full male qualifications.[25]

In some aboriginal groups in Africa, South America, Australia, and the Pacific Islands (Polynesia and the Melanesian cultures) the circumcision ceremony further includes also subincisions of various body parts or the penis. Although this additional practice is often regarded as a part of the rite of

[19] Abu-Sahlieh, 160.

[20] In a survey conducted in Nigeria, 89.9 percent of the respondents rooted circumcision of their male children in cultural reasons, whereas only 10.7 percent referred to Biblical ones. O. B. Borofice, "Women's Attitudes to Men's Sexual Behaviour," *Health Transition Review* 5 (1995): 75, http://htc.anu.edu.au/pdfs/Boroffi1.pdf. For the estimated rates of circumcision among the male population in Nigeria, see Halperin and Bailey, 1814.

[21] Soori Nnko, Robert Washija, and J. Ties Boerma, "Dynamics of Male Circumcision Practices in Northwest Tanzania," *Sexually Transmitted Diseases* 28, no. 4 (2001): 214; Godfrey B. Tangwa, "Circumcision—An African Point of View," in *Male and Female Circumcision—Medical, Legal and Ethical Considerations in Pediatric Practice*, ed. George C. Denniston, Frederick Mansfield Hodges, and Marilyn Fayre Milos (New York: Kluwer Academic/Plenum Publishers, 1999), 217.

[22] Chessler, 586.

[23] The anthropological literature points out that there is also a large belt of noncircumcising tribes running from southern Sudan through Uganda, West Kenya, Rwanda, Burundi, part of eastern Zaire, and through western Tanzania to Malawi, Zambia, Zimbabwe, and southern Namibia. Recent studies, however, show an increase in the rate of the practice also among previously noncircumcised communities. Nnko and others, 214; Tangwa, 259.

[24] Tangwa, 185.

[25] S. K. Hellsten, "Rationalizing Circumcision: From Tradition to Fashion, From Public Health to Individual Freedom—Critical Notes on Cultural Persistence of the Practice of Genital Mutilation," *Journal of Medical Ethics* 30, no. 3 (2004): 251.

passage into adulthood, it was reported as also being performed on children six to ten year olds.[26]

Among Western countries the culturally based male circumcision was practiced, historically, as a punitive measure, as a curative procedure for insanity, as a mark of slavery, or for cosmetic reasons.[27] Some also point out that, during the nineteenth century, Britain and other English-speaking countries further advanced the practice as a preventive method for masturbation.[28] By the twentieth century, the practice became even more widespread. Presumably for medical, hygienic, and cosmetic rationales, it became remarkably prevalent in Western countries such as the United States, Canada, and Australia, and it was even incorporated as a part of routine neonatal practice of the hospital and the physicians.[29] Furthermore, other countries such as South Korea followed the Western influence and adopted it as well.[30]

In past decades, there has been another shift, with a visible decline in the prevalence of the practice in Western states. In the United Kingdom, for instance, the rate of male circumcision has dropped significantly (from about 30 percent to about 6 to 7 percent), and it no longer enjoys the support of major medical associations.[31] In the United States, records show a decline from 86 percent of male newborns to 65 percent, though it varies regionally.[32] Some explain this drop in the change in attitude of medical associations in leading Western countries. Despite the supposed medical benefits that have been associated with circumcision, including improved penile hygiene, reduction in urinary tract infections (UTIs), protection from penile cancer,[33] and, most significantly, protection from sexually transmitted diseases (STDs), particularly

---

[26] Geoffrey P. Miller, "Circumcision: Cultural—Legal Analysis," *Virginia Journal of Social Policy & Law* 9, no. 3 (2003): 510; Ashley Montagu, "Mutilated Humanity," *Humanist* 55, no. 4 (1995): 13.

[27] For example the castrati, which is the practice that existed in Italy between the seventeenth and nineteenth centuries to circumcise male children with high singing ability around the ages of eight to ten, as a means of securing their singing voice for the church and cathedral choirs and for opera roles. See information on the castrati on the Web: *All You Would Like to Know About the Castrati,* http://www.cix.co.uk/~velluti/cast.htm; Queensland Law Reform Commission, *Circumcision of Male Infants Research Paper* (Brisbane, 1993), http://www.cirp.org/library/legal/QLRC/01.html, section 2(a). (hereafter *Circumcision of Male Infants Research Paper.*)

[28] Marie Fox and Michael Thomson, "Short Changed? The Law and Ethics of Male Circumcision," *International Journal of Children's Rights* 13, no. 1–2 (2005): 169–72; Christopher Price, "Male Circumcision: An Ethical and Legal Affront," *Bulletin of Medical Ethics* 128 (1997): 13.

[29] Christopher R. Fletcher, "Circumcision in America in 1998—Attitudes, Beliefs, and Charges of American Physicians," in *Male and Female Circumcision—Medical, Legal and Ethical Considerations in Pediatric Practice,* ed. George C. Denniston, Frederick Mansfield Hodges, and Marilyn Fayre Milos (New York: Kluwer Academic/ Plenum Publishers, 1999), 259; *Circumcision of Male Infants Research Paper,* sections 2(b), 2(c).

[30] D. S. Kim, J. Y. Lee, and M. G. Pang, "Male Circumcision: A South Korean Perspective," *BJU International* 83 (Suppl. 1 1999): 28.

[31] Fox and Thomson, 162, n. 3.

[32] Ibid., 162.

[33] It was reported that the risk of uncircumcised men to have penile cancer is three-fold greater than circumcised men. Edgar J. Schoen, Thomas E Wiswell, and Stephen Moses "New Policy on Circumcision—Cause for Concern," P*ediatrics* 105 (2000): 620.

hepatitis and HIV,[34] neither is overwhelmingly supportive of a universal public policy on neonatal circumcision.[35]

The controversial nature of these medical benefits may account for the reluctance of medical associations to endorse the practice as public policy guidance. Opponents of the practice question the validity and the accuracy of studies attempting to establish the connection between circumcision and optimal penile hygiene and between circumcision and reduced rates of UTIs.[36] They emphasize the rarity of both UTIs and penile cancer in the first place (the latter is estimated to be, at most, 1 percent) and the contribution of sexual practices and other behavioral factors such as drug injection and smoking to the development of penile cancer and the transmission of STDs.[37] Finally they point to the inverse effect that previous support for circumcision has had on the spread of STDs, mostly HIV. In many African and other communities, the procedure is still carried out in accordance with its traditional method, which involves a traditional local expert (*mohel* for Jews, *ngariba* for Muslims, or other traditionally authorized personnel) and the usage of various tools as well as sharpened fingernails.[38] Particularly among African communities, the procedure is further carried out simultaneously on a group of adolescents, using a shared razor blade.[39] And while the Western surgical procedure performed by licensed physicians with sterilized and specially made devices in health facilities is on the rise,[40] the health facilities in many such rural and traditional communities are a far cry from those envisioned in the West.[41]

---

[34] Based on properties of the foreskin and its increased sensitivity, some studies suggest a lower risk of STDs, such as syphilis and HIV (up to one-third) for circumcised men. Stephanie Clark, "Male Circumcision Could Help Protect Against HIV Infection," *Lancet* 356, no. 9225 (2000): 225.

[35] R. V. Short, "Male Circumcision: A Scientific Perspective," *Journal of Medical Ethics* 30 (2004): 243.

[36] Lannon and others, 686–93.

[37] Robert C. Bailey and Daniel T. Halperin, "Male Circumcision and HIV Infection," *Lancet* 355, no. 9207 (2000): 927; Lannon and others, 689–91.

[38] Among Jews, the practice is carried out by a *mohel*, an observer Jew who acquired his expertise by observation. His training was specifically to perform the circumcision, and he normally had no other medical training besides that. After the removal of the tip of the prepuce, the remaining lining of the prepuce was torn off the glands with a sharpened fingernail, removing all the inner lining of the prepuce. This was followed by the *mohel*'s sucking of the blood out of the wounded part, taking a mouthful of wine and spurting it on the wound. Ilan Katz, "Is Male Circumcision Morally Defensible?" in *Moral Agendas for Children's Welfare*, ed. Michael King (New York: Routledge, 1999), 92–93; Chessler, 558, n. 7; *Circumcision of Male Infants Research Paper*, sec. 3.

Among Muslims, male circumcision is traditionally obtained from a *ngariba*, an Arab expert from the community, though the mothers themselves and other traditional professionals such as nurses, dispensaries, and traditional birth attendants would at times carry out the practice as well. Nnko and others, 217.

[39] Quentin Gausset, "AIDS and Cultural Practices in Africa: the Case of the Tonga (Zambia)," *Social Sciences & Medicine* 52 (2001): 511, 513.

[40] Boroffice, 75, 76; Nnko and others, 217.

[41] Both proponents and opponents of the practice add other arguments, including: reference to improvement and reduction of sexual practice and sensation; lower incidence of cervical cancer among women with circumcised partners; short and long psychological effect of the procedure; and the possible complication following the procedure. Overall, however,

There are also political and economic rationales that play a role in the preservation—and ironically, also the decline—in the prevalence of the practice. On the one hand, considering the power Jews and Muslims have politically, financially, or numerically, it is hard to imagine how a prohibition to carry out a religiously mandated practice would endure. Moreover, there is an economic dimension that cannot be ignored: both traditional experts and Western physicians have economic incentives in the practice. For traditional experts, the circumcision may be their main or only source of income, hence it is essential to their living (along with the social honor that is often attributed to those who carry out the practice).[42] For Western physicians, the interest is both to medicalize and to privatize the procedure. As private medical interventions are more profitable than publicly funded ones, they have no financial incentive to advocate for a universal neonatal policy of circumcision (unless, such a policy will provide them with such benefit, as may be the case in developing countries). Furthermore, in a market-oriented culture and as insurance companies gradually withdraw their medical coverage for religio-culturally based circumcision, the sums of money that can be obtained for the private procedure and for the accompanying pharmacological products rise. Yet, while under a well-regulated medical system, this would not eventually erect a barrier for those who follow the practice for religious rationales, it remains out of reach for many who lack such justification and cannot afford it.

2. Tribal Marks

Tribal marks are among the most long-standing bodily practices documented in anthropology, ethnography, and medical research. Originating in third world societies and observed in various states in Latin America, southwest Asia, and Africa, markings play a significant role in maintaining social identities and a sense of belonging for members of the group. In the past few decades, elements of tribal marks dispersed and were also adopted by many other communities worldwide. In the twentieth century, they can be found in both Western and non-Western states, including the United States, the United Kingdom, and others.

A tribal mark is an umbrella term used to describe a few practices that change the appearance of human skin. Two of the main practices under this concept are tattooing and scarification. Both are closely related to one another, involving an intentional and potentially irreversible disruption of the surface of the skin by using sharp instruments. The distinction between them is at times blurred, as the traditional method used may be quite similar. Thus, the literature often considers the practices together, using the terms interchangeably and

---

the incidence of such complications is low (estimated between 0.2 percent and 2 percent), most of the complications that occur are minor, and death is a rare complication. Marilyn F. Milos, and Donna Macris, "Circumcision: A Medical or A Human Rights Issue?" *Journal of Nurse-Midwifery* 37, no. 2 (Suppl. 1992), Library of Circumcision Information and Resource Pages, http://www.cirp.org/library/ethics/milos-macris/; Lannon and others, 688–89; Anna Taddio and others, "Effect of Neonatal Circumcision on Pain Responses During Vaccination in Boys," *Lancet* 345, no. 8945 (1995): 292.

[42] This point has also been one of the main obstacles in the international campaign to abolish female circumcision. See, for example, Hellsten, 252.

without referring to which of the two is actually practiced. Each of these traditional bodily practices is briefly described, and then the cultural context in which they occur is explained.[43]

a. Tattooing

The practice of tattooing involves the puncturing of the skin with a sharp tool and the insertion of pigment into it. Historically, the toothed tool was made of bone or shell from animals, and the pigment was prepared from burned candlenut or oily nuts diluted with water.[44] After dipping the teeth of the tool into the pigment, the tattooist placed them on the skin, tapping the handle of the tool with a stick. The stroke was followed by a small quantity of blood that, once healed, left visible blue or black colored marks on the skin.[45]

For the most part, this traditional method of tattooing has been transformed into a more hygienic and colorful one. The traditional tool was replaced with remodeled electrical razors in which the blade can be detached and discarded after each tattoo session. Instead of the traditional green-black ink, ink tattoo companies now supply various ink colors that can be used.[46] Such a shift occurred in various aboriginal communities, most notably the facial tattoos of the Maori of New Zealand (the *Ta Moko*).[47] However, the traditional method of tattooing is still commonly used in Papua New Guinea,[48] for example, and the shapes, forms, and designs of tattoos still often follow their traditional connotation or at least incorporate elements of them.[49]

---

[43] Piercing of the earlobes, lips, and nose are other types of "tribal marks," which will not be discussed here because they do not involve a permanent body modification (the hole closes if the rings are removed). In this context, tattooing, scarification, and branding that are commonly accepted (e.g., one tattoo, etc.)in the new subcultures that have developed in recent years in various countries (mainly Western, but also in China, for example), which endorse excessive tattooing, scarification, and piercing as their identification marks will also not be discussed here. The reason is that they do not follow the concept of "traditional practices" as defined above. Particularly, they lack the "generational" element that makes the practice "long lasting, resistant to change and embedded within the cultural fabric of a community," and, hence, beyond the scope of this study.

[44] Makiko Kuwahara, *Tattoo: An Anthropology* (Oxford: Berg Publishing, 2005), 62–63.

[45] Ibid., 62–63.

[46] Ibid., 66–67.

[47] Ngahuia Te Awekotuku, "Ta Moko: Maori Tattoo," in *Goldie: the Art of Charles F. Goldie*, ed. Roger Blakely and David Bateman (Auckland: David Bateman, 1997), 113, http://psychology.waikato.ac.nz/mpru/pubs/articles/1997awekotuku.pdf.

[48] UNICEF East Asia and Pacific Regional Office (EAPRO), *The Mekong Partnership and Beyond: Papua New Guinea*, http://www.unicef.org/eapro-hivaids/general/overview.htm.

[49] For discussion on the endorsement of traditional types of tattoos, see, for example, Shannon Bell, "Tattooed: A Participant Observer's Exploration of Meaning," *Journal of American Culture* 22, no. 2 (1999): 53–54; Daniel Rosenblatt, "The Antisocial Skin: Structure, Resistance, and 'Modern Primitive' Adornment in the United States," *Cultural Anthropology* 12 no. 3 (1997): 287–334; Margo DeMello, "'Not Just for Bikers Anymore': Popular Representations of American Tattooing," *Journal of Popular Culture* 29, no. 3 (1995): 37–52.

b. Scarification

The procedure of scarification, also called cicatrisation, involves cutting of the skin and allowing the wound to heal so that it leaves a permanent scar. The tools and methods used to create the scar vary in different societies and depend on the desired shape and design. To make a raised globular scar, a hook is inserted into the skin and pulled upward so that it can be cut across with a blade. For the creation of linear scars, nails or simple blades are often used. The practice is common in Papua New Guinea, in countries of sub-Saharan Africa, such as Nigeria and Togo,[50] and among the Garrisa community of Kenya.[51]

In some cultures, substances such as fruit acid, clay, or ash are inserted into the cuts, irritating the wound and creating bumps known as keloids. This practice is common, for instance, among people in eastern and middle Nigeria and among the people of Papua New Guinea.[52] When the insertion of substances results in changes in skin color, it creates a mark that is similar to a tattoo (as observed, for example, among the Yoruba group of Nigeria).[53] In others, the scar is created after the surface of the skin has been burned (branding). These burns can be applied on various parts of the body, using flame, hot objects, and even herbs such as garlic. This practice was documented, for example, in Nigeria, Ghana, among various Asian cultures such as Vietnam, and in Israel among children of Yemenite origin.[54] There is variation as to who carries out the practice. While traditional healers and the elderly are often the ones authorized to perform the practice, or to provide the recommendations for those who can, parents and other relatives may carry it out as well.[55] In the Ashanti region of Ghana, for example, the practice was performed predominantly by siblings and friends.[56]

The cultural reasons for both tattooing and scarification vary among the groups in which they are performed. Some of the most prevalent rationales, however, are a mark of identification, a rite of passage into adulthood, a reflection of life experience and development, and a means of beautification. In southwestern Nigeria, for example, some of the ethnic groups wear facial marks to prove royal lineage or ethnic origin.[57] Among the Maori groups in New

---

[50] Committee on the Rights of the Child, *Concluding Observations: Nigeria,* paragraphs 56–58, U.N. Doc. CRC/C/15/Add.257 (April 13, 2005); Committee on the Rights of the Child, *Concluding Observations: Togo,* paragraph 56, U.N. Doc. CRC/C/15/Add.255 (March 31, 2005).

[51] Garissa is a district of the northern province of Kenya. Akunga and others, 35.

[52] Olubimpe Ayeni, "Observations on Medical and Social Aspects of Scarification in Sub-Saharan Africa," http://www.med.uottawa.ca/medweb/hetenyi/ayeni.htm.

[53] Ibid.; Ayodele Samuel Jegede, "The Yoruba Cultural Construction of Health and Illness," *Nordic Journal of African Studies* 11 no. 3 (2002): 331; Erid Schildkrout, "Inscribing the Body," *Annual Review of Anthropology* 33 (2004): 323.

[54] Garty Ben-Zion, "Garlic Burns," *Pediatrics* 91 (1993): 659.

[55] Kennth W. Feldman, "Pseudoabusive Burns in Asia Refugees," *American Journal of Diseases of Children (AJDC)* 138 (1984): 768.

[56] Samuel Forjuoh, "Pattern of Intentional Burns to Children in Ghana," *Child Abuse & Neglect* 19, no. 7 (1995): 838, 839.

[57] A. E. Obiechina and A. O. Alutayo, "Attitudes to Facial marks in South Western Nigeria," *Odonto-Stomatologie Tropicale* 23, no. 91 (2000): 23.

Zealand, the traditional facial tattoo (*Ta Moko*) "seemed to identify rank, to give recognition to achievers and to provide identifiable authority structure."[58] After years of oppression, the custom is ever more associated with a sense of cultural authenticity and sacredness, and acquiring a facial tattoo is a great source of symbolism of Maori pride and identity among the members of the group.[59] In various communities in Papua New Guinea, scarification along with nose bleeding, tongue cutting, and incision of the penis are a few of the traditional practices that young men go through as a part of their initiation rite.[60] Girls in the northern part of Tiv land in Nigeria receive stomach scars at about the age of puberty, and children of the group are often seen with mouth scars.[61] Scarification of both male and female youngsters' bodies is still performed as an initiation rite among the Macondes community in the northeastern part of Mozambique.[62] Among the Kanuiri ethnic group in Niger, children received face marks and their uvula is removed during the naming ceremony on the eighth day after birth.[63]

Tattooing and scarification are also performed, however, as healing and protective rites. Collective healing rituals, including scarification, are known to be prevalent in various communities in sub-Saharan African countries, such as Zambia and Nigeria, Togo, Zaire, the middle belt of Nigeria, and others.[64] Tattooing for therapeutic reasons was previously documented among the Arab population in Iraq, where tattooing of one child aimed at securing the survival of consecutive siblings.[65] The Yoruba ethnic groups in Nigeria commonly use scarification and marks as a measure of protection from disease or for healing,[66] and with an emphasis on familial relations, a large triangular pattern of cicatrices is stamped on the abdomen of an elder sibling from the Egnu/ Egbado Yoruba group to complement the incision of facial marks of a younger

[58] Mohi Rua, "Contemporary Attitudes to Traditional Facial Ta Moko," in *Maori and Psychology: Research and Practice—The Proceedings of a Symposium Sponsored by the Maori and Psychology Research Unit,* ed. N. Robertson (Hamilton, New Zealand: Maori & Psychology Research Unit, 1999), http://wfass-trinity.fass.waikato.ac.nz/docushare/dsweb/Get/Document-999/rua.pdf, 2.

[59] Ibid.

[60] Sione Latukefu, "Noble Traditions and Christian Principles as Nations Ideology in Papua New Guinea: Do Their Philosophies Complement or Contradict Each Other?" *Pacific Studies* 11, no. 2 (1988): 84, 87.

[61] Laura Bohannan, *The Tiv of Central Nigeria* (London: International African Institute, 1953), 66–67, http://www.yale.edu/hraf/collections.htm.

[62] Tore Saetersdal, "Symbols of Cultural Identity: A Case Study from Tanzania," *African Archaeological Review* 16 no. 2 (1999): 124, 130.

[63] Ronald Cohen, *The Structure of Kanuri Society* (Ann Arbor, Michigan: University Microfilms, 1960), 150, http://www.yale.edu/hraf/collections.htm.

[64] Gausset, 513; Boroffice, 68; Roy Baskind and Gretchen Birbeck, "Epilepsy Care in Zambia: A Study of Traditional Healers," *Epilepsia* 46, no. 7 (2005): 1124; Oladunni Osowole and others, "A Survey of Treatment Practices for Febrile Illnesses Among Traditional Healers In the Nigerian Middle Belt Zone," *African Journal of Traditional, Complementary and Alternative Medicines* 2, no. 3 (2005): 339.

[65] Winifred Smeeton, "Tattooing Among the Arabs of Iraq," *American Anthropologists, New Series* 39 no. 1 (1937): 55.

[66] Avondale S. Tegade, "The Yoruba Cultural Construction of Health and Illness," *Nordic Journal of African Studies* 11, no. 3 (2002): 331.

brother.[67] Finally, at least in Zambia and Nigeria, the practices are particularly observed in the context of treatment for epilepsy.[68]

Interestingly, although the existence of these practices as curative and protective measures is known, the information on the rates and prevalence of the practices is lacking. Existing scholarship often merely points out that the practices are common, and the literature is more likely to stress the gender of the subject who is traditionally subjected to the practices but less his or her age. Thus, for example, among the Shan tradition in Burma and Thailand, tattooing is customarily performed on men for both religious (spiritual) and cultural or social reasons (as a mark of men's maturity or as a weapon of magical protection and invulnerability).[69] However, it is not clear at what age the initiation or the magical rite actually takes place.

It is not clear whether tattooing, scarification, and branding have any significant health implications in and of themselves. The medical literature notes infections of the wounds as being potentially harmful. More significantly, it points to higher risk of contracting infectious diseases, specifically mentioning HIV and various types of hepatitis due to the usage of unsterilized and shared instruments with which the practices are performed.[70] These, however, are essentially side effects of the practices, and without precise data on the rate of which contamination actually happened during these practices, establishing such a connection is difficult. This is particularly so considering the various possible explanations including sexual behavior, other traditional practices, general unhygienic conditions, etc., that contribute to the transmission of HIV and other infectious diseases, making the differentiation rather complex.[71]

3. Milk Teeth Extraction

The practice of milk teeth extraction has been reported in medical literature since the 1960s, though it is believed to date back to prehistoric times. Originating in northern Uganda, it spread to other communities in sub-Saharan and eastern Africa and has been observed among the Garissa community in Kenya, in Eritrea, among the Molepolole in eastern Botswana, Angola, Somalia, Sudan, Tanzania, and others.[72] In a report published in 1998, it was also documented in Myanmar,[73] among immigrant communities from Uganda and Sudan in

---

[67] Ayeni, note 52.

[68] Baskind and Birbeck, 1124.

[69] Nicola Tannenbaum, "Tattoos: Invulnerability and Power in Shan Cosmology." *American Ethnologist* 14, no. 4 (1987): 695.

[70] Olive Shisana and others, *HIV Risk Exposure Among Young Children—A Study of 2–9 Years Old* (Pretoria, South Africa: Human Sciences Research Council Press, 2005), 3, http://www.hsrc.ac.za/media/2005/4/20050405_1Report.pdf.

[71] Gausset, 513.

[72] Akunga and others, 77; Zuberi, 68; Paul S. Landau, "Explaining Surgical Evangelism in Colonial Southern Africa: Teeth, Pain and Faith," *Journal on African History* 37 (1996): 276; Henne O. Mogensen, "False Teeth and Real Suffering: the Social Course of 'Germectomy' in Eastern Uganda," *Culture, Medicine & Psychiatry* 24 (2000): 331.

[73] *Evaluation Report: Participatory Qualitative Evaluation of Life Skills and HIV/ AIDS Training for Youth and Women* (UNICEF/ Myanmar, Population Council (Thailand) Inc., June 1998), 20. http://www.unicef.org/spanish/evaldatabase/files/MYN_98-01_part1.pdf.

the United Kingdom and the United States, and among Ethiopian Jews who immigrated to Israel.[74]

The practice refers to the removal of canine tooth buds among young children and infants as a therapeutic and protective measure against childhood illnesses such as diarrhea and fever that the unerupted primary canine teeth are believed to cause (referred to as "killer teeth").[75] In northern Uganda, the practice has been "generally considered as one of the most common idioms of distress in relation to the sickness of children before the age of teething."[76] In Ethiopia, the traditional belief holds that such ailments are due to worms in the gum that risk the child's life, and hence removal is essential.[77] Similar beliefs were found also among the rural Kenyan Maasai and in Tanzania.[78] The Jop'Adhole of eastern Uganda attribute additional symptoms such as vomiting, refusal to eat, and biting the mother's breast to the presence of "false teeth" in the child's gum that, if left untreated, would result in the child's death.[79] Although such symptoms may occur for other reasons, the light color of the gums (whitish or yellowish), their softness, and irritation are believed to distinguish the phenomena of false teeth from other types of children's illnesses.[80] The maggot, or the yellow fluid, is believed to be the *entity* that causes the illnesses, and the fact that it can be seen verifies the existence of the disease and allows—and also requires—its removal.[81]

The practice has different names in the various places in which it is performed. In its place of origin, northern Uganda, it is known as *ebino* (in English translated as "false teeth"). Other terms in other Ugandan communities and especially across the border, however, are used as well. In Acholi, it is *two lak*; in Lango, it is *gidog;* in Luganda, it is *ebinyo*; in Runyenkole, it is *ebiino*; in Lusoga, it is *bino*; in Iteso, it is *Ikela/Icela*; and in Jop'Adhole, it is *lake jo marak* (spelled also *lakijo marach* (in English translated as bad teeth) or *gire kwanya* (referring to the teeth that were removed).[82] In Tanzania, the practice is called *meno ya nailoni* or *meno ya plastiki* (in English translated as plastic teeth) connoting the association with the milky appearance of the tooth buds that are removed;[83] and among the Somali people, it is known as *Ilko Nacowo* (in English

---

[74] Sandro Accorsi and others, "The Burden of Traditional Practices, Ebbino and Tea-Tea on Child Health in Northern Uganda," *Social Sciences & Medicine* 57 (2003): 2189; S. N. Dewhurst and C. Mason, "Traditional Tooth Bud Gouging in a Uganda Family: A Report Involving Three Sisters," *International Journal of Paediatric Dentistry* 11 (2001): 296.

[75] Dewhurst and Mason, 292

[76] Mogensen, 331.

[77] Andres Jeppsson, Mequanent Tesfu, and Lars-Ake Persson, "Health Care Providers' Perspectives on Harmful Traditional Health Practices in Ethiopia," *Ethiopian Journal of Health Development* 17, no. 1 (2003): 37, http://www.cih.uib.no/journals/EJHD/ejhdv17-no1/ejhdv17-n1-page33.pdf.

[78] Accorsi and others, 2188.

[79] Mogensen, 333.

[80] Mogensen, 333; Accorsi and others, 2188.

[81] Mogensen, 340.

[82] Accorsi and others, 2184; Mogensen, 331.

[83] Accorsi and others, 2188; Mogensen, 336.

translated as "fox teeth").[84] Finally, dentists recently medicalized the practice, terming it germectomy.[85]

As a medical cure for various childhood ailments, milk teeth extractions are normally performed on children before the age of two. In more rural areas, the age is even younger, carried out on infants that are only a few months old.[86] The practice is sometime performed, however, as a measure of protection, even if no illnesses have yet occurred.[87] In such cases, alternative and less intrusive methods may be used, such as rubbing the gums with herbs.[88] At other times, the removal of teeth may be performed at an older age as a treatment of poor growth,[89] and in some cultures it is performed as a rite of passage. Among the Nkumbi and Herero communities, for example, the practice is set after the onset of puberty as a mark of the person as a social being. Similarly, in Angola the custom constitutes a part of the age-group initiation rites.[90] Nonetheless, the practice is most common before the age of teething, often when the infant is a few months old.[91]

Local healers, parents, or elderly women (often the grandmothers) are traditionally the ones to carry out the procedure. It is conducted with various tools, ranging from fingernails to sharpened handles of teaspoon, without the use of aseptic techniques or local analgesics.[92] In the Sudan, it has been reported that the procedure is carried out with a heated instrument;[93] and in northern Uganda, *ebino* may be performed simultaneously with another custom, known as the *tea-tea.* The latter consists of making systematic incisions on the chest wall of the infant as a means to cure difficulties in breathing due to acute respiratory tract infection, anemia, or severe malaria. The incisions, vary in depth, are aimed at removing the "miller grains" that are perceived as causing the illness.[94]

The reasons given for the emergence of the practice and for its spread varies. Primarily, it has been attributed to the importance and the symbolism of teeth in the respective communities. Teeth mark the transition from helpless

---

[84] Helen D. Rodd and Lesley E. Davidson, "'Ilko Dacowo': Canine Enucleation and Dental Sequelae in Somali Children," *International Journal of Paediatric Dentistry* 10 (2000): 295.

[85] Mogensen, 331

[86] Dewhurst and Mason, 292; Mogensen, 333; Accorsi and others, 2186.

[87] Mogensen, 336.

[88] Ibid.

[89] Jeppsson, Tesfu, and Persson, 37.

[90] Landau, 276.

[91] Makonnen Asefa, Jenny Hewison, and Robert Drewett, "Traditional Nutritional and Surgical Practices and Their Effects on the Growth of Infants in Southwest Ethiopia," *Paediatric & Perinatal Epidemiology* 12 (1998):194; Dewhurst and Mason, 292–93. In medical studies the case definition of *ebino* generally refers to children up to five years old. Accorsi and others, 2185.

[92] Dewhurst and Mason, 292.

[93] Ibid.

[94] In a study of 740 infants who were subjected to the *ebino* in the Gulu district, northern Uganda, 112 of them were also subjected to the practice of *tea-tea.* Robert Iriso and others, "'Killer' Canines: The Morbidity and Mortality of *Ebino* in Northern Uganda," *Tropical Medicine & International Health* 5, no. 10 (2000):709; See also Accorsi and others, 2184.

baby to social member of the group. They signal the "capacity of the child to act and to be acted upon in socio-cultural processes" which replaced the previous dependence on the mother.[95] The development of healthy teeth is therefore important as it symbolizes that "the child is moving from a mere bodily being to clan identity."[96] As symptoms such as diarrhea and fever indicate illness, the practice developed as a means to cut off what appears to be jeopardizing the child's healthy development.[97]

The cultural construction of false teeth as connoted with the child's development and health has been further entrenched within the local communities due to the power it granted young mothers in their familial relations. According to Henne O. Mogensen, the state of false teeth conveys many hardships and problems in the everyday life of those who care for the child. Yet, in contrast to the customary hierarchical matrimonial relations by which the elder women provide the diagnosis and the treatment for an illness, the diagnosis of false teeth has been placed in the hands of the young mothers. Assumed to have the experience and knowledge to identify the existence of the threat, the child's body constitutes an important medium of communication through which young mothers renegotiate their place. The state of false teeth presumably allow the mothers to have greater independence and enables them to express discontent, distress, and unhappiness with their familial and other environment that they could not have expressed otherwise. It further allocates the responsibility for the child's ailment from the mothers to other family members, particularly the mothers-in-law, allowing simultaneously for others to comment on the mothers' fulfillment of their role as mothers, wives, and daughters-in-law.[98] The belief in false teeth and in the treatment that is needed was thus reinforced in the politics of local families.

The evolution of the practice, however, has been often associated with the years of political unrest and with local resistance. With the arrival of the Christian missionaries to the African continent during the nineteenth century, new "modern" therapeutic practices were introduced. Treating physical effects as an individual's sins and providing surgeries that were not previously common repudiated the local understanding of health and pain as a collective rather than individual ailment and required adjustment.[99] In some places, the rise in the practice was further exacerbated by the missionaries' efforts to halt initiation rites, which opened "a space for a cultural coming-to-terms."[100] In Angola, for example, it has been argued that the missionaries' contempt for male circumcision tacitly directed the local communities to replace the now prohibited practice with the custom of milk teeth extraction.[101] The teeth pulling appeared as a substitute practice that allowed the medical missionaries

---

[95] Mogensen, 337.
[96] Ibid.
[97] Ibid., 338.
[98] Ibid., 345, 347.
[99] Landau, 278.
[100] Ibid., 276.
[101] Ibid.

to be involved; it also enabled the preservation of the relationship with the local priest-healer and of the symbol for passing to a new status through some form of body modification.[102]

Regardless of the causal explanation for the emergence of the practice, it clearly spread rapidly from northern Uganda to other regions in the country and to its neighboring countries, cutting across social and ethnic groups. In Sudan, for example, it is estimated that 22 percent of children have been subjected to the practice;[103] among Kenyan Maasai, the estimation stands at about 87 to 90 percent; in two subsequent studies in Tanzania (reported in 1992 and in 1997), 31.4 percent and 37.4 percent of children up to five years old were believed to have been subject to the practice, respectively.[104] In a fieldwork conducted in 1995–96 on the Jop'Adhola Nilotic group in the county of Tororo district of eastern Uganda, the researcher states that all children who she followed in their first year of their life were subjected to the practice, even if only in a lesser form than the entire removal of the teeth buds.[105] Furthermore, scholars point to the high and still increasing prevalence of the practice among different ethnic groups in eastern Africa. Thus, for example, in comparison to the first reported case of *ebino* in northern Uganda in 1969, in 1996, 16.1 percent of the children only in the Acholi district were reported as being subjected to the practice. In 2003, the prevalence rose to almost 33 percent of the children studied in the Gulu district of northern Uganda.[106] A reported increase in the occurrence of the practice was also documented among Maasai children in Kenya in the years between 1991 and 1992 and in 1998 (an increase from 35 percent to 87 percent).[107] Among children in Addis Ababa, the rate of the practice was reported as 15 percent in 1993; in 2005, it has been estimated to be 89 percent.[108]

There is relatively little scholarship on the medical implications of milk teeth extraction. In what has been documented, the main implications mentioned were infections (especially sepsis),[109] anemia, tetanus, and bleeding,[110]

---

[102] Ibid., 276–77.

[103] Dewhurst and Mason cite a study conducted in Sudan in 1992 which found 22 percent of the children as being subjected to the practice (Dewhurst and Mason, 292); Accorsi and others cite a study from 1994 in which 45 percent of the illiterate mothers and 10 percent of literate mothers who responded were reported as using teeth buds extraction for treating diarrhea in children (Accorsi and others, 2188).

[104] Accorsi and others, 2188.

[105] Mogensen, 336 (She conducted fieldwork in three rural communities in the county of Tororo district, Uganda, inhabited by Jop'Adhola, a Nilotic group of about 200,000 people. She studied the mother's interpretation of their children's symptoms and their use of various treatment options. Included in the children's group were some preschool children, but most were infants of a few months old (ibid., 333)).

[106] The survey conducted in 1996 was carried out in four districts in Uganda (Acholi, Toro, Kigezi, and Bugisu), and the practice of milk teeth extraction was found only in the Acholi district. Accorsi and others, 2188.

[107] Accorsi and others, 2188.

[108] Zuberi, 75.

[109] Sepsis is a medical condition caused by a severe infection leading to a systematic inflammatory response, which may further lead to acute organ dysfunction and to septic shock.

[110] Accorsi and others, 2187. The implications of the *tea-tea* custom were reported as

which were also reported as linked with children's mortality rates.[111] Other implications mentioned are weight loss[112] and dental anomalies, some of which are permanent. These include absence, enamel defects, and loss of vitality in the adjacent teeth to which the practice has been performed.[113] Among a group of Somali children in the United Kingdom, mild to severe fluorotic-like lesions were common (33.5 percent), and compared to other populations, the prevalence of missing lower permanent lateral incisors was, according to the researchers, "very high" (5 percent).[114] Finally, the use of unsterilized tools, often on several infants at a time, was also raised as potentially promoting the transmission of infections, most acutely hepatitis and HIV.[115]

Notwithstanding these results, however, a few points of caution are needed. Most of the studies conducted were carried out on rather small samples, often limited to hospital settings and based on the researchers' interpretation of the discharge records from the hospital. Thus, while they may provide some indication of the complications following the removal of teeth buds, they are not necessarily sufficiently representative. Considering the overall poor economic, sanitary, and nutrition deficiencies in most of the African continent, not all children can actually reach hospitals. On the other hand, children who were admitted to hospitals commonly had other significant ailments such as malaria, pneumonia, and others for which the teeth extraction was undertaken in the first place. This starting point may have further exacerbated the complications due to *ebino*.[116] Mogensen also points out the inaccuracy in using child's mortality rates to evaluate medical implications. Despite the appearance of objectivity of this standard, she argues, the rate of a child's survival should also be taken into account as an objective sign of the community's health, as this is the day-to-day contextual struggle to life. Excluding from consideration the question of general morbidity, she argues, dooms the mortality rates to be "objective yet invalid," obscuring rather than clarifying the actual condition of the child's health.[117] Indeed, as S. N. Dewhurst and C. Mason point out, "it is important to remember that children that undergo tooth bud gauging as a

---

less severe, as "the operation . . . is executed in a less traumatic way, using mainly a new razor blade."

[111] Iriso and others reported that the medical complications related to *ebino* lead "to hospital death in more than one fifth of all infants admitted for *ebino*" (Iriso and others, 708). Dewhurst and Mason also cite a study conducted in Juba area of Sudan in 1989 in which two out of fifty-six children attending the emergency department following the removal of the "Lugbaba" (canine) teeth died due to infection and tetanus (Dewhurst and Mason, 296).

[112] Asefa, Hewison, and Drewett, 194.

[113] In one study, the prevalent damage to the permanent successor was stated as 7 percent (Dewhurst and Mason, 293); Rodd and Davidson, 293; Jeppsson, Tesfu, and Persson, 37.

[114] Rodd and Davidson, 295.

[115] Accorsi and others, 2187; Iriso and others, 708.

[116] Children admitted to hospitals often had other illnesses rather than complications from *ebino* and *tea-tea,* such as malaria and pneumonia. In one study, 740 out of 40,564 children who were admitted to the St. Mary's Hospital Lacon in Gulu district (northern Uganda) between 1992 and 1998 were admitted for *ebino* implications. These admissions, however, corresponded to the admissions for malaria and malnutrition, which were the two leading causes for hospitalization. Iriso and others; Accorsi and others, 2185.

[117] Mogensen, 332.

treatment will usually survive their illnesses."[118] In fact, observations of medical records that are not generally designed for research but for patient care should be made with caution. The accuracy of the prescription in the hospital reports differs among physicians and over time, and it may also be naturally biased towards the services that are available at the particular hospital.[119] Drawing general conclusions from such data thus requires prudence. Finally, it is important to note the researchers' clear cultural bias. While providing the cultural background of the practice, they nevertheless use blatant wording to reflect their contempt. Commonly used terminology includes words such as "crude," "traumatic," and labeling traditional healers with quotation marks, which logically can only lead to "severe consequences."[120] Conversely, however, improvement in sanitation, nutrition, and vaccination may achieve culturally sensitive and quicker results.[121]

4. Neck Elongation: The Case of the "Padaung Girls"

The term "neck elongation," which refers to the practice of the hill tribes of Myanmar (previously Burma) and Thailand of draping rings over the women and girls' necks, is somewhat misleading. Literally, the concept of elongation describes the traditional practice of *stretching* body parts, particularly by piercing the body tissue and inserting jewelry and other instruments that over time expand the original puncture. The practice of the so-called giraffe women, however, is different. In contrast to earlier anthropological work,[122] and despite the appearance of a long neck, in fact, it is not the neck itself that is elongated, but rather a combination of physical and visual factors. The brass rings around the neck from chin to shoulder that are placed from an early age force the chin upward, while the weight of the coils compresses the shoulder bones and the ribcage downwards, thus creating the illusion that the neck is longer.[123]

The practice originated with the Padaung (or Pa-dong) tribe of the Karen ethnic group of Myanmar.[124] Following the military dictatorship in Myanmar in 1962, however, many of the Padaung fled to the Burma-Thailand border and settled in the Ban Nam Piangdin, Ban Huay Seuthao, and Ban Nai Soy refugee camps in the Mae Hong Son district in Thailand.[125] According to the custom,

---

118 Dewhurst and Mason, 296. They make this point negatively, though, that is: because children are likely to survive, it perpetuates the local belief that the practice was curative.

119 Accorsi and others, 2190.

120 Accorsi and others, for example, describe the practices as follows: "the operation of *ebino* is generally done by a local practitioner in a very traumatic way, without anesthetic, and under very crude conditions, leading to severe consequences" (Accorsi and others, 2187.)

121 Dewhurst and Mason, 296.

122 Harry Ignatius Marshall, *The Karen People of Burma* (Ohio: University of Columbus, 1922), 44.

123 Andrew Marshall, *The Trouser People* (Washington DC: Counterpoint, 2002), 148; Jack Picone, "The Ring Cycle," *MATP (Australian Nationwide News)*, June 14, 2003, Magazine, 20, http://www.lexisnexis.com.

124 The Padaung tribe is also called the Kayan (Pascal Khoo Thwe, *From the Land of Green Ghosts: A Burmese Odyssey* (New York: Harper Collins: 2002), 10). According to Scott, "the Paduang call themselves "*Kekawngdu*," but no one else does" (James George Scott, *Burma and Beyond* (London: Grayson & Grayson, 1932), 96).

125 Satha Cheewin, "Rights: Governor Denies Karens Exploited," *Bangkok Post*, December 11, 1997, 3, http://www.lexisnexis.com.

only Padaung girls who were born on a Wednesday of a full moon wore the brass coils. The girls begin wearing coils before puberty. The first one-kilogram ring is commonly adorned at the age of five, adding rings gradually to take up the space of natural growth.[126] The upper limit is twenty to twenty-eight rings for a mature woman.[127] Traditionally, the second and third rings are added at the ages of ten and fifteen, and two more rings before the age of twenty, making the total of five rings. In recent years, all girls of the tribe have undergone the practice and at an increasing rate. Some attributed this change to the tourist attraction that the custom created, particularly among the refugee hill tribes in northern Thailand.[128] Thus, it has been reported that some girls start wearing the coils at ages as young as two, or, in any case, the addition of rings is hastened, wearing the second ring at the age of eight, the third by the age of thirteen, and the final two by the time the girls reach fifteen.[129] Only the elder women of the village are assumed to have the knowledge and the right to change the brass rings. The procedure evidently requires the aid of several women and takes a few hours.[130]

There is no one traditional explanation of the time or the motivation behind the development of the brass rings custom.[131] In his memoir, *From the Land of Green Ghosts,* Pascal Khoo Thwe remarks that the reasons he was given for the practice vary and that they were "a mixture of pure myth and mythical history."[132] The rationales range from providing protection against animal attacks to serving as symbols of wealth and status.[133] One explanation describes a beautiful dragon with a long neck that was impregnated by the wind to produce the first Padaung people.[134] The custom is thus a means of keeping alive the tribe's Dragon Mother mystical descent.[135] Another theory is that the practice is

---

[126] There is some flexibility with the age in which the practice takes place. According to Marshall, a Padaung girl is likely to have the first ring between the age of six and ten. Marshall, *The Trouser People,* 247. According to Scott, by contrast, there is no "minimum age": it is done "as early as it is possible for [the girl] to bear them." Scott, *Burma and Beyond,* 98.

[127] There is no consensus on the exact number of rings a mature woman has. Some argue that the limit is twenty, others claim it is twenty-five, and still others point out that "the record is 28 brass rings." See Marshall, *The Trouser People,* 149; Picone, 20. Also, the accumulation of rings is not made separately by adding one or two additional rings every once in a while but by a brass ring that is changed for a longer one when the time arrives. See "The Pa Dong Village of Nai Soi: A Visit to the Long Necked Women," May 14, 2001, http://www.sunbaytours.com/ePadong.html.

[128] Canela A. Jaramillo, "Defining 'Comfort': Padaung Women in Thailand," *Standards* 7, no. 2 (2001), http://www.colorado.edu/journals/standards/V7N2/EDITORIAL/editorial.html; Marcus Rose, "Human Zoo: Neck-Ringing Refugees," *New Internationalists,* February 1995, sec. 264, 4, http://www.lexisnexis.com. Marshall describes his meeting with two Padaung girls aged five and fourteen years old in northern Thailand, who already had twelve and seventeen rings, respectively. Marshall, *The Trouser People,* 147.

[129] Jaramillo, note 128; Rose, 4.

[130] J. Borrell, "Last of the Long Necks," *Herald Sun,* May 29, 1992, sec. Travel (Suppl.), 37. http://www.lexisnexis.com.

[131] Scott, 101.

[132] Thwe, 18.

[133] Marshall, *The Trouser People,* 151.

[134] Denis D. Gray, "Long-Necked Tourism: 'Human Zoo' or Boon to the Poor?" *Associated Press,* March 30, 1998, International News, http://www. lexisnexis.com.

[135] Marshall, *The Trouser People,* 9; Thwe, 18.

primarily a custom of beautification. Accordingly, the longer the neck appears, the more appealing it is.[136] It has also been argued that Padaung men began placing rings around the women's neck to prevent them from marrying out of their tribe and to make them less attractive to foreign men.[137] According to Thwe, however, the custom emerged as a measure of protection of the women during times of anarchy, when foreign tribes, including Burmans, "used to raid the villages and carry off [our] women."[138] Some have also suggested that the performance of the practice at a young age aimed at warding off evil sprits or "to protect themselves from attacks of wild animals such as tigers, which tended to seize the necks of their victims."[139] Regardless of the historical roots for the practice, women and girls from the tribe who were interviewed for media articles simply rationalize it as a matter of tradition, pride in their culture, and as a symbol of their identity.[140] This also complements Thwe's last explanation for the custom, by which the women wore the brass rings to preserve the identity of the tribe and as a symbol of solidarity with it.[141]

Even if some of the claims are spurious,[142] the reality that needs to be taken into account is more complex. The interest the long-necked women and girls generate is not new. The custom of wearing brass rings fascinated Western culture for many years and troops of long-necked women were exhibited as part of the famous Bertram Mills Circus in England in the 1930s.[143] However, globalization and the political upheavals experienced particularly in Myanmar necessitate another set of considerations.

While in exile, many traditional ways of life changed tremendously. As refugees, the Padaung's previous livelihood of agriculture and farming was limited. Lacking citizenship rights, they are denied the privileges of full Thai nationality. They are confined to villages and therefore cannot look for employment or other opportunities outside it.[144] At the same time, at least since the 1990s, the Tourism Authority of Thailand promoted enthusiastically the display of the Padaung women and girls as a national tourist attraction.[145] Not

---

[136] Marshall, *The Karen People of Burma*, 44.

[137] Scott, 101. Scott notes that although there is liberty of marriage among the Padaung people, and that both man and women are allowed to choose outside the tribe, the women's "formidable armour . . . seems to deter suitors other than the men of their own race." See also "The Pa Dong Village of Nai Soi: A Visit to the Long Necked Women."

[138] Thwe, 18.

[139] Ibid.; Noel Grove, "The many Faces of Thailand," *National Geographic Magazine* 189, February, 1996, 82–105, http://www.hwwilson.com/Databases/omnifile.htm.

[140] Picone, 20.

[141] Thwe, 18.

[142] Jaramillo, note 128.

[143] Marshall, *The Trouser People*, 146. Thwe's story in this regard is particularly interesting. His grandmother joined the trip to England, bringing back with her experiences and photographs that were taken during her trip "in a big village called London." Years later, when he escaped Myanmar as a refugee and attended Cambridge University in England, he happened to meet a couple who held a painting of his grandmother from her circus experience. Thwe, 28, 294–95.

[144] Sara Hemingway, "Tourism and Women's Human Rights in South East Asia," *International Journal of Human Rights* 8, no. 3 (2004): 281.

[145] An estimation of 10,000 Thais and foreigners is said to visit the Pa-Dong villages each

only did tour operators begin to take tourists to see them in their villages, but some of them also traveled to Japan to promote Thai tourism at trade fairs.[146] The main, and often only, source of income for members of the Padaung tribe became selling hand-made merchandise and money received from being photographed by tourists. While this state of affairs enables them to be better off than all other refugees from Myanmar, they are essentially compelled to follow the custom, mutated for tourist satisfaction, despite the fact that it is arguably dying out in Myanmar.[147]

Despite the interest the Padaung girls has generated, the medical literature on the implications of the practice is limited. It has been reported that x-ray examination of women and girls' necks from the tribe conducted by *National Geographic* in 1996 showed that the weight of the metal coils squashes the ribs and the collarbones.[148] Others reported that the Padaung women have high pitched and strangled voices due to the changes in the larynx.[149] It has also been argued that after years of wearing the brass rings, the neck muscles become extremely weak and can no longer hold the head alone. Thus, if the coils are removed, it is believed that the women's head flops over, resulting in deformation or suffocation.[150] The extent to which these outcomes are accurate, however, is unclear. Contrary to these medical reports, it has been argued that: collapse of the neck if the brass coils are removed is merely an unfounded claim;[151] rehabilitation of the neck bones and muscles is feasible;[152] and, in any case, but for some general discomfort, the brass coils cause no other health complications to occur whether the coils remain on or are taken off.[153] These counterarguments also fit with Thwe's testimony that some women decided to give up the custom in old age and that it took his own grandmother "a couple

---

year. They are required to pay a fixed fee for the ferry boat, which takes them to the villages, but not to tour in the village itself. However, they are expected to pay for photographs and in order to mingle with the Pa-Dong women and girls. See Jaramillo, note 128.

[146] Agence France Press, "Thai "Longneck" Ethnic Group Losing Identity: Governor," October 11, 2002, International News, http://www.lexisnexis.com.

[147] Hemingway, 278; Ian S. McIntosh, "State Sanctions Child Abuse in Thailand," *Cultural Survival Voices* 1, no. 1 (2001), http://209.200.101.189/publications/csv/csv-article.cfm?id=3&highlight=McIntosh. However, the disappearing of the practice in Myanmar may be attributed to the political persecution of the tribe rather than to voluntary or natural cultural change. Under the specific civil and political circumstances, the brass rings make fighting less comfortable and also exposes the members of the tribe to common viewers. Additionally, the availability of brass rings has been reduced significantly due to the difficulties in manufacturing brass coils, on the one hand, and the custom of burying women with their coils on their neck, on the other hand. See Philip Smucker, *Burma: Longnecks in Exile Fight to Stay Alive,* IPS-Inter Press Service, January 20, 1989, http://www.lexisnexis.com; Borrell, "Last of the Long Necks."

[148] Marshall, *The Trouser People,*" 148.

[149] Scott, 99; Borrell, note 130.

[150] Gray, note 134, Scott, 98; Smucker, note 147.

[151] Mary Braid, "The Long Road to Freedom," *Independent,* November 7, 1998. http://calbears.findarticles.com/p/articles/mi_qn4158/is_19981107/ai_n14191470.

[152] Rose, 4.

[153] Scott, 99–100 (points to the long life expectancy, large families, and general good health).

of days" to recover and to be able to support her head once she decided to take off her rings.[154]

C. CONCLUSION

Clearly, there are multiple factors that play a role in the preservation and reinforcement of the four practices described above. These include religious and cultural sources of identification, presumable medical benefits, social constructions of childhood and of what is a healthy development of members of the community, beautification, economic incentives, and political contexts. Most of these factors are interrelated, and there is often some overlap among them. While a particular factor may occasionally take a prominent role in the continuity of a specific practice, it is generally their combination in one sort or another that carries on the tradition.

In Western culture, male circumcision may be the best practice to illustrate how the medical custom is tied to cultural identity. A primary symbol of identification, it is performed as a determination of community membership and as a mark of belonging to a particular age group. It was then intertwined with and translated into aesthetic and medical rationales, which, in turn, are translated into financial incentives that reinforce political, religious, and cultural justifications. But these connections exist in the other practices that are observed, depending on the particular social, cultural, and medical constructions of the local communities. The fact that milk teeth extraction, for example, continues to take place among minority groups in Western countries shows that it is not only the civil and political turmoil as well as the lack of economic resources that leads to the perpetuation of the practice. It is rather the cultural construction of how best to nurture the healthy development of a child from a status of dependency to a social member of the community. It also illustrates the micropolitics that reinforces the practice as young mothers renegotiate their own status and identification as mothers, wives, and daughters-in-law. As individuals whose development is contingent on others, children inherently absorb this environment, in all its aspects. To what extent have these factors been taken into account in the international human rights discourse? Moreover, how are the children configured into the human rights discussion in view of these traditional biomedical practices? The next chapter provides a philosophical and legal analysis of the international biopolitical discourse on children's rights in the context of traditional bodily practices.

---

[154] Thwe, 9 and 19. He also mentions that the term they used to "tease" women who had given up wearing the rings is "ex-copper angel." Thwe, 59.

CHAPTER 4

CHILDREN'S BIOETHICS AND THE FRAMEWORK OF ANALYSIS

The interest in harmful traditional practices started gaining momentum during the 1980s. Led by the women's rights movement, the international community was called upon to assume its responsibility to protect women and children from such practices that may be detrimental to their health. This initiative instigated a series of international ventures, which have expanded ever since, to address the issue. Starting with the dialogue on female genital cutting under the Working Group on Slavery of the Subcommission on Prevention of Discrimination and Protection of Minorities in 1981, the issue evolved into a much broader project. In 1984, two members of the subcommission were entrusted "to conduct a comprehensive study on the phenomenon of traditional practices affecting the health of women and children."[1] In 1986, the Working Group on Traditional Practices Affecting the Health of Women and Children submitted a preliminary comprehensive study of the issue to the Commission on Human Rights.[2] In 1988, the UN subcommission appointed Mrs. Halima Embarek Warzazi as Special Rapporteur, mandated "to study traditional practices affecting the health of women and children and to consider measures to be taken at the national and international levels to eliminate the practice."[3] Her appointment was extended annually until 2005, after which the main consideration of the issue was transferred to the Special Rapporteur on Violence against Women, Its Causes and Consequences.[4]

[1] U.N. Economic and Social Council, Commission on Human Rights, *Report of the Working Group on Traditional Practices Affecting the Health of Women and Children,* 42nd Sess., Item 19, paragraphs 1–5, 15–18, U.N. Doc. E/CN.4/1986/42 (February 4, 1986).

[2] U.N. Economic and Social Council, Commission on Human Rights, *Report of the Working Group on Traditional Practices Affecting the Health of Women and Children,* 42nd Sess., Item 19, U.N. Doc. E/CN.4/1986/42 (February 4, 1986).

[3] Hereafter "Special Rapporteur on Traditional Practices." The Special Rapporteur was appointed by the UN Subcommission on Prevention and Discrimination and Protection of Minorities pursuant to Resolution 1988/34 on September 1, 1988. The resolution followed the request of the UN Commission on Human Rights (Resolution 1988/57). U.N. Commission on Human Rights, Subcommission on Prevention and Discrimination and Protection of Minorities, *Study on Traditional Practices Affecting the Health of Women and Children, Preliminary Report by the Special Rapporteur,* 41st Sess., Agenda Item 4, 3, U.N. Doc. E/CN.4/Sub.2/1989.

[4] Mrs. Halima Embarek Warzazi submitted her ninth and final report in 2005, where she also recommended that the main mandate on the issue will be in the hands of the Special Rapporteur on Violence against Women, Its Causes and Consequences (hereafter Special Rapporteur on Violence against Women) (U.N. Commssion on Human Rights, Subcommission on the Promotion and Protection of Human Rights, *Ninth Report and Final Report on the*

The formal legal consideration of the issue paralleled these developments. The first provision protecting children from "practices of religion or belief that are injurious to their physical or mental health or their full development" had already been incorporated in the UN Declaration on the Elimination of All Forms of Intolerance and of Discrimination Based on Religion or Belief.[5] Other declarations and resolutions were passed over the years, calling for the elimination of such practices. The adoption of the explicit and unequivocal reference to harmful traditional practices in Article 24(3) of the International Convention on the Rights of the Child (Children's Convention or Convention),[6] however, brought the issue to the fore and formally and legally bound it to state responsibility. Requiring states "to take all affective and appropriate measures with a view to abolishing traditional practices prejudicial to the health of children," the statement called for decisive action and catalyzed further developments within the international human rights discourse.

Subsequent international treaties incorporated provisions in a similar spirit, most notably in the African Charter on the Rights and Welfare of the Child (African Charter).[7] Article 21 of the African Charter, entitled, "Protection against Harmful Social and Cultural Practices," requires states

> to take all appropriate measures to eliminate harmful social and cultural practices affecting the welfare, dignity, normal growth and development of the child and in particular: (a) those customs and practices prejudicial to the health or life of the child; and (b) those customs and practices discriminatory to the child on the grounds of sex or other status.

Subparagraph (2) contains specific reference to the prohibition and measures to be taken with regards to child marriage and the betrothal of girls and boys.[8] Consensual declarations and platforms of actions adopted in various international conferences specifically call upon states to give priority to "developing programmes and policies that foster norms and attitudes of zero

---

Situation Regarding the Elimination of Traditional Practices Affecting the Health of Women and the Girl Child, 57th Sess., Agenda Item 6(a), 94, U.N. Doc. E/CN.4/Seb.2/2005/36). While Ms. Radhika Coomaraswamy, the Special Rapporteur on Violence against Women in the years between 1994 and 2003 also studied the issue of harmful traditional practices, the explicit mandate referencing to specific practices such as female circumcision was given in 2003 (see U.N. Commission on Human Rights (Resolution 2003/45), *Elimination of Violence against Women,* 59th Sess., U.N. Doc. E/CN.4/RES/2003/45). Since 2006, the Special Rapporteur on Violence against Women, Dr. Yakın Ertürk, reports to the Human Rights Council (rather than to the Human Rights Commission).

[5] Article 5(5) of the Declaration on the Elimination of All Forms of Intolerance and of Discrimination Based on Religion or Belief, G.A. Res. 36/55, 36 U.N. GAOR Supp. (No. 51), at 171, U.N. Doc. A/36/684 (1981). On the rationales and discussions that took place during the formulation of this provision, see Chapter 2, Section E.

[6] Convention on the Rights of the Child, G.A. Res. 44/25, annex, 44th Sess., 61st plenary meeting, U.N. GAOR Supp. (No. 49), at 167, U.N. Doc. A/44/49 (1989), entered into force September 2, 1990, reprinted in 28 I.L.M. 1448 (1989).

[7] African Charter on the Rights and Welfare of the Child, OAU Doc. CAB/LEG/24.9/49 (1990), entered into force November 29, 1999.

[8] Ibid., Article 21.

tolerance" for harmful and discriminatory attitudes and practices and to their eradication.[9] Regional committees, such as the Organization of African Unity (OAU) and the Council of Europe, convened conferences, workshops, and seminars to study the various bodily traditional practices affecting the health of children and to provide policy guidance. Particularly active in this regard has been the Inter-African Committee (IAC) on Traditional Practices Affecting the Health of Women and Children, a nongovernmental organization (NGO) that, in collaboration with grassroots organizations, has worked not only to formulate policy statements, but has also taken a leading role in the advocacy and the work within the various communities to address the issue.[10] The impact of the international campaign against harmful traditional practices also expanded to national states, many of which (including the United Kingdom, the United States, and Sweden) enacted specific laws aimed at eradicating harmful traditional practices, particularly in reference to female genital cutting.[11] Yet these developments did not take an easy, straightforward path. As the practices are often a part of, and integral to, community life, webs of relations and particular contexts, interventions into the traditional performance of the practices often faced substantial opposition on the local and community levels. How were the practices discussed within the international human rights framework? What are the considerations taken into account? And to what extent are they compatible with the new conceptualization of children's rights?

Typically, the issue of harmful traditional practices was discussed within the scope of two main contexts. The first revolves around the question of who is an appropriate and acceptable subject to hold rights under the law (international law or any other legal system). It questions whether under a concept of liberal pluralism a cultural group can demand, *as such*, to be endowed with the possession and exercise of rights or if the subjects of rights can be only

---

[9] See Commitment 6(y) of the Copenhagen Declaration on Social Development and paragraphs 79(a, b) of its Programme of Action of the World Summit for Social Development (Copenhagen, Denmark, March 6–12, 1995, in *Report World Summit for Social Development*, U.N. Doc. A/CONF.166/9 (1995)); paragraphs 106(h), 124(i), 276(a-d), 277(a-d), 283(d) of the Beijing Platform of Action Platform of Action of the Fourth World Conference on Women (Beijing, China, September 4–15, 1995, U.N. Doc. A/CONF.177/20 (1995) and A/CONF.177/20/Add.1 (1995), annexes 1–2, U.N. Sales No. E.96.IV.13, reprinted in 35 I.L.M. 401, 407 (the Declaration), 409 (the Platform)); paragraphs 40, 42, and 48 of the Key Actions for the Further Implementation of the ICPD Programme of Action of the International Conference on Population and Development (ICPD + 5), U.N. G.A. 21st Special Sess., Agenda Item 8, addendum U.N. Doc. A/S-21/5/Add.1 (1999); paragraphs 69(e), 96(a-d), 98(d) of Further Actions and Initiatives to Implement the Beijing Declaration and Platform for Action (Beijing + 5), U.N. G.A. 23rd Special Sess., Agenda Item 10, annex, U.N. Doc. A/Res/S-23/3 (2000).

[10] The IAC functions as a network made up of twenty-eight national committees as well as European group sections with headquarters in Addis Ababa, Ethiopia, and an international liaison office in Geneva, Switzerland. It is the only African NGO and NGO network to address the problems of harmful traditional practices. For more information on the IAC, see http://www.iac-ciaf.com/.

[11] In addition, the criminal codes of various states may cover some harmful traditional practices, even if not explicitly pointing to female genital cutting. See Womenaid International, *Female Genital Mutilation: Governments Respond*, http://www.womenaid.org/press/info/fgm/fgmgov.htm.

individuals as private entities. This query is particularly pertinent considering the collective-communal aspect of traditional bodily practices and their importance to the preservation of the cultural group, on the one hand, and the potential clash with individual rights, on the other. Although the potential risk involved surely encompasses adults and children, the latter raises greater concern as the stakes, in terms of the potential damage they implicate (severity and permanency wise), are much higher. The second and closely linked context is the examination of the issue of multiculturalism, referring to the extent to which states are expected to tolerate and accommodate (or conversely, prohibit and eradicate) such biomedical practices that are accepted by minorities within their borders yet differ from those held by the dominant culture. This latter discussion goes beyond the philosophical debate as it is expected to bring into the equation a practical solution. It is one thing to draft an abstract solution for the cultural encounter, but it may be very different when it is eventually concretely applied.

Both frameworks are important for the discussion. They provide a central locale for the entire discourse on human rights and are, in fact, an ongoing attempt to resolve cultural encounters. Yet how are children configured into these contexts? The case of children's bioethics is particularly illuminating as, for them, the concept of group rights may well extend to many others who claim a right to make biomedical decisions on their behalf. Examining the international discourse concerning decision making about health adds another dimension as it provides a glimpse at the construction of children as citizens of the world.

Accordingly, the next three chapters are organized as follows. The present chapter is divided into two parts. The various theoretical arguments raised with regard to collective (group) rights versus individual rights are surveyed, and their application in the context of children is examined (Section A). Moving from theory to practice, the second part (Section B) explores the models suggested to resolve the tension associated with applying the theoretical framework to particular bodily practices. Pointing to the deficiencies and lacunas of this debate, Chapter 5 considers the meaning of children's rights in the context of biomedical practices. Providing an in-depth analysis of specific rights, it is argued that the conventional rights-based approach that has been taken, so far, to address biomedical practices involving children is flawed. While it is still overwhelmingly preoccupied with the protective/welfare model of children, its view of children as subjective rights holders ultimately overlooks their peculiar status. Chapter 6 suggests an identity-based alternative framework to discuss children's bioethics.

A. THEORETICAL FRAMEWORK OF HUMAN RIGHTS

1. Group Rights and Human Rights

The scholarly debate on group rights emerged out of the reality of multi-culturalism particularly in liberal democracies and in light of the increased political mobilization of cultural minorities asserting a collective character and demanding rights. Traditionally, the liberal (and Western) concept of human rights was based on two main assumptions. First, human rights are presumed to be claims made by individuals against society and the state. They are assumed to have universal applicability, giving the rights to individuals merely on the merit of being human. The second postulation is that human rights are private, individualized, and autonomous.[12] Individuals are expected to be free to be the authors of their own lives.[13] The claim of group rights as falling within the scope of this liberal theory of human rights thus appears to challenge both assumptions. It focuses on collectives of individuals who are understood to have shared interests and aims at protecting cultures, ways of life, and practices that are presumably not sufficiently protected by the assertion of individual interests.[14] This hypothesis claims one's freedom to follow one's own internal regulations and carry out practices such as scarification as a part of the group's right to preserve its culture and identity. As the beliefs and practices of such minority groups may not, and often do not, correspond to those of the majority's culture, the concept of group rights puts to the test the extent to which liberal democracies can follow their fundamental principles of tolerance and respect. This is all the more so given that the groups subject to protection may themselves be intolerant of differences.

Opponents of group rights ("absolute liberalists") express a few concerns in endowing rights to groups.[15] First, they stress what Ayelet Shachar termed "the paradox of multiculturalism vulnerability":[16] group rights would subjugate individual freedoms and rights to the interest of traditional communities.[17] It would enable continuing norms of paternalism, patriarchy, and discrimination against members of the group,[18] hence contradicting the notion of color-blind and individualized rights as envisioned by the liberal human rights regime.[19] Secondly, opponents caution that if cultural groups are endowed with rights, *as such*, cultural justifications would be used as a pretext for discriminatory manners, even if the culture does not require so and with great difficulties proving the

---

[12] Rhoda E. Howard, "Dignity, Community and Human Rights," in *Human Rights in Cross-Cultural Perspectives: A Quest for Consensus,* ed. Abdullahi Ahmed An-Na'im (Philadelphia: University of Pennsylvania Press, 1992), 82.

[13] Michael McDonald, "Should Communities Have Rights? Reflections on Liberal Individualism," in *Human Rights in Cross-Cultural Perspectives: A Quest for Consensus,* ed. Abdullahi Ahmed An-Na'im (Philadelphia: University of Pennsylvania Press, 1992), 140.

[14] Ibid., 134.

[15] Susan Okin, Yael Tamir, Jack Donnelly, and Rhoda Howard are considered among the leading opponents of groups' rights. See Susan M. Okin, "Is Multiculturalism Bad for Women?" in *Is Multiculturalism Bad for Women?* ed. Susan M. Okin (Princeton, NJ: Princeton University Press, 1999), 7–20; Yael Tamir, "Siding with the Underdogs," in *Is Multiculturalism Bad for Women?* ed. Susan M. Okin (Princeton, NJ: Princeton University Press, 1999), 47–52; Jack Donnelly, *Universal Human Rights in Theory and Practice,* 2nd ed. (Ithaca, NY: Cornell University Press, 2003); Howard, note 12.

[16] Ayelet Shachar, *Multicultural Jurisdiction: Cultural Differences and Women's Rights* (Cambridge: Cambridge University Press, 2001), 3.

[17] Howard, 83.

[18] Okin, 12, 22.

[19] Howard, 83, 93.

culture's authenticity otherwise.[20] Overall, then, not only would group rights unnecessarily duplicate rights, some argue, but they would also do so without providing the best protection for the individual.[21] Finally, commentators argue, group rights frustrate the natural development of cultures from taking place. In order for a minority group to qualify as a cultural group, leaders of the group would have to exhibit a "unified front," even at the cost of excluding and silencing other dissenting members of the group.[22] Consequently, rather than allowing for the dynamic and changing character of culture to take its natural course, the institutionalization of a particular position within the culture will freeze its development. It would protect and strengthen the privileged ones in the community on the backs of the powerless and marginalized members of the group and would block nonconformists and reformers from leading to internal change.[23] This artificial interest is thus undesirable not only from a cultural point of view, but also because it will further exacerbate discrimination in the way in which the community handles its functions.

Some scholars insist that the burden cannot be resolved by simply dismissing groups' claims. In his eloquent essay, "The Politics of Recognition," Charles Taylor argues that the occurrence of collective rights claims emerged from developments within human rights discourse. A shift from a concept of honor to dignity combined with the development of the modern notion of authentic identity has given an egalitarian edge to demands for cultural recognition. The first established the universal notion of equal respect and nondiscrimination;[24] the second provided that *everyone*, individuals or groups, should be recognized for their unique identity and their distinctness from everyone else.[25] Put differently, group rights, he argues, are built into the political theory of liberal democracies. Hence, the same principles of liberal human rights should be applied and be able to provide an effective method for handling the "politics of difference."[26] The question is, how and under what conditions?

Chandran Kukathas provides one such model. Siding with the previous scholars, Kukathas upholds the supremacy of individual rights and rejects any moral or political rights that collectives may claim.[27] Culture, he asserts, "is not fundamental . . . for the constitution of group identity," nor does it provide "some ineluctable prerequisite for an identity to come into being."[28] However, acknowledging that culture provides an important (albeit *post facto*) content to

[20] Alison D. Renteln, *The Cultural Defense* (Oxford: Oxford University Press, 2004), 11. Alison Renteln suggests using the services of expert witnesses to testify about particular norms within a culture in judicial proceedings that involve members of minority groups who may have a "cultural defense."

[21] McDonald, 146; Howard, 97.

[22] Tamir, 48; Howard, 98.

[23] Tamir, 48, 52.

[24] Charles Taylor, "The Politics of Recognition," in *Multiculturalism*, ed. Amy Gutman (Princeton, NJ: Princeton University Press, 1994), 42.

[25] Ibid., 38–39.

[26] Ibid., 60–61.

[27] Chandran Kukathas, "Are There Any Cultural Rights?" *Political Theory* 20, no. 1 (1992): 107–08, 111.

[28] Ibid., 111.

group identity, he advocates for toleration of different ways of life and to a policy of laissez faire.[29] For him, individuals can join together and cede their individual rights to the group without state intervention and regardless of the group's endorsement of liberal ideology, or inversely, the discriminatory manners in which the group follows. The only limitation he sees in this regard is that one's "right to exit" is upheld. As he argues, the only fundamental right that needs state protection and cannot be forfeited is one's right to exit. All other rights, in contrast, are either derivative of it or can be granted to the community. He thus concludes, "if members of a cultural community wish to continue to live by their beliefs, the outside community has no right to intervene to prevent those members acting within their right."[30]

Will Kymlicka offers another model for reconciling the principles of liberal democracies and group rights. He argues that the idea of collective cultural rights should be recognized without necessitating a denial of the liberalists' individualistic premise.[31] Social and cultural structures are important. They are intertwined with individuals' selves[32] and provide the contexts within which individuals can make meaningful choices. As such, group rights necessarily *promote* individual choice and autonomy as well as liberal equality, which entitle them to both special protection against the larger community (yet not against their own members) and to differential rights.[33]

Others have further emphasized the states' responsibilities to accommodate groups within their borders. Taylor, for example, rejects the notion that constitutional recognition of cultural group claims is sufficient. The politics of difference, he argues, must go beyond the procedural conceptualization of equal rights. The insistence on uniform application of the rules defining these rights and the suspicion of collective goals reflect the hegemonic culture, and are practically inhospitable to difference.[34] If one takes group claims seriously, it is necessary to create a substantive democracy where nondiscrimination means not only equal treatment, but differential treatment,[35] which will "not only let [cultural groups] survive, but acknowledge their worth."[36] This, according to Taylor, is the essence of the demand for recognition as it gives the members of the cultural group the room for their own judgments about what makes a good life.[37]

Adeno Addis is even more willing to accommodate the question of group rights. In contrast to previous scholars, Addis rejects the possibility that cultural rights can be understood in terms of individual rights.[38] Rather, he insists that a

---

[29] Ibid.

[30] Ibid., 117.

[31] Will Kymlicka, "The Rights of Minority Cultures: Reply to Kukathas," *Political Theory* 20, no.1 (1992): 142; Chandran Kukathas, "Cultural Rights Again: A Rejoinder to Kymlicka," *Political Theory* 20, no. 4 (1992): 680.

[32] Kymlicka, "The Rights of Minority Cultures," 140.

[33] Ibid., 141–42.

[34] Taylor, 43, 62, 60.

[35] Ibid., 39.

[36] Ibid., 64.

[37] Ibid., 61.

[38] Adeno Addis, "Individualism, Communitarianism, and the Rights of Ethnic Minori-

cultural right is a group right as "by its very nature, culture is a communion of its members rather than the sum of the attitudes and life-projects of the various individuals within the group."[39] Adopting what he terms a "critical pluralist" approach, he advocates for a mutually contingent accommodation approach by which "[as individuals], the group has a moral right to have the condition and the framework necessary for making choices."[40] Thus, he calls not only for providing necessary resources to ensure the maintenance and development of the cultures of the minority group, but also for institutional structures that will enable the minority group to participate in the dominant culture and to prosper.[41]

The flaws of these models have been already widely debated in scholarly literature. Some scholars point out, for example, that the assumed separation between the individual and his or her cultural group as Susan M. Okin, Kukathas, and others suggest, is artificial and in effect impossible.[42] Individuals do not live in isolation but within cultural contexts. Every cultural context consists of various factors and systems of belief that are interlaced and integrated with one another to comprise a whole.[43] Every society is built upon a process of enculturation by which individuals absorb the cultural configuration of their community and identity as their own.[44] Viewed in this way, then, the discussion on individuals' rights, they argue, cannot be separated from their collectives or from their construction of what is considered infringement on their rights.

Others contend that conceptualizing group rights as a question of autonomous choice imposes a liberalization policy, which essentially misses the point. While Kymlicka, for example, is seemingly willing to grant minority groups special rights against the larger community to preserve and develop their culture,[45] he allows so only as long as these communities endorse concepts of liberalism, personal choice, and the individual's supremacy over the collective.[46] Such a precondition, however, is at the heart of the debate about whether there are any group rights at all. Many minorities do not share the liberal view of individual

---

ties," *Notre Dame Law Review* 67 (1992): 658.

39 Ibid.

40 Ibid.

41 Ibid., 650. This cultural dialogue is also advanced by Ayalet Shachar. No longer even questioning the existence of minority groups' claim, she suggests an accommodative approach that will facilitate what she terms "the paradox of multiculturalism vulnerability," where the interests of the individual clash with those of the community. Accordingly, she calls for a constitutive dialogue between the majority and the minority cultures as a condition for recognition of minority's autonomy. Ayelet Shachar, "The Puzzle of Interlocking Power Hierarchies: Sharing the pieces of Jurisdictional Authority," *Harvard Civil Rights & Civil Liberties Law Review* 35 (2000): 385–426.

42 Jill E. Korbin, "The Cross Cultural Context of Child Abuse and Neglect," in *The Battered Child,* 3rd ed., ed. Henry C. Kenpa and Ray Helfer (Chicago: University of Chicago Press, 1980), 27–28.

43 Ibid.

44 Renteln, 12; McDonald, 151.

45 Kymlicka, "The Rights of Minority Cultures," 140, 142.

46 Ibid., 142; Kukathas, "Are There Any Cultural Rights?" 119; Chandran Kukathas, "Cultural Rights Again: A Rejoinder to Kymlicka," *Political Theory* 20, no. 4 (1992): 680.

autonomy or of enhancing one's possible choices.[47] The liberalization condition may thus undermine the core rationale of group rights to preserve and develop its culture *as it is*. Furthermore, as it practically gives the decision of the extent of liberalization of a particular cultural group and its appropriateness to the majority, Kymlicka is in fact not bestowing any rights on the cultural group as such but a gesture, if the majority finds it fit.

Others in contrast, critique the complexity of the process of identity formation, thrusting aside the notion of cultural identity as a shared commodity of the individual members of the group (both as individuals and as a collective). Collective identity, or "life scripts," as Kwame A. Appiah terms it, is the imposition of collective identity, which does not necessarily reflect the individual's self. In reality, there is tension between individual and group identities and an ongoing dialogue to negotiate personal identity.

> It is in dialogue with other people's understandings of who I am that I can develop a conception of my own identity, . . . my identity is crucially constituted through concepts and practices made available to me by religion, society, school, and state, and mediated to varying degrees by the family."[48]

Yael Tamir further rebuffs the notion of the collective's identity as a target of cultural survival and preservation. It is erroneous to assume, she insists, that in order to retain identity, all members of the tribe must adopt the traditional practices and preserve the cultural identity *as is*. Considering the dynamic and changeable character of culture and cultural identity, she contends, such an assumption embeds a great deal of paternalism. "It assumes that while 'we' can survive change and innovation and endure the tensions created by modernity, 'they' cannot; that 'we' can repeatedly reinvent ourselves, our culture, our tradition, while 'they' must adhere to known cultural patterns."[49]

The extent to which these models of "politics of difference" can (or should) apply to children has not yet been yet fully explored elsewhere. Yet, as the question of group rights is often assumed to be at the heart of the discussion on the preservation of religio-cultural bodily practices, the status of children in this discourse merits further consideration.

2. Group Rights and Children

In the literature, absolute liberalists such as Okin, Kukathas, Kymlicka, and others often come across as standing in opposition to one another.[50] A central

---

[47] Kukathas, "Are There Any Cultural Rights?" 120–21.

[48] Kwame A. Appiah, "Identity, Authenticity, Survival: Multicultural Societies and Social Reproduction," in *Multiculturalism*, ed. Amy Gutman (Princeton, NJ: Princeton University Press, 1994), 154.

[49] Tamir, 51.

[50] Particularly, they differ on the basis of their focal subject of rights (individuals versus collectives) and their insights on the place of culture. For further discussion on the points of divergent among these scholars, see a collection of essays in *Is Multiculturalism Bad for Women?* ed. Susan M. Okin (Princeton, NJ: Princeton University Press, 1999).

argument that is shared by all, however, is the notion of autonomous decision making. While autonomous decision making may encompass an enormous number of fields and interests, its most fundamental dimension is reflected in the concept of the right to exit. Kukathas is the most unequivocal supporter of this approach, though the others include, explicitly or implicitly, variations of it. To the extent that one decides consciously to remain with a cultural group (a point that is debated in itself),[51] communicates alternative options with the larger group, or participates in any type of negotiation on the group's recognition, one still has the option of choosing to opt out of the group.

Even as this option may be attractive to resolve multicultural tensions, it is nevertheless flawed on both general and particular levels. On the general level, for individuals who are born in any given community, the cultural norms are a simple fact of existence and a natural part of their development rather than a matter of choice or coercion.[52] Although this does not mean a predetermined and unchangeable position,[53] the mental capability of opting out of a given cultural group is neither a universally physical or desirable alternative. The preconditions for making such a decision, including the realization of individual autonomy, exposure to liberal ideology, etc., may be missing as well.[54] Furthermore, economic, geographic, and other circumstances prevent individuals from opting out of a group.

The reality of children's lives adds an additional layer. Born into an existing political and legal group, they are the central targets of the process of enculturation. They internalize the group's cultural characteristics unconsciously and even prior to the cognitive process of *post facto* content on which Kukathas's understanding of culture is built. Children's capability to exit is limited further by their physical immaturity as well as by their dependency on family and others for their survival. It is for these reasons, and in contrast to adults,[55] that children's starting points are not only one of a *lack* of autonomy, but also one of a *lack* of capacity to make (right) choices. One interesting example is the condition of street children. The phenomenon has been regarded as an appalling pandemic in many developing states, and international agencies have made great efforts in recent years to eradicate it—albeit increasing reports of children who choose to leave the familial communities in favor of independent

---

[51] Rainer Baubock, "Cultural Minority Rights for Immigrants," *International Migration Review* 30, no. 1 (1996): 207.

[52] McDonald, 151; Kymlicka, "The Rights of Minority Cultures," 143.

[53] Renteln, 12.

[54] Cass R. Sunstein, "Should Sex Equality Law Apply to Religious Institutions?" in *Is Multiculturalism Bad for Women?* ed. Susan M. Okin (Princeton, NJ: Princeton University Press, 1999), 88; Kymlicka, "The Rights of Minority Cultures," 143.

[55] There is a need to distinguish here between legal capacity to act and autonomy. Adults are generally assumed to have both autonomy and the legal capacity to exercise it, unless found "unfit," as it is often argued in the case of people with mental disabilities, for example. Children, in contrast, are assumed to have neither, and while autonomy is taken as a part of a developmental process, full legal capacity to act is often granted to children only when they reach majority (as conceptualized within the particular society), commonly in Western societies, between the ages of eighteen and twenty-one.

living on the street.[56] Leaving aside that, for many children, such an alternative is basically not viable, for others, who purport to make an autonomous choice, it is often perceived as an incomprehensible one. It follows, then, that even if ignoring, for the moment, all the above-mentioned flaws in the thesis of the right to exit, its endorsement can take place only because, and as long as, children are essentially excluded from the discourse.

The notion of making an autonomous decision to opt out creates yet another difficulty in the case of children. Scholars point out the unreasonable and undesirable zero-sum choice that the application of the right to exit as the basis for granting collective/cultural rights places on individuals: either accept all group practices (even if they infringe on their individual rights) or leave. The discomfort arises as one's disagreement with some elements of his or her given culture does not necessarily mean a desire to opt out of it. In-group members may prefer and strive to change the culture from within,[57] and just as opting out of the majority's cultural group for some disagreements seems unreasonable, there is no reason to assume that it is any different in the context of minority groups.[58] Some have even argued that it is, in fact, exactly this ability to participate (regardless of the outcome, in the short run) that plays a key role in determining one's identity.[59]

Theoretically, children's rights to participate under Article 12 of the Children's Convention could be regarded as analogous to the participation of members of minority groups. The article acknowledges that all children capable of forming a view are entitled to be involved in the process of establishing a space in which they can play a role in the modification or preservation of cultural traditions. In practice, however, the reality of children is often very different. In many societies, children are still viewed as those who should be seen but not heard. Their objections are often dismissed, assuming that further education and enculturation will suffice. Also in societies where children can express their own views, the extent to which they can actually participate, and, moreover, have their views taken seriously, is quite limited. Furthermore, without discounting entirely the novelty and significance of Article 12, adults are still the ones who retain the responsibility and the final say.[60] The situation is more complicated because it is also adults who make decisions about the welfare of children in the first place.

---

[56] Rachel Burr, "Global and Local Approaches to Children's Rights in Vietnam," *Childhood* 9, no. 1 (2002): 52–55, 57–59.

[57] Martha Nussbaum, "A Plea for Difficulty," in *Is Multiculturalism Bad for Women?* ed. Susan M. Okin (Princeton, NJ: Princeton University Press, 1999), 107; Shachar, "The Puzzle of Interlocking Hierarchies," 400–03; Joseph Raz, "How Perfect Should One Be? And Whose Culture Is?" in *Is Multiculturalism Bad for Women?* ed. Susan M. Okin (Princeton, NJ: Princeton University Press, 1999), 97–98.

[58] Raz, 97.

[59] James Tully, "The Challenges of Re-imagining Citizenship and Belonging in Multicultural and Multinational Societies," in *The Postnational Self: Belonging and Identity,* ed. Ulf Hedetoft and Mette Hjort (Minneapolis: University of Minnesota Press, 2002), 153, 174.

[60] Gerison Lansdown, *The Evolving Capacities of the Child* (Florence, Italy: UNICEF & Innocenti Research Centre, 2005), 21.

This setback is intertwined with another flaw in the minority groups/cultural rights discourse: which minority groups merit recognition and protection under the liberalist models of multiculturalism?[61] There are two particular contexts that are pertinent to the discourse on children's bioethics. The first revolves around the type and origin of the minority group. Kymlicka, for example, makes a distinction between native groups and immigrant groups, whereby only the first warrants the full yielding of group rights.[62] Unlike native groups whose minority status was imposed on them, he views immigrant communities as comprised of individuals who chose a different cultural environment from their original one. They can thus be expected to assimilate over time in the new cultural group, and their claims for group rights should be limited both in terms of scope and time.[63]

Kymlicka's theory fails to appreciate the distinctive context of children. Even if his line of analysis (mainly, voluntary immigration, difference of opportunities, and individual autonomy) can be applied in the case of adults, an issue that is itself contested,[64] it cannot justifiably apply to children. Children commonly have little or no say at all in their parents' decision to immigrate.[65] Furthermore, whether the children will assimilate into the culture of the new country or maintain their traditional practices is essentially unpredictable.[66] Although they are assumed as more likely to adopt the culture and the practices of the larger group, Rainer Baubock points out that it is in fact the second (and even third) generations of immigrants who are most inclined to demand recognition of their ways.[67] Thus, while the zero-sum solution may be indeed a bad choice for all individuals who challenge their cultural backgrounds, for children, the alternative of participation, either for the purpose of challenging or for upholding the cultural tradition, cannot be taken for granted.

The second context has to do with the type of human rights violation that would justify denying the group liberal recognition and protection. For Kymlicka, for instance, only intentional, overt, and formal forms of human rights violations

---

[61] This question in the specific context of biomedical practices will be elaborated on in Section B. The discussion here is limited to the discourse on group versus individual rights.

[62] Will Kymlicka's distinction includes religious groups as a third type of minorities. However, unlike native and immigrants groups who generally have the right of recognition and of cultural protection, albeit differences in scope and time, religious minorities are likely to fail his requirements for "group rights" as they seek to protect their boundaries by constraining their members rather than providing them with choice. Will Kymlicka, *Multicultural Citizenship: A Liberal Theory of Minority Rights* (Oxford: Clarendon Press, 1995), 35–44.

[63] Ibid., 76, 89, 96, 167–70.

[64] Rainer Baubock, for example, rejects Kymlicka's rationalization for fewer cultural rights of immigrant groups. In reality, he argues, immigration is not always voluntary, and it may be forced, for example, by groups'/individuals' displacement, dissidents, asylum seekers, and others. Also when it is perceived as "voluntary migration," he continues, it may in fact be a result of economic opportunities or a desire to join relatives and family. Either way, he points out, the members of the group are likely to carry with them their origin's set of values, beliefs, and practices, and have some shared identity characteristics that qualify them for the purpose of recognition. Baubock, 207–08, 214–23 (discussing immigration and emigration).

[65] Baubock, 221.

[66] Rentlen, 214.

[67] Baubock, 224–25.

would exclude the particular group from the liberalist protection. James Tully also concentrates his participatory model on public institutions, proposing a "democratic approach" in which "citizens come to imagine themselves as free and equal members of the *demos* or *civitas* by means, and as a result, of the freedom to participate in public life, either directly, by participating themselves, or indirectly, by identification with their trusted representatives."[68] Even Taylor, while pointing out that recognition has become familiar on both private and public spheres, focuses his discussion on the "'politics of difference" only on the latter. Yet, as women's advocates correctly show in the context of the feminist movement, much of the discrimination against women may be informal, covert, and take place in the private sphere.[69] It is this type of discrimination that often erects a barrier to the possibility of exercising their other rights.[70] Thus, they argue, without recognizing and strengthening the link between the private and the public shares, the public solution is only partial, unjustly excluding an array of discriminatory practices from state protection.

This lack is pertinent, and even more so in the context of children and biomedical practices. Even if endorsed by the entire cultural community, biomedical practices are private in nature, often take place within the familial/close environment (parents, grandparents, siblings, and even friends), and hence they are difficult, from a policy perspective, to track down.[71] In most cases the practices are performed on children with benign intentions. Aside from the different cultural constructions of what is harm, practices such as scarification and the extraction of milk teeth are generally performed as measures of protection and care for the child and his or her development, and there is clearly no intention to harm.[72] The sphere of medical treatment has been traditionally conceptualized as falling within the parental and other caregivers' authority, and while there is familiarity with disputes over the correctness of the caregivers' decision making, the challenge is not normally based on a notion of discrimination but of protection.

The deficiency is broader than the biomedical context however. Regardless of how and where cultural communities delineate their understanding of childhood, the general assumption is that the status of a child merits different treatment from adults. Whether it is conditioned on age, as is often the case in Western dualistic thought, or by other factors, as it is in many African cultures,[73] discrimination against children (intended and unintended) is still

---

[68] Tully, 153.

[69] Okin, 22.

[70] Kymlicka gives the example of land rights of indigenous groups. According to the Dawes Act, indigenous land cannot be sold to and by individuals as it is an essential feature for the group's survival. However, this limitation practically deprives the individual members of the group from their economic right, requiring them to cede it—or its value—to the group, and thus substantially hamper their ability to exit. Janet E. Halley, "Culture Constrains," in *Is Multiculturalism Bad for Women?* ed. Susan M. Okin (Princeton, NJ: Princeton University Press, 1999), 102.

[71] See Chapter 1, Section C.

[72] See Chapter 3.

[73] Rachel Murray, *Human Rights in Africa: From the OAU to the African Union* (Cambridge: Cambridge University Press, 2004), 167.

often overlooked. The difference in treatment is often not perceived in any way as discrimination at all. Thus, for example, while a suggestion that children's participation under Article 12 of the Children's Convention, essentially meant to be used only in such "events occurring in the (private) life of children" and not in any public debate,[74] may resonate with some conceptualization of children, it unjustly reinforces the rigid private/public dichotomy with all its flaws. It also ignores the successful stories of children's participation in the public sphere, on the local and national levels, such as in the development of child-appropriate health programs and hospital design, educational curricula, and others.[75]

There is of course a need to distinguish children as a subgroup from adults. Infants cannot be assumed to be capable of participating, nor can they be compared with older children and youngsters, although capacities certainly evolve over time.[76] Children's exercise of rights requires special measures of assistance and protection that are not generally assumed as needed for adults. If not provided, their rights to physical and spiritual development may be hampered, and the fear of abandoning children to their rights may turn into a monstrous reality. But where these differences may be particularly relevant for the purpose of determining what weight should be attached to the child's views,[77] the point of departure is still one of subordination rather than of participation, hence oftentimes turning Article 12 to mere rhetoric.

Finally, the concentration on minority groups misses the point that children are citizens of the world. It is not only children belonging to minority groups who are at risk from biomedical practices that may be harmful to their development. It is not only these children who are subjected to practices purporting to establish and maintain their ("right") cultural identity, which they may have little say about. Culture is a universal feature of humanity, and although it is an integral part of a group's claims for recognition, it is not synonymous with group rights or limited to a minority group's claims for recognition.[78] While, in most cases, the majority's culture does not need to reassert its cultural rights or

---

[74] This understanding is based on the lack of any of the usual limitations to civil liberties in Article 12 (Marie-Francoise Lucker-Babel, "The Right of the Child to Express Views and to Be Heard: An Attempt to Interpret Article 12 of the UN Convention on the Rights of the Child," *International Journal of Children's Rights* 3 (1995): 395.).

[75] For a survey of public projects carried out by children in various places around the world, which were highly evaluated in their impact on their and the community's advancement of rights, see Gerison Lansdown, *Promoting Children's Participation in Democratic Decision-Making* (Florence, Italy: UNICEF & Innocenti Research Centre, 2001) and Lansdown, *The Evolving Capacities of the Child.*

[76] Yet the right of a child who is capable of forming his or her views to express them is not limited to verbal opinions; the child may also use nonverbal ones. Lucker-Babel further argues that in order for infants to be useful to the decision, trained specialists to interpret the child's feelings must be used (Lucker-Babel, 397). However, the practicality of this proposal is limited, especially as the application of Article 12 of the Children's Convention is contingent on the principle of "evolving capacity," stipulated in Article 5 of the Children's Convention.

[77] Lansdown, *The Evolving Capacities of the Child*, 21.

[78] Lyndel Prott, "Understanding One Another on Cultural Rights," in *Cultural Rights and Wrongs*, ed. Halina Nieć (Paris: UNESCO Publishing, 1998), 268; Renteln, 214–15.

claims for recognition, all children essentially belong to (and are subordinated to) some sort of cultural minority group. For them, it is not only traditional communities that make decisions on their behalf, but also other substitute cultural communities, such as international agencies, the international community at large, the extended family, the nuclear family, or even just the parents. All of them eventually comprise a small-scale cultural community for the child, with collective interests to promote and entrench. Thus, a discussion of children's bioethics needs to be taken beyond the question of group versus individual rights or the policy approach of liberal democracies toward minority groups within its national borders.

B. BODILY PRACTICES AND CULTURAL CONFLICTS

This section examines questions regarding the proper scope of government regulation of children's health. To what extent and under what conditions should liberal democracies intervene in biomedical practices performed on children in the private sphere of minority groups? When is such interference in sovereign states justified on the international level?

1. Cultural Bodily Encounters on the National Level

Responding to the questions above, scholars have tried to draw a fine line between enabling cultural groups to flourish in accordance with their own judgments without abandoning the fundamental rights of individual members of such groups to (small-scale) totalitarian regimes. For the most part, the discussion remained on the abstract level. With the exception of female circumcision and other mostly gender-related practices that have been widely discussed,[79] only a few analysts have actually taken steps to apply their models specifically, broadly, and/or to do so from a comparative perspective.[80] The scholar addressing this issue most comprehensively is Bhikhu Parekh.

Parekh proposes a concept of "society's operative public values" to resolve disagreements about which traditional practices to allow and which to ban.[81] These operative values constitute the shared moral structure of society's public life. They give the context and are the only acceptable starting point for a debate. Such an approach, he assumes, would lead to a dialogue between the various groups as well as within the groups themselves, theoretically allowing for a change in both the minority's practices or the society's operative public values. Parekh's model advances in three stages of debate. First, the spokesmen of the minority group have to defend the contested practice within the practice's authority and cultural context. This stage requires explaining the importance

[79] The United Nations and other international bodies generally focused on a few categories of harmful traditional practices: (1) female genital cutting; (2) son preference; (3) female infanticide; (4) early marriage and dowry; (5) early pregnancies, food taboos during pregnancies, and damaging childbirth practices; and (6) violence against women (*Fact Sheet No. 23: Harmful Traditional Practices Affecting the Health of Women and Girls,* Part I).

[80] The paramount concentration of the discussion surrounds national policies versus minority groups. See my reservation to this concentration below.

[81] Bhikhu Parekh, *Rethinking Multiculturalism: Cultural Diversity and Political Theory* (Cambridge, MA: Harvard University Press, 2000), 267.

of the contested practice to the cultural group, its relevance to the way of life, and its binding character on the group. If the practice seems to violate society's operative public values, the spokesmen must explain how "the practice is interlocked with other valuable practices and central to their way of life, which would be undermined if it were to be disallowed."[82] If the majority is not persuaded, the minority group moves to the second stage, offering a defense of the practice from outside its cultural authority and context. In this stage, the spokesmen of the cultural group appeal to values to which the wider society itself subscribes or can be persuaded to share. They present "comparable practices" that exist in the majority's culture or point to the value their contested practice holds for the enrichment of the diversity in the wider society. Finally, if no agreement can be reached, the minority group has to cede the practice, giving way to the operative public values of the wider society to prevail.

Aside from the theoretical model, Parekh's work is particularly significant as he provides a practical dimension by applying it to a number of traditional practices. Analyzing them in the three stages and the possible arguments the relevant minority groups are likely to raise, he finds the Hindu burial practice of scattering the ashes of the dead in the river, the Jewish and Muslim animal slaughtering practices, and the Asian arranged marriage custom as acceptable practices that require accommodation. Female circumcision and polygamy, by contrast, he opposes because they violate the operative public value in liberal democracies of equality.[83]

Although Parekh's "dialogical consensus" for culture conflicts is laudable, there are several difficulties that surface particularly in the context of children. First, while presumably there is a process of negotiation between society at large and its minority groups, ultimately, if not persuaded otherwise, the majority comes out ahead. This resolution, however, seems to undermine the entire approach. While arguably any set of legally established values inherently reflect the hegemonic culture,[84] the *a priori* determination that the outcome in case of disagreement would be necessarily in favor of the majority contradicts the principle of equality that is fundamental to both his analysis and the essence of negotiations. Instead of finding a middle ground, it is eventually only the minorities that may have to surrender their cultural rites (and rights).

It is perhaps for this last reason that his discussion ultimately comes across as biased. His justifications for vetoing the practices, for the most part, on the assumption of discrimination against women, seem to merely endorse the arguments raised by Western feminists that received widespread publicity in media coverage and other outlets. The power imbalance between men and women, boys and girls, is viewed as the source of all ills (female circumcision, polygamy, and *Sati*), and, constructed as such, he draws the conclusion that they need to be uprooted from the ground and entirely banned.

---

[82] Ibid., 272.

[83] Parekh does not ban the most lenient form of female circumcision. Parekh, 276

[84] Taylor, 43.

While inequality certainly has an impact on women and girls' rights, two objections to Parekh's discrimination-based approach can be made. First, is the implied conditional comparison with men/boys. Neither of the practices that Parekh actually discussed, and allowed, bear direct impact on the living body, and seemingly all of them apply equally to both men and women (see above). However, the fact that a particular practice is performed on men/boys does not, in itself, justify approving the parallel practice when performed on women. Parekh's reference to the background and context of the practices performed on men/boys is particularly limited, giving an impression that they are simply fine. The most illuminating example is Parekh's comparison between male circumcision and female circumcision in its less severe form. The latter, he contends, "involves minimum physical harm and does not seem to be very different from male circumcision." Remarking that male circumcision "has sometimes been criticized on medical and more recently on psychological grounds and involves some degree of physical mutilation" he points out that, "it is widely allowed" and concludes that, "unless female circumcision [of this lenient form] is shown to cause graver harm, there is no obvious reason to treat it differently."[85]

This mere reference to "some criticism," however, does not in any way clarify why he chose one stance over the other, implying that the fact that it is "widely allowed"[86] played a determinative role. If a standard of harm is to be used, the comparison need not be the relative harm that is caused to boys in traditional bodily practices, in comparison to that caused to girls, but rather more general criteria of harm. While he argues that the principle of no harm is "largely unproblematic [to ban a practice] when physical harm is involved,"[87] he does not clarify why the criticism concerning medical and psychological impact as well as the "degree of physical mutilation" with regard to male circumcision has no force.[88]

Another objection to Parekh's approach relates to a double standard of equality. If equality is the point of departure, then one may as well argue that the performance of the rite of male circumcision among Jews as the primary symbol of membership in the community and the everlasting covenant between men and God discriminates against Jewish women who cannot attain these goals. The performance of male circumcision as a means of separating the boy from his family (particularly, ties to the mother) as has been documented in a number of African tribes[89] may be argued as being discriminatory against boys, disallowing them to retain the softer features of connectedness. The fact

---

[85] Parekh, 276

[86] Ibid.

[87] Ibid., 267.

[88] Except for the gender lines, Parekh's criteria which practices to examine are somewhat unclear. Aside from male circumcision, the other bodily practice that he mentions that relates also to boys is scarification. While he specifically comments in his discussion about the "harm principle" that scarification of children "raise[s] interesting issues," he does not provide any further elaboration beyond that (ibid., 265, 267).

[89] Eric K. Silverman, "Anthropology and Circumcision," *Annual Review of Anthropology* 33 (2004): 425.

that the practice is performed to show the bravery of men[90] arguably reinforces traditional sex roles between men and women; yet only young men are called upon to play this role. With respect to women and girls, Parekh does not seem to question the capacity of the young men, in view of their cultural background, to make a choice of this sort. He thereby supports the traditional presumption that only boys, yet not girls, have agency. Finally, his exclusion from the discussion and his approval of mild female circumcision is inconsistent with his general reasoning. If, as he argues, the reason for banning the practice is grounded in society's operative public value of girls' equality, it is not clear why allowing the practice *in any form* should be accepted as the rationale for its performance.

There is yet another, more general, critique of Parekh's model that needs to be put forward. Although Parekh advocates the need to protect children from being subjected to harmful traditional practices, he seems to overlook their status as active rights holders. To what extent are children involved in the decision making of rites of passage? It is not clear. Particularly in traditional societies, children are not assumed to have a representative capacity. To what extent can the adult members of the minority group actually speak for the children of the group? This is also unclear. Adults, especially women, are assumed to have the responsibility to enculturate the children. A part of their own social values and dignity is calculated according to the cultural values they ask for, leading to a more rigid approach.[91] Furthermore, regardless of their cultural background, children are increasingly acknowledged as having their own voices, interests, and concerns. Parekh does not explain where and how children are involved in the dialogical process, aside from being passive targets of protection. In view of his infantilizing approach to women with regard to traditional practices, there is doubt if he could have taken the childrens' views into account.[92]

Alison D. Renteln provides a more inclusive discussion of bodily practices involving children in her provocative book, *The Cultural Defense.* She advocates using the principle of "irreparable (physical) harm" to determine which traditional practices should be banned. Aware of the lack of universal consensus as to what would constitute harm, she defines the principle as those traditions that cause death or permanent disfigurement.[93] Accordingly, she precludes the performance of both female and male circumcision, as well as ritual scarification and cosmetic surgeries performed on children. The issue at stake, she argues, is

---

[90] Ilan Katz, "Is Male Circumcision Morally Defensible?" in *Moral Agendas for Children's Welfare*, ed. Michael King (New York: Routledge, 1999), 90.

[91] Okin, 126–27.

[92] See, for example, his discussion on women's decision to be circumcised and on the Indian practice of *Sati*, where he rationalizes the ban by women's inability, due to their general status in Hindu society, "to think independently and decide for themselves between alternative ways of understanding their cultural traditions." Parekh, 278–79, 281–82. In contrast to his fervent claim to women's equality, he practically relegates such women to the mere status of "body without mind," discarding any agency role they posses. His rejection of polygamy further adds a sense of uneasiness as it eventually comes across as a mere disrespect to different ways of family and life styles. Ibid., 282–92.

[93] Rentlen, 217.

whether it is the parents or the state that has the final say in the shaping of the child's identity, and endorsing individual choice as guiding principle, she opts for the latter.[94]

While there is little argument with regard to the exclusion of practices that cause death, the exclusion of practices that cause consequential permanent body change should be examined further. The body, as Elizabeth Grosz nicely summarizes it, is an "imaginary autonomy,"

> an internalized image or map of the meaning that the body has for the subject, for others in its social world, and for the symbolic order conceived in its generality (that is, for the culture as a whole). It is an individual and collective fantasy of the body's forms and modes of action.[95]

Similarly, for those communities who follow bodily rites, the point is the meaning they convey to one's (and the group's) identity. The bodily change is a reflection of it, the family's "memory made flesh," as Katharine Young termed it, and an integral part of the psychological process in which children construct their identities. It is a (moral) judgment about how to relate to the world by which children, and essentially, also all other human beings, shape a corporeal self.[96] While certainly not all bodily practices should be allowed, further clarification is needed to determine *why* the practices' potential extinction is justified. Is it the Western (Christian-based) notion of human dignity and its dislike of body modification?[97] Is it a question of the aesthetic and discomfort body diversity may arouse? Or is there a need for any additional long-term health implications? The answers are not clear.

The criterion of irreparable harm combined with the preference for individual choice is further problematic because it is too vague a point of departure to discuss children's bioethics.[98] Correctly, Renteln does not stipulate an age of majority. While this corresponds to the existence of various constructions of childhood, it essentially leaves open the question at what age (if ever) can a child make an autonomous decision to follow a particular rite, without being overridden by state officials? Can a four-year-old Muslim boy decide to be circumcised? Can eleven-, twelve-, or even fifteen-year-olds decide to have their faces scarred? Can a five-year-old girl decide to wear neck brass?

---

[94] Ibid., 217–18.

[95] Elizabeth Grosz, *Volatile Bodies: Toward a Corporeal Feminism* (Bloomington: Indiana University Press, 1994), 39–40, quoted in Katherine Young, "The Memory of the Flesh: The Family Body in Somatic Psychology," *Body & Society* 8, no. 3 (2002): 26.

[96] Young, 26.

[97] Paul S. Landau, "Explaining Surgical Evangelism in Colonial Southern Africa: Teeth, Pain and Faith," *Journal on African History* 37 (1996): 276.

[98] A point of clarification on Renteln's work is essential here. Renteln's discussion revolves around cultural conflicts within the court system mainly in the United States. Her thesis is that the cultural context of one's behavior needs to be allowed in legal proceeding to ensure that justice, also with regards to minority groups, is done. Her discussion on biomedical practices involving children is thus "on the defense." It focuses on adults who are charged for performing biomedical practices on children, and the question of children's rights per se is only subsidiary.

The inclination toward the principle of freedom to choose in this context does not resolve the difficulties but, in fact, further complicates the issue. To enable one to make (presumably, individual) choices, merely securing the development of the child's faculty of choosing is not enough.[99] It also requires the development of a sense of what is morally good and bad, and consistent exposure to the particular preferable way of life. As scholars emphasize, values, especially religious and culturally based ones, "cannot usually simply be told to a child, they have to be *lived*."[100] It is in this vein, then, that reference to one's freedom to choose is inapt. Some may indeed have the sense of loss of freedom when a child is not educated in the Western spirit of choosing among alternative lifestyles, careers, and so on. Yet, as Stephen Frosh explains,

> is there not a similar loss of freedom when one does not instill in a child religious and communal values which are part of her or his family tradition? How easily can one "choose" to join a community for which one does not have a deep, lived appreciation? Could I, when my children are seventeen or eighteen, say to them, "I have not taught you anything, but now you are free to become whatever you like"?[101]

This relates back to the discussion on the development of a corporeal self. As identity starts to develop at a very young age, the preclusion of practices affecting children is, in reality, likely to lead to permanent loss of the practices.

2. Evaluating Cultural Bodily Practices on the International Level

a. *The Majority/Minority Rule on the International Level: An Acceptable Analogy?*

Moving to the international sphere, to what extent are these approaches applicable on the international level? Within liberal democracies, limitations of the minority's practices may be justified on the basis of the principle "when in Rome do as the Romans do" (despite its flaws). The assumption is that it is only reasonable to expect that immigrants and minority groups somewhat adjust their customs to conform to the majority's rule. But this expectation cannot be idiosyncratically assumed to apply to all societies in the world. Clearly, not all nation-states follow the Western model of liberal democracies. With the exception of the European Union, membership as nation-states in the United Nations and in other international (regional) bodies *does not* require liberal and democratic political regimes. Members of the United Nations exhibit an array of political regimes and pluralism also among the liberal and democratic ones. There are significant differences not only between developing and developed states, but also among developed states themselves. Furthermore, in many states the majority of the population is rural. The national structure is thus

---

[99] Ze'ev W. Falk, "Rights and Autonomy—Or the Best Interests of the Child?" in *Children's Rights and Traditional Values,* ed. Gillian Douglas and Leslie Sebba (Burlington, VT: Ashgate Publishing, 1998), 115.

[100] Stephen Frosh, "Identity, Religious Fundamentalism and Children's Welfare," in *Moral Agendas for Children's Welfare,* ed. Michael King (New York: Routledge, 1999), 207; David Archard, *Children: Rights and Childhood* (London: Routledge, 1993), 56, quoted in Falk, 115.

[101] Frosh, 205.

essentially comprised of predominantly minority groups, making it virtually impossible to define any majority's guiding set of principles and beliefs. Thus, the appropriateness of the intention to simply extend this liberal majority's rule to encompass all children around the world needs consideration.

Although somewhat simplistic, one may draw an analogy between the international community and Western liberal democracies. According to this analogy, the UN system (assumed to be the most inclusive international system) parallels a liberal nation-state with its fundamental principles of equality, tolerance, and human rights, and each state is a cultural minority group within it. This brings into the discussion a whole set of other relevant questions, such as to what extent the Western foundations of the international instruments can and should be assumed as a consensual basis of all states. As many of the current members of the United Nations were only colonies and did not exist as independent states at the time when some of the main instruments were drafted, the answer is not obvious. Are the international instruments expected to apply similarly in the various states? If not, where is the line drawn between acceptable and unacceptable applications? Even if the treatment of minority groups within liberal democracies may be inevitably somewhat ethnocentric,[102] simply duplicating it on the international level might amount to colonialism.[103] These questions touch upon not only the known debate between universalism and relativism, but also on the impact of globalization, on the various economic, social, historical, and political forces that play a role, interestingly, in both the evolution of traditional bodily practices and the advancement of human rights. As such, they are necessarily intertwined with the particularly contentious contemporary debate on the construction of national, subnational, and other identities.

These complicated issues are discussed in more detail in Chapters 5, 6, and 8. For the time being, the discussion now turns to the question of how to examine and evaluate, on the international level, particular traditional practices without being charged with cultural imperialism. What are the considerations international agencies take into account throughout the process of their decision making to veto particular traditional practices? Moreover, to what extent do these international bodies, and the Monitoring Committee under the Children's Convention (Children's Committee or Committee) in particular, actually incorporate the notion of children as subjects of rights in the international discourse? As those who are responsible to set the standard for children's rights worldwide, the Committee's interpretation of what counts as a harmful traditional practice bears critical weight.

b. International Cross-Cultural Evaluation, Bodily Practices, and Imperialism

The issue of cultural imperialism is not new in the international human rights context. The question of whether one set of norms can be equally applicable and transferable to all people, regardless of cultural and religious

[102] Renteln, 218.

[103] Theoretically, all states have an equal voice under the international system.

contexts, accompanied the global entrenchment of "rights talk" that took place in the past decades.[104] Voices, mainly from non-Western countries, challenged the assumption of equal applicability and criticized the international human rights corpus as harmful, alien, and destructive to traditions, social structures, and human diversity.[105] Makau Mutua even specifically charges it as Western imperialism attempting to translate historical physical power into one specific set of political and ideological values.[106] Thus, despite the growing domestic and international rights talk, no consensus about the nature and substantive scope of the proclaimed rights is in sight. As Henry J. Steiner and Philip Alston point out,

> Whether human rights are to be viewed as divine, moral or legal entitlements; whether they are to be validated by intuition, custom, social contract theory, principles of distributive justice, or as a prerequisite for happiness; whether they are to be broad or limited in number and content—these and kindred issues are [still] matters of on-going debate with little probability of resolving soon.[107]

Regardless of one's endorsement of a universalist or relativist approach to human rights, however, there seems to be a growing consensus that cross-cultural evaluation is not only possible but also unavoidable. The justifications vary, running from a notion of "shared consciousness of vulnerability"[108] to a suggestion that it is motivated by an inherent feature of human beings based on compassion for our fellow human beings.[109] Jack Donnelly grounds cross-cultural evaluation on the responsibility to follow *our* (i.e., Western) moral precepts. "To refuse to act on our own precepts simply because others reject them," he argues, "is to fail to give proper weight to our own moral beliefs."[110] Furthermore, cross-cultural judgment is increasingly viewed as an integral part of the politics of difference. As Renteln clarifies, there is a distinction between recognition of cultural differences and their endorsement. Disparate cultural moral codes and norms of behavior should be acknowledged as a part of the principal of equality and justice, but this acknowledgment need not necessarily be translated into the outcome.[111] And as Taylor emphasizes, while the politics

---

[104] Michael Goodhart, "Origins and Universality in Human Rights Debates: Cultural Essentialism and the Challenge of Globalization," 4 *Human Rights Quarterly* 25 no. 4 (2003): 938, 940; Kukathas, "Are There Any Cultural Rights?" 108.

[105] Henry J. Steiner and Philip Alston. *International Human Rights in Context: Law, Politics, Morals* (New York: Oxford University Press, 1996), 167.

[106] Makau Mutua, "The Complexity of Universalism in Human Rights," in *10th Annual Conference on "the Individual vs. the State" Central European University*, Budapest, June 14–16, 2002, http://www.ceu.hu/legal/ind_vs_state/Mutua_paper_2002.htm, part 2.

[107] Steiner and Alston, 169–70.

[108] The principle of "shared consciousness of vulnerability" suggests that when the evaluation is made on the basis of a value or norm that is widely accepted by "the widest range of cultural tradition," the less it would be charged with ethnocentrism or cultural imperialism. Corinne A. A. Packer, *Using Human Rights to Change Tradition: Traditional Practices Harmful to Women's Reproductive Health in Sub-Saharan Africa.* (Oxford: Antwerpen Intersentia, 2002), 100.

[109] Ibid., 100.

[110] Donnelly, 93.

[111] Renteln, 15; Taylor, 69.

of difference requires recognizing cultural worth, refusal to endorse another's cultural judgment has nothing to do with the validity or invalidity of the judgment.[112] When and on what grounds do biomedical practices reach the point at which the international community finds them so incomprehensible that they undermine the values of tolerance, equality, and respect on which the concept of liberal democracy is built?

Discussing the issue of cross-cultural judgment on the international level, Donnelly charts a grid with the various practices as a means to resolve when pressing negative external judgment is "not only permissible but also demanded."[113] He proposes mapping internal (local) and external (international) moral judgments according "to the relative importance that is attached to them." Placing these moral judgments against one another, he describes four possible scenarios and the action that the international community is expected to press ahead with. Case 1 includes practices that are morally unimportant, both externally and internally, and thus whether one maintains his or her condemnation is of little interest. Case 2 includes practices that are externally unimportant and internally important, and thus imposing negative external judgment would be inappropriate and "at best, insensitive." Case 3 includes practices that are externally very important and internally unimportant and thus present "the best occasion to press an external judgment." The most complicated practices to handle are those contained in Case 4. In this rubric Donnelly locates practices such as human sacrifice, trial by ordeal, extrajudicial execution, and female infanticide, which hold great moral importance both internally and externally, yet one side will have to surrender. In such cases, Donnelly argues, the inherent universality of basic morals (of the West) requires the international community to support a negative judgment and to act toward the eradication of the practices.[114]

Donnelly does not provide any other guidelines to assist in the classification of various practices in the rubrics, with the exception of Case 4, nor does he provide any examples of practices that fall, in his mind, in Cases 1 to 3. This opens a substantial gap in his model as it leaves the most pressing question unanswered: what counts as an internal or external moral judgment, and how to evaluate its relative worth? Corinne Packer, for example, proposes her categorization as follows: neck elongation as an example of a practice that is morally unimportant both internally and externally (Case 1); mourning practices for widows, facial scarification, and male circumcision as examples of practices that are internally important but externally unimportant (Case 2); and incisions, dietary taboos, and other practices that "moral arguments are rarely given for their practice or continuation, but rather arguments of superstition (arguably based on ignorance)"[115] as examples of practices that are internally unimportant but externally important (Case 3). Yet, while this classification may reflect the particular context of sub-Saharan Africa that was

[112] Taylor, 69.
[113] Donnelly, 93.
[114] Ibid., 93–94.
[115] Packer, 3, 103–05.

her regional focus (no information on sources is provided),[116] its application in other communities around the world is doubtful.

One example is the practice of neck elongation. As a practice of beautification, it may not evoke any particular moral judgment, hence coinciding with Packer's classification as lacking internal moral worth. However, at least in the context of the Padaung girls, the practice clearly also has social, political, and economic significance. Taking into account the group's struggle for self-determination, it may also be argued that it holds moral implications for the Karen group in general. It is a visible and unequivocal symbol of support, admiration, and pride in their national/ethnic identity, hence qualifying it as holding a significant internal moral judgment.

The extent to which these have been calculated in the decision making of the various international agencies (if at all) is not clear. The approach taken by Ms. Halima Embarek Warzazi, the Special Rapporteur on Harmful Traditional Practices, seems to endorse the first, that is, that the practice of neck elongation among the Padaung girls in Thailand does not hold internal moral importance. Referring to the practice in a statement she delivered at the United Nations in 1998 on "Obstacles to Development," she essentially attributed its continuance only to the economic burden of the tribe. The practice, she stated, "might be ended if alternate means of a living could be provided to the inhabitants of the village where it occurred; the sad fact was that the village attracted tourist and tourist income because of this practice."[117] The Children's Committee's classification of neck elongation among the Padaung and the Kareni tribes in Myanmar as harmful traditional practice in 2004 was done under the cloak of medical rationales. Criticizing Myanmar's government for not doing enough to raise awareness about the harmfulness of the practice, the Committee noted, "the practice can result in sudden death or serious damage to the spinal cord, *if . . . removed* [emphasis added]."[118] Moving to the arena of Article 24(3) of the Children's Convention, the Committee practically calls for the elimination of the practice and refers to the state's obligation to do so. By that, it explicitly identifies the practice of neck elongation as falling into either Case 3 or Case 4, endorsing the Special Rapporteur's comment on internal moral unimportance, or the opposite, acknowledging its internal importance, yet nevertheless calling for its abolishment without further clarification.

Another example is the practice of milk teeth removal. Although Packer does not mention the practice, based on her reasoning, it seems likely to fall into either Case 3 or Case 4. While the international campaign has been to press ahead with a negative moral judgment,[119] the evaluation of the internal moral

[116] Packer focuses on traditional practices bearing influence on women's reproductive health in sub-Saharan Africa. Packer, 3.

[117] U.N. Press Release, *Sub-Commission Completes Debate on Obstacles to Development*, U.N. Doc. HR/SC/98/14 (August 13, 1998)

[118] Committee on the Rights of the Child, *Concluding Observations: Myanmar*, paragraphs 58–59, U.N. Doc. CRC/C/15/Add.237 (June 30, 2004).

[119] See, e.g., Committee on the Rights of the Child, *Concluding Observations: Ethiopia*, paragraph 64, U.N. Doc. CRC/C/15/Add.144 (February 21, 2001). See also Federal Demo-

judgment attributed to the practice certainly depends on the observer. The practice may be perceived as entirely superstitious considering the arguable connection between childhood's ailments and worms in the gums, the belief that the yellow fluid is an entity (the maggot) that endangers the child's life, and the obvious contradiction between the practice and Western medicine, which would qualify it under Case 3. As such, according to Donnelly, it presents the optimal case on which to pass a negative external judgment. However, children's development and upbringing practices are contingent on the moral codes of the societies in which they live.[120] Viewed in this way the practice of milk teeth extraction could also fall under Case 4 as it is carried out in order to cut off what appears to jeopardize the child's development. Put differently, not providing the necessary protection to children who are among the most vulnerable members in the community may be regarded as both internal and external moral judgment, hence resolved in a confrontational clash.

The international agencies that addressed the practice did not reveal whether these considerations influenced the final determination to press ahead with the negative external judgment.[121] Consigning the practice to the category of harmful traditional practices in the context of Ethiopia, both the Children's Committee and Mrs. Radhika Coomaraswamy, the UN Special Rapporteur on Violence against Women, merely referred to it as an issue of concern mentioning a report submitted by the National Committee on Traditional Practices in Ethiopia (NCTPE). How they assessed the internal moral worth of the practice is unclear, and the Children's Committee's conclusion on the matter is vague. The Committee simply recommended that "the State Party take advantage of the experience gained by other countries [to end it]."[122] Considering that the Committee itself did not address the practice in any other country, the extent to which this recommendation is actually helpful remains in doubt.

The difficulty in judging the relative moral judgment both internally and externally is evident as evaluating others' cultural practices is always influenced by one's own cultural conceptualization.[123] It not only directs the determination of the correctness of a practice toward one's own, but also affects (and often underestimates) the weight and significance others attribute to their practices. As Herodotus nicely summarizes it,

---

cratic Republic of Ethiopia, "Response to the Questionnaire on Violence Against Children Submitted to the UN Secretary General's Independent Expert on the Study on Violence Against Children," paragraph 8 (May 2005), available at http://www2.ohchr.org/english/bodies/CRC/docs/study/responses/Ethiopia.pdf.

[120] Jill E. Korbin, "Children, Childhood, and Violence," *Annual Review Anthropology* 32 (2003): 434.

[121] *Concluding Observations: Ethiopia,* paragraph 64; Commission on Human Rights, *Report of the Special Rapporteur on Violence Against Women, Integration of the Human Rights of Women and the Gender Perspective: Violence Against Women,* Economic and Social Council, 59th Sess., Item 12(a), paragraph 241, U.N. Doc. E/CN.4/22003/75/Add.1 (February 27, 2003).

[122] *Concluding Observations: Ethiopia,* paragraph 65.

[123] Raimundo Pannikar, "Is the Notion of Human Rights a Western Concept?" *Diogenes* 120 (1982): 84–88.

> if one were to put before all men the suggestion that out of all customs they should choose the best, each people would examine them and then pick their own; so accustomed are they to think that their own customs are far the best . . . there are many proofs to show that all men customarily hold this attitude towards customs.[124]

Still, the natural bias towards one's cultural practices and beliefs does not and should not justify surrendering the evaluation of traditional bodily practices to Western imperialism. Rather than dismissing the complexity, scholars and the international agencies should strive to take a comprehensive and contextualized approach before pressing ahead with a negative moral judgment. This includes consideration of the various interests at stake, including not only the individual child, but also his or her familial and communal environments, the meaning that is given to the various bodily practices within the particular cultural context, and the relationships between them. Taking such an approach is imperative as it is the only way for the child's voice to be heard.

C. CONCLUSION

The two common theoretical frameworks in which harmful traditional practices are commonly discussed raise a number of difficulties in the context of children. It can be argued that the philosophical debate about groups' rights and about the politics of difference is unsuitable to address children's rights. Ultimately, the conventional liberal model builds on an assumption of (autonomous) individuals who can participate in the public debate and can decide to exercise their right to exit. Children, in contrast, are assumed to lack these characteristics in the first place. They are born into a reality in which they do not choose, and their efforts to decide for themselves are often dismissed on the basis of their immaturity. Moreover, the concentration on minority groups ignores the reality of all children—they all belong to small, nonvoluntary associations: the families.

With regard to the second framework on multiculturalism, the scholarly efforts to resolve cultural encounters in a manner that fits the liberal notions of toleration and accommodation on both the national and international levels are considered. While Parekh's "dialogical consensus" is significant, his actual address of traditional bodily practices concerning children is limited. His excessive attention to gender equality overlooks the fact that boys, too, are subject to bodily practices that may be harmful. Moreover, although Parekh advocates for the protection of children from harmful traditional practices, his discussion ignores them as subjects. Renteln's principle of irreparable (physical) harm is helpful, as it provides a clear initial guideline: practices that cause death should be excluded. This principle does not answer, however, other critical questions, particularly, why every physical modification should be disallowed, and how to evaluate the point at which a child can make bodily related decisions on his or her own. This omission is substantial as many traditional bodily practices

---

[124] Herodous, *The Histories* (Harmondsworth,UK: Penguin Classics, 1954), Book III, part 38, quoted in Packer, 85.

are carried out at a young age especially to inscribe cultural identity into the child. Thus, the practical implication of their preclusion is likely to lead to their permanent loss.

Scholarly efforts to establish universal criterion for cross-cultural moral evaluation to draw the line between harmful traditional bodily practices and other cultural customs is also lacking. Donnelly's scheme leaves a rather wide gap for subjectivity in the determination of the harmfulness of a biomedical practice. The evaluation of other's practices is always tainted with one's own construction of correctness of any given practice, and, furthermore, it may also be dependent on a variety of external factors that play a role in the construction of the wrongness of the practice. Once the assessment is contingent on moral evaluation, it is essentially impossible to press ahead with a judgment without some sort of paternalism and, in the context of liberal democracies, also Eurocentrism. While some may argue that it is unavoidable, and actually justified, it seems that taking a more comprehensive and contextualized approach would be preferable for mollifying some of the cultural tensions. This, in return, requires consideration of the question of which rights of the child are arguably violated. What are the states' responsibilities in this regard? Does this discourse reflect the new conceptualization of children as subjects of rights? And to what extent are children's particular voices, views, and beliefs as social and cultural agents actually incorporated into the discussion on *their* bioethical rights?

CHAPTER 5
BIOMEDICAL PRACTICES AND THE CHILD: RIGHTS IN QUESTION

The two theoretical frameworks in which harmful traditional practices are commonly discussed and the difficulties with their application in the context of children were considered in the preceding chapter. It was argued that the scholastic debate about minorities, the question of state accommodation, and the cross-cultural moral evaluation were not suitable to fully address children's bioethical (and other) rights. For the most part, the discussion was in the abstract, and the rights of the child that are in question were not elaborated. However, to establish the content of states' duties in the context of children and biomedical practices, it is essential to specify which rights are violated. It is also imperative to evaluate whether the approach taken by states and the international agencies in this area is the most appropriate and effective for the promoting children's rights.

International and national analyses of traditional biomedical practices have typically fallen under the umbrella of children's protection rights. Specifically, scholars and human rights activists raise the following rights of the child as being violated: abuse/neglect; freedom from torture, cruel, inhuman, and degrading treatment; and freedom from violence. These are often intertwined with the reference to the child's right to health and to his or her right to life. Literature in the twenty-first century also brought some of the so-called participatory rights into the discussion. Building on the international trend and the Western underlying principle of an individual's autonomy, scholars refer to the child's right of self-determination as *the* basic source for analysis. Particularly in the context of religio-cultural bodily practices, they emphasize the child's right to religious freedom and point to complexities related to the doctrine of informed consent.

This chapter examines the arguments raised for and against each of these rights. The appropriateness of using the protective (or welfare) approach and the question of the suitability of the participatory model for resolving biomedical conflicts concerning children is examined, yet neither approach is found adequate to the task of handling such complex issues. Drawing on the anthropological and sociopolitical literature, as well as the international legal interpretation of the various traditional bodily practices under consideration (i.e., male circumcision, scarification, extraction of milk teeth, and neck elongation), it can be argued that these models tend to be not only unhelpful, but also destructive in the way they approach children's bioethical rights.

A. ABUSE AND NEGLECT

Both Article 19 of the International Convention on the Rights of the Child (Children's Convention or Convention)[1] and Article 16 of the African Charter on the Rights and Welfare of the Child (African Charter)[2] stipulate that states have the responsibility to protect the child from all forms of abuse, neglect, and maltreatment, with specific reference to such acts that cause physical or mental harm and including sexual abuse.[3] Accordingly, if male circumcision, scarification, the extraction of milk teeth, and neck elongation are defined as abusive, states are required to protect the child, with specific legislative, administrative, social, and educational measures, against the parents, legal guardians, or any other persons responsible for the care of the child who allow the practices to take place. The general question then is whether the customs under consideration indeed fall within the scope of these articles.

William Brigman is one of the scholars who answers the question in the affirmative.[4] He makes an explicit comparison between male circumcision and other bodily modifying rites, such as the removal of earlobes, fingers, and toes, the binding of female feet, infanticide, ritual sacrifice, and "other disfiguring practices around the world," arguing that they all fall within the scope of the term "abuse," from which children are entitled to be protected. "Despite the great concern about child abuse among scholars and legislators in the past twenty years," he charges, "the same type of cultural astigmatism which prevented past generations from perceiving their actions as child abuse prevent contemporary American from perceiving or acknowledging the most widespread form of child abuse in society today: child mutilation through routine neonatal circumcision of males."[5] Charles A. Boner and Michael J. Kinane, Jacqueline Smith, and others make similar accusations, equating circumcision and other forms of ritual body modification with child abuse, hence calling for intervention and legal prohibition.[6]

Whether this is the case, however, is open to debate. To begin with, the concept of child abuse and neglect is hard to pin down, particularly within the international context. The variations in child-rearing beliefs and practices are substantial both across cultures and also within cultures. Just as various

---

[1] Convention on the Rights of the Child, G.A. Res. 44/25, annex, 44th Sess., 61st plenary meeting. U.N. GAOR Supp. (No. 49), at 167, U.N. Doc. A/44/49 (1989), entered into force September 2, 1990, reprinted in 28 I.L.M. 1448 (1989).

[2] African Charter on the Rights and Welfare of the Child, OAU Doc. CAB/LEG/24.9/49 (1990), entered into force November 29, 1999.

[3] Article 19 of the Children's Convention; Article 16 of the African Charter.

[4] William Brigman, "Circumcision as Child Abuse: the Legal and Constitutional Issues," *Journal of Family Law,* 23 no. 3 (1984–85): 337, Library of Circumcision Information and Resource Pages, http://www.cirp.org/library/legal/brigman/.

[5] Ibid.

[6] Charles A. Bonner and Michael J. Kinane, "Circumcision: the Legal and Constitutional Issues," in *2nd Internatonal Symposium on Circumcision,* San Francisco, California, April, 30–May 3, 1991. http://www.nocirc.org/legal/bonner2.php; Jacqueline Smith, "Male Circumcision and the Rights of the Child," 1998, Library of Circumcision Information and Resource Pages, http://www.cirp.org/library/legal/smith/.

initiation rites such as genital operations, facial scarification, and others may be considered in Western eyes as child abuse, so the individualized child-rearing practices in the West are perceived as bizarre, exotic, and damaging to the child's welfare in the eyes of non-Westerners.[7] Judgments are culturally bound, making cross-cultural comparison nearly impossible,[8] and thus precluding the possibility of assuming the validity of a universal standard for child-rearing practices as well as for child abuse and neglect.[9]

Secondly, while a distinction between types of abuse seems to have support, drawing the line between them is complicated. The orthodox definition of child abuse considers four subcategories as falling within the scope of the term: physical abuse, physical neglect, sexual abuse, and emotional abuse.[10] But how are traditional bodily practices configured into these categories? Jill Korbin differentiates in this context between three levels at which the cultural and social context come into play in defining child abuse and neglect. The first level includes child-rearing practices that may be viewed as acceptable by one group but as unacceptable and abusive by another (positive *emic* perspective, negative *etic* perspective). The second level addresses what counts as deviant behavior within the group. It involves, "what more validly may be considered child abuse and neglect. . . . the idiosyncratic departure from culturally and socially acceptable standards that result in harm to a child or compromise his or her physical, emotional, cognitive, social and cultural development." This level is where most agreement between the *emic* and the *etic* perspectives are likely to occur. Finally, the third level deals with child abuse as a symptom of the "sick society." In such cases, the induced harm to children is viewed beyond the control of individual parents and caretakers. Social conditions, such as poverty, unemployment, inadequate housing, poor health care, few educational opportunities, etc., are seen as powerful factors contributing to the incidence of child abuse and neglect.[11]

Traditional bodily practices, however, are not fully compatible with either. They do not fit entirely with the concept of "child rearing practices" as merely the way "to bring up and care for (a child)"[12] because they implicate more than educational measures or the provision of nourishment and support. Different from child-rearing practices such as corporal punishment, traditional bodily practices generally aim at transferring local beliefs (not only knowledge) that

[7] Jill E. Korbin, "The Cross Cultural Context of Child Abuse and Neglect," in *The Battered Child*. 3rd ed., ed. Henry C. Kenpa and Ray Helfer (Chicago: University of Chicago Press, 1980), 23.

[8] Peter Newell, *Children and Violence* (Florence, Italy: UNICEF ICDC, 1997), 5.

[9] Korbin, "The Cross Cultural Context of Child Abuse and Neglect," 23; Jill E. Korbin, "Child Maltreatment in Cross-Cultural Perspective: Vulnerable Children and Circumstances," in *Child Abuse and Neglect: Biosocial Dimensions,* ed. Richard J. Gelles and James B Lancester (New York: Aldin De Gruyter, 1987), 34; David Archard, "Can Child Abuse Be Defined?," in *Moral Agendas for Children's Welfare,* ed. Michael King (New York: Routledge, 1999), 84; Richard J. Gelles and Claire P. Cornell, "International Perspectives on Child Abuse," *Child Abuse & Neglect* 7 (1983): 377.

[10] Archard, 80.

[11] Korbin, "The Cross Cultural Context of Child Abuse and Neglect," 22–23.

[12] *Concise Oxford Dictionary,* 10th ed., s.v. "Rear."

are expected to be internalized in one's self. Furthermore, although both child-rearing practices/educational measures and traditional bodily practices aim at future development, the first often contains institutionalized forms of adult-child dichotomy. They connote power relations whereby adults pass on the knowledge to the younger members of the community who are subordinated to them.[13] Traditional bodily practices, by contrast, aim at enculturation and participation, and while the power relations from the *etic* perspective may at times exist, they are not necessarily perceived as such from the *emic* perspective at all. Some traditional bodily practices are also carried out by the child's peer group (e.g., scarification), and as friends are often credited with substantial impact on his or her development, the two contexts are different. The general discourse on peer relations has to do with documenting children's relationships among themselves as they break away from the parental/adults' authority. The context of traditional bodily practices reflects the children's endorsement of the traditional practices.

With regard to the second level, Korbin argues that there seems to be a general device to distinguish between traditional practices that involve pain and suffering from idiosyncratic forms of maltreatment. However, she also emphasizes that the attempt to compare the various practices, which is inherently contingent on the eyes of the beholder, obscures the issue rather than clarifies it.[14] A similar act of facial scarification, for example, may convey significantly different meanings in different cultures. While among the Maori of New Zealand it is a form of beautification and of ethnic identification, for others it is an unacceptable mutilation.[15]

Finally, traditional bodily practices cannot be generally assumed to exist merely because of poverty, unemployment, and other difficult social conditions. These external factors may have implications for the ways in which the practices are carried out. With regard to male circumcision, scarification, and milk teeth extraction, for example, the Monitoring Committee under the Children's Convention (Children's Committee or Committee) was notified about significant health implications, including the increase in the transmission of HIV/AIDS and hepatitis C infection among young boys and infants who were subjected to the practices in unsterilized conditions by unskilled practitioners in various developing African countries as well as economically disadvantaged

[13] Although power relations within the educational system are generally universal, there have been efforts in the past few years to institute other types of educational systems, such as "democratic schools," "home-schooling," and others. According to Lansdown, the democratic school model has proved to be quite successful. The provision of a supportive and an encouraging environment to children, she argues, was shown to result in a better and more participatory development. Gerison Lansdown, *The Evolving Capacities of the Child* (Florence, Italy: UNICEF & Innocenti Research Centre, 2005), 59–60.

[14] Korbin, "Child Maltreatment in Cross-Cultural Perspective," 3.

[15] Archard, 84; Mohi Rua, "Contemporary Attitudes to Traditional Facial Ta Moko," in *Maori and Psychology: Research and Practice—The Proceedings of a Symposium Sponsored by the Maori and Psychology Research Unit,* ed. N. Robertson (Hamilton, New Zealand: Maori & Psychology Research Unit, 1999), 2, http://wfass-trinity.fass.waikato.ac.nz/docushare/dsweb/Get/Document-999/rua.pdf.

Muslim groups in developed ones.[16] However, it would be insensitive simply to conceptualize religio-cultural bodily practices *as* grounded in a sick culture/ society. It seems unreasonable that the scarce financial resources or other challenging social conditions would not play a role in the continuance of the practices, unless other cultural and moral justifications for the performance of the practices exist. In fact, it may prove the opposite, as *despite* the risky environment, communities and individuals still insist on maintaining the practices.

The issue is still more complicated, as anthropological research and social studies demonstrate that some traditional bodily practices have evolved due to and as a response to other sociopolitical factors. The extraction of milk teeth, for example, is arguably one such practice, where its spread throughout Africa has been attributed to political and social unrest.[17] The practice of neck elongation among the Padaung girls may have originated in the fear of intermarriage and a desire to protect women from abduction.[18] The Makadone group's replacement of their traditional bodily practices of scarification, teeth filling, lip-plug, facial tattoos, and others with "the Muslim version of these rites, with its emphasis on circumcision" has been associated with their immigration from northeastern Mozambique to Tanzania throughout the twentieth century and with their subsequent release from the Portuguese's colonizing power thereby.[19]

Aside from the difficulty of distinguishing between practices that emerge *because* of social ills and those that were historically grounded in religio-cultural rationales, the helpfulness of such assertion is further limited for another reason. Regardless of the origin of the practices, their importance has to be examined as it is construed in a specific historic era. While neck elongation of the Padaung girls is viewed, by some, as completely contingent on economic necessity and historical gender-based discrimination,[20] from the *emic* perspective, the practice today is clearly a matter of ethnic and tribal identification.[21]

---

[16] Committee on the Rights of the Child, *Third Periodic: Finland*, paragraphs 395–398, U.N. Doc. CRC/C/129/Add.5 (January 5, 2005); Committee on the Rights of the Child, *Concluding Observations: South Africa*, paragraph 33, U.N. Doc. CRC/C/15/Add.122 (February 23, 2000); Committee on the Rights of the Child, *Concluding Observations: Lesotho*, paragraphs 43–44, U.N. Doc. CRC/C/15/Add.147 (February 21, 2001); Committee on the Rights of the Child, *Concluding Observations: Zambia*, paragraphs 46–47, U.N. Doc. CRC/C/15/Add.206 (July 2, 2002). See also Jim Rutenberg and Andy Newman, "Mayor Balances Hasidic Ritual Against Fears of Babies' Health," *New York Times*, January 6, 2006, A1, http://www.nytimes.com/2006/01/06/nyregion/06rite.html (discussing neonatal contraction of herpes following circumcision of Ultra-Orthodox Jewish boys in Brooklyn, NY).

[17] Paul. S. Landau, "Explaining Surgical Evangelism in Colonial Southern Africa: Teeth, Pain and Faith," *Journal on African History* 37 (1996): 278.

[18] See "The Pa Dong Village of Nai Soi: A Visit to the Long Necked Women." *Sunbbaytours*. May 14, 2001. http://www.djparadisetour.com/MaeHongSon/ePadong.html.

[19] Tore Saetersdal, "Symbols of Cultural Identity: A Case Study from Tanzania," *African Archaeological Review* 16, no. 2 (1999): 124, 130.

[20] Canela A. Jaramillo, "Defining "Comfort": Padaung Women in Thailand," *Standards* 7, no. 2 (2001), http://www.colorado.edu/journals/standards/V7N2/EDITORIAL/editorial.html.

[21] Jack Picone, "The Ring Cycle," *MATP (Australian Nationwide News)*, June 14, 2003, Magazine, 20, http://www.lexisnexis.com/.

From an *etic* perspective, milk teeth extraction may appear as merely a reflection of the general poor environment in the respective African (developing) nations in which the practice takes place. As such, it may come across as a practice that can be easily eliminated if proper education is provided and if health services are improved.[22] However, the fact that it persists also among members of these groups who moved to Western states, where theoretically, the illness that is attributed to the general society disappears, implies that it is *now* a far more integral element within the specific sociocultural context than the mere construction of what is proper child-rearing practice.

Ultimately, because bodily practices are integral to ostensibly all cultures, banning or condemning one particular practice is likely to either drive the practice underground (as was the case during the first years, for example, with female circumcision) or have it replaced by another bodily practice of one sort or another. Again, the emergence of milk teeth extraction in Angola as a way to get around the missionaries' condemnation of male circumcision[23] is a case at point. Another case in point is the changes that occurred within the Makadone group of Northeastern Mozambique (see above). This suggests that targeting specific practices may merely lead to the endorsement of another harmful practice rather than to the elimination of those practices that violate children's rights in general.

Finally, another shortcoming with the classification of traditional bodily practices as child abuse has to do with the complexity of finding a criterion by which to evaluate the prospective harm. Children may suffer from a variety of harms such as illness, disease, genuine accident, and the like. Yet these harms do not necessarily constitute child abuse in the sense that they establish a direct state responsibility, nor do these harms give rise to the moral obligation to act.[24] David Archard suggests that there are two underlying principles on which the concept of child abuse is constructed. One is the occurrence of a significant or "particularly serious" kind of harm that befalls children. The second is one's (individual or group) responsibility for the harm. However, while there may be consensus on the necessity of these two factors for the definition of child abuse, what actually constitutes this "significant harm," and who is the "human agency" who can be held responsible are controversial.[25]

The complexity of reaching a consensus on what constitutes significant harm is a derivation of the discussion on how child abuse is conceptualized in the first place. It is closely linked with the question of what is, or what should be, the general and universally applicable standard of harm. On the international level, this question is often raised under the auspices of the child's right to life or of the child's right to health. Both rights are stipulated in all international human rights instruments, including general ones, that pertain to all individuals,

---

[22] Sandro Accorsi and others, "The Burden of Traditional Practices, Ebbino and Tea-Tea on Child Health in Northern Uganda," *Social Sciences & Medicine* 57 (2003): 2190.

[23] Landau, 276–77. See also the discussion in Chapter 3.

[24] Archard, 75, 76.

[25] Ibid., 76–77, 81–87.

and child-specific ones.[26] But are these objective and neutral routes?

Most bodily practices do not aim, in themselves, at killing the child or at risking the child's life.[27] The most substantial life-related arguments often raised against male circumcision, scarification, and milk teeth extraction are that when they are carried out without sterilized tools or in an unhygienic environment, there is a greater risk for transmission of HIV/AIDS, hepatitis C, etc. (and yet there are no statistics or information on the number of cases in which the risk

---

[26] Among the general articles about one's right to life are: Article 3 of the Universal Declaration of Human Rights (hereafter UDHR), adopted and proclaimed by G.A. Res. 217 A (III), U.N. Doc A/810, (1948); Article 6 of the International Covenant on Civil and Political Rights (hereafter ICCPR), opened for signature December 16, 1966, G.A. Res. 2200A (XXI), 21st Sess., U.N. GAOR Supp. (No. 16), at 52, U.N. Doc. A/6316 (1966), 999 U.N.T.S. 171, entered into force March 23, 1976; Article 2 of the European Convention for the Protection of Human Rights and Fundamental Freedoms, 213 U.N.T.S. 222, entered into force September 3, 1953, as amended by Protocols Nos. 3, 5, 8, and 11, which entered into force on September 21, 1970, December 20, 1971, January 1, 1990, and November 1, 1998, respectively; and Article 4 of the African [Banjul] Charter on Human and Peoples' Rights, adopted June 27, 1981, OAU Doc. CAB/LEG/67/3 rev. 5, reprinted in 21 I.L.M. 58 (1982), entered into force October 21, 1986 (hereafter African [Banjul] Charter). Both the Children's Convention and the African Charter restate the child's right to life in Articles 6 and 5, respectively.

The main provision for the general right to "the highest standard of health" is stipulated in Article 12 of the International Covenant on Economic, Social and Cultural Rights (hereafter ICESCR), adopted Dec. 16, 1966, G.A. Res. 2200A (XXI), 21 Sess., U.N. GAOR Supp. (No. 16), at 49, U.N. Doc. A/6316 (1966), reprinted in 993 U.N.T.S. 3, entered into force January 3, 1976. An array of other international treaties include provisions on this right as well, including: Article 25 of the UDHR, Article 12 of the Convention on the Elimination of Discrimination against Women (hereafter CEDAW), G.A. Res. 34/180, 34 U.N. GAOR Supp. (No. 46), at 193, U.N. Doc. A/34/46, entered into force September 3, 1981; Article 16 of the African [Banjul] Charter; and Article 11 of the European Social Charter, 529 U.N.T.S. 89, entered into force February 26, 1965. The child's right to the "enjoyment of the highest attainable standard of health" is also restated in the child-specific conventions, in Articles 24(1) and 14 of the Children's Convention and of the African Charter, respectively. See, however, that the wording of the latter is somewhat different, stating in Article 14(1) that "Every child shall have the right to enjoy the best attainable state of physical, mental and spiritual health."

Interestingly, under both the ICCPR and the International Convention on the Protection of Immigrant Workers and Their Families, G.A. Res. 45/158, annex, 45 U.N. GAOR Supp. (No. 49A), at 262, U.N. Doc. A/45/49 (1990), entered into force July 1, 2003, the references made are not to individuals' health but to *public* health, providing a justification to limit other individuals' rights (such as liberty of movement, manifestation of one's religion, and freedom of expression). The only reference to *individuals'* health under the latter convention is in Article 28, which does not follow the wording of "the enjoyment of the highest attainable standard of health" as in the other international treaties, but states the right "to receive any medical care that is urgently required for the preservation of irreparable harm to their health on the basis of equality with nationals of the state concerned. Such emergency medical care shall not be refused them by reason of any irregularity with regard to stay or employment."

[27] See the discussion on the health implications of the various practices in Chapter 3. With the exception of neck elongation, which some have argued may result in death, if removed (yet others insist it is only a myth), male circumcision, scarification, and the extraction of milk teeth are not presumed to have such complications. Even if they may exacerbate the transmission of infectious diseases, they are not carried out for this reason, but rather are a side effect of unsterilized medical and other environments.

actually materialized into life-threatening situations). Similarly, the classification by the Children's Committee on the dangers of neck elongation among the Padaung and the Kareni tribe under Article 24(3) of the Children's Convention is ultimately also somewhat moot. The Committee refers to "sudden death or serious damage to the spinal cord" to justify this categorization. Regardless of the debate as to whether these complications are real or not,[28] the potential hazards, also by the Committee's observation, are not claimed as probable unless the rings are removed. Yet why should they be removed?

In the context of the Padaung tribe in Thailand, some feminists called for the abolition of the practice, charging that it is exploitative, providing "relative economic comfort" at the price of the women and girls' physical *discomfort.*[29] Testimonies of Padaung women from Myanmar where no tourist value to the practice exists, however, do not support that. Their main concern was that they are easily recognized as members of the tribe because of the brass rings, which renders them easier targets for governmental persecution, rather than any particular discomfort that is associated with the practice itself.[30] Instead of the child's right to life, per se, then, an entirely different set of questions, revolving around one's quality of life and the extent to which states are responsible for the unhealthy lifestyles or risky behaviors of its members arise. These, however, may be better addressed through the umbrella of developmental and/or participatory rights, as otherwise the discussion retreats to the paternalistic notion of state-parents-child relations that characterized and preoccupied the discourse prior to the "children's rights revolution."

Approaching traditional bodily practices merely via a concept of risk to one's health is also flawed. It basically endorses a Western/scientific standard of evaluating one's life, although this standard is not universally shared. For individuals who carry out the practices for religious rationales, the performance of any given practice is not a question at all: they follow the practice as a mandatory, religiously ordained rite.[31] Even for secular individuals who follow religiously based bodily practices, there is much more at stake than the evaluation of the (Western) medical justification of the perceived risk or harm. As for the question of harm, children may suffer not only physical harm, but also "a range of other [emotional] harms, such as damage to the child's identity, innocence, integrity, self-confidence, etc.," which the preclusion of these religious and culturally ingrained practices would cause.[32]

---

[28] See Chapter 3.

[29] Jaramillo, note 20.

[30] Daw Pee, "It's a Curse to Be a Women," *Women in Action* 72, no. 1–2 (2000), http://www.isiswomen.org/wia/wia100/index.html. Some may argue that as is often the case in national struggles for self-determination, women tend to subordinate their rights to the national efforts; hence, the lack of reference to any health complication of the practice or to substantial discomfort that it creates should be understood merely as a political stance. Such an argument, however, is too simplistic. External factors of one type or another always play a role in the maintenance of traditional practices. Concluding that the practice should be blamed on this ground, then, would only yield quite a different women's voice.

[31] Ilan Katz, "Is Male Circumcision Morally Defensible?" in *Moral Agendas for Children's Welfare*, ed. Michael King (New York: Routledge), 92.

[32] Ibid., 91–92; Michael King, "Images of Children and Morality," in *Moral Agendas for*

Despite the child's explicit right to preserve his or her identity,[33] these considerations are conventionally never taken into account. The result is that medical justifications for the bodily practice in question are often only used as smokescreens. For minority groups (or, on the international level, for national groups), medical rationales are only a means to defend the practice in the groups' appeal to the "other's" recognition and acceptance, having nothing to do with the cultural groups' adherence to it.[34] For the majority/liberalist groups, such medical justification are either a generic means to rationalize their banning of other's practices or to justify their own bodily practices, which may have not gained sufficient public support as yet (after all, the pursuit of scientific developments is also a culture).

Analyzing the second underlying principle of child abuse of accountability, that is, who is accountable for such abuses, is problematic as well. The most natural response may be to hold the parents or the others who care for the child responsible for carrying out the practice. Still, with customs that are religiously based or that have become so culturally ingrained, the question of who is to blame seems to need a broader address. It does not help in this context, as Archard points out, to try and translate the collective responsibility into a "reduced story" that refers only to certain actions of individuals (mostly the parents). The question rather should be whether children who are harmed while living under certain social and political arrangements are *wronged* by so living.[35] The answer to this question, however, is not at all obvious. Is it wrong for the Padaung girls to have brass rings and to participate and contribute to the familial and communal economic needs? Do the body modifications following circumcision and scarification destine the children to "wronged lives," *because* of the practice? Put more bluntly, is it possible to reach a neutral and objective determination that the child's best interests is to be Jewish, Muslim, Maori, or an atheist? This brings us back to the initial problem of "whose morality?" in the determination of harm should count, which the paternalistic humanist/liberalist alone cannot resolve.

B. TORTURE, CRUEL, INHUMAN, AND DEGRADING TREATMENT

The right to be free from torture, cruel, inhuman, and degrading treatment is stipulated in an array of international instruments, including international human rights law, which is applicable at all times, and humanitarian law, which pertains to armed conflict situations (the Law of War).[36] Additionally, both the

---

Children's Welfare, ed. Michael King (New York: Routledge, 1999), 22.

[33] Article 8 of the Children's Convention.

[34] Katz, 99.

[35] Archard, 83.

[36] Article 5 of the UDHR is the prototype provision. It forbids the use of torture and cruel, inhuman, or degrading treatment or punishment, and it has served as a basis for several subsequent legally binding treaties. Most notable are: the Convention against Torture and Other Cruel, Inhuman or Degrading Treatment or Punishment, G.A. Res. 39/46, annex, 39 U.N. GAOR Supp. (No. 51), at 197, U.N. Doc. A/39/51 (1984), entered into force June 26, 1987; Article 7 of the the ICCPR; and other regional human rights instruments such as Article 5(2) of the American Convention on Human Rights, opened for signature Nov. 22, 1969, O.A.S.T.S. No. 36, 1144 U.N.T.S. 123, entered into force July 18, 1978, reprinted in

Children's Convention and the African Charter contain an explicit stipulation of the right.[37] The prohibition to subject one to such acts is designed to protect all individuals irrespective of their religion, race, nationality or lack of, etc.,[38] and it is generally recognized as binding customary international law.[39]

Traditionally, the prohibition against torture, cruel, inhuman, and degrading treatment was formulated to prevent public officials from utilizing abusive interrogatory methods to extract information from individuals held in custody. The notion has expanded to include states' responsibilities to protect those under their jurisdictions not only from torturous acts "inflicted by people acting in their official capacity," but also from those inflicted by people "outside their official capacity, or in a private capacity."[40] The Human Rights Committee emphasizes that the prohibition relates to both acts that cause physical pain and mental suffering, including corporal punishment, particularly in the context of children.[41] In this vein, scholars and children's activists such as Smith, Abbie J.

Basic Documents Pertaining to Human Rights in the Inter-American System, OEA/Ser.L.V/II.82 doc.6 rev.1, at 25 (1992); Article 3 of the European Convention for the Protection of Human Rights and Fundamental Freedoms, 213 U.N.T.S. 222, entered into force September 3, 1953, as amended by Protocols Nos. 3, 5, 8, and 11, which entered into force on September 21, 1970, December 20, 1971, January 1, 1990, and November 1, 1998, respectively; the European Convention for Prevention of Torture and Inhuman or Degrading Treatment or Punishment, E.T.S. 126, entered into force February 1, 1989 (amended according to the provisions of Protocols No. 1 (ETS No. 151) and No. 2 (ETS No. 152), entered into force on March 1, 2002); Inter-American Convention to Prevent and Punish Torture, Dec. 9, 1985, 25 I.L.M. 51; and Article 5 of the African[Banjul] Charter. The prohibition is also explicitly stipulated in the Four Geneva Conventions of 1949 and their Protocols I and II. See Metthew G. St. Amand, "Public Committee Against Torture in Israel v. The State of Israel et al: Landmark Human Rights Decision by the Israeli High Court of Justice or Status Quo Maintained?" *North Carolina Journal of International Law & Commercial Regulation* 25 (2000): 669; See Suzanne M. Bernard, "An Eye For an Eye: The Current Status of International Law on the Humane Treatment of Prisoners," *Rutgers Law Journal* 25 (1994): 770.

[37] Article 37 of the Children's Convention; Article 16 of the African Charter.

[38] John Quigley, "International Limits on Use of Force to Elicit Confessions: A Critique of Israel's Policy on Interrogation," *Brooklyn Journal of International Law* 16, no. 3 (1988), 485, 491.

[39] Bernard, 789.

[40] Human Rights Committee, *Prohibition of Torture and Cruel Treatment or Punishment (General Comment No. 20)*, 44th Sess. (1992), reprinted in *Compilation of General Comments and General Recommendations Adopted by Human Rights Treaty Bodies*, paragraph 2, U.N. Doc. HRI/GEN/1/Rev.1, at 30 (1994) (hereafter *General Comment No. 20 (Torture)*.)

[41] *General Comment No. 20 (Torture)*, paragraph 5. The context in which the prohibition occurs in these international instruments pertaining to children varies, and it is also different from its address under the ICCPR. Under the African Charter, it is stipulated in the same article that addresses child abuse and neglect; in the Children's Convention it is placed in the context of criminal justice and the right to liberty and security; under the ICCPR, in contrast, it is stipulated in a separate article and includes a particular reference to the prohibition of subjecting one to medical or scientific experimentation without his or her free consent. Whether this placement has any further implications on the scope of the freedom is doubtful. Walter H. Bennett, discussing the 1986 draft of the Children's Convention, argued that this placement is limiting as it appears to create an exclusive link only between children in delinquency procedures and their right to be free from torture, cruelty, etc., and fails to recognize that such abuses exist also in other state-run settings, such as the educational system, child care, treatment facilities, and others. (Interestingly, he does not include the familial, private,

Chessler, James G. Dwyer, and others argue that parents and others who carry out traditional bodily practices such as circumcision and scarification on their children violate their children's rights to be free from torture, cruel, inhuman, and degrading treatment.[42] Specifically with regard to male circumcision, they advance this argument because of the way in which it often takes place and because of the "intense and unwarranted pain that accompanies it."[43]

The *general* international (rather than child-specific) focus on most of the practices under consideration provides some support for such charges. With the exception of neck elongation, all the practices in this present study were raised among the various international agencies in the context of torture, cruel, etc., treatment. In two reports released by the United Nations, male circumcision was mentioned as a human rights violation.[44] The committee monitoring the International Convention on the Elimination of All Forms of Racial Discrimination (ICERD) also enumerated, among the torturous behaviors perpetrated by Serbs against Bosnians, castration, bodily mutilation, and the extraction of teeth. The committee under this treaty found that the various acts constituted criminal acts against humanity and international law.[45] At least in the context of male circumcision, the practice was remarkably mentioned as providing grounds for granting asylum.[46] In a decision delivered

---

setting.) However, children's right to be free from torture, etc., is established also under the general human rights treaties, and Article 41 of the Children's Convention guarantees that "provisions which are more conducive to the realization of the rights of the child" in either national or international law will have precedence. Walter H. Bennett, "A Critique of the Emerging Convention on the Rights of the Child," *Cornell International Law Journal* 20, no. 1 (1987): 13.

[42] Smith, note 6; Abbie J. Chessler, "Justifying the Unjustifiable: Rite v. Wrong," *Buffalo Law Review* 45 (1997): 594, http://www.cirp.org/library/legal/chessler; R. S. Van Howe, J. S. Svoboda, J. G. Dwyer, and C. P. Price, "Involuntary Circumcision: the Legal Issues," *BJU International* 83 (Suppl. 1 1999): 64, http://www.cirp.org/library/legal/vanhowe5/#n27.

[43] Smith, note 6.

[44] M. Cherif Bassiouni and others, "Rape and Sexual Assault: Final report of the United Nations Commission of Experts established Pursuant to Security Council Resolution 780 (1992)," UN Security Council, S/1994/674/Add.2, vol. V, annex IX (1994), http://www.ess.uwe.ac.uk/comexpert/ANX/IX.htm.

[45] Committee on the Elimination of Racial Discrimination, *Documents Submitted in Compliance with a Special Edition of the Committee: Bosnia and Herzegovina (Additional Info from State Party)*, U.N. Doc. CERD/C/247/Add.1 (April 11, 1995).

[46] Cases are distinguished here between those in which the practice *itself* was considered under the rubric of the prohibition of torture, cruel, inhuman, and degrading treatment as establishing sufficient grounds for asylum, and other asylum cases in which the *existence* of the practice created "risk factors" for persecution. The first cases deal with the impact of the bodily practices themselves, whereas the focal point of the latter cases is the discriminatory manner in which minority groups are treated. Such cases raise issues of ethnic cleansing and hatred towards the "other" with no particular relevance to the traditional bodily practices that these other groups follow. This is the case, for example, with the persecution of the Karen group (including the Padaung tribe in Myanmar). Such cases of asylum seekers were raised in at least two communications submitted to the UN Committee against Torture where two applicants requested to be granted asylum in the Netherlands and in Canada, respectively, contending that their scars constitute a risk factor, since they can cause suspicion of involvement in the Tamil Tigers (LTTE) by the Sri Lankan authorities and expose the claimers to intensive and torturous interrogations. In both cases, however, the Committee against

by the German Federal Administrative Court in 1991, a Christian Turkish man was granted political asylum once his fear of being circumcised against his will in compulsory military service was deemed sound.[47]

One could argue that this analysis should apply to traditional bodily practices that are carried out on children. If male circumcision, extraction of teeth, etc., constitute a violation of one's right to be free from torture, cruel, and degrading treatment when carried out on adults, presumably they should be prohibited also when performed on children. After all, the physical harm, pain, and infringement on one's bodily integrity that are associated with the practices, without one's consent, appear similar. Yet while such an argument is generally acceptable, the equation between the two seems to be immensely erroneous. First, it is important to point to the general circumstances of warfare in which the practices were dealt with under the auspices of the committee monitoring the ICERD. The UN reports dealt with massive violations of humanitarian law. In the former Yugoslavia, these included a whole range of sexual assaults including rape, forced and coerced sexual acts, and amputation of sexual organs. Similarly, the report describing forced bodily interventions of Bosnian Serb soldiers was part of the committee's consideration of "torture of prisoners." It was the entire context of prisoners who were subjected to the range of such acts, including the extraction of teeth and circumcision (which also appears to have taken a much more invasive form of mutilation than the neonatal one) that was evaluated and classified as constituting torture. Neither of the practices was singled out as constituting a torturous act in and of itself.

Second, the rationales for carrying out traditional bodily practices such as circumcision, scarification, teeth extraction, and others are vastly different in the two contexts. When the practices are performed within the context of warfare, the practices are inherently a deviant activity. They are perpetrated by individuals, either privately or institutionally, who use their powerful positions with the aim of exploiting and humiliating others. When traditional bodily practices are performed on children, in contrast, they are legitimized as an integral part of one's religious and cultural beliefs, and no such institutionalized intention of humiliation can be assumed.[48] Unlike the warfare and asylum cases that aim at showing the out-group's status of the victims, traditional bodily practices that are performed on children aim at their inclusion within the respective community, albeit with differences in the way in which appropriate inclusion practices are conceptualized. They are performed with a notion of empowerment in mind,

---

Torture rejected the application on the basis of insufficient evidence for such risk. See *S. T. v. the Netherlands,* Communication No. 175/2000, Committee against Torture, 27th Sess., U.N. Doc. CAT/C/27/D/175/2000 (November 23,2001); *V. v. Canada,* Communication No. 47/1996, CAT, 20th Sess., U.N. Doc. CAT/C/20/D/47/1996 (May 19, 1998).

[47] Judgment of November 5, 1991, BverwG, Bundesverwaltungsgericht, Federal Administrative Court, 107 DVBI 828-830 (1992), cited in Steven J. Svoboda, "Attaining International Acknowledgment of Male Genital Mutilation as a Human Rights Violation," in *Male and Female Circumcision—Medical, Legal and Ethical Considerations in Pediatric Practice,* ed. George C Denniston, Frederick Mansfield Hodges, and Marilyn Fayre Milos (New York: Kluwer Academic/Plenum Publishers, 1999), 460.

[48] Katz, 100.

even if the adult-child relationship is a part of it. They provide the historical roots and the sociocultural connectedness that are inherent to human nature, welcoming the child into the responsibilities that membership within the group entails. Simply restating these conclusions is thus wrong, as it constructs (only some) cultures as prisons and parents/communities as vindictive military guards, yet neither is generally correct. All cultures constrain,[49] yet portraying external intervention to prohibit a traditional cultural bodily practice as liberating not only overlooks one's *own* cultural constrains, but also ignores the other's *liberating* cultural characteristics. And perhaps the higher costs are that such conceptualization ultimately undermines the only or the predominant sense of care and trust among parents and children, yet without providing any real replacement and alternatives.

Again, this does not mean that all bodily practices should be allowed. Absolute "cultural relativism" may be totalitarian in terms of advancing children's rights just as much as an absolute cultural "'universalist" approach may be. The "lack of intention to humiliate" or the contrary, the intention to benefit the child, do not in and of themselves protect a traditional practice from being categorized as a human rights violation and abuse. Yet the general context and rationales must be taken into account. It is particularly so as Geraldine Van Bueren points out,

> although it may be true that there is global recognition that the attaching of electrodes to children in detention in Turkey amounts to torture, there is not universal agreement when one moves away from the more extreme forms of direct state action, particularly when one considers practices, for which the state may be liable, initiated within the family.[50]

Considering the utmost moral condemnation acts of torture, cruel, inhuman, and degrading treatment demand, holding these traditional bodily practices to the same classification *within* the family runs the risk of tearing down, unjustly, the basic unit on which individuals, societies, nations, and international citizens are built.

C. FREEDOM FROM VIOLENCE

There is no explicit right to be free from violence. Traditionally, it has been built on a combination of a few other explicitly stated rights, including human dignity and bodily integrity, the right to liberty and security, freedom from slavery, the right not to be subject to torture, inhuman, or degrading treatment or punishment and abuse.[51] It has been further constructed as a right that is

---

[49] Janet E. Halley, "Culture Constrains," in *Is Multiculturalism Bad for Women?* ed. by Susan M. Okin (Princeton, NJ: Princeton University Press, 1999), 100.

[50] Geraldine Van Bueren, "Children's Rights: Balancing Traditional Values and Cultural Plurality," in *Children's Rights and Traditional Values,* ed. by Gillian Douglas and Leslie Sebba (Burlington, VT: Ashgate Publishing, 1998), 16.

[51] Corinne A. A. Packer, *Using Human Rights to Change Tradition: Traditional Practices Harmful to Women's Reproductive Health in Sub-Saharan Africa* (Oxford: Antwerpen Intersentia, 2002), 63.

broader than the mere reference to child abuse or to the prohibition against torture, cruel, inhuman, and degrading treatment. Thus, although both these two categories were found inappropriate, there is still a need to examine whether addressing religio-cultural bodily practices could and should be under the umbrella of a general right to be free from violence.

Violence against children is commonly defined as "deliberate behavior by people against people liable to cause physical or psychological harm."[52] It includes sexual abuse and exploitation, a wider range of other societal forms of violence (poverty, child labor, lack of adequate health care, and education, etc.), unintentional neglect by the state, parents, and other caretakers, and, interestingly, also self-inflicted violence by children as perpetrators of violence.[53] This definition seems to have evolved from the one adopted in the context of violence against women. It is broader, however, as the latter merely builds on a gender-based rationale.[54] Some argue that the definition in the context of children reflects the intention to avoid some of the cultural relativism defense and to include, within the scope of the term, the "many other forms of violence that are harmful to children [yet] lie outside common definitions of child abuse."[55] It remains unclear, however, to what extent using the category of violence to address traditional bodily practices that are carried out on children is useful.

Discussing harmful traditional practices affecting women's reproductive health, Corinne Packer points out the substantial flaw in the existing work on traditional practices and violence. Although the definition used encompasses "any act of gender-based violence that results in or is likely to result in, physical, sexual or psychological harm or suffering to women . . . whether occurring in public or in private life,"[56] the inclusion of harmful traditional practices has been made by what she termed the "blanket gender-violence approach." With the exception of female circumcision that is explicitly mentioned, other traditonal practices are grouped together as "other traditional practices harmful to women,"[57] assuming that the only reason for their performance is gender discrimination, and without any further explanation "which other rights, beyond those protecting from violence, may be drawn upon."[58] Consequently, all harmful traditional practices are automatically equated with violence against women, which, given the obvious erroneous nature of such a statement, dooms it to fail. The result of this approach, she explains, is that:

---

52 Newell, 2.

53 Ibid., 2, 5–8, 11, 14.

54 Under the international human rights system, references explicitly prohibiting violence against women are stipulated mainly in "soft law" documents, including: the Declaration on the Elimination of Violence against Women G.A. Res. 48/104, 48 U.N. GAOR Supp. (No. 49), at 217, U.N. Doc. A/48/49 (1993); Committee on the Elimination of Discrimination against Women, *Violence against Women (General Recommendation 19),* 11th Sess. (1992), U.N. Doc. A/47/38, at 1 (1993), reprinted in *Compilation of General Comments and General Recommendations Adopted by Human Rights Treaty Bodies,* U.N. Doc. HRI/GEN/1/Rev.6, at 243 (2003); and others.

55 Newell, 2.

56 Article 1 of the Declaration on Violence against Women.

57 Article 2 of the Declaration on Violence against Women.

58 Packer, 64–65.

> [I]t is difficult both to convince the skeptical and to devise practical strategies and programmes to effect changes of behavior. It also fails to provide or indicate any criteria by which important distinctions might be made among various traditional practices, some of which might not always be harmful or, even if harmful, not in all cases violent or, ultimately, human rights violation.[59]

Thus, it is evidently inapt to deliver any appropriate remedy or to advance the human rights discourse on harmful traditional practices.

The discussion of traditional bodily practices and violence in the context of children follows, to a great extent, the discourse on violence against women. There is often an explicit comparison between women and children as vulnerable victims of violence. This is particularly so within the family/private sphere, where historical inequality (and, in the context of children, also their dependency) prevented an appropriate address.[60] Harmful traditional practices are regarded as just one among many violent acts committed against children, such as infanticide, physical assault, sexual abuse, and illicit transfer and abduction of children.[61] However, it gives no particular account of the differences in what constitutes these various categories, although the motivation and rationales for corporal punishment and male circumcision, for example, are clearly substantially different.

Similar to the discourse on violence against women, traditional practices performed on a child are simply assumed as involving an invasion of the child's bodily integrity and are equated with violence.[62] Furthermore, ostensibly all internationial bodies addressing the issue of harmful traditional practices have focused predominantly, and commonly also exclusively, on women and girls. This includes not only the international bodies specializing in the rights of women/girls, but also the Children's Committee and the UN Secretary-General's Independent Expert on the Study of Violence Against Children.[63] There is

---

[59] Ibid., 66.

[60] Newell, 2.

[61] Ibid., 4–8.

[62] Ibid., 8.

[63] The UN Secretary-General's Independent Expert on the Study of Violence against Children, Mr. Paulo Sérgio Pinheiro, was appointed in 2003 "to conduct an in-depth study on the question of violence against children and to put forward recommendations for consideration by Member States for appropriate action." He submitted his first comprehensive report to the General Assembly on August 19, 2005, and a second report on October 11, 2006. He delivered a statement as a follow-up Progress Report in October 2007. In his 2005 report, the independent expert referenced only female circumcision and other harmful traditional practices carried out on girls (see paragraphs 17, 32, 44 and 53). While his 2006 report mentions also "scarring, burning, branding," and other harmful traditional practices, he relies mainly on the documentation of the Special Rapporteur on Harmful Traditional Practices (paragraph 46). In his statement to the General Assembly in 2007, he did not make any explicit reference to harmful traditional practices. U.N. General Assembly, *Report of the Independent Expert for the United Nations Study on Violence against Children,* 60th Sess., U.N. Doc. A/60/282 (August 19, 2005); U.N. General Assembly, *Report of the Independent Expert for the United Nations Study on Violence against Children,* U.N .General Assembly, 61st Sess., U.N. Doc. A/61/299 (August 29, 2006); *Statement by Mr. Paulo Sérgio Pinheiro, Independent Expert for the United Nations Secretary-General's Study on Violence against Children,* U.N. General Assembly, 62nd Sess., http://

thus a false impression that these practices are carried out only on girls *because* of a gender bias against them. Not only does such an approach relegate the discusson to a much narrower one than it should be (practically, ignoring the entire group of boys), but it is also not necessarily supported in the literature.

Anthropological studies have shown that culturally sanctioned rites are often not perceived even by the children themselves as abusive, violent, or, even if violent, as violating their rights to bodily integrity or of any other rights.[64] As Korbin points out, however painful and terrifying some of the traditional practices may be, both adults who perform and perpetuate the rites and children who are subjected to them, view them as having a positive long-term value that outweighs the physical pain and the emotional fear.[65] Thus, for example, testimonies of boys who were circumcised and of girls who were scarified as rites of passage have expressed, along with the fear and pain, the excitement, pride, and dignity that these practices provided them.[66]

Given these expressed views and rationales, it is apparent that the notion of a violent act as the forceful usage of physical power against another with an intention to hurt, damage, or kill, does not apply.[67] This does not mean that all traditional bodily practices should be allowed or defensible if they have a significant collective value. However, the moral condemnation of such practices as violent acts and abuse and the accompanying call to act and eradicate them are unsuitable.

D. FREEDOM OF THOUGHT, CONSCIENCE, AND RELIGION

Freedom of thought, conscience, and religion is considered to be one of the most fundamental human rights. For some, it is even *the* most basic right, the "mother of rights" from which all others rights are to be derived.[68] It should thus come as no surprise that the freedom of thought, conscience, and religion is explicitly stipulated in many general international human rights treaties, most significantly the Universal Declaration of Human Rights (UDHR), the International Covenant on Civil and Political Rights (ICCPR), and the 1981 Declaration on the Elimination of All Forms of Intolerance and of Discrimination Based on Religion or Belief (Declaration on Religious Freedom or Belief), as well as in those pertaining specifically to children.[69]

---

www.violencestudy.org/IMG/pdf/62_UNGA_statement.pdf.

[64] Heidi Gengenbach, "Boundaries of Beauty: Tattooed Secrets of Women's History in Magude District, Southern Mozambique," *Journal of Women's History* 14, no. 4 (2003): 115–21. Such studies will be discussed in Section E.2.

[65] Korbin, "Children, Childhood, and Violence," 434.

[66] Katz, 90; Gengenbach, 119, 136.

[67] The *Concise Oxford Dictionary* defines violence as "behavior involving physical force intended to hurt, damage or kill" (*Concise Oxford Dictionary,* 10th ed., s.v. "violence").

[68] James E. Wood, "An Apologia for Religious Human Rights," in *Religious Human Rights in Global Perspective—Religious Perspective,* ed. Johan D. van der Vyver and John Jr. Witte (The Hague: Martinus Nijhoff Publishers, 1996), 475.

[69] Article 18 of ICCPR; Article 18 of the UDHR; Declaration on the Elimination of All Forms of Intolerance and of Discrimination Based on Religion or Belief, G.A. Res. 36/55, 36 U.N. GAOR Supp. (No. 51), at 171, U.N. Doc. A/36/684 (1981). See also Article 12 of the International Convention on the Protection of the Rights of All Migrant Workers and Mem-

Both Article 14 of the Children's Convention and Article 9 of the African Charter stipulate that "everyone has the right to freedom of thought, conscience and religion," following the wording of Article 18 of the UDHR and of the ICCPR. Under the general human rights instruments, the stated right includes also the freedom to have and to adopt religion or belief by one's choice and "to manifest one's religion or belief in worship, observance, practice and teaching."[70] True to its spirit, the latter is further allowed to take place either alone, in community with others, in public, or in private. The communal aspect of the freedom is also explicitly stressed with regards to individuals belonging to ethnic, religious, or linguistic minorities in both the ICCPR and the Children's Convention, restating their right "to enjoy their own culture, to profess and practice their religion and to use their language."[71]

Although there seems to be consensus on the importance of the right, the context of children is more complicated. At least a part of the argument against traditional bodily practices revolves around the question of what does it actually mean that the child has a right to freedom of thought, conscience and religion. Scholars and human rights activists raise, in particular, two main charges. One is that devout parents are unable to acknowledge and accept that their child may develop along different paths than theirs or hold different opinions and beliefs than them.[72] Thus, so the argument further goes, carrying out the traditional bodily practices unreasonably infringes on the right of the child to religio-cultural self-determination. They coerce children into a religious or cultural system and deprives them of the right to make their *own* religious and cultural judgments. As such, they contradict Article 18(2) of the ICCPR that prohibits subjecting one to coercion that impairs his or her choice of religion or belief. They are destructive of the natural development of the child's own cultural identity.[73]

The other argument has to do with the concern that the preservation of religiously based bodily practices comes at the price of the child as an autonomous individual and as an end in him or herself. Allowing parents and the community to carry out such practices on their children, it is argued, also accords them control over the life and body of another person. As Dwyer contends, it allows them to "simply adopt an instrumental view of children, treating them as mere means to the furtherance of other persons' ends [i.e., to the community's religious preservation]."[74] This result, however, breaches the most fundamental moral and legal principle by which one cannot in any way be considered or treated as the property of another.[75]

---

bers of Their Families.

[70] Article 18 of the UDHR; Article 18(1) of the ICCPR; and Article 1(1) of the Declaration on the Elimination of All Forms of Intolerance and of Discrimination Based on Religion or Belief.

[71] Article 27 of the ICCPR; Article 30 of the Children's Convention. Interestingly, the African Charter does not contain a parallel provision on the rights of minority groups.

[72] James G. Dwyer, "Parents' Religion and Children's Welfare: Debuking the Doctrine of Parents' Rights," *California Law Review* 82 (1994): 1440–41.

[73] Ibid., 1410.

[74] Ibid.

[75] Ibid.

On these grounds, scholars and human rights activists have advocated in recent years for a prohibition of religio-cultural bodily practices that are carried out on children. Their underlying assumption is that upholding the *child's* autonomous and independent right to religious freedom will remedy both concerns. The first question is hence whether the child's religious freedom is, indeed, an autonomous and independent right. The more crucial one, however, is whether the conceptualization of religion and religious rights, including their forms of manifestation, coincides with the child's *own* voice, and, in view of that, whether it is the suitable approach to take.

1. Children's Religious Freedom as an Autonomous Right

Discussing religion and children's right in the post-Children's Convention era, Philip Veerman and Caroline Sand argue that "Article 14 of the Children's Convention relates to the child as the subject of rights and it is clearly the *child* who exercises this right to freedom of religion."[76] Others also emphasize that under the Convention, parents are viewed only as *trustees of the state.* They are given a role in enforcing the child's independent right but not the independent right to entrench *their* religious convictions on their child.[77] This approach is rooted in the liberalist notion of individualism, where even the family, "is increasingly seen not as separate entity, but rather 'as simply the sum of its component parts, as a collective of individuals united temporarily for their mutual convenience and with rights against one another'."[78] Yet whether children have an autonomous and independent right to religious freedom under the international system is open to debate.

Indeed, others, by contrast, believe that the restatement of the right was not intended to establish an autonomous and independent religious freedom of children. The objection is grounded in a few rationales. First, many of the religious groups do not adhere to the individualistic notion of liberalism. According to Christianity, for example, the family is a collective institution, with its own integrity, destiny, purpose, and responsibilities before God.[79] Rights are God-mandated, "something given and conferred on others by active obedience to god."[80] Religious guidance is considered one such obligation, a part of the parental responsibility and duty of which one is accountable to God.[81] Similarly, even if, biblically, children are subjects with rights, those rights should be balanced with their responsibility to God and obedience to their parents as primary caregivers.[82]

---

[76] Philip Veermen and Caroline Sand, "Religion and Children's Rights," *International Journal of Children's Rights* 7, no. 4 (1999): 386.

[77] Rex J. Ahdar, "Children's Religious Freedom, Devout Parents and the State," in *Law and Religion in Contemporary Society: Communities, Individualism and the State,* ed. Peter W. Edge and Graham Harvey (Aldershot, UK: Ashgate Publishing, 2000), 98.

[78] Ibid., 99.

[79] Ibid., 101.

[80] Paul Stephenson, "Describe the "Rights" of the Child and the Christian Response to It," http://www.viva.org/?page_id=267.

[81] Rex J. Ahdar, "The Right of the Child to a Godly Future," *International Journal of Children's Rights* 10, no. 1 (2002): 97.

[82] Stephenson, note 80.

For others, religion is perceived as innate, a characteristic that one cannot dispense with. In Judaism, for instance, the child's religion is a birthright that follows the mother's religion, and under the religious law, no conversion can ever fully take place. For Muslims, the child's religion follows the father's, and the child has no autonomous and independent say about it at all.[83] This argument was explicitly raised during the drafting of the Children's Convention and was in fact also the main reason for diverting from the terminology adopted in other general human rights instruments addressing religious freedom.[84] Thus, unlike the UDHR, the ICCPR, and the Declaration on Religious Freedom or Belief, the Children's Convention does not contain a reference to the child's right to adopt a religion or belief by his or her choice. Theoretically, this omission cannot take away from the child's already guaranteed right under other international instruments. Yet, ostensibly, all Muslim states have placed specific reservations on this matter to prevent such an option from materializing.[85] Thus, in practice, the number of children who are legally entitled to an independent right to religious freedom is clearly far from universal.

Second, parents hold a recognized interest, and even a right and a duty, to entrench their *own* religious convictions on their children. This is most evident in the context of education. Article 18(4) of the ICCPR requires states to "respect the liberty of parents, and when applicable, legal guardians, to ensure the religious and moral education of their children in conformity with their own convictions." Article 5(2) of the Declaration on Religious Freedom or Belief is more unequivocal. Although referring to the *child's* right to have access to education in the matter of religion or belief and to the right not to be compelled to receive teaching on such matters, the right is contingent on the wishes of his or her parents or legal guardians. Yet the parental influence role on the child's religious freedom goes far beyond mere religious education. The principle of respect for family autonomy is well established in international law[86] and, in the particular context of children, parents or legal guardians explicitly hold primary responsibility for the upbringing and direction of the child. Article 5(1) of the Declaration on Religious Freedom or Belief explicitly stipulates the right of parents (or legal guardians) "to organize the life within

---

[83] Sharon Detrick, ed., *The United Nations Children's Convention: A Guide to the "Travaux Preparatoires"* (Dordrecht: Martinus Nijhoff, 1992) 244–48.

[84] U.N. Economic and Social Council,, *Report of the 1989 Working Group on a Draft Convention on the Rights of the Child,* 45th Sess., Agenda Item 13, paragraphs 16, 280–291, U.N. Doc. E/CN.4/1989/48 (March 2, 1989) (*Legislative History* on Article 14 (Religious Freedom), 11, 19–20.

[85] For the list of reservations on Article 14 of the Children's Convention, see http://www.unhchr.ch/html/menu3/b/treaty15_asp.htm.

[86] See Article 17 of the ICCPR, Article 8 of the European Convention for the Protection of Human Rights and Fundamental Freedoms, and Article 11 of the African Charter. The international "soft law" further establishes this principle. See, for example, Human Rights Committee, *The Rights of the Child (General Comment No. 17),* 35th Sess. (1989), reprinted in *Compilation of General Comments and General Recommendations Adopted by Human Rights Treaty Bodies,* U.N. Doc. HRI\GEN\1\Rev.1, at 23 (1994). See also the Preamble of the Children's Convention, upholding the family as "the fundamental group of society and the natural environment for the growth and well-being of all its members, and particularly children." The Preamble does not have legally binding force as do the articles of the Convention.

the family *in accordance with their religion or belief.*" Taking into account, as scholars point out, that religious values and beliefs cannot be simply told to a child but have to be lived,[87] separating the parental right and responsibility from the child's autonomous religious freedom is clearly artificial.

Finally, the child's exercise of his or her religious rights is fatally intertwined with and largely dependent on others' interests, rights, and duties. While this constraint is not necessarily limited only to children's exercise of their religious rights,[88] it is more clear, and acute, in their regard. Parents or other legal guardians have the primary responsibility to provide direction to the child *in the exercise of his or her religious right.*[89] When the family is perceived as failing, state officials are presumed to have the justification to do so on the child's behalf. Either way, it is other adults (parents, grandparents, communities, courts, and other state agencies) who make the child's exercise of his or her religious right feasible.

Rex J. Adhar's study of the case law is most illuminative in this regard. Examining courts decisions delivered in the United States, England, New Zealand, and others where conflicts between the parents and the child's religious freedom occurred,[90] he found that while there is an increasing tendency to hear the child's views, evidently all courts voted for the "orthodoxy" conceptualization of religious right. There has not been one case, so far, he stresses, in which the courts accepted a child or adolescent's claim for religious adherence that is distinguished from the parental one.[91] While in "fractured family" or "spiritual custody" cases children's views on their religious preferences appear as receiving greater weight (in comparison to views of children from intact families),[92] the

---

[87] Stephen Frosh, "Identity, Religious Fundamentalism and Children's Welfare," in *Moral Agendas for Children's Welfare,* ed. Michael King (New York: Routledge, 1999), 207.

[88] The communal feature of religious community and the interdependency among its members are, by definition, it is safe to say, a part of what religious freedom is all about. One could even argue that without the collective gatherings, ceremonies, religious rites, and other communal practices that are associated with particular faiths, no religious freedom, in general, can be exercised. In Orthodox Judaism, for example, some of the prayers can be carried out only if there is a *minyan* of ten men, including boys from the age of thirteen.

[89] Under Article 14(2) of the Children's Convention, the parents have the "right and duty" to provide guidance and direction to the child's exercise of right, whereas under the African Charter, only the parental *duty* is stated.

[90] The information available on such conflicts and their resolution is quite sparse, especially in Africa, Asia, and the Middle East. Two of the reasons that come to mind are the difficulties children have in approaching legal institution and the Islamic concept by which the child follows the father's religion and has no right to change it.

[91] Ahdar, "Children's Religious Freedom," 94–95.

[92] Yet see, in contrast, Ronen's comparative discussion on spiritual custody cases in Canada and in Israel. Both revolved around spiritual custody cases, in which one parent became a member of the Jehovah's Witnesses subsequent to the divorce, yet the courts reached opposite results, both seemingly ignoring, in practice, the children's own views. Thus, for example, the Canadian court ruled on the basis of the child's best interests, upholding the father's request, although the children expressed that they do not want to be exposed to his new religious tenets. Justice Shamgar of the Israeli Supreme Court, in contrast, although using children's rights terminology and the child's right to religious freedom, "interpreted" the children's views that they want to have the parental conflict over with, and their lack of explicit expression of a desire to join the mother's new religious community (although

choice given essentially remained between the religions of the parents rather than a separate religious choice of the child.[93] In practice, then, the decisions remained greatly paternalistic. Regardless of the terminology courts use (the child's best interests or the child's right to religious freedom), ultimately, they follow their own underlying ideology. This includes not only the traditional assumption that adults know better, but also a question of what conforms to the majority's views (rather than tolerance to pluralism) and to the national preference.[94]

In the end, then, a discussion of the child's autonomous and independent right to religious freedom, or any other individual for that matter, simply seems to miss the point. Whether the child's religious preferences are indeed given sufficient weigh, if they are accepted or dismissed on the basis of the child's best interests or on the principle of the child's evolving capacity, the child's "autonomous and independent" exercise of his or her religious freedom is protected only to the extent that he or she is permitted to do so as determined by others.

2. Children's Views of Religion

In view of the emerging concept of children as individual subjects of rights, there is yet still another question to address: to what extent do children's views on religion actually correspond to those of adults?

Studies of children in a variety of contexts have shown that children have their own views and concerns that are distinct from those expressed by adults. Although there is only limited research conducted on children's views on religion and religious freedom, the little that exists demonstrates that there is no reason to assume that it is otherwise. Thus, for example, research with Christian children showed that their images of Jesus are substantially different from adults. Children view Jesus as more human than divine, more of a healer, leader, and great teacher rather than the common image of Jesus as God's son or as a savior.[95] In another cross-cultural study conducted among children (mean

they remained in her custody) as a preference to continue with their Jewish education. Ya'ir Ronen, Ya'ir, "The Child's Right to Identity as a Right to Belong," *Tel Aviv University Law Review* 26, no. 3 (2003): 966–69.

93 Ahdar, "Children's Religious Freedom," 95. The question whether courts enforce children's independent right to religious freedom is different from the question whether such an independent right exists. Courts' decisions are an issue of public policy that can develop and change over time, whereas fundamental rights either exist or not. See for example, Alison D. Renteln, *The Cultural Defense* (Oxford: Oxford University Press, 2004). The reluctance of courts to allow for "cultural evidence" does not undermine the existence of minority's cultural rights, although the principle of justice, in her view, requires that they allow so.

94 Bilsky's essay, "*Child-Parent-State: the Absence of Community in the Courts' Approach to Education*," discussing courts' cases in Israel, is most compelling in this regard. Among the rationales Israeli courts provide are, for example, "Here in Israel, as opposed to the Diaspora, a Jewish child who lives among his own people should not be made to feel so very different from his peers." See Leora Bilsky, "Child-Parent-State: the Absence of Community in the Courts' Approach to Education," in *Children's Rights and Traditional Values*, ed. Gillian Douglas and Leslie Sebba (Burlington, VT: Ashgate Publishing, 1998), 134–59. See also Ronen, 966–67.

95 Karen Walshe, "What do Young People Today Really Think About Jesus?" *British Jour-*

age, eleven years old) in Finland, Hong Kong, and Bahrain, the researchers found that children are more interested in spiritual issues than in religious ones,[96] that girls were more interested in religious questions than boys, and that gifted children (regardless of sex) were generally more interested in scientific questions than religious ones.[97]

Whether these childish views should make a difference in courts' decisions in favor of one religious upbringing or another may be open to debate. One should be careful not to infer any conclusions from these views as to the practical and behavioral aspect of religious manifestation. Claims of this sort would be highly speculative, perhaps also culturally inappropriate, and even impossible.[98] These differences in adults' and children's views, however, do call into question whether concentrating on conflict resolution between the parental religious liberty to entrench their beliefs in their child and the religious freedom of the child, or between the state's set of beliefs versus the parental one, goes hand in hand with the Children's Convention and with children's right hitherto. Once again, it may be the case that by taking on this path, it is not the child's religious freedom that is actually upheld but how and what it is assumed to be by those who decide on his or her behalf. If this is so, then endorsing this path undermines what has been the cornerstone of the children's rights revolution.

E. INFORMED CONSENT

Another argument commonly raised is that traditional bodily practices contravene the well-established doctrine of informed consent. This section will examine this contention.

1. Doctrine of Informed Consent—Historical Context

The doctrine of informed consent first emerged in the practice of medicine. It developed in response to the shocking testimonies of Holocaust survivors in the era following World War II and represents the struggle to give the patient a voice in medical decision making and to level the playing field between patients and their physicians. It grants the patient the right to decide whether to subject him or herself to medical procedures, outlawing those that do not meet the doctrine's requirements. Particularly, the doctrine necessitates the existence of two conditions. One is that the patient is informed, that is, that he or she receives all relevant information on the procedure (expected benefits, possible risks and complications, alternative medical treatments, etc.) to enable him or her reach the second condition, namely that of consent (and by implication, also of refusal to consent).[99] The underlying principle of the doctrine is rooted

nal of Religious Education 27, no. 1 (2005): 66, 74.

[96] Spiritual issues were seen as "broader than religious ones, and they are not necessarily linked to any traditional religion." Kirsi Tirri, Mary K. Tallen Runnels, and Petri Nokelainen, "A Cross-Cultural Study of Pre-Adolescents' Moral, Religious and Spiritual Questions," *British Journal of Religious Education* 27 no. 3 (2005): 212.

[97] Ibid., 212–213.

[98] See Section E.2 on children's informed consent.

[99] Whether the right to consent to medical treatment includes the right to refuse to consent is controversial. Some argue that granting one a right to refuse life-saving medical

in the notion of respect for an individual's choice and to his or her right to self-determination in health care decision making.[100] Thus, without an informed consent, any voluntary physical contact by another person, even if no harm was done, may give rise to a civil claim (for assault) or to a criminal assault charge.[101]

The application of the doctrine of informed consent in the context of children's bioethics has been highly contentious. Unlike adults, the underlying assumption is that children lack autonomy. They have been conceptualized as incapable of receiving the necessary information and, all the more so, going through the process of translating it into a rational choice. Thus, a proxy's substitute consent (traditionally, consent of the parents or other legal guardians) was generally required on the child's behalf, assuming that he or she would make a decision that is in the child's best interests. Although states have the power to intervene and override the proxy's decision as the child's *parens patria,* if the parents and others who are responsible for the child fail to do so,[102] they commonly reserved this option only to extreme ones, most notoriously those revolving around the proxy's *refusal* to consent to a proposed medical treatment on the basis of religio-cultural beliefs.[103]

With the children's rights revolution, however, at least the legal approach has changed. States are expected to be more active in the protection of the child's rights, and, furthermore, the manner in which the child is to participate in medical decision making and provide consent is on the agenda. The issue was one of the key themes discussed during the drafting process of the Children's Convention, with proposals to integrate it both under "respect to the views of the child" (Article 12) and under a paragraph dealing with medical interventions and experimentation in the context of the child's right to health (Article 24). Although no explicit reference eventually remained in the Convention, it was

---

treatment on the basis of one's autonomy undermines in itself the concept of autonomy of the patient and makes it meaningless. Overriding the latter is thus arguably easier to justify. See, for example, Marc Stauch, "Rationality and the Refusal of Medical Treatment: A Critique of the Recent Approach of the English Courts," *Journal of Medical Ethics* 21 (1995): 164.

[100] Carole M. Lannon and others, "Circumcision Policy Statement," *Pediatrics* 103, no. 3 (1999): 686.

[101] Queensland Law Reform Commission, *Circumcision of Male Infants Research Paper* (Brisbane, 1993), Library of Circumcision Information and Resource Pages, http://www.cirp.org/library/legal/QLRC/, sec. 4.

[102] Clare Dyer, *Doctors, Patients and the Law* (Oxford: Blackwell Scientific Publishing, 1992), 83.

[103] The focus here is on the question of parental and others' *positive* consent for bodily intervention carried out on their child. There is ample literature addressing courts' decisions overriding parents' refusal of medical treatment for their child on the basis of their religious convictions. See, for example, Adam Lamparello, "Taking God Out of the Hospital: Requiring Parents to Seek Medical Care for Their Children Regardless of Religious Belief," *Texas Forum on Civil Liberties & Civil Rights* 6 (2001): 47–115; Elizabeth A. Lingle, "Treating Children by Faith Colliding Constitutional Issues," *Journal of Legal Medicine* 17 (1996): 301–30; Martha Swartz, "The Patient Who Refuses Medical Treatment: A Dilemma for Hospitals and Physicians," *American Journal of Law & Medicine* 11 (1985): 147–94; Ahdar also refers to such cases from the United States, England, New Zealand, and others. Adhar, "The Right of the Child to a Godly Future," 96–97.

understood that the doctrine is inherently included at least within Article 12.[104]

On a general level, there is no doubt that the Children's Committee has made a considerable effort to incorporate the doctrine into the context of children's bioethics. Requiring a shift towards a notion of children as active agents, the Committee formulated two specific guidelines to address the issue of medical treatment and children's participation. In its General Guidelines for Article 1 on the definition of the child, it made a straightforward request that states provide information on the minimum national legal age for medical treatment or surgery without parental consent.[105] In its General Guidelines for Article 24 on health, it further requested states "to indicate the measures adopted to ensure respect for the general principles of the Convention," including respect for the child's views.[106]

The Children's Committee also emphasized the importance of children's agency in its General Comments. It referred to children's entitlement to participate in raising awareness and in developing policies and programs to address HIV/AIDS;[107] in its consideration of children with disabilities, the Committee emphasized the importance of involving them in the process of decision making with regard to policies related to them and to their needs in various bodies such as parliament, committees, and other forums where they may voice views on such matters[108]; in the context of adolescent health, the Committee required that states set minimum ages of, among others, medical consent that "closely reflect recognition of the status of human beings under the ages of 18 as rights holders in accordance with their evolving capacity age and maturity";[109] and in its General Comments on "Implementing Child's Rights in Early Childhood," the Committee accentuated that

> the right to express views and feelings should be anchored in the child's daily life at home (and including, when applicable, the extended family) and in his or her community; within the full range of early childhood health, care and education facilities, as well as in legal proceedings; and in the development of policies and services, including through research and consultations.[110]

---

[104] See discussion in Chapter 2.

[105] Part II, paragraph 24 of the Committee on the Rights of the Child, *General Guidelines Regarding the Form and Contents of Periodic Reports to be Submitted by States Parties under Article 44, paragraph 1(b) of the Convention,* U.N. Doc. CRC/C/58 (November 20, 1996) (hereafter General Guidelines).

[106] Part VI, part B, paragraph 93 of the General Guidelines.

[107] *General Comment No. 3 (HIV/AIDS),* paragraph 12; Committee on the Rights of the Child, *Adolescent Health and Development in the Context of the Convention on the Rights of the Child* (*General Comment No. 4*), 33rd Sess., paragraph 39, U.N. Doc. CRC/GC/2003/4 (2003). (hereafter *General Comment No. 4 (Adolescent Health).*)

[108] Committee on the Rights of the Child, *The Rights of Children with Disabilities* (*General Comment No. 9*), 43rd Sess. paragraph 32, U.N. Doc. CRC/C/GC/9 (2007) (hereafter *General Comment No. 9 (Children with Disabilities).*)

[109] *General Comment No. 4 (Adolescent Health),* paragraph 9.

[110] Committee on the Rights of the Child, *Implementing Child Rights in Early Childhood (General Comment No. 7),* 41st Sess., paragraph 11(b), U.N. Doc. CRC/C/GC/7 (2005) (here-

"Young children," the Committee emphasized, "are themselves able to contribute to ensuring their personal health and encouraging healthy lifestyles among their peers, for example through participation in appropriate, child-centered health education programmes."[111]

In practice, however, states display divergent views of children's participation in the context of medical treatment. Moreover, despite the Children's Committee's comments, its own message is dual and somewhat ambiguous. A few examples will suffice to clarify this point. According to the states' reports submitted to the Committee, a minor of seventeen years in New Zealand can consent to medical treatment without parental consent. In Togo, it is allowed only for those who are "emancipated," and it is fixed for either sex at the age of twenty-one years.[112] In Nigeria, medical treatment without parental consent can be legally carried out from the age of twenty-one, although the explicit expressed approach is to refrain from stipulating a minimum age for medical counseling as "there is a bond between parents and children until they die."[113] In neither of these cases did the Committee make explicit remarks on the age of majority for the purpose of medical treatment; it made only general recommendations for further harmonization of the national law with the Children's Convention. It calls for further efforts to overcome the "prevailing attitudes in the family, in school, in other institutions and in society that hinder the enjoyment" of the child's right to participation,[114] without stipulating an upper age limit for medical treatment. In contrast, however, the Swedish regulations allowing a child of seven years to accept medical counseling without parental consent received the Committee's criticism, recommending Swedish officials to "reassess the advisability" of such a permission.[115] Thus, the extent to which the doctrine of informed consent has actually established a universal standard for children's bioethics and its practical implications is doubtful.[116] Still, to what extent do these apply to the context of traditional religio-cultural bodily practices?[117]

after *General Comment No. 7 (Early Childhood)*).

[111] *General Comment No. 7 (Early Childhood),* paragraph 27(b).

[112] Committee on the Rights of the Child, *Initial State Report: Togo,* paragraph 3, U.N. Doc. CRC/C/3/Add.42 (February 27, 1996).

[113] Committee on the Rights of the Child, *Second Periodic Report: Nigeria,* paragraphs 42–43, U.N. Doc. CRC/C/70/Add.24 (September, 17, 2004).

[114] Committee on the Rights of the Child, *Concluding Observations: Togo,* paragraphs 19, 35–37, U.N. Doc. CRC/C/15/Add.83 (October 10, 1997); *Second Periodic Report: Nigeria,* paragraph 34.

[115] Committee on the Rights of the Child, *Initial State Report: Sweden,* paragraph 46, U.N. Doc. CRC/C/3/Add.1 (September 23, 1992); Committee on the Rights of the Child, *Concluding Observations: Sweden,* paragraph 11, U.N. Doc. CRC/C/15/Add.2 (February 18, 1993).

[116] The difficulties with "age limitation" are discussed in Chapter 6.

[117] The extent to which religious adherence differs from a cultural one and the relationship between the two concepts is controversial. Some view religion as only one aspect included within the general concept of culture, whereas others contend that it is the other way around, or, at least, that religion is a separate category. They insist that the roots, rationales, and motivations behind religious adherence merit a distinctive response. The issue was not resolved on the international level, despite ongoing efforts since the 1960s. For discussion on the relationship between religion and culture, see Yvonne M. Donders, *Towards a Right to Cultural Identity?* (Antwerp: Intersentia, 2002), 72; Philip Hefner, "The Spiritual Task of Religion

Furthermore, as such practices are often perceived as elective ones, who is the most suitable to consent?

2. Children's Religio-Cultural Bodily Practices and Informed Consent

Particularly in light of the children's rights revolution, some have argued that parental/proxy consent to carry out religio-cultural bodily practices on children should be outlawed.[118] They contend that such consent is inherently incompatible with the doctrine of informed consent as it violates the child's rights.[119] This claim is based on several assumptions:

1. Religio-cultural bodily practices are similar to medical interventions as they involve the amputation or the incision of what otherwise is considered a healthy tissue. As such, assuring the informed consent of the individual involved, in this case the child, is necessary;
2. Due to age and immaturity, the child is unable to give such an informed consent;
3. Consent of the parents on behalf of their child is insufficient as:
   a. Their religious and cultural beliefs prevent them from considering the practice objectively and/or from properly balancing the medical complications and risks. The element of informed is therefore missing from their consent; and
   b. Religio-cultural bodily practices such as male circumcision and scarification violate an array of the rights of the child, including abuse and neglect, torture, etc., as well as the right to life, health and privacy. They are thus not in the child's best interests, in contravention with one of the primary and overreaching principles of both international and national standards. Hence, such religio-cultural bodily practices should be prohibited.[120]

---

in Culture: An Evolutionary Perspective," *Zygon* 33, no. 4 (1998): 540; Azizah Y. al-Hibri, "Is Western Patriarchal Feminism Good for Third World/Minority Women?" in *Is Multiculturalism Bad for women?* ed. Susan M. Okin (Princeton, NJ: Princeton University Press, 1999), 43; Daniel G. Scott, "Spirituality in Child and Youth Care: Considering Spiritual Development and 'Relational Consciousness,'" *Child & Youth Care Forum* 32, no. (2003): 117–31. See also Jeremy T. Gunn, "The Complexities of Religion and the Definition of 'Religion' in International Law," *Harvard Human Rights Journal* 16 (2003): 189–215 (distinguishing between three facets of religion: religion as belief, religion as identity, and religion as a way of life). For a comprehensive discussion on the international address of religious freedom, see Natan Lerner, *Religion, Beliefs, and International Human Rights* (Maryknoll, NY: Orbis Books, 2000); Bahiyyah G. Tahzib, *Freedom of Religion or Belief: Ensuring Effective International Legal Protection* (The Hague: Kluwer Law International, 1996). See Chapter 6, Section E.2.

[118] Smith, note 6; Chessler, 598.

[119] Les Haberfield, "Informed Consent and Infant Male Circumcision," *Australian Law Teachers Conference,* Sydney, New South Wales, Australia, October 3, 1997, Library of Circumcision Information and Resource Pages, http://www.cirp.org/library/legal/haberfield/; Ross Povenmire, "Do Parents Have the Legal Authority to Consent to the Surgical Amputation of Normal, Healthy Tissue From Their Infant Children?: The Practice of Circumcision in the United States," *Journal of Gender, Social Policy and the Law* 7 no.1 (1998–99): 103–06.

[120] There is a place to distinguish between parents' refusal to consent to a proposed medical treatment for their child because of their religious conviction and traditional bodily

Whether that should be the approach, however, is questionable for a few reasons. First, this set-up of assumptions is an overstated generalization. Most parents do care for their child and consider what is in his or her best interests. In fact, objectors of traditional bodily practices also would not normally charge that it is a matter of a lesser duty of care.[121] They rather place their thrust at the point of *causation*, arguing that, "the more compliant a parent is to religious doctrine, the more likely the parent is to consent to the circumcision regardless the risk."[122] Yet, this not only assumes a level of homogeneity within groups, which is hard to imagine ever exists, but it also ignores the fact that religiously based practices are often followed for *cultural* rather than religious rationales.

In Nigeria, for example, where it is estimated that more than 80 percent of the male population is circumcised, the most prevalent rationales given for the practice of male circumcision are cultural. This is so although Nigeria is a generally Muslim-oriented society; hence, one would assume that following the rite would be for religious reasons.[123] The justifications are mostly ritual practice, but they are also aesthetic—the belief that the practice enhances fertility or sexual pleasure and for other health reasons.[124] Ilan Katz in his essay on circumcision of Jewish boys is also illuminative. He describes the agony of decision making that *secular* Jewish parents (different from religious ones) go through when contemplating the various choices that accompany the rite. It is not that the risks of physical damage to the child are not taken into account, he argues, but rather that these are evaluated as opposed to the risks of the child being ostracized from the community and the damage to the community itself.[125] Thus, although they may (and often do) eventually opt for the practice, it is not because of relinquishing their faculty of thought but because their balance between the risks, consequences, and, eventually, the moral argumentation, differs from the Western humanist approach.[126]

---

practices that are carried out for religio-cultural rationales. Refusal of medical treatment such as a blood transfusion by members belonging to the Jehovah's Witnesses community is made "on the principle," and it is limited in its application to specific time and place in which the treatment is requested. Religio-cultural bodily practices, in contrast, aim at inscribing an identity into the child's body, which is beyond the immediate context. This distinction is different from and goes beyond the debate whether one's right to consent to medical treatment includes the right to forgo it. Stauch, 164.

[121] See also Korbin's distinction between parental/others' acts that deviate from the communal (*emic*) code of parental conduct, which may be due to lack of parental care, and traditional bodily practices that are within the *emic* boundaries of child-rearing practices, albeit their different conceptualization from an outsider's (*etic*) perspective. Korbin, "The Cross Cultural Context of Child Abuse and Neglect," 22.

[122] Haberfield, note 119.

[123] O. B. Boroffice, "Women's Attitudes to Men's Sexual Behaviour," *Health Transition Review* 5 (1995): 75, http://htc.anu.edu.au/pdfs/Boroffi1.pdf; Daniel T. Halperin and Robert C. Bailey, "Male Circumcision and HIV Infection: 10 Years and Counting." *Lancet* 354, no. 9191 (1999):, 1814.

[124] Soori Nnki and others, "Dynamics of Male Circumcision Practices in Northwest Tanzania," *Sexually Transmitted Diseases* 28, no. 4 (2001): 217.

[125] Katz, 103.

[126] Ibid., 92.

Putting aside that this set-up of assumptions is a rather narrow and prejudicial conceptualization of religio-cultural groups, it also does not seriously advance the child's best interests or the autonomous exercise of his or her rights. However defined, children all around the world are not assumed to have the autonomy and its accompanying chain of individual choice. This is particularly so when the practice is carried out at a very early age or in infancy. Practically, then, children are subjected to the substitute decision making of others, thus essentially redirecting the issue back to the question whether it is the parents, the community, or the state who should have the final say in the construction of the child's identity.[127] This, however, is a very different question. Religious and cultural bodily preferences are not such that one is born with or can develop autonomously and individually regardless of one's cultural environment. Neither the parents nor the state can objectively determine in advance that a particular identity is more in the child's best interests than another. More importantly, and in light of the child's *own* participatory right, it is impossible to assume in any way that an infant would *want* to be circumcised, scarified, follow any other religio-cultural bodily practice—or forgo them altogether—as a part of *his or her* sense of identity and membership in any given community. The reliance on the doctrine of informed consent as the ultimate mark of one's autonomy, on the one hand, and its presumed balance with the child's best interests, on the other, is thus utterly misleading. As Dena S. Davis nicely portrays the complexity, "these are two very different values, and comparing and weighting them invites the proverbial analogy of apples and oranges."[128] In the case of religio-cultural bodily practices, the determination eventually falls on the parents, the community, or the state's preference of taste.

The case may be different if children's views on the issue were on hand, as their opinions and feelings could have clarified whether they had or have a preference.[129] Such inquiry, however, is extremely difficult to obtain. Children's personal accounts of religious bodily practices that they were subjected to when a few days old or at a very young age are not available, and the interpretation of the nonverbal expression of views (which is included within the scope of Article 12) is highly subjective. Opponents of neonatal male circumcision, for example, often reference the emotional effect the rite has on newborns. In one study, researchers tested pain responses of circumcised and uncircumcised boys at the age of four to six months when routinely vaccinated for diphtheria-

[127] Renteln, 217.

[128] Dena S. Davis, *Genetic Dilemmas: Reproductive Technology, Parental Choices, and Children's Future: Reproductive Technology, Parental Choices, and Children's Future* (New York: Routledge Publishing, 2001), 23.

[129] Many human rights activists also dismiss adults' decisions to go through a traditional bodily practice. This has been raised and debated in the context of female circumcision, where adult women who request to be circumcised in Western countries are turned down on the assumption that their general cultural background prevents them from reaching a "rational choice" (the argument of "false conscience"). See, for example, Bhikhu Parekh, *Rethinking Multiculturalism: Cultural Diversity and Political Theory* (Cambridge, MA: Harvard University Press, 2000), 278–80 (arguing that women's decision to be circumcised should be banned, as their general status in society prevents them "[from thinking] independently and decid[ing] for themselves between alternative ways of understanding their cultural traditions").

pertussis-tetanus (DPT).[130] Using randomized controlled trial and post hoc analysis, they concluded that "[neonatal] male circumcision was associated with increased infant pain response to routine vaccination. . . . [With] significantly longer crying bouts and higher pain scores."[131]

The extent to which these findings can be generalized or utilized for the purpose of drawing a general prohibition, however, is doubtful. One's reactions and emotional development are influenced and shaped by various social, cultural, economic, and other factors. Different events trigger one's emotional state, including natural tendency. Singling out one rite as *the* cause for one's emotional stress is thus oversimplistic. Thus, for example, the fact that pain scores and cry duration for the first vaccine (the first other medical intervention after the circumcision) did not differ among circumcised and noncircumcised boys[132] may imply that other factors intervened. Interestingly, the researchers excluded from their study infants who had undergone painful procedures that are not routine (such as a surgery) or infants who were in discomfort before the vaccination and showed "natural" behavioral pain scores that were relatively high.[133] While extensive surgical interventions may indeed not be comparable, on the physical level, with a rite such as male circumcision, the lack of further clarification as to what counts as a nonroutine procedure and its exclusion from the sample seems to suggest that the findings were somewhat biased in advance.

Retrospective studies of *adults* who underwent traditional biomedical practices at a young age, on the other hand, which could be an alternative to the option of having children's views heard directly, are also too limited in their general applicability. In a singular self-portrait of his life, Nelson Mandela describes the feelings of excitement, pain, and pride that accompanied his circumcision ceremony as a rite of passage.[134] Yet again, as Korbin points out in her survey of anthropological literature, whereas some children express positive long-term value in religious and culturally sanctioned rites, others do not.[135] Furthermore, it is not implausible to assume that the passage of time has romanticized the ceremony especially as the process of enculturation has taken root, and hence may easily deflect the results.

The best option would be to examine data of children who have matured enough to form their views. Although such studies are still quite sparse, the following surveys were found. In a study conducted in three communities in Oyo and Akinyele, southwestern Nigeria, among respondents who had facial marks, the ten- to nineteen-year-old age group was the one least likely to express liking of the marks. A large percentage of the respondents (87.01 percent)

---

[130] Anna Taddio and others, "Effect of Neonatal Circumcision on Pain Responses during Vaccination in Boys," *Lancet* 345, no. 8945 (1995): 291–92.

[131] Ibid., 292.

[132] Ibid.

[133] Ibid., 291–92.

[134] Nelson Mandela, *Long Walk to Freedom: The Autobiography of Nelson Mendela* (Randburg, South Africa: Macdonals Purnell, 1994), 25–26, quoted in Katz, 90.

[135] Korbin, "Children, Childhood, and Violence," 434.

expressed a dislike of the facial marks and a desire to have them removed. The reasons given were that the marks were embarrassing (62.12 percent) and that "the marks made them unhappy" (37.88 percent).[136] No further clarification was given about what the sources for the embarrassment were or what factored into the respondents' "unhappiness." The researchers ascribe this finding to the fact that the practice is uncommon among this age group.

Examining the data, however, other reasons may account for this result as well. For example, although the majority of the respondents had their facial marks for purposes of identification with their tradition, culture, or their royal lineage (76 percent overall—46.56 percent for tradition/culture, and 29.99 percent for royal lineage)—the remaining respondents provided less positive motives. These included: family decision (7.11 percent), claim of ownership of the child in paternity disputes (5.5 percent), and as an act of naturalization for immigrants who want to express identification with the local people (1 percent).[137] The researchers do not provide any further account on the distribution of these reasons among the various age groups. Yet if traditional/cultural marking is not common among children in these groups, it may be the case that the children-respondents' embarrassment and unhappiness was in fact because of the negative connotation that was attached to their marks for reasons of which they could not be proud. In other words, were the practice prevalent among their peer group and associated with their group's cultural identity, the children's views may have been different.

A compelling support for this line of reasoning can be derived from cross-cultural comparison of children's views on facial marks. Perhaps the most known cultural community to follow the practice is the Maori group throughout the eastern islands of Polynesia and particularly, nowadays, New Zealand. The facial marks (the *Ta Moko*) were originally performed as a traditional and cultural rite of passage to symbolize social status and sexual attraction. Following the arrival of the Christian missionaries and the European (British) colonization around the middle of the nineteenth century, the practice was morally condemned and legally prohibited.[138] Consequently, for a few decades past the beginning of the twentieth century, the number of Maori men following the practice reduced significantly. Conversely, as Maori women remained mainly at home, they kept on with the practice, and in the past few decades, it enjoyed a substantial revival.[139] The interesting point for this discussion is the Maori children's views and role in the process.

---

[136] A. E. Obiechina and A. O. Alutayo, "Attitudes to Facial Marks in South Western Nigeria," *Odonto-Stomatologie Tropicale* 23, no. 91 (2000): 24.

[137] Ibid., 14.

[138] Ngahuia Te Awekotuku, "Ta Moko: Culture, Body Modification, and the Psychology of Identity," *Proceedings of the National Maori Graduates of Psychology Symposium* (2002): 123–24, http://waikato.researchgateway.ac.nz/bitstream/10289/869/1/NMGPS_2002_TeAwekotuku.pdf.

[139] The outlawing of the practice was also dropped following the regulation and change of the technology in which it was performed (from chisels to electric machines). Linda Waimarie Nikora, Mohi Rua, and Ngahuia Te Awekotuku, "In Your Face: Wearing Moko—Maori Facial Marking in Today's World," *Tatau/Tattoo: Embodied Art and Cultural Exchange Conference* 2003, http://waikato.researchgateway.ac.nz/bitstream/10289/463/1/content.pdf.

In one study the researchers collected the opinions, experiences, and views of children whose parents followed the practice. Their data from those who commented on the children's reactions and feelings in seeing their parents with the (new) tattoo suggested that "children are far more accepting and encouraging of the transformations their parents and grandparents are choosing than other family members."[140] Other studies have gone further, crediting the young generation of Maori for the revival of the *Ta Moko* since the 1970s. "Motivated by an assertion of identity," the researchers argue, the children reclaimed the right to the practice, bringing about its current renaissance.[141] This observation coincides also with testimonies of aged Maori people in New Zealand at the beginning of the twentieth century (when the practice was prohibited yet still seen) who "recall their childhood and teenage years looking in awe at the face markings on a venerable ole man's face."[142] In contrast to Western thought, then, by which the child's best interests require the avoidance of religio-cultural bodily practices, children's views, particularly among cultural groups in which the practices are common, may be different. In this light, if indeed it is children's rights that are argued to be upheld, at least their own opinions should be incorporated into the discourse. The problem is of course that due to the time (age wise) in which many of the traditional religio-cultural bodily practices are carried out, such data may not be obtainable at all. Thus, as much as it would be nice to uphold a concept of children's participatory rights, practically, it may be impossible. The question is then whether there is an alternative model that could provide a better response. As is suggested in Chapter 6, such a model should contain the shared characteristics of human beings, which are essentially built on interdependency, relationships, and development—as are reflected in one's identity.

F. CONCLUSION

The general tendency by national and international scholars and agencies to address the issue of harmful traditional bodily practices under the umbrella of children's protection rights should be reconsidered. The concepts of (1) child abuse, (2) torture, cruel, inhuman, and degrading treatment, and (3) violence against children are both culture bound and vague. The concepts preserve the traditional approach toward children as passive vessels who need to be rescued; they extend the objective of child savers beyond parental/individual malfunction to entire families, communities, and cultures; and considering the moral condemnation that accompanies such classifications, it mistakenly endangers the very basic characteristics of human beings—social actors who develop and are constructed within culture through webs of relationships, which provide the content of one's development, life, and identity. Thus, and aside from the erosion and loss of effectiveness that overusage of these categorizations may incur, a different approach needs to be adopted.

---

140 Ibid.

141 Te Awekotuku, 113.

142 See the comment about possible bias in adults' expression of memories from their childhood, above. Nikora, Rua, and Te Awekotuku, note 139.

The alternative and novel participatory approach that has characterized the children's rights' discourse in the past few decades is also somewhat impotent to provide satisfactory address. The crux of the question is to what extent the child's self-determination rights, particularly, autonomy and independent religious freedom and partaking in biomedical decision making, advance the discourse on children's bioethics. As has been shown, the rubric of participatory rights, that is, self-determination rights, particularly autonomy and independent religious freedom and partaking in biomedical decision making, *is not* the appropriate vehicle to provide address to the issue. Infants and young children have little agency role in the decision making when such traditional bodily practices are carried out at a young age. Religio-cultural views of older children and adolescents often cave in to the protective approach (either from others or from themselves), and their singular voice is overlooked. While Gerison Lansdown may be correct that "the realization of children's rights is not contingent on the ability to exercise agency, or on the acquisition of a given age,"[143] the practical questions remain. This, thus, goes back to the first set of questions. Which criteria, or whose morality, should be employed? Who among the parents, community, and state should have the final say? And do they in any case, anyway, reflect the child's own voice?

The complexities involved here are plenty. A determination based on the moral value (both internally and externally) is predisposed to be biased, as the evaluation can be made only through the views of the observer. Within the international human rights discourse, the result is often Eurocentric, yet without providing any particular reliable justification. A moral condemnation is also not likely to present a long-term solution. As bodily practices are an inherent part of human interactions, a condemned practice will find its way back in one alternative form or another. The medical criterion of harm is also inapt to resolve the tension. The concept of harm is culturally constructed, and transplanting one understanding to a significantly different cultural setting may be simply not feasible. If nevertheless enforced, it is again likely to be Eurocentric, endorsing definitions that corroborate the Western emphasis on physical harm but neglect the emotional and mental injuries.

Lending a hand to the principle of the child's best interests or to the child's evolving capacity does not advance the discourse any further as they are, from adults' perspective, the easy way out. Both principles practically give into the subjective discretion of the decision maker who factors the balance between the various values by his or her taste and choice. The subsequent attempt to balance between parental, national, and other interests against the child's best interests and his or her evolving capacities, though, is impossible, as it evaluates incomparable factors.

In any case, the examination must go beyond that. The debate, it cannot be emphasized enough, is not only about children belonging to minority groups or about religio-cultural bodily practices that are carried out on children in non-Western states and of which the Western international orientation does

[143] Lansdown, 5.

not approve. It is also not about the religio-cultural bodily practices themselves on which biomedical cultures collide. It is rather about which identity one eventually wants the child to construct. Acknowledging that it is ultimately a conflict about the right identity(ies), it becomes clear why both the protective and self-determination/participatory approaches cannot be practically resolved. Hiding behind medical rationales, calling for the principle of autonomy, and upholding the child's best interests are simply not enough. The discussion thus now turns to the child's right to cultural identity. As the center in which the various factors that play a role in the child's development converge, it is here where the discourse on children's bioethics has to commence.

CHAPTER 6
RIGHTS DISCOURSE, CHILDREN, AND BIOETHICS

The previous chapters showed the complexities raised by the discussion on children's bioethics. The paramount emphasis on children belonging to minority groups fails to grasp the broader picture in which all children belong, in one way or another, to a minority group. Although both scholastic and activist work on the national and international levels discuss the issue of harmful traditional practices (mainly in the context of girls), children as subjects are still practically excluded from the discourse. The focus remained only on the minority's participation in the public sphere. Also when referring to the private one, children are presumed to be invisible and, often, merely those who need protection. Jack Donnelly's effort to craft international criteria to distinguish between such traditional bodily practices that require acting upon versus others that do not is also problematic. It is inherently subjective and likely to follow the (Western) spirit alone.[1]

Analyzing the specific rights of the child that are presumably violated, both the protective and the participatory (self-determination) approaches have been critiqued as being culturally insensitive or unable to give an accurate account of the experience of children. No alternative model to understand traditional bodily practices has been provided, although it has been mentioned it is rooted in cultural identities. In this vein, this chapter deconstructs the concept of rights in an effort to adjust it to the particular status of children. The argument advanced is that traditional bodily practices are integral to one's culture and, hence, also fall within the scope of his or her cultural rights. In the context of children, the argument has to be understood in light of their rights to cultural identity.

To advance this argument, Sections A and B look at the concepts of culture, cultural rights, and cultural identity, and highlight some of the problems associated with their analysis. To what extent do biomedical practices fall within the scope of internationally recognized cultural rights? This is followed by the more specific investigation in Section C: even if biomedical practices are integral to one's cultural rights, to what extent are they compatible with the *child's* cultural rights? To answer that, one needs to consider the broader question whether children have rights. Examining leading scholastic theories on the issue, the section shows the role identity plays in the children's exercise of their rights and ties it to children's bioethics. Thus, in Section D, some of the scholarship concerning the child's cultural identity, as well as the address

[1] See Chapter 4, Section B.2.b.

of the Monitoring Committee under the Children's Convention (Children's Committee or Committee), is discussed. Finally, Section E considers the implications of the child's right to (biomedical) cultural identity for international law: how should biomedical/identity conflicts be translated into state policies and responsibilities?

A. CULTURE, CULTURAL RIGHTS, AND CULTURAL IDENTITY

The concepts of culture, cultural rights, and the right to cultural identity are elusive. Perhaps because "the cultural" is often a given, the need to explain, defend, and preserve it appears to be at odds. But cultures and the underlying derivatives of cultures are far more complex. As the boundaries between cultures and cultural identities are intrinsically a matter of an ongoing negotiation, it should thus come as no surprise that what counts under cultural rights, what cultural identity means, and especially what recognition of such rights would entail are all unclear.

The focus of the traditional study of culture on exotic and remote ways of life is partly responsible for this oversight. This concentration has, even if only obliquely, connected the concept of culture only with simple and presumably homogenous societies.[2] Indeed, it was not until the last few decades when anthropologists, sociologists, and others realized that *their* culture should and could equally be the subject of study. The "cultural turn," as it has been termed,[3] clarified that, although invisible, the concept of culture applies to all human beings and to all societies.[4]

Another reason for the peculiarity of the cultural turn has to do with the way in which rights are conceptualized. If being a rights holder means, at least, and as it has been traditionally understood under Western discourse of human rights, that another should not interfere with culture, formulating a concept of cultural rights and, all the more so, of a right to cultural identity, implicitly assumes that culture can be deprived. This, however, does not seem to resonate well with the nature of culture as a universal and most intrinsic feature of humanity. After all, culture is possibly what distinguishes human beings from animals,[5] and, so, how can one be deprived of culture and cultural identity? This is a majoritarian approach, however, assuming that culture and cultural identity are something that one simply has. It is often not the case though for minorities who need to attest to their cultural rights and identity(ies). As policies to remove children belonging to indigenous groups from their homes during the 1950 and 1960s in various Western countries around the world[6]

---

[2] Clyde Kluckhohn and William H. Kelly, "The Concept of Culture," in *The Science of Man in the World Crisis*, ed. Ralph Linton (New York: Octagon Books), 79.

[3] Austin Sarat and Jonathan Simon, "Beyond Legal Realism?: Cultural Analysis, Cultural Studies and the Situation of Legal Scholarship," *Yale Journal of Law & Humanities* 13, no. 1 (2001): 5.

[4] Kluckhohn and Kelly, 79.

[5] Philip Hefner, "The Spiritual Task of Religion in Culture: An Evolutionary Perspective," *Zygon* 33, no. 4 (1998): 536.

[6] The phenomenon of "stolen generation" was documented in Australia, Israel, and other countries.

and the increase in the number of spiritual custody cases[7] in recent years have highlighted, there is indeed a need for both their negative and positive protection.

Still another part of the discomfort emerges in view of the multifaceted yet inherent complexities that these concepts of culture, cultural rights, and cultural identity raise. Scholars and human rights activists point to the vagueness of the terms and their ongoing change, which complicates the task of determining their content.[8] Culture can have at least three meanings: "culture as capital," referring to the accumulated material heritage of mankind; "culture as creativity," referring to the process of artistic and scientific creation; and "culture as a total way of life," referring to the anthropological concept, that is, the sum total of the material and spiritual activities and products of a given social group that distinguishes it from other similar groups.[9] What constitutes cultural rights also varies. As Lyndel Prott points out, cultural rights can be interpreted as "rights *relating to* culture," referring to the sense of creativity, including all sort of freedoms of expression, of religion, and of language. They can mean a "right *to* culture," that is, the right to preserve, exercise, or have access to a culture, including the right to restitution of cultural, intellectual, religious, and spiritual property. Or they can also mean a "right to *the survival* of cultures," referring to the need to ensure that minorities can assemble and participate in ceremonies as a part of their communal survival.[10] Yet how is the right to cultural identity derived?

Others express particular concern about the tension between the collective and the individual that these concepts implicate. Since culture "lives in and is sustained and developed by [both] collectives and the individuals,"[11] it is hard to pin down how to weigh these two inextricable dimensions without abandoning the rights of the individual members.[12] Scholars also point to the difficulties in ascertaining whether the claimants are the true representatives of the cultural group, whether a particular claim for culture and cultural identit(ies) is indeed authentic as claimed (if such authenticity of culture ever exists),[13] and, in any

---

[7] "Spiritual custody" cases refer to cases in which the parents are of different religions and, following divorce, the noncustodial parent requests that the court would award him or her spiritual (religious indoctrination) one. See Alison D. Renteln, *The Cultural Defense* (Oxford: Oxford University Press, 2004), 135–38; Annie Bunting, "Elijah and Ishmael: Assessing Cultural Identity in Canadian Child Custody Decisions," *Family Court Review* 42, no. 3 (2004): 471–84; Ya'ir Ronen, "The Child's Right to Identity as a Right to Belong," *Tel Aviv University Law Review* 26, no. 3 (2003): 935–84.

[8] Halina Nieć, "Casting the Foundation for the Implementation of Cultural Rights," in *Cultural Rights and Wrongs*, edi. Halina Niec (Paris: UNESCO Publishing, 1998), 178, 182; Lyndel Prott, "Understanding One Another on Cultural Rights," in *Cultural Rights and Wrongs*, ed. Halina Nieć (Paris: UNESCO Publishing, 1998), 164–65.

[9] Rodolfo Stavenhagen, "Cultural Rights: A Social Science Perspective," in *Cultural Rights and Wrongs*, ed. Halina Nieć (Paris: UNESCO Publishing, 1998), 4–5.

[10] Prott, 165.

[11] Douglas Sanders, "Collective Rights," H*uman Rights Quarterly* 13, no. 3 (1991): 383.

[12] Prott, 167.

[13] Kobena Mercer, "Welcome to the Jungle: Identity and Diversity in Postmodern Politics," in *Identity: Community, Culture, Difference,* ed. Jonathan Rutherford (London: Lawrence & Wishart, 1990), 65.

case, where does the group versus the individual's cultural rights and cultural identity start and end.

These intricacies are more complicated given the contention about the actual link between culture, cultural rights, and a right to cultural identity. Some question whether the right to cultural identity is simply a deduction of cultural rights, if it should be stated as a separate right, or perhaps not be conceptualized as a right at all. Scholars note in this context that cultural rights have a "transversed character": they overlap the categories of civil, political, economic, and social rights.[14] The address of a right to cultural identity merely as a part of one's cultural rights is thus doomed to be insufficient.[15] Others also mention that the main goal of cultural rights was to elevate inequalities between individuals, hence falling short of providing appropriate state responsibilities to protect and guarantee cultural rights (and their derivatives).[16] Still others contend that the various definitions of culture and of cultural rights make any determination of the content of a right to cultural identity ostensibly impossible. Considering also its dynamic character, it thus appears as precluding the option of having a separate right to cultural identity that is grounded with sufficient legal force.[17]

Legal theorists of rights base this argument on a distinction between the legal, philosophical, and political dimensions of rights.[18] This distinction holds that only when claims ripen into enforceable ones can they gain the full status of a right. Cultural rights, following this line of thought, cannot be habitually assumed as reaching this point. They may have moral strength (i.e., a philosophical dimension), but an expectation that states will have to set out a public policy strategy to enforce them (i.e., the political aspects) or provide a remedy for their violation (i.e., the legal aspect) is unreasonable.[19] As Donnelly simply remarks, cultural rights and particularly the right to cultural identity are

---

[14] Yvonne M. Donders, *Towards a Right to Cultural Identity?* (Oxford: Antwerpen Intersentia, 2002), 71.

[15] Ibid.

[16] Ibid., 75.

[17] Prott, 164–67; Donders, 75–76.

[18] Prott, 161–62.

[19] Maurice Cranston, "Are There Any Human Rights?" *Daedalus* 112, no. 4 (1984): 14. Cranston explains this point in terms of "injustifiability." He stages a three-prong test to determine whether rights are universally recognized with legal force under the international human rights law. One is a practical test, questioning whether the right is enforceable or not. The simple assumption is that "if it is impossible for a thing to be done, it is absurd to claim it as a right." The second test is its universal applicability. A universal right, he argues, must be such that it pertains to every human being. Finally, the third prong is the test of paramount importance. Assuming that universal rights entail a *moral duty* to act in order to protect a right of another, he calls for "common sense" to be the determinative force. Following the three tests, Cranston thus argues that only civil and political rights can qualify as universal rights under the international human rights system, whereas economic, social, and cultural rights, in contrast and, even more so, the so-called third generation of rights (including the right to identity and developmental rights) cannot. He rationalizes that the economic, political, and other circumstances in developing countries necessitates the conclusion, as a matter of "common sense," that the enforceability of cultural rights is unreasonable. Ibid., 13–14.

"not a good, service or status that can be given [by the state] to people."[20]

Consequently, some scholars suggest setting aside the rights approach in the context of cultural rights and cultural identity. Prott, for example, stresses that an assertion of legally binding cultural rights could be damaging to the general discourse on human rights. Insisting that they exist in law, she argues, runs the risk of voiding the value of other rights because it would not provide proper enforcement nor any remedy.[21] Yvonne M. Donders proposes the recognition of cultural identity as a general value but not as "a right."[22] In her view, such an approach acknowledges the importance of cultural identity to human dignity that is worth preserving, yet presumably avoids the slippery slope of efforts to resolve the complexities associated with cultural issues.[23]

Whether these approaches actually settle the conflicts, however, is debatable. It is precisely because identity claims are viewed as merely having general (albeit undisputable) value that distorts, in practice, the vision of the actual interests that are involved. "Identity-related interests and values of individuals and groups still often remain central to cultural disputes," Avigail Eisenberg points out correctly, and the efforts to ignore them or to present them as though they no longer contain the identity debate offers only indirect and most likely inadequate means of resolving such disputes.[24] This is particularly so in the context of children whose world is mostly built on their semilegal orders of relationships (rather than on formal rules) that are reflected and projected into their identities.

The discussion of medical cultures and biomedical practices in the context of the child's cultural rights and the right to cultural identity strikes at the heart of these debates. Medical cultures are contingent on individuals' and groups' systems of knowledge and belief. They include one's entire understanding of his or her relationship with others, with the group, and with the cosmos. They include the rationale that mobilizes individuals and groups in their decision making and actions. Moreover, they reflect the intentional effort to inscribe a cultural identity into the body. As such, medical cultures are inherently interlaced with a person's and group's identities, and as children are the prime targets of enculturation, identity-based procedures are especially crucial for them. Yet, whereas most would surely concede that biomedical practices are cultures, the question is to what extent they fall within the scope of cultural rights. Furthermore, are they integral to the child's cultural rights and to his or her right to cultural identity?

---

[20] Jack Donnelly, "Human Rights, Individual Rights and Collective Rights," in *Human Rights in a Pluralist World,* ed. J. Berting and others (Westport, CT: Meckler, 1999), 58, quoted in Donders, 5.

[21] Prott, 162–67.

[22] Donders, 75–76.

[23] Prott, 94; Donders, 79, 340.

[24] Avigail Eisenberg, "Identity and Liberal Politics: the Problem of Minorities within Minorities," in *Minorities within Minorities: Equality, Rights and Diversity,* ed. Avigail Eisenberg and Jeff Spinner-Halev (Cambridge: Cambridge University Press, 2005), 249.

B. BIOMEDICAL PRACTICES *AS* CULTURAL RIGHTS

Whether biomedical practices are or can be claimed as cultural rights requires addressing two main questions. On the general level, there is first a need to determine which elements of culture are included within the scope of cultural rights and ought to be taken into account.[25] Specifically, the question is whether biomedical practices as a feature of culture fall within the scope of internationally recognized cultural rights. The second and more complicated question requires assertion as to whether a concrete practice that is generally covered by the right to culture should be protected.

Theoretically, the most straightforward approach to answering the first question is using existing international human rights instruments as a basic source of reference. The most cardinal legally binding ones are Articles 22 and 27 of the Universal Declaration of Human Rights (UDHR),[26] Article 15 of the International Covenant on Economic, Social and Cultural Rights (ICESCR)[27] and Article 27 of the International Covenant on Civil and Political Rights (ICCPR).[28] Children's rights to active participation in cultural life are restated in both the International Convention on the Rights of the Child (Children's Convention or Convention) and the African Charter on the Rights and Welfare of the Child (African Charter),[29] and they include an explicit separate reference to children with disabilities.[30] Additionally, the provision addressing children belonging to religious, ethnic, and linguistic minority groups was also restated in the exact wording in Article 30 of the Children's Convention.[31]

These sources, however, are generally vague, either stipulating a general right to culture and cultural life without elaboration or tackling a specific dimension of it such as cultural property, education, and artistic expression.[32]

---

[25] Renteln, 213.

[26] Universal Declaration of Human Rights, adopted and proclaimed by G.A. Res. 217 A (III), U.N. Doc./ A/810 (1948). Although the UDHR is not an international treaty, it is believed to have gained the status of customary international law.

[27] International Covenant on Economic, Social and Cultural Rights (ICESCR), adopted Dec. 16, 1966, G.A. Res. 2200A (XXI), 21 Sess., U.N. GAOR Supp. (No. 16), at 49, U.N. Doc. A/6316 (1966), reprinted in 993 U.N.T.S. 3, entered into force January 3, 1976.

[28] International Covenant on Civil and Political Rights, opened for signature December 16, 1966, G.A. Res. 2200A (XXI), 21st Sess., U.N. GAOR Supp. (No. 16), at 52, U.N. Doc. A/6316 (1966), reprinted in 999 U.N.T.S. 171, entered into force March 23, 1976

[29] Article 31 of the Convention on the Rights of the Child, G.A. Res. 44/25, annex, 44th Sess., 61st plenary meeting. U.N. GAOR Supp. (No. 49), at 167, U.N. Doc. A/44/49 (1989), entered into force September 2, 1990, reprinted in 28 I.L.M. 1448 (1989); Article 12 of the African Charter on the Rights and Welfare of the Child, OAU Doc. CAB/LEG/24.9/49 (1990), entered into force November 29, 1999.

[30] Article 23 of the Children's Convention; Article 13 of the African Charter.

[31] The right to culture is formally recognized also in regional agreements such as the Inter-American and the Africa systems. See, for example, Article 14 of the Additional Protocol to the American Convention on Human Rights in the Area of Economic, Social and Cultural Rights, "Protocol of San Salvador," O.A.S. Treaty Series No. 69 (1988), entered into force November 16, 1999, reprinted in *Basic Documents Pertaining to Human Rights in the Inter-American System,* OEA/Ser.L.V/II.82 doc.6 rev.1 at 67 (1992); Article 14 of the African Charter.

[32] As Nieć points out, even this provision is stipulated without the extent of specification that would allow deriving the concrete entitlement and obligations that these categories entail. Nieć, 181.

Article 15 of the ICESCR, the most legally binding and persuasive provision on cultural rights within the international human rights framework, provides a few general categories of rights: participation in cultural life; enjoyment of the benefits and application of scientific progress; benefiting from the protection of the moral and material interests resulting from scientific, literary, or artistic production; and conservation, development, and diffusion of science and culture. The only reference to biomedicine *as* culture is thus in the context of "scientific progress," a reference that, unlike the general category of "cultural and artistic life," was not restated in the children-specific instruments at all. Even the UN Declaration on the Elimination of All Forms of Intolerance and of Discrimination Based on Religion or Belief does not explicitly mention bodily practices,[33] including some of the most fundamental bodily manifestations of religion or belief such as burial and dietary practices.[34] The list is nonexhaustive,[35] however, and the extent to which bodily practices carried out for medical treatment or for "inscribing cultural identity" onto one's body remains open to debate.

Despite the ambiguity, there are several reasons why bodily practices should be included within the concept of cultural rights under international law. First, their inclusion is intuitive. Differences in some of the most basic means of communication, such as bodily gestures, facial expressions, and even laughter or a smile can be discerned among cultures and across time.[36] The body and bodily practices are often regarded as primary reflections of social structures and identification.[37] They are often key means of participation in the cultural lives of individuals and groups; they are inherently intertwined with cultures and with cultural identities.

In her discussion on minority right to culture under international law, Alison D. Renteln elucidates the point that basing the validity of rights on its

---

[33] Declaration on the Elimination of All Forms of Intolerance and of Discrimination Based on Religion or Belief, G.A. Res. 36/55, 36 U.N. GAOR Supp. (No. 51), at 171, U.N. Doc. A/36/684 (1981) encompasses both religious and cultural beliefs and prescribes in Article 1 four external manifestations of religion or belief that are guaranteed individually or in community with others, in public or private: worship, observance, practice, and teaching. Article 6 of the declaration lists nine specific illustrations of these external manifestations, including assembly (Article 6(a)), the right to make, acquire, and use the necessary articles and material related to the rites and customs of a religion or belief (Article 6(c)), the freedom to teach a religion or belief (Article 6(e)), and others. See, in this regard, the comment on the difficulties in discerning between religious and cultural practices and beliefs in Chapter 5, note 117.

[34] Bahiyyah G. Tahzib, *Freedom of Religion or Belief: Ensuring Effective International Legal Protection* (The Hague: Kluwer Law International, 1996), 183.

[35] The chapeau of Article 6 of the declaration reads: "In accordance with article I of the present Declaration, and subject to the provisions of article 1, paragraph 3, the right to freedom of thought, conscience, religion or belief shall include, inter alia, the following freedoms."

[36] Fred E. H. Schroeder, "Say Cheese! The Revolution in the Aesthetic of Smiles," *Journal of Popular Culture* 32, no. 2 (1998): 108, 110; Katherine Young, "The Memory of the Flesh: The Family Body in Somatic Psychology," *Body & Society* 8, no. 3 (2002): 25.

[37] Nick, Crossley, "Embodiment and Social Structure: A Response to Howson and Inglis," *The Sociological Review* 49, no. 3 (2001): 320; Chris Shilling, "Embodiment, Experience and Theory: In Defense of the Sociological Tradition," *Sociological Review* 49, no. 3 (2001): 332.

statement in an international instrument is too limiting. "If there were no Article 27 of the ICCPR, would that mean that there was no right to culture?"[38] This rhetorical question seems to be most applicable in the context of biomedical practices. If cultures and bodily practices as expressions of cultures are universal (which they are), and if they are integral to one's dignity and identity (which they also are), then acknowledging the *right to be different* also in the physical form is the correlative that cannot be taken away. And whether this right is explicitly stipulated has nothing to do with the essence and existence of the right.[39] Thus, the lack of particular reference in the international instruments to "traditional biomedical practices" *as* culture/cultural rights and as integral to one's (cultural) identity does not and should not detract from their validity.

Second, there is a growing consensus that the right to participate in cultural life should be interpreted broadly. In a Day of General Discussion on the right to participate in cultural life that the committee under the ICESCR held in December 1992, scholars observed a greater willingness on the international level to endorse the anthropological meaning of culture as a way of life, "being more than cultural manifestations, to include language, literature, clothing, shelter, arts, customs and traditions."[40] Biomedical practices clearly fall within this understanding, as the body and its rituals are a central medium between the individual and his or her social group. In this vein, the participants also declined to incorporate an explicit provision excluding harmful cultural practices, although the issue was raised with concern.[41]

The international bodies monitoring the conventions also endorsed this approach. Although the committee under the ICESCR did not go so far as to issue a general comment on Article 15,[42] its broad interpretation of the right to participate in cultural life can be learned from its revisions to the guidelines for states' reports on the issue. In its revised guidelines on Article 15, the committee requests that states provide information on the legislative and other measures taken to fulfill the right of everyone to take part in cultural life and to

---

[38] Renteln, 216.

[39] It is a different question whether the concept of right is appropriate altogether to advance the discourse. This is elaborated on in Section C. Also, it is interesting to note in this regard that Article 3(d) of the Convention on the Rights of Persons with Disabilities (Disability Rights Convention), G.A. Res. A/61/611 (2006), stipulates, among others, and for the first time in a "core" human rights treaty, the general principle of "Respect for difference and acceptance of persons with disabilities as part of human diversity and humanity." The argument advanced with regard to biomedical practices and the right to be different goes beyond the disability context, however.

[40] Donders, 154, 157. The Day of General Discussion was held in the presence of the members of the committee, a few external experts, including UNESCO and the International Movement for Rights and Humanity. Donders, 154.

[41] Ibid., 156.

[42] The only aspect of Article 15 that the committee under the ICESCR has addressed is with respect to "the production of the moral and material interest resultng from any scientific, literary or artistic production." See Committee on Economic, Social and Cultural Rights, *The Right of Everyone to Benefit from the Production of the Moral and Material Interests Resulting from Any Scientific, Literary or Artistic Production of which He or She Is the Author (General Comment No. 17)*, 35th Sess., U.N. Doc. E/C. 12/GC/17 (2006).

manifest their culture.[43] It requires information, *inter alia*, on steps taken on the conservation, development, and diffusion of science and culture, and on the promotion of awareness of cultural diversity (minority and indigenous groups). The committee also incorporated a reference to the collective dimension of culture and explicitly requests information on "the promotion of cultural identity as a factor of mutual appreciation among individuals, groups, nations and regions." By that it makes a direct and clear link between Article 15 on culture, cultural participation (i.e., cultural rights), and cultural identity.[44]

The Human Rights Committee under the ICCPR has further established the link between bodily practices as culture and cultural rights (broadly defined) in its general comment on the freedom of thought, conscience, and religion (1994). In paragraph 4, the committee stipulates that the freedom to manifest religion or belief encompasses a broad range of acts, including "not only [ritual and] ceremonial acts but also such customs as the observance of dietary regulations, . . . participation in rituals associated with certain stages of life, and the use of a particular language customarily spoken by a group."[45] It thus explicitly endorses traditional bodily practices within the scope of the right to religio-cultural freedom.

Finally, there is now an array of international treaties that support this approach. To begin with, the child-specific international instruments establish a link between bodily practices, culture, and cultural rights. Article 24(3) of the Children's Convention refers, generally, to "traditional practices," which clearly include those having either religious or cultural origin; and the parallel article of the African Charter refers to "social and cultural practices."[46] However, as both stipulate states' obligations to abolish harmful traditional practices, the right to (bodily) traditional practices can be derived by means of deduction: if states are obligated to abolish (*only*) harmful traditional practices, individuals have a right to all others.

The UNESCO Convention on the Protection and Promotion of the Diversity of Cultural Expressions (UNESCO Convention on Cultural and Artistic Expressions) adopted in 2005 gives an additional boost to the argument that biomedical practices are cultural rights.[47] The convention forms

---

[43] *Revised General Guidelines Regarding the Form and Contents of Reports to be Submitted by States Parties under Articles 16 and 17 of the International Covenant on Economic, Social and Cultural Rights*, annex, U.N. Doc. E/C.12/1991/1 (June 17, 1991). Cynthia P. Cohen, "The United Nations Convention on the Rights of the Child: Involvement of NGOs," in *The Legitimacy of the United Nations: Towards an Enhanced Legal Status of Non-State Actors*," ed. Theo C. van Boven, Cees Flinterman, Fred Grunfeld, and Rita Hut (Utrecht, the Netherlands: SIM., 1997), 171–172, 176, http://www.uu.nl/content/14Price.pdf (hereafter ESCR Report Guidelines).

[44] Donders, 150.

[45] Human Rights Committee, *The Right to Freedom of Thought, Conscience and Religion (General Comment No. 22)*, 48th Sess. (1993), *Compilation of General Comments and General Recommendations Adopted by Human Rights Treaty Bodies*, U.N. Doc. HRI\GEN\1\Rev.1, at 35 (1994) (hereafter *General Comment No. 22 (Religious Freedom)*).

[46] Article 21 of the African Charter.

[47] The UNESCO Convention on the Protection of the Diversity of Cultural Contents and Artistic Expressions was adopted in the 33rd session of UNESCO's General Conference

an international normative instrument, reinforcing the idea that cultural diversity is a defining characteristic of humanity, a form of "common heritage of humanity . . . [that] should be cherished and preserved for the benefit of all."[48] The convention reaffirms the links between culture, development, and dialogue, and explicitly stipulates among its objectives the protection and promotion of the diversity of cultural expressions, the promotion of respect for and raising awareness of, the diversity of cultural expressions on all levels of governance (local, national, and international), and the "recognition to the distinctive nature of cultural activities, goods, and services as vehicles of identity, values and meaning."[49] Article 4 of the convention provides a list of relevant definitions in which biomedical practices can be taken. It takes a broad definition of cultural diversity as "the manifold ways in which the cultures of groups and societies find expression. These expressions are passed on within and among groups and societies." It defines cultural expressions as "those expressions that result from the creativity of individuals, groups and societies, and that have cultural content," delineating cultural content as "the symbolic meaning, artistic dimension and cultural values that originate from or express cultural identities."[50] As cultural expressions inherently include bodily ones, both naturally and intentionally, biomedical practices could easily fall within the scope of this convention.[51]

Finally, both the explicit reference to scientific progress and the treaties pertaining specifically to the issue of bioethics further reinforce the legally binding nature of the international recognition of the link between bodily practices, culture, cultural rights, and identity. Most of these conventions are recent developments in the international human rights arena.[52] They were all crafted within the European Union's regulations (rather than on the international-UN level), with the archetype convention, the European Convention on Human Rights and Biomedicine, entering into force only in December 1999.[53]

---

in October 2005. It was the result of three years of negotiations and was adopted by 148 states, with four abstentions, and only two voting against (the United States and Israel). The convention entered into force on March 18, 2007. See UNESCO's Web site for more information, http://portal.unesco.org/en/ev.php-URL_ID=28354&URL_DO=DO_TOPIC&URL_SECTION=201.html.

[48] Preamble of the UNESCO Convention on Cultural and Artistic Expressions.

[49] Article 1(a), 1(e) and 1(g) of the UNESCO Convention on Cultural and Artistic Expressions.

[50] Article 4(1), 4(3) and 4(2) of the UNESCO Convention on Cultural and Artistic Expressions.

[51] Whether that would be the case in practice, is yet to be seen. The UNESCO Convention on Cultural and Artistic Expressions was originally drafted in order to promote the flow of information across borders, in view of technological developments in this field. Its explicit provisions on "cultural expressions" were essentially an effort to protect the cultural heritage of indigenous groups. However, as international law is developing and as a "living document," its interpretation ultimately depends on the opinions and trends of the time.

[52] The rubric of "bioethics" and the protection of human rights generally include also the Geneva Conventions, pertaining to medical treatment of the wounded, sick, and others in the context of war. The discussion on these conventions is beyond the scope of this study.

[53] Convention for the Protection of Human Rights and Dignity of the Human Being

Their relevance is in the explicit link between biomedicine, human rights and identity.[54] Whereas all other international human rights instruments stipulate the goal of guaranteeing the enjoyment of all rights and freedoms enunciated in the conventions, the Bioethics Conventions state as their purpose and objective the protection of "dignity and identity of all human beings."[55] Although these instruments were drafted with scientific-technological developments in mind within the general human rights discourse,[56] once one accepts that the scientific revolution is also "a (medical) culture,"[57] it would be difficult to justify that such protection applies only selectively to these practices.

C. CHILDREN AS BEARERS OF (BIOMEDICAL) CULTURAL RIGHTS

Assuming that biomedical practices qualify as cultural rights under international human rights law, there is still a need to examine the extent to which they are compatible with the *child's* cultural rights. Conceptually, there is an assumption that one's participation in cultural life and/or manifestation of religio-cultural beliefs, including in the form of biomedical practices, is

with Regard to the Application of Biology and Medicine: Convention on Human Rights and Biomedicine (the Oviedo Convention) (ETS No. 164), entered into force December 1, 1999; Additional Protocol to the Convention for the Protection of Human Rights and Dignity of the Human Being with regard to the Application of Biology and Medicine, on the Prohibition of Cloning Human Beings (ETS No. 168), opened for signature on January 1, 1998, entered into force March 1, 2001; Additional Protocol to the Convention on Human Rights and Biomedicine, on Transplantation of Organs and Tissues of Human Origin (ETS No. 186), opened for signature on January 24, 2002, entered into force May 1, 2006; Additional Protocol to the Convention on Human Rights and Biomedicine, concerning Biomedical Research (ETS No. 195), entered into force September 1, 2007 (hereafter the Convention on Human Rights and Biomedicine or the Oviedo Convention, interchangeably; Additional Protocol on the Prohibition of Cloning, the Additional Protocol on Transplantation of Organs and Tissues; and Additional Protocol on Biomedical Research, respectively. The term "Conventions on Biomedicine" will be used to refer to this set of conventions together.

[54] An exception is the Additional Protocol on the Prohibition of Cloning. However, this convention contains only one substantial provision, stipulating an absolute prohibition of cloning, defined as "any intervention seeking to create a human being genetically identical to another human being, whether living or dead." Article 2 defines "genetically identical" to another human being as "human being sharing with another the same nuclear gene set." See Article 1 of the Additional Protocol on the Prohibition of Cloning.

[55] Article 1 of the Convention on Human Rights and Biomedicine. Articles 1 of the other additional protocols include this reference as well. See also the references made in the Disability Rights Convention that link between a physical trait and identity. Article 24(3)(b) of the Disability Rights Convention refers to states' obligations in the context of education to facilitate "the learning of sign language and the promotion of the linguistic identity of the deaf community," and Article 30(4), dealing with participation in cultural life, stipulates the right of persons with disabilities "to recognition and support of their specific cultural and linguistic identity, including sign languages and deaf culture." That said, the reference to scientific research and development is not stipulated as one's right but as part of states' obligations with regard to international cooperation (Article 32).

[56] The right to "scientific progress" is included within the scope of Article 15(2) of the ICESCR. While this book focuses on "culture as a way of life" (see the Introduction), it is argued that scientific progress is also part of that culture, rather than a separate category of "culture."

[57] See Chapter 1, Section B. See also Deborah Lupton, *Medicine as Culture* (London: Sage Publications, 2003), 84–112, discussing medicine as culture in more detail.

contingent on one's free choice. Article 27 of the UDHR on cultural rights and Articles 18 and 27 of the ICCPR on religious freedom and on ethnic, linguistic, and religious minorities, respectively, all stipulate the element of free and noncoercive participation. The committee under the ICESCR also interpreted the right to take part in cultural life to include this element ("which he or she considers pertinent").[58] Both child-specific instruments contain the word freely with regard to the child's cultural participatory rights as well as the wording of religious freedom.[59] This terminology raises difficulties with children, however, as they are not ordinarily perceived as having freedom of choice. Furthermore, as discussed earlier, children's autonomous religio-cultural freedom is completely intertwined with and contingent on others' interests, rights, and duties.[60] The fear is that by simply stating the child's right to cultural rights and to cultural identity, the right is only equated with the parental/communal one, eschewing the child's own individual voice.[61] For this reason, some argue that there is no need, as a matter of policy, to recognize the child's right to culture or to cultural rights at all.[62]

This assertion requires two subsequent examinations. First one touches upon the broader issue of whether children actually have rights. Despite the widespread use of the rights rhetoric, some argue that children's universal incapacity precludes them from being bearers of rights. The second question is how does it translate with regard to the child's right to identity and, in any case, whether there are any justifications for the preservation of the child's culture and cultural identity in the context of biomedicine that are valued more than choice.

---

[58] Paragraph 1 under Article 15 of the ESCR Report Guidelines.

[59] Article 14 of the Children's Convention, Article 9 and 12 of the African Charter. Article 27 of the UDHR stipulates "everyone has the right to freely participate in the cultural life of the community"; Article 31(1) of the Children's Convention and Article 12(1) of the African Charter state that "State parties recognize the right of the child . . . to participate freely in cultural life and arts." Article 15 of the ICESCR, as well as Articles 23 and 13 of the Children's Convention and of the African Charter, respectively, on children with disabilities, in contrast, do not include the explicit wording "freely participate." The omission may be reflective of the (mistaken) social perceptions of the drafters at the time when the conventions were drafted, by which persons with disabilities, in general, and all the more so children with disabilities, were presumed to lack a capacity to make such free choices. The Disability Rights Convention aimed at remedying this omission, however, as it requires the equalization of the human rights of persons with disabilities with others. In the context of the ICESCR, Article 15 originally only aimed at increasing accessibility to "high culture" rather than the broader understanding of "culture" as understood today. Donders's overview of the work of the committee under the ICESCR and its discussion on the right to participate in cultural life under Article 15 emphasize the element of personal choice and one's own sense of identification as well. Donders, 144–62.

[60] See Chapter 5, Sections D and E.

[61] Harry Brighouse, "What Rights (If Any) Do Children Have?" in *The Moral and Political Status of Children*, ed. David Archard and Colin M. Macleod (Oxford: Oxford University Press, 2002), 50.

[62] Ibid.

1. Do Children Have Rights?

The debate about the extent to which children have rights preceded the children's rights revolution and has continued since. It revolves, in particular, around the meaning and the function of rights in the context of children, with traditional "power/will" theorists and "interest" scholars holding both extremes. According to the first, which follows the (Western) human rights tradition, a right has been conceptualized as "power that a person posses to control or claim or do something."[63] The focus has been on rational and autonomous beings having the capacity to make decisions and claims on their own behalf. Under this power/will theory, for one to be regarded as a rights holder, one needs to have a certain level of competency, that is, rationality combined with at least some agency (i.e., self-sufficiency and autonomy).[64] In other words, only those who are capable of claiming, demanding, or waiving rights can be bearers of rights.

From this vantage point, the question of children's bioethical cultural rights can hardly be contested. At least so far as very young children are concerned, but also more generally in the discussion on children as a subgroup, children cannot be assumed to have an individual will, capacity of rational decision making, and ability to exercise any rights. They are universally, unavoidably, and naturally dependent on those who care for them and practically have power over their lives.[65] Hence, followers of the power/will theory argue that it is only a matter of reasonable deduction that children are not in any way bearers of rights.

Interest theorists, in contrast, build on children's inherent moral worth to justify children's status as rights holders. According to this line of thought, because children's moral rights are equal to those of adults, it would be difficult to justify denying them positive rights as well.[66] As Tom D. Campbell insists, the essence of rights has to do primarily with the "normative defense and furtherance of interests," regardless of one's capacity and rationality or their lack thereof.[67] The question to ask, then, is whether children's interests provide "the basis for having rules which require others to behave in certain ways of identifying these interests and arranging and enforcing duties which meet the requirement that they set."[68] If so, one can and should be regarded as a rights holder. In the particular context of children, as children have interests like all other human beings, they are intrinsically also bearers of rights.[69]

---

[63] James Griffith, "Do Children Have Rights?" in *The Moral and Political Status of Children*, ed. David Archard and Colin M. Macleod (Oxford: Oxford University Press, 2002), 19.

[64] Robert Noggle, "Special Agents: Children's Autonomy and Parental Authority," in *The Moral and Political Status of Children*, ed. David Archard and Colin M. Macleod (Oxford: Oxford University Press, 2002), 99–101.

[65] Onora O'Neill, "Children's Rights and Children's Lives," in *Children, Rights and the Law*, ed. Philip Alston, Stephen Parker, and John Seymour (New York: Oxford University Press, 1995), 38–39.

[66] Tom D. Campbell, "The Rights of the Minor: As Person, as Child, as Juvenile, as Future Adult," in *Children, Rights and the Law*, ed. Philip Alston, Stephen Parker, and John Seymour (New York: Oxford University Press, 1995), 9.

[67] Ibid., 5.

[68] Ibid.

[69] Ibid.

Scholars from both strands of thought provide further philosophical considerations to justify their respective result. Onora O'Neill, for instance, one of the leading power/will theorists, defends her argument by referencing to the traditional legal discourse of rights and duties. She draws a distinction between perfect and imperfect obligations,[70] by which *perfect obligations* include specified obligations that one has to *all* others as well as specified obligations one has for *specified* others. *Imperfect obligations*, in contrast, are specified obligations for unspecified others, but not for all others.[71] Only as long as one remains in the realm of perfect obligations, that is, when there are specified agents and the recipient of their application (albeit differences in the scope, or universality), she contends, is it possible to retain the concept of fundamental rights and of rights holders. It is not the case, however, under circumstances of imperfect obligations, as no such specificity exists. Yet, when one considers children's interests, she argues, one is likely to remain within this latter realm. The examples she has in mind include being kind and considerate in dealing with children, developing their talents, and bestowing upon them a lively attitude in their upbringing. While society certainly views such instances as critical obligations to uphold in children's interests, the recipients of the obligation are not specified. Children's interests are thus located outside of the realm of perfect obligations, and no rights holders (or rights waivers) can be assumed.[72] To bridge between the traditional legal model of rights and the peculiar status of children, she thus suggests stepping aside from the focus on "children's fundamental rights," and instead, securing children's interests in a matrix of fundamental obligations that regulates adults' duties towards children in a more comprehensive way.[73]

Laura M. Purdy, another vocal opponent of the concept of children's rights, calls attention to utilitarian considerations to bolster the power/will model. She argues that children are morally different from adults not only because they lack instrumental reasoning, but also because they lack prudential and moral action. These latter qualifications hold great importance for both the individual and society at large, however, and thus their absence, as far as children are concerned, merits the status of nonrights holders.[74] While adults often have inadequacies in these respects, she contends, it is a price that a liberal society should be willing to pay. But "adding many actors to the scene

[70] O'Neill, 25.

[71] Ibid., 27.

[72] Ibid.

[73] The so-called constructive model. Ibid., 25–27.

[74] Laura M. Purdy, "Why Children Shouldn't Have Equal Rights?" *International Journal of Children's Rights* 2 (1994): 227–28. In this contex, see also Noggle, note 64. Noggle examines—and dismisses—an analogy between trustee (fiduciary) and family relations. He bases his argument on a distinction between cognitive (simple) and moral (global) agency. While children at a relatively young age may have some cognitive, simple, agency, he argues, they lack moral agency. For both reasons relating to the individual child and to the community's interests in having moral and independent, self-sufficient, members, he argues, this latter factor of moral (global) agency is what qualifies one as full membership in the community. He thus concludes that parental authority over their children is justified on the the basis of the moral incapacity of the child.

who suffer from even more extensive deficiencies [i.e., children] will make [the world] still more difficult to cope with the problems now facing humanity."[75] If children were to be granted equal rights, she thus warns, the world would be at a disadvantage, and, worse still, it would risk the survival of a "worthwhile civilization" altogether.[76]

Interest theorists, on the other hand, present their own set of philosophical argumentation to advance the notion that children are bearers of rights. For one thing, as Campbell counters, rights are not granted in order to increase altruism, as Purdy suggests, but to defend self-interests.[77] Children of all ages are thus entitled to positive rights, and, generally, a broader view of social interests cannot and should not prevail. Other scholars draw on the work of leading legal theorists such as Ronald Dworkin and John Rawls to further ground children's interests, moral worth, and hence rights. Michael Freeman, for example, adjusts Dworkin's theory of rights to the context of children by adding to the fundamental concepts of equality of dignity and of respect for persons the "normative value of autonomy," the latter including mere potential capacity for autonomy.[78] Referencing also Rawls's theory of justice, he explains that "equality is . . . best expressed as an original position of equal beings: autonomy as the putative choice of those beings under a 'veil of ignorance'."[79] The assumption is thus that if one had to decide whether to grant children rights without knowing one's own status (i.e., while behind the "veil of ignorance"), the answer would likely be affirmative, notwithstanding some acceptable paternalism so as to ensure that children's interests are protected from themselves.[80]

The debate between the power/will approach and the interest one is important to the general philosophical discourse on children's rights, and one should contemplate their respective strengths and weaknesses. However, the extent to which it makes a practical difference in the particular context of children's bioethics is rather limited. To begin with, it is interesting to note that the gap between them is not as wide as one may think. Ultimately, both strands seem to uphold a separate moral and legal order from which one's interests can be derived and translated into laws. For O'Neill, it is a separate system of obligations that is naturally located outside the scope of state law. Its inclusion within the formal state law in the form of codified adults' responsibilities is nevertheless essential to secure the desired goal of children's protection. For Purdy, it is the moral obligation not to abandon children to their rights that necessitates, in her view, rejecting children as bearers of rights. For Campbell, it

[75] Purdy, 229.

[76] Ibid.

[77] Tom D. Campbell, "Really Equal Rights? Some Philosophical Comments on 'Why Children Shouldn't Have Equal Rights' by Laura M. Purdy," *International Journal of Children's Rights* 2 (1994): 262.

[78] Michael D. A. Freeman, "Taking Children's Rights More Seriously," in *Children, Rights and the Law,* ed. Philip Alston, Stephen Parker, and John Seymour (New York: Oxford University Press, 1995), 64, 66.

[79] Ibid., 64.

[80] Ibid., 67.

is a separate system of moral worth that precedes and parallels the formal legal system. Its translation into codified interests in the form of rights is nevertheless crucial to secure, at least, the child's protective rights. Freeman's reliance on Dworkin's and Rawls's theories is also entirely based on a claim of morality, which is translated into law and rights in order to repudiate utilitarian calculations.[81] Either way, the core of the argument is morally based. It is some sort of a moral order that originated outside and beyond the formal legal system yet that its codification as a mandatory one may be in place. Thus, whether one takes the position of the power/will theorists (by which the rights talk is adult-centered rather than reflecting children's own voice)[82] or the view expressed by interest scholars (by which whichever rhetoric one uses to discuss children's interests, be it interests, rights claims, others' obligations towards them, and so forth), it is ultimately still a question of rights,[83] the essence of the debate is moral, and how, if at all, it would be best to codify it in law. This, however, is also at the essence of bioethical standards, and all the more so in the particular context of children, where sociocultural considerations about children, childhoods, and medical cultures have left the moral-translated-into-legal norms themselves contested.

The second important reason why the application of both strands is limited in the context of children's bioethics is because the evolution of others' duties and responsibilities (whether grounded in the child's interests and rights or in adults' obligations) is inherently contingent on the child's relationships with others and can thus have no meaning if taken, explored, and codified in the abstract or in isolation.

In a sense then, both will/power and interest theories of children's rights seem to miss the point. While to an extent both may be correct, neither actually captures the more complex lived experiences of children *as children* nor the informal and mutual relationships in which children are involved with and which provide them the *legal* organization of their daily lives.[84] Under the power/will theory, children ultimately remain as merely dependent subjects whose interests are protected if an external force obligates adults to do so.[85] State responsibility to uphold the child's rights under interest theories position the child in between an adversarial state-parents/community relationship, a lose-lose situation. While the centrality of the latter to the child's development

---

[81] Ibid., 64.

[82] O'Neill, 38.

[83] Campbell, "The Rights of the Minor," 15.

[84] John Griffith coined the term "legal pluralism" to explain the phenomena of the existence of multiple levels of legal orders by which individuals have, simultaneously, a sense of loyalty and obligation to follow. He argues that social action always takes place in a context of multiple overlapping semiautonomous social fields. Thus, the legal and social organizations of any given society are two complementary systems rather than subsumed within one system. John Griffith, "What Is Legal Pluralism?" *Journal Legal Pluralism & Unofficial Law* 24 (1986): 38.

[85] Barbara Arneil, "Becoming versus Being: A Critical Analysis of the Child in Liberal Theory," in *The Moral and Political Status of Children*, ed. David Archard and Colin M. Macleod (Oxford: Oxford University Press, 2002), 77–78.

as a cultural human being is unequivocal, the rights discourse sets boundaries between them and fails to secure their various meaningful interactions.

Yet it is in between these relationships or orders where children absorb the particular cultural context and the morality that adjoins the various practices. It is within these multiple informal sociolegal orders where children are provided with the sources of attachment and relationships with those around them, particularly with those who care for them and *for whom they care for* that is vital for their development.[86] It is also within these orders, where children as subjects are in the process of developing their autonomy, however conceptualized in any given culture, of which cultural identity is not only an integral part but also a precondition to the child's exercise of his or her rights and freedoms.[87] Putting international and national formal legal instruments aside, then, it is within these semilegal orders where children internalize and negotiate their cultural background in the process of constructing their identities—and hence also their duties and rights. The omission of these indispensable factors by both approaches is a serious one.

2. The Relational Approach/Ethic of Care

Feminist discourse on rights offers a viable alternative. At the heart of this discourse is the assumption that individuals develop within a matrix of relationships. It emphasizes the contextual interdependency and responsibilities and calls for a discussion of rights in view of these relationships.

The "relational theory of rights," or what some have termed "feminist ethic of care,"[88] came about as the other voice to the conventional human rights discourse. It builds on the work of the feminist sociologist, Carol Gilligan, about the differences between the sexes and challenges the preconditions for being a rights' bearer with rationality and autonomous decision-making capacity.[89] Such emphasis, feminists argue, is built on a distorted outlook of society. It views society as comprised of isolated individuals, in which autonomy can presumably be achieved only "by erecting a wall (of rights) between the individual and those around him."[90] In reality, however, individuals are intrinsically interdependent, and autonomy is possible only through relationships.[91] As Anne McGillivray elucidates,

---

86 Ibid., 91.

87 Leora Bilsky, "Child-Parent-State: the Absence of Community in the Courts' Approach to Education," in *Children's Rights and Traditional Values,* ed. Gillian Douglas and Leslie Sebba (Burlington, VT: Ashgate Publishing, 1998), 144–45.

88 Martha Minow, "Rights for the Next Generation: A Feminist Approach to Children's Rights," *Women's Law Journal* 9 (1986): 15; Jennifer Nedelsky, "Re-conceiving Autonomy: Sources, Thoughts and Possibilities," *Yale Journal of Law & Feminism* 1 (1989): 7–36; John O'Manique, *The Origins of Justice: the Evolution of Morality, Human Rights and Law* (Philadelphia: University Pennsylvania Press, 2003); Tom Cockburn, "Children and the Feminist Ethic of Care," *Childhood* 12, no. 1 (2005): 71–73; Samantha Brennan, "Children's Choices or Children's Interests: Which Do Their Rights Protect?," in *The Moral and Political Status of Children,* ed. David Archard and Colin M. Macleod (Oxford: Oxford University Press, 2002), 53–69.

89 Campbell, "The Rights of the Minor," 17.

90 Nedelsky, 12.

91 Anne McGillivray, "Why Children Have Equal Rights: in Reply to Laura Purdy." *International Journal of Children's Rights* 2 (1994): 256; Nedelsky, 12.

> we are communal species dependent from conception to death on complex web of relationships, socialized first to the mother, then to the small community of the family and the increasingly wider communities of friendship, society and governance. 'Individual' can [thus] have meaning only with reference to collectivity. It follows that rights can have meaning only in terms of the collective.[92]

Advocates of the relational theory also contest the paramount importance that the conventional discourse on human rights grants to reason and to rational decision making as the ground for granting rights. As John O'Manique argues persuasively, such an approach subjects the essence of humanity to reason and to the capacity "to analyze and calculate, to induce and deduce" although it is not the whole, nor even the paramount, of it.[93] Instead, much greater attention needs to be given to contextual responsibilities, emotions, and other intuitive characteristics of human nature.[94]

The relational approach has been long advocated by feminists such as Martha Minow, Jennifer Nedelsky, McGilivray, and others in the context of women's rights. It is, however, particularly appealing and even with greater force in the context of children. It casts aside the conventional reflection of (male) adults' perception of rights as a question of authority, status, and power. Focusing instead on the emotional and intuitive aspect of relationships, it thus also brings into the discourse the domestic (feminine) private sphere, encapsulated in the concept of care, which better reflects the status of children.[95]

Specifically, there are three main and related implications in taking this approach. First is that children's rights are understood as a question of relationships and (moral) responsibilities rather than formal rules. It thus recognizes that even though rights are valuable, "they are not sufficient as moral principles underpinning our relations to children."[96] The second implication is that it binds the discourse on children's rights to the informal and contextualized (rather than the abstract) environment. It thus allows for a discourse on children's right to cultural identity as constructed within their sociocultural milieu to take place. The third implication is that the emphasis on connectedness and relations as a means to one's exercise and realization of rights necessarily steps aside from the Western construct of a world of dichotomies: female/male, child/adult, Western/Eastern, I/the "other," private/public, normal/abnormal, victim/aggressor, culture/individual. As such, the relational approach opens a discussion on children of all ages as active participants and as citizens of the world.

This latter consequence is particularly important when one considers the gap that otherwise exists between the conceptualization of childhood and

[92] Ibid., 255–56.
[93] O'Manique, 57–58.
[94] O'Manique, 58–59.
[95] Arneil, 88
[96] Arneil, 89. Arneil suggests this analogy in her comparison between the feminist relational theory of morality and Rawls' (traditional) theory of justice.

of children as bearers of bioethical (and other) rights. Article 1 of both the Children's Convention and its African counterpart define a child as "every human being below the age of eighteen years unless under the law applicable to the child, majority is attained earlier." This formulation reflects the drafters' dual objectives: first, as a matter of public policy, to identify the category of people under the conventions' protection and second, to explicitly recognize that maturity varies depending on the issue or procedure at stake.[97]

Yet, as we saw, the extent to which the rights stipulated in the conventions apply to all children, regardless of age, has been a contentious point. Advocates of the power/will theory hold firmly that granting rights to children who are assumed to have no agency capacity is meaningless. While neither specifies a "childhood age limit" in which children would be considered as having sufficient agency to be granted rights, the underlying assumption is that agency is built on straightforward developmental stages of which children only need "to grow out of." Their acquisition of rights corresponds with their "agency development"[98] and hence is obtained only gradually as well. Accordingly, infants who are assumed to lack any agency capacity have no rights, children who are assumed to have some agency capacity have some rights, and adolescents can usually be assumed as having most of adults' agency capacity and rights.[99] In other words, the emphasis is on "children as becoming," human beings who are ultimately defined by the end product, that is, the adult the child will become.[100]

The result of this line of thought, however, seems to undermine the spirit of the Children's Convention according to which all children are bearers of all the rights listed in it. It also contrasts with contemporary sociological and anthropological studies on childhood and on children's agency, which emphasize that development and participation are not merely an individual process, as conceived under a scientific approach, but a question of interaction.[101] This was found to be reflective of children's own voices as well.

In an ethnographic study of nine- to twelve-year-old children, for example, Helga Kelle observed that children's construction of development is as social praxis, depending on the acceptable social practices and on the children's relations with others, both peer group and adults. She also noticed that children's reflections on gender relations are the main source of influence on their own measure of development.[102] In another study, James J. Dilon highlighted that children's agency can be observed from infancy. Children are

---

[97] U.N. Economic and Social Council, *Report of the 1989 Working Group on a Draft Convention on the Rights of the Child*, 45th Sess., Agenda Item 13, paragraph 80, U.N. Doc. E/CN.4/1989/48 (March 2, 1989).

[98] O'Neill, 39; Noggle, 100; Griffith, "Do Children's Have Rights?" 24

[99] O'Neill, 39.

[100] Arneil, 71; Griffith, "Do Children's Have Rights?" 22.

[101] Helga Kelle, "The Discourse of "Development": How 9-to-12-year-ld Children Construct "Childish" and "Further Developed" Identities within their Peer Culture," *Childhood* 8(1) (2001): 96–97; Judith A. Chafel, and Carin Neitzel, "Young Children's Ideas about the Nature, Causes, Justification, and Alleviation of Poverty," *Early Childhood Research Quarterly* 20 (2005): 434, 447–48.

[102] Kelle, 100–101, 109, 111.

influential actors, he emphasized, not only individually and indirectly (such as, by the power of crying and eye contact), but also on a broader level, having impact on the political values, views of life, and general development of adults around them.[103] In a similar vein, Priscilla Alderson, Joanna Hawthorne, and Margaret Killen further extended children's participatory capacity in the context of medical care from children of seven years old to premature babies.[104] They suggest that rather than assuming that the parents/adults are the ones who allow or support the babies' survival and that the children themselves are mere receivers of support, the crying and amount of energy and concentration these babies put into surviving should be viewed as active participation.[105] Regardless of whether one accepts these particular reconceptualizations of participation, it nevertheless becomes clear that the emphasis of the discussion on children and children's rights should refocus on children *as beings*, present individuals who influence and are influenced by their sociocultural web.

The relational approach naturally corresponds to these observations. Instead of defining children according to an autonomous capacity that they lack, it conceptualizes their capacity as "autonomy-in-relations" or as "autonomy with others." It acknowledges that boundaries and power relations between parents/adults and children are an ongoing dynamic process of negotiation with mutual impact on their development.[106] Indeed, it is only in this sense that such contemporary studies on the participation rights of infants and young children make sense. Moreover, this understanding of participation is the only path that allows analyzing present children as *beings* rather than as *becomings*,[107] which was a core principle of the Children's Convention.

A question that still requires consideration is how the relational approach advances the particular discourse on children's bioethics, which is examined in the next section.

a. *The Relational Approach and Children's Bioethics*

Taking the relational approach makes particular sense in the context of children's bioethics as it overpasses some of the more acute difficulties that arise. First, as was discussed in Chapter 5, Section E, the principlism approach to bioethics and its key component of the doctrine of informed consent have been entirely based on the traditional notion of rational decision making made by separate individuals claiming their autonomy. They emerged from an external (Western) source as a principal reflection of one's inherent dignity and moral worth, and as an effort to regulate physicians and individuals' relations. The

---

[103] James J. Dilon, "The Role of the Child in Adult Development," *Journal of Adult Development* 9, no. 4 (2002): 270.

[104] Priscilla Alderson, *Children's Consent to Surgery* (Buckingham, UK: Open University Press, 1993), 190; Priscilla Alderson, Joanna Hawthorne, and Margaret Killen, "The Participation Rights of Premature Babies," *International Journal of Children's Rights* 13 (2005): 34.

[105] Alderson, Hawthorne and Killen, 39, 43.

[106] Smiljka Tomanović, "Negotiating Children's Participation and Autonomy within Families," *International Journal of Children's Rights*, 11 (2003): 51.

[107] Both the provision and the protection approaches leave children as mere dependent subjects with an emphasis on the potential agents they will become. See Arneil, 80.

Western medical ethics as encapculated in the principlism approach and the doctrine of informed consent, however, is only one possible way of regulating physician/individuals' relations, and it cannot be universally applied.[108] Even when it is applied, the extent to which children have the rights to, or the interests in, exercising informed consent under the Children's Convention is limited.

As discussed in Chapter 2, an explicit requirement of the child's informed consent was excluded from the final text of the Children's Convention's and so it is not legally codified in the child-specific instrument on the international level. The failure to include such a provision, especially considering the awareness and concerns that were raised in this context, theoretically, implies that children do not have this right. This is the case also under the European Conventions on Biomedicine. While the Convention on Human Rights and Biomedicine requires informed consent for any biomedical intervention, the assumption with regard to children is that they are "persons not able to consent."[109] The right to provide informed consent is thus given to the child's representative or others authorized by law.[110] The Children's Committee's requirement that states provide it with information on the issue and the European requirement that the child's opinion will be heard "taking into consideration as an increasingly determining factor in proportion to his or her age and degree of maturity" (though without determinative power)[111] are thus based on the moral value that is assumed to be inherent to the discourse.[112]

But the problem with the doctrine of informed consent in the context of children goes beyond that. Even when it exists, it is inherently dependent on the child's relationships with those around him or her. Although studies have

---

[108] See discusion in Chapter 1.

[109] Title of Article 6 of the Convention on Human Rights and Biomedicine. The article includes also adults who according to law, do not have the capacity to consent to an intervention "because of mental disability, a disease or for similar reasons" (Article 6(3)).

[110] Article 6(2) of the Convention on Human Rights and Biomedicine.

[111] Article 6(2)) of the Convention on Human Rights and Biomedicine. As mentioned in Chapter 2, this explicit provision in the Convention on Human Rights and Biomedicine is, in a way, a step ahead of the Children's Convention. Still, note that the Convention on Human Rights and Biomedicine did not grant the child any determinative power but settled on a rather low model of children's participation. Scholars point to four main models of child's participation—being informed, expressing a view, influencing the decision, and being a main decider. Michael Freeman, "Children's Health and Children's Rights: An Introduction," *International Journal of Children's Rights* 13, no. 1–2 (2005): 2; Gerison Lansdown, *The Evolving Capacities of the Child.* (Florence, Italy: UNICEF & Innocenti Research Centre, 2005), 16–17. See also Gerison Lansdown, *Promoting Children's Participation in Democratic Decision-Making* (Florence, Italy: UNICEF & Innocenti Research Centre, 2001), 16. The European provision as it stands thus seems as taking only the second level.

[112] One could of course argue that children have this right through the general human rights instruments, particularly, Article 7 of the ICCPR, and as "reserved" in Article 41 of the Children's Convention. Yet as the Convention aimed at drafting an instrument that is comprehensive and that addresses children's lives from all aspects (including these that are already recognized in other "general" human rights treaties (such as the right to life, freedom from torture, etc.)), the omission of a reference to the question of informed consent is significant.

found that given the appropriate environment and communication, children as young as seven are capable of giving an equally rationalized informed consent as adults would,[113] others (such as the parents, community, courts, and medical professionals) are still the ones making the decision regarding the child's capacity and maturity on his or her behalf. The inevitable result is that these others compete on the "right" biomedical choice. To avoid such confrontational conflict, the approach toward children's bioethics, thus, has to be beyond the question of informed consent and parental/professional/courts' choice. Applying the ethic of care and its emphasis on moral responsibilities, in contrast, provides an alternative, proactive, and problem-solving approach as it brings them together. Instead of retaining the biomedical conflict between the parents/community and the medical professional, or between the parents'/community's duty to *fulfill* and the state's to *enforce*, all parties now concentrate on working together on what aspects of care they might best provide.[114] As such, it also allows room for the child's voice.

More than that, the relational approach allows for the determination of risks and benefits of bodily practices to be contextualized. This is important because society's moral order is not built on individual subjects, but rather on the collective.[115] Stressing physical implications of a biomedical procedure is thus insufficient to justify parental (and other relevant others') choice or its dismissal. Parents and others who care for the child have an invaluable expertise and knowledge of their child that no objective doctor or court can acquire during the short interaction each has with the child.[116] Their decision to carry out such bodily practices on their child may be genuinely concerned with the mental implications and benefits that the child would gain, mostly, one's rootedness, sense of communal belonging, and identity.[117] A holistic, relational, approach to the interpretation of children's rights is thus crucial, and it is particularly so in the context of bioethics. Considering the indisputable connection between the body, society, and culture, and between these and the individual and his or her identity, children's bioethical rights cannot be seriously discussed by excluding their sociocultural sources of influence, but rather by acknowledging and involving their autonomy-in-relations with these webs around them.

This also leads to the argument that there is yet a further adjustment in the relational approach that needs to be made in the context of children.[118] Once

---

[113] Alderson, *Children's Consent to Surgery*, 190.

[114] Arneil, 90.

[115] Stephen Frosh, "Identity, Religious Fundamentalism and Children's Welfare," in *Moral Agendas for Children's Welfare*, ed. Michael King (New York: Routledge, 1999), 206

[116] See also, in this regard, Bridgeman, discussing court cases in the United Kingdom and the European Court of Human Rights revolving around children with disabilities. Particularly in view of the recent *Glass* case, she stresses the need to opt out of the "all objective medical expertise approach" in favor of a more flexible and relational one that acknowledges parental expertise. Jo Bridgeman, "Caring for Children with Severe Disabilities: Boundaried Relational Rights," *International Journal of Children's Rights* 13, no. 1–2 (2005): 99–119.

[117] Frosh, 205; Katz, 93, 99.

[118] See also, in this context, Cockburn, 80. He suggests adjusting the feminist ethic of

it is acknowledged that children's legal orders are completely immersed in the sociocultural ones, children's autonomy as rights holders has to reflect their own experiences. The question is what would be the best way to do so.

One option is to translate children's autonomy into children as "future-oriented" consenters. According to this approach, adults' interference with children's autonomy by making decisions on their behalf is justified as the children would retrospectively appreciate and accept the interference.[119] This option is too limited, however. It assumes that the child will necessarily adopt similar values to those that led the adults to make the concrete decision on his or her behalf, although that is not always the case. For instance, children raised as Christian Scientists, who rely exclusively on faith healing, would not appreciate imposed medical treatment as they mature unless they are instilled with values that remove them from their entire familial and communal religious setting. While not supporting in any way a child's death, one still must remember that such cultural displacement may be devastating not only to the family and the community, but to the child as well. Furthermore, it still does not view children's experiences from their points of view, but rather from the experiences of other adults.

A persuasive alternative is suggested by Leora Bilsky. Her argument is based on the assumption that children are subjects who are simultaneously *in the process of* developing their autonomy as well as their cultural identity. Both processes of development, however, are intrinsically influenced by the children's communities and hence necessitate that one provides an explicit space for children's autonomy *as* identity. She thus suggests reconceptualizing autonomy, whereby adults' rights will remain conceptualized in terms of autonomy and freedom, and children's autonomy would be analyzed as a question of identity.[120] The relationship between these two notions of autonomy, she holds, allows for a more qualified understanding of the interaction between children and their relationships as a forum in which they will ultimately exercise their rights.[121]

Although Bilsky's discussion was in the context of education, having reviewed the studies on children, her proposal is appealing also in the context of children's bioethics. Medical cultures establish the criteria of autonomy as appropriate for their respective communities and they are inherently intertwined with the group's and the individual's sense of identity.[122] Furthermore, considering the important role children's webs of relations play in their lives, such an approach also seems to better reflect children's own voices in the construction

---

care in the context of children so it avoids the construction of children as mere recipients of care, hence acknowledging the reality in which children often care for others (without attributing any sort of suffering to it). Cockburn, 82. He also points out correctly that there is a need to increase research on the voice of those who are "cared for," which goes beyond the conventional studies so far, which focused on the concept of care and on the power relations between the caregivers and the "cared for" with an emphasis on the first.

[119] Freeman, "Taking Children's Rights More Seriously," 68.

[120] Bilsky, 145.

[121] Ibid.

[122] See the discussion in Chapter 1.

of the concepts of development, participation, autonomy, and also rights. The reconceptualization of autonomy as identity as far as children's bioethics is concerned is thus in place.

b. Arguments against the Relational Approach

Some caution against espousing a moral system that is built on the ethic of care in the context of children is necessary. For instance, Campbell warned that it would create an inevitable asymmetry between children's equal moral worth and their lack of rights.[123] McGillivray specifically charges that any such effort should be suspect. Her assumption is that rights transform the child from a "thing" to a member of his or her respective community and provide the framework for the relationship. This is especially so in view of the hegemony of the rights rhetoric: if children cannot make rights claims, their status will be consigned to the status of slaves.[124] As the argument thus goes, proposals to replace rights with care/relations may thus be viewed as only reflecting adults' fear of losing control and power over children and, hence, should be dismissed.[125]

This line of thought is limited though, for two main reasons. First, it seems to assume that the approach to ethic of care inherently replaces the rights discourse, although this is not necessarily the case. There is nothing inherent in the centrality of the complex web of relations, intuitions, and emotions as advocated by the relational approach that precludes a complementary discourse on rights.[126] Similarly, there is nothing in the approach's interpretation and contextualization of the place of the family, parents, and children that demands such a result. Rather, it may only remove the point in which rights are evoked, questioning where the "good fences" should be placed, yet not thrusting them aside altogether. They should be, as Barbara Arneil points out, "nothing more than a fallback position should the ties of affection, care and kinship fail."[127]

Second, insisting on the rights talk is problematic as it relegates issues to legal categories, although they are far more complex than an abstract discussion on rights. Contrary to the conventional argument, it is often not age, autonomy, capacity, rationality, or the ability to claim that make an individual a citizen with rights and duties within his or her respective community. Among many African cultures, for instance, one's membership is based on a combination of social and economic factors in which the child participates, in the passage of physical initiation ceremonies (particularly the circumcision rituals), and in the various constructs of childhood that apply to the individual, including his or her relationships and responsibilities and duties to others.[128] A similar

---

[123] Campbell, "The Rights of the Minor," 9.

[124] McGillivray, 246.

[125] Ibid., 244.

[126] Cockburn, 78. See, furthermore, that the concept of care is in itself often built on power-relations of carer givers and those who are being "cared for." Cockburn, 80–81.

[127] Arneil, 83.

[128] Alice Armstrong, Matrine Chuulu, Chuma Himonga, and Puleng Letuka, "Towards a Cultural Understanding of the Interplay between Children's and Women's Rights: An Eastern and Southern African Perspective," *International Journal of Children's Rights* 3 (1995): 336, 338.

mingling of responsibilities and duties, subordination, and power is also prevalent among Pacific Island cultures.[129] A conceptualization of the entire discourse on children's bioethics needs to recognize the relational experiences of children,[130] their dependency, and their attachments to both individuals and collectives who constitute their communities of reference.[131] These ultimately have to be conceptualized in terms of the child's cultural identity, which is discussed in the next section.

D. CHILDREN'S CULTURAL IDENTITY

Although human rights discourse seems to have been obsessed with the question of identity in the past few decades, the discourse on children's cultural identity began only in the 1990s. This oversight is odd because in order for cultural groups to endure, they must convey their traditions to children who serve as the ultimate carriers of the culture's future.[132] While the complexities associated with multiculturalism have been discussed extensively, the ongoing efforts to sustain boundaries and hence identities[133] seem to have ignored the role of children. Thus, although the identity crisis has been characterized as "symptomatic of postmodern predicament of contemporary politics,"[134] children's rights to identity as both the source of the conflicts and as a possible cure has been overlooked.

This is all the more peculiar considering that although an array of international instruments, declarations, resolutions, and judicial decisions acknowledge the prominent *value* of cultural identity,[135] the Children's Convention was the first and most explicit international legally binding instrument stipulating this right.[136] Article 8 of the Convention states that, "States Parties undertake to respect the right of the child to preserve his or her identity, including nationality, name and family relations as recognized by law without unlawful interference."[137] Article 8(2) further sheds light on state responsibility in this regard, stating that "where a child is illegally deprived of some or all of the elements of his or her identity, States Parties shall provide appropriate assistance and protection, with a view to re-establishing speedily his or her identity." Theoretically, then,

---

[129] Clifford R. O'Donnell, "The Right to a Family Environment in Pacific Island Cultures," *International Journal of Children's Rights* 3 (1995): 90–91.

[130] Anne Donchin, "Understanding Autonomy Relationally: Towards a Reconfiguration of Bioethical Principles," *Journal of Medicine. & Philosophy* 26, no. 4 (2001): 367.

[131] Arneil, 91.

[132] David Archard, "Children, Multiculturalism and Education," in *The Moral and Political Status of Children*, ed. David Archard and Colin M. Macleod (Oxford: Oxford University Press, 2002), 142.

[133] Tharaileth K. Oommen, *Pluralism, Equality and Identity: Comparative Studies* (New Delhi: Oxford University Press, 2002), 29.

[134] Mercer, 43.

[135] Donders, 329–31.

[136] Donders, for example, in her extensive study questioning whether there is an international trend towards an explicit legally binding right to cultural identity does not have any reference to the Children's Convention.

[137] Interestingly, although the African Charter incorporated various provisions stipulating the child's right and duty to follow African morals, traditional values, and cultures, it does include an explicit right to identity as the Children's Convention.

the separate provision in the Convention should have overcome some of the ambiguity that surfaces in the general debate on cultural rights and cultural identity.

The omission seems to be a result of a few contrasting views on identity claims, particularly in the context of children. A part of it may also be the result of a (mistaken) impression that contestations of boundaries and identities take place mostly on the macro (political and national) levels.[138] This may also reflect the traditional emphasis on minority groups and hence also the related question whether identity claims, which inherently contain subjective elements, are proper subjects of public and political assessment.[139] Either way, as children are commonly viewed as players only in the private/micro sphere, their identities seem to be less subject to political manipulation.

Another part has to do with the (Western) assumption that identities are to a great extent a matter of "pick and choose." This understanding evolved on the back of the indisputable characteristics of cultural identities as ongoing processes that are open to change. Identity is viewed as the conjunction of one's past with the social, cultural, and economic relations in which one lives and a site in which the interrelationships of differences are marked by translation and negotiation.[140] As a thing that is negotiable, the supposition has thus been that there is always a space for personal choice, "reinvention,"[141] and, furthermore, that it is almost a question of one's own preference. It is in this vein that Donders, for example, draws an analogy between the right to religious freedom and advocates for recognition of one's right to "freedom of identity."[142]

Framed in this way, the child's right to identity raises theoretical difficulties. On the one hand, children were not traditionally conceived as pickers and choosers. Ordinarily they were merely ascribed their parental or stereotypical identities based on assumptions about religion, culture, race, or ethnicity. They were not perceived, however, as having—not to mention being the creators of—their own identities at all.[143] Their identity was essentially understood in contrast to adults, to what they are not as yet but who they will (presumably) eventually become.[144] Interestingly, the formulation of the child's right to *preserve* his or her identity under the Children's Convention may also be seen as supporting this argument. The idea of preservation may come across as reinforcing parental/communal power of indoctrination over the child and connote that children's identity is otherwise fixed. On the other hand, psychological and social studies

---

[138] See Chapter 4.

[139] Eisenberg, 162.

[140] Jonathan Rutherford, "A Place Called Home: Identity and the Cultural Politics of Difference," in *Identity: Community, Culture, Difference*, ed. Jonathan Rutherford (London: Lawrence & Wishart, 1990), 19–20, 26.

[141] Martha Minow, *Not Only For Myself: Identity, Politics, and the Law* (New York: New Press, 1997), 23

[142] Donders, 340.

[143] Bunting, 473.

[144] Lucia Rabello De Castro, "Otherness in Me, Otherness in Others: Children's and Youth's Constructions of Self and Other," *Childhood* 11, no. 4 (2004): 471.

on children's identity have established that children have their own identities that differ from the identities of their parents.[145] Scholars point out that children have a range of shifting cultural identities to which they switch depending on the contexts.[146] Marc Jans even argues that the child's cultural identification is essentially the one characteristic that distinguishes citizenship of the child from adults. Whereas, for adults, national (political) citizenship is a primary aspect of identity, children, he argues, possess a much broader capability of creating informal networks and identifying themselves with multiple and larger social groups and communities.[147] Children are thus increasingly viewed as producers rather than mere recipients of culture and of cultural identities.[148]

On the basis of such findings (Western) scholars have increasingly emphasized the need to guarantee the child's capacity to make identity choices on his or her own. Harry Brighouse, for instance, advocates for policy goals that aim at protecting the child's interests to have "emotional and intellectual resources to revise their identities to be congruent with their own personalities."[149] He cautions that if we assume that the child's right to culture intrinsically follows the parental culture, we only grant protection to acquiring "unchosen, difficult to shrug off, identities" (or give paramount importance to it). It would thus stand in contrast to the child's right or interest to acquire an identity that is grounded in choice.[150] Judith Ackroyd and Andrew Pilkington make a similar point, arguing that instead of advocating for a right of the children to a cultural identity, children need to have a right to construct their own cultural identities.[151]

There are three main difficulties that these assumptions of "identity authorship" raise, however. First, on the general level, there is perhaps no better example than the human body that exemplifies the mingling between the public and the private spheres in the process of identity construction. While the body is presumably under the individual's control, in practice, as Michel Foucault and other social scientists observed a long time ago, it turned out to be

> the ultimate site of political and ideological control, surveillance and regulation. . . . Through the body and its behaviors, state apparatuses such as medicine, the educational system, psychiatry and the law define the limits of behavior and record activities, punishing those bodies which violate the established boundaries and thus rendering bodies productive and politically and economically useful.[152]

---

[145] Bunting, 480.

[146] Judith Ackroyd and Andrew Pilkington, "Childhood and the Construction of Ethnic Identities in a Global Age," *Childhood* 6, no. 4 (1999): 445.

[147] Marc Jans, "Children as Citizens: Towards A Contemporary Notion of Child Participation," *Childhood* 11, no. 1 (2004): 39.

[148] Ackroyd and Pilkington, 444, 453.

[149] Brighouse, 50.

[150] Brighouse examines children's rights to religion, culture and freedom of expression as falling within the scope of the child's cultural rights. Brighouse, 50.

[151] Ackroyd and Pilkington, 453.

[152] Lupton, 25.

These characteristics of the body, as a locale of social and political control, remain inextricably entwined with issues of identity.[153] The power to label bodies as deviant or normal, as hygienic or unhygienic, as controlled or needing control,[154] and as beautiful or ugly, castrating and repugnant[155] is inherently intertwined with the private sphere, as one's identity is made in relation to such public proclamations. As Tharaileth K. Oommen points out, if previously one's identity was under the individual's search for his or her self-determination, the social attribution of identity now invades all areas that were traditionally protected by the "private sphere." [156]

Second, the assumption of "self-invention" has to be made with caution. As Rainer Baubock,[157] Stephen Frosh,[158] and others emphasize, there is no such thing as a completely free decision about identity or culture. Culture must be regarded as both a context and as something that can be chosen, but it is always constrained by one's present cultural affiliations and by the need to gain recognition from the alternative culture.[159] This is particularly so in the case of children whose dependency on the various communal attachments and contexts is critical for their constitutive development of self.[160] Attention should also be given to the fact that the liberal construction of autonomy as the ability to revise one's identity is only partial. Autonomy does not provide one only with the ability to change his or her conception of good (i.e., culture), but also with the equivalent value of fostering the capacities to decide to *adhere* to a conception of good.[161] Thus, even if one upholds the liberal emphasis on choice, a more qualified approach necessitates creating a space in which one can retain traditional values.[162] This argument is valid for the broader discourse on culture and on cultural identity, and even with greater force in the context of children who are, ultimately, the bearers of *all* cultural identities.

There is still another issue that one should consider in this context, however: the value given to choice itself. The underlying assumptions in the

---

[153] Hillel Steiner, "Silver Spoons and Golden Genes: Talent Differntials and Distributive Justice," in *The Moral and Political Status of Children*, ed. David Archard and Colin M. Macleod (Oxford: Oxford University Press, 2002), 187.

[154] Michel Foucault, *The History of Sexuality, Volume One: An Introduction* (London: Penguin, 1979), 54, quoted in Lupton, 25.

[155] Richard Shweder, "What About FGM?" And Why Understanding Culture Matters in the First Place?" in *Engaging Cultural Difference: The Multicultural Challenge in Liberal Democracies*, ed. Richard A. Shweder, Martha Minow, and Hazel Rose Markus (New York: Russell Sage Foundation, 2002), 224.

[156] Oommen, 38.

[157] Rainer Baubock, "Cultural Minority Rights for Immigrants," *International Migration Review* 30, no. 1 (1996): 203–50.

[158] Stephen Frosh, "Identity, Religious Fundamentalism and Children's Welfare," in *Moral Agendas for Children's Welfare*, ed. Michael King (New York: Routledge, 1999).

[159] Baubock, 207.

[160] Arneil, 91.

[161] Eamonn Callan, "Autonomy, Child-Rearing, and Good Lives," in *The Moral and Political Status of Children*, ed. David Archard and Colin M. Macleod (Oxford: Oxford University Press, 2002), 118, 130.

[162] Callan raises this argument in the context of children's religious education.

discourse of children's rights to culture and cultural identity have ultimately been that rational decision making is a necessity to "shrug off identities" or to "retain identities,"[163] and that one's choosing of culture and identity is a good in itself. Western scholars addressing this issue provide two main rationales for this line of argument. One is grounded in the interest of the community at large (presumably, the liberal state) in developing citizens that are capable of rational and autonomous choice.[164] Others also point to the interest of the child in developing such autonomous cultural and identity decision making, separate and different from the states' interests.[165] They ground this position in what Joel Feinberg, Dena Davis, and others conceptualized as "the child's right to an open future" and propose policies that aim at maximizing the child's possible life choices.[166]

This emphasis on choice, however, is and should be only a part of the picture. Choice is not only a matter of rational adherence to or rejection of a conception of good that one has an interest in acquiring. Another inherent part of human choice is also the reliance on the intuitive and emotional adherence to or rejection of a conception of good. Furthermore, autonomous choice is itself not an absolute value of all or nothing, nor is it valued similarly across the board. In other words, not all things can be chosen; some things can be chosen, but not by us; and, furthermore, not all has to be chosen. This, so it seems, is where the discourse on the relational approach, medical cultures, cultural identities, and children needs to be examined.[167] To what extent is the sociopsychological discourse on the child's identity applicable to the legal discourse on the "right of the child to preserve his or her identity, including nationality, name and family relations"?[168] How does it come about in the work of the Children's Committee, particularly in the context of biomedical practices?

1. The Child's Right to Identity under the Children's Convention

If one examines the historical legislative process of the child's right to preserve his or her identity, one sees that the provision was drafted with both legal and sociocultural identities in mind.[169] The originators of the provision,

---

[163] Brighouse, 50; Callan, 118.

[164] Noggle, 112.

[165] Archard, "Children, Multiculturalism and Education," 153–54.

[166] Feinberg stamped the concept of the child's right to "an open future" in his work in the 1980s, and it has been used and referenced to by others scholars since. Joel Feinberg, "The Child's Right to an Open Future," in *Whose Child? Children's Rights, Parental Authority, and State Power,* ed. Will Aiken and Hugh La Falleete (Totowa, NJ: Littlefield, Adams, 1980), 125–27. Dena S. Davis, "Genetic Dilemmas and the Child's Right to an Open Future," *Hastings Center Report* 27, no. 2 (1997): 12; Archard, "Children, Multiculturalism and Education," 156.

[167] This touches upon the broader question of how to balance between the collective and the individual dimensions of culture, cultural rights, and cultural identity, which is elaborated on later on in Section E.2 and Chapter 8, Section C.

[168] Article 8 of the Children's Convention.

[169] See Chapter 2.

the Argentinean delegation and its supporters, were explicit about it, proposing the wording the child's "inalienable right to retain his true and genuine personal, legal and family identity."[170] Although the provision as it currently stands diverges from this wording, its formulation, "including nationality, name and family relations as recognized by law" suggests that this intention was retained. This conclusion also makes sense in light of the various political forces that played a role during the drafting of the Children's Convention.

As in every legislative process, the article was drafted so as to avoid unnecessary redundancy. In fact, this was also the initial and main objection raised to Argentina's proposal to include the provision on the child's right to identity. After all, Article 7 of the Children's Convention already specifically stipulates "the right from birth to a name, the right to acquire a nationality and, as far as possible, the right to know and be cared for by his or her parents." Settling on the formulation in Article 8, which makes explicit reference only to elements that were already recognized and protected under another provision in the Convention,[171] is thus not accidental, and it has to be viewed as an effort to ensure elements that were beyond that. Moreover, one needs to appreciate the extent to which this formulation reflects the disagreements that occurred among the state delegates regarding the scope of the provision and the ambiguity that the sociocultural aspects of identity raise. Delegates indeed requested further clarifications on the terminology of the original proposal, stipulating the child's right to preserve his or her "true and genuine" identity. They also raised questions about its interpretation. Even if some delegates originally preferred to limit the provision to legal elements of identity, however, the decision to go ahead with wording that inherently allowed for broader interpretation necessitates the conclusion that they were ultimately willing to accept more than just legal identity. This is particularly so when one recalls the consensual basis for the work of the working group.[172] If they were not persuaded, they could have retained their objection, and the working group would not have adopted a choice of words that implied other sociocultural aspects of identity. But as the final text of the Convention demonstrates, they refrained from doing so. To what extent has the Children's Committee taken note of these interests?

2. The Children's Committee Analysis

The Children's Committee's analysis of the child's right to preserve his or her identity under Article 8 of the Children's Convention is narrow. In its

[170] U.N. Economic and Social Council, *Report of the 1985 Working Group on a Draft Convention on the Rights of the Child*, 41st Sess., Agenda Item 13, paragraph 9 and annex II, U.N. Doc. E/CN.4/1985/64 (April 3, 1985) (*Legislative History* of Article 8 (Identity), 4; Sharon Detrick, *A Commentary on the United Nations Convention on the Rights of the Child* (Dordrecht: Martinus Nijhoff, 1999), 160.

[171] See also, in this regard, Articles 9–10 of the Children's Convention (dealing with family relations and family reunification), Article 18 (parental responsibilities for the upbringing and development of the child), Articles 20–21 (alternative family environment and adoption).

[172] Cohen, 171. For further discussion of the Children's Convention, see Chapter 2, Section E.2.c.

General Guidelines for States' Reports, the Committee classifies its analysis under the theme of "civil rights and freedoms" and requires states "to provide relevant information, including the principal legislative, judicial, administrative or other measures in force; factors and difficulties encountered and progress achieved in implementing the relevant provisions, and implementation priorities and specific goals for the future."[173] The General Guidelines provide no further clarification, however, on the elements that constitute the child's "preservation of identity."[174] The Committee thus seems to have taken, on the formal level, a passive stance in this context.

Analysis of the Children's Committee's list of issues, summary records, and concluding observations sheds little light on the matter. In some cases, the Committee merely cites the provision. In its list of issues to Croatia, for instance, it requires that further information be provided about the "implementation in practice of the provisions of Articles 7 and 8 of the Convention, particularly on how national legislation ensures that the child's right to preserve his/her nationality and his or her identity is fully respected and protected."[175] In its list of issues to Argentina, it also required information on the steps taken to ensure that "in case of illegal deprivation of elements of the child's identity, all appropriate assistance and protection is provided to re-establish such identity."[176]

In others, and as has been for the most part, the Children's Committee completely tied up the discussion on the child's right to preserve his or her identity with Article 7, which stipulates state responsibility to ensure the child's right to birth registration, the child's right to a name, the child's right acquire nationality, and "as far as possible, the right to know and be cared for by his or her parents." Accordingly, its reference to the issue in its list of issues and summary records often revolves only around the formal legal documentation of the elements of identification with regard to birth registration, name, and nationality.[177] Similarly, its concluding observations often merely express a

[173] Paragraph 15(b) of the *Guidelines Regarding the Form and Contents of Periodic Reports to be Submitted by States Parties under Article 44, paragraph 1(b) of the Convention,* U.N. Doc. CRC/C/58 (November 20, 1996) (hereafter General Guidelines).

[174] This lack of clarification exists also in the more recent general comment the Committee issued on The Rights of Children with Disabilities (Committee on the Rights of the Child, *The Rights of Children with Disabilities (General Comment No. 9),* U.N. Doc. CRC/C/GC/9 (2007) (hereafter *General Comment No. 9 (Children with Disabilities)*). Paragraph 34 of the general comment repeats the child's right to preserve his or her identity, but it does not provide further elaboration.

[175] Committee on the Rights of the Child, *List of Issues: Croatia.* U.N. Doc. CRC/C.11/WP.1 (November 27, 1995).

[176] Committee on the Rights of the Child, *List of Issues: Argentina,* paragraph 18, U.N. Doc. CRC/C.6/WP.1 (February 17, 1994).

[177] See, e.g., Committee on the Rights of the Child, *Summary Record: Ukraine,* U.N. Doc. CRC/C/SR.240 (November 7, 1995). The Children's Committee requested further information on the measures taken to ensure the child's right to preserve his or her identity under Article 8. It stressed that it was not merely a legal concern but that the lack of sufficient legal provision facilitated activities such as trafficking in children (paragraph 9). The Committee was also unsatisfied with Ukraine's delegates' response that it is protected by the national law on citizenship, hence leading to its remark, in its concluding observations, that it is "con-

concern about states' insufficient implementation of "Articles 7 and 8 of the Convention," with particular reference only to the above-mentioned formal elements of identity. Thus, for example, the Committee made specific note when birth registration or the naming of the child are influenced by his or her status of legitimacy and hence affected the application of equal rights.[178] On a few occasions, the Committee expressed its concern that states' policies on adoption, anonymous birth,[179] and anonymous sperm donors in assisted reproductive methods may be in violation of the child's right to identity. Yet, even in such latter instances, the Committee has only focused on "truth telling" and on the legal regulations that are insufficient to protect the child's right to know his or her biological parents.[180] The question whether the scientific-medical practices themselves violate in any way the child's sense of identity, in contrast, was not raised.[181]

The Children's Committee's reference to children's cultural identity has been almost exclusively in its address of children belonging to minority groups,[182]

---

cerned about the absence of any law prohibiting the sale and trafficking of children, and the fact that the right of the child to have his/her identity preserved is not guaranteed by the law" (Committee on the Rights of the Child, *Concluding Observations: Ukraine,* paragraph 11, U.N. Doc. CRC/C/15/Add.42 (November 27, 1995)). However, once the Ukraine delegate provided information on its legal measures to ensure the child's right to name and nationality in its next periodic report, it seems to have satisfied the Committee's previous concerns, as neither the list of issues, the summary records, nor the concluding observations raised it again. See Committee on the Rights of the Child, *List of Issues: Ukraine,* U.N. Doc. CRC/C/Q/UKR/2 (June 14, 2002); Committee on the Rights of the Child, *Summary Record: Ukraine,* U.N. Doc. CRC/C/SR.821 (October 1, 2002); Committee on the Rights of the Child, *Concluding Observations: Ukraine,* U.N. Doc. CRC/C/15/Add.191 (October 9, 2002).

[178] Committee on the Rights of the Child, *Concluding Observations: Malawi,* paragraphs 31–32, U.N. Doc. CRC/C/15/Add.174 (April 2, 2002).

[179] There is a distinction between *anonymous birth* and *secrecy birth.* Anonymous birth refers to the situation in which mothers are allowed, by law, to deliver a child without providing any identifying information on them. Such policy exists, for example, in France, as was originated in an effort to elevate the problem of mothers who give birth secretly and abandon their children. Secrecy births, in contrast, require mothers to provide their identifying information, although it is kept secret. Children are often allowed to have access to at least some of the information, depending on the mother's request at the time of birth, once they reach a certain age of maturity (as determined by each state).

[180] Committee on the Rights of the Child, *Concluding Observations: Switzerland,* U.N. Doc. CRC/C/15/Add.182 (June 7, 2002); Committee on the Rights of the Child, *Concluding Observations: Monaco,* U.N. Doc. CRC/C/15/Add.158 (June 8, 2001); Committee on the Rights of the Child, *Concluding Observations: Denmark,* U.N. Doc. CRC/C/15/Add.33 (February 15, 1995); Committee on the Rights of the Child, *Concluding Observations: France,* U.N. Doc. CRC/C/15/Add.20 (April 25, 1994); and Committee on the Rights of the Child, *Concluding Observations: Norway,* U.N. Doc. CRC/C/15/Add.23 (April 25, 1994). In the context of adoption, for example, see Committee on the Rights of the Child, Kyrgyzstan, paragraph 38, U.N. Doc. CRC/C/15/Add.127 (August 9, 2000).

[181] For an interesting comparison in this context, see the approach taken by the European Court of Human Rights in the case of *X, Y and Z v. the UK* (Application no. 21830/93, European Court of Human Rights, Judgment of April 22, 1997). The case raised the question of the child's identity in a social family comprised of a biological mother, a female-to-male transgender father, and an anonymous-donor in vitro fertilization child. See Chapter 7.

[182] See paragraph 64 of the *General Comment No. 9 (Children with Disabilities)*, which emphasizes the importance of including a child with disabilities in the education system as a

particularly indigenous groups.[183] This attitude gained particular momentum since 2003, after the Committee held a Day of General Discussion on the rights of children belonging to indigenous groups. During this day, the Committee heard representatives of the Working Group on Cultural Diversity and of the Working Group on Nondiscrimination who emphasized, among other issues, the importance of cultural identity. Ms. Nicolaisen, the moderator of the Working Group on Cultural Diversity, expressed her concern with regard to the invisibility of indigenous cultures and stressed the negative impact it has on the self-esteem and lack of sense of identity that children belonging to indigenous groups have. She stressed that it is necessary to find ways to ensure ownership of culture and to adopt legislation to protect indigenous languages, overcome the conflict between traditional values and human rights rhetoric, and empower indigenous youth groups.[184]

The Special Rapporteur of the Working Group on Nondiscrimination also commented on indigenous children and identity. She emphasized the enormous psychological damage that indigenous children and indigenous communities in general suffer due to "the loss of indigenous families and communities through institutionalization, removal for adoption, disappearance or armed conflict." She also stressed the collective right of indigenous peoples to their land and its importance "in order to provide children with negotiating power and identity."[185]

The Children's Committee has indeed taken into account these recommendations in later observations, for example, of Brazil.[186] Taking particular note of Brazil's new constitutional recognition of the "social organizations, customs, languages, creeds and traditions" of indigenous communities and its abolishment of discrimination, the Committee also made explicit reference to the child's right to cultural identity. The Committee recommended that: "the State take adequate measures in order to provide protection for the rights of indigenous children, in particular their rights to preserve historical and

---

means of showing that the child has "recognized identity and belongs to the community of learners and citizens." Considering that the discrimination against children with disabilities has often resulted in the lack of their birth registration, the latter paragraph may refer mainly to the legal aspects of identity. It is still to be seen how the committees under either the Children's Convention or the Disability Rights Convention will address state reports in this regard.

183 See, for example, Committee on the Rights of the Child, *List of Issues: Finland,* paragraph 20, U.N. Doc. CRC/C/Q/FIN/2 (June 26, 2000). The Committee requested additional information on "the measures envisaged to maintain the Sami and the Roma children's cultural identity, in particular in the social services structure," and it paid particular emphasis to its follow-up on the issue of general education and language. See Committee on the Rights of the Child, *Concluding Observations: Finland,* paragraphs 59–60, U.N. Doc. CRC/C/15/Add.132 (October 16, 2000).

184 Ms. Nicolaisen, the Moderator of the Working Group on Cultural Diversity. Committee on the Rights of the Child, *Day of Discussion: Indigenous Groups,* paragraph 2, U.N. Doc. CRC/C/SR.899 (September 26, 2003).

185 Ms. Pinto, the Special Rapporteur of the Working Group on Non-Discrimination, paragraphs 5, 11, U.N. Doc. CRC/C/SR.899 (September 26, 2003).

186 Committee on the Rights of the Child, *Concluding Observations: Brazil,* paragraph 71, U.N. Doc. CRC/C/15/Add.241 (November 3, 2004).

cultural identity, customs, traditions and languages in accordance with the Constitution." This analysis is of particular importance in the international discourse on the right to health, as indigenous medical cultures are the only other medical culture (aside from the scientific one) that has been officially recognized as constitutive to the individuals and to the indigenous groups as a whole.[187]

Still, the Children's Committee's analysis of cultural identity of children belonging to indigenous groups also inherently reflects its limitations. It reinforces the common assumption that culture is only associated with exotic and remote ways of life; that, generally, it is not something that nonindigenous children can be deprived of; and that, ultimately, the preservation of the child's identity requires protection of something that is fixed. Whereas the cultural identities of indigenous children necessarily contain elements of their medical cultures, the Committee refrained from making any further general link between medical cultures, cultural rights, and the individual child's right to preserve his or her identity. In view of the discourse on children's bioethics throughout this work, however, such interconnections are pertinent to all children. After all, as has been implied all along, children are always some sort of a minority group.

3. Children as a Minority Group

The extent to which children should be viewed as a minority group has been one of the questions legal theorists of children's rights debate. Some reject the analogy, arguing that the presumed shared characteristic of powerlessness is insufficient to establish a comparison between the rhetoric of children and minority rights. They argue that whereas other minority groups such as women and other cultural and social groups have been discriminated against for political and social rationales, childhood is a universal and natural stage of life. Children's dependency, particularly among younger ones, is unavoidable, and the consequent subordination has nothing to do with being an artificial product of monarchs or oppressors' whims.[188] Different from other socially discriminated groups, then, the main remedy for children is to grow up.[189] Others retort that such a view is limited as it only looks at the "historical role of the rhetoric of rights" to stimulate an action from people who were oppressed. In more contemporary discourse, in contrast, one should see not only the more active role that children themselves take in order to advance their rights,[190] but also the value of the language of rights beyond one's action: it identifies one's interests, which are at the core of one's rights.[191] Thus, even if children may not

---

[187] Committee on Economic, Social and Cultural Rights, *The Right to the Highest Attainable Standard of Health (General Comment No. 14)*, 22nd Sess., Agenda Item 3, U.N. Doc. E/C.12/2000/4 (2000), reprinted in *Compilation of General Comments and General Recommendations Adopted by Human Rights Treaty Bodies*, U.N. Doc. HRI/GEN/1/Rev.6, paragraph 27, at 85 (2003) (hereafter *General Comment No. 14 (Health)*).

[188] O'Neill, 36–40.

[189] Ibid., 39.

[190] Freeman, "Taking Children's Rights More Seriously," 57.

[191] See, for example, Campbell, "The Rights of the Minor," 15; Freeman, "Taking Children's Rights More Seriously," 58–59.

be able to make claims on their own, the importance of recognizing their rights is akin to that of any other minority group.

These arguments are well taken and, clearly, not all disputable. Indeed, a perfect analogy between children and minority groups may be inappropriate for both natural and moral rationales.[192] It seems, however, that their relevance is only to the extent that one deliberates whether the rhetoric of rights in the context of children is applicable at all. It does not detract, in contrast, from the social and moral essence of the argument that children are essentially always members of minority groups. Not all minority groups are discriminated against; not all members belonging to minority groups are powerless. Yet, the social construct of minority groups conceives them as such. While the rationale for children's dependency is rooted justly in some natural and universal characteristics, it is also, nevertheless, the case that childhood and children as powerless and subordinates are social constructs.[193] Thus, at least on social and moral nexus, children are always members of minority groups. Moreover, children's senses of attachment, belonging, identification, and ownership with their entire environment, as has been established in social studies on children,[194] seem to resemble some of the unique characteristics of indigenous groups, specifically, the connection of indigenous groups with their entire cosmos, including objects, subjects, the living and the dead, as well as with the land and the spirit. It is thus suggested that children should be conceptualized as (universal) members of indigenous groups.

Yet, what are the practical implications of such conceptualization? Or, how should the child's right to cultural identity be reflected in the context of biomedical practices?

E. CHILDREN'S BIOETHICS IN PRACTICE

Perhaps the greatest challenge facing children's bioethics is the question of how to put the principles into practice. To state the obvious, there can be no fixed criteria to determine which biomedical practices should be protected by the child's right to culture and to cultural rights. Traditionally, the child's right to health was examined against the cultural rights of the parents and/or community, focusing on the autonomy of the child (often represented by others) versus the autonomy of those who make decisions on his or her behalf. As I have shown, the child's cultural rights, including religious freedom, religio-cultural minorities, and culture in general, in contrast, lag behind. Furthermore, while identity claims are often a part of the general discourse,

---

[192] See, in this regard, Purdy, note 74, and Noggle, note 64.

[193] There is increasing literature, for example, taking up the issue of not only "children at risk," but also of "children as risk." See Sharon Stephens, ed., *Children and the Politics of Culture* (Princeton, NJ: Princeton University Press, 1995); Mark Ensalaco and Linda C. Majka, *Children's Human Rights: Progress and Challenges for Children Worldwide* (Oxford: Rowman & Littlefield Publishing, 2005); Kristine A. Bentley, "Can There Be Any Universal Children's Rights?" *International Journal of Human Rights* 9, no. 1 (2005): 114–17.

[194] See in this regard, for example, Ronen, calling for a separate recognition of "the right of the child to belong" on the basis of children's web of emotional sense of attachment, belonging and identification with their entire environment, including family, community, objects, animals and other aspects of their lives.

they have not commonly received sufficient attention. However, as has been argued throughout this work, a child-centered approach to children's rights can have meaning only through the lens of their identity. Thus, at the very least, there needs to be an official forum in which identity claims are discussed and evaluated. The practical question is then how should such biomedical/identity conflicts be translated into state policies and responsibilities?

1. States Responsibilities to "Respect, Protect, and Fulfill"

Under international human rights law, states commonly have both positive and negative obligations to implement the various rights stipulated in the treaties. States must refrain from violating the rights recognized by the treaties, and when restrictions on rights are made, they have to be permissible: they must be necessary and proportionate to the pursuance of the legitimate aims. States are also required to adopt legislation, judicial administrative, education, and other appropriate measures to fulfill their legal obligations and to provide remedies when illegal violation of rights takes place.[195]

The committees authorized to enforce the international human rights treaties provide further interpretation of these responsibilities.[196] Specifically, they read these dual obligations as imposing three levels of commitments: to respect, to protect, and to fulfill (the "tripartite typology"). The obligation *to respect* requires states to refrain from interfering with the enjoyment of rights under the conventions. The obligation *to protect* requires states to prevent violations of such rights by third parties. The obligation to *fulfill* requires states to take appropriate legislative, administrative, budgetary, judicial, and other measures toward the full realization of such rights. Each of these obligations to respect, to protect, and to fulfill contains both elements of the obligation of conduct and the obligation of result. The *obligation of conduct* requires action reasonably calculated to realize the enjoyment of a particular right, including, at the very least, the "core content" or the "minimum essential levels of each of the rights."[197] *The obligation of result* requires states to achieve specific targets to satisfy a detailed substantive standard.[198] In the particular context of children,

---

[195] Human Rights Committee, *Nature of the General Legal Obligation on States Parties to the Covenant (General Comment No. 31)*, U.N. Doc. CCPR/C/21/Rev.1/Add.13 (2004); Committee on Economic, Social and Cultural Rights, *The Nature of States Parties' Obligations (General Comment No.3)*, 5th Sess., annex III, at 86, U.N. Doc. E/1991/23 (1991), reprinted in *Compilation of General Comments and General Recommendations Adopted by Human Rights Treaty Bodies*, U.N. Doc. HRI/GEN/1/Rev.6, at 14 (2003) (hereafter *General Comment No. 3 (States' Obligations)*).

[196] The Children's Committee explicitly endorsed the general comments of the other monitoring bodies under the treaties as a part of its working procedures. The general comments on "the Highest Attainable Standard of Health" (issued by the Committee under the ICESCR) on the "Freedom of Thought, Conscience and Religion" and on "The Rights of Minorities" (issued by the Human Rights Committee under the ICCPR) thus apply to the discourse on children as well. (Human Rights Committee, *The Rights of Minorities (General Comment No. 23)*, 5th Sess. (1994), reprinted in *Compilation of General Comments and General Recommendations Adopted by Human Rights Treaty Bodies*, U.N. Doc. HRI\GEN\1\Rev.1, at 38 (1994).)

[197] Paragraph 9 of the Maastricht Guidelines on Violations of Economic, Social and Cultural Rights (Maastricht, January 22–26, 1997), reprinted in*Human Rights Quarterly*, 20 (1998): 691–704 (hereafter Maastricht Guidelines).

[198] Paragraph 7 of the Maastricht Guidelines.

these, in return, are also subject to the overreaching requirement that states' duties have to be read in light of the four core principles of the Children's Convention, namely nondiscrimination (Article 2), the child's best interests (Article 3), the child's right to life, survival, and development (Article 6), and the child's right of participation (Article 12).[199] How are these states' responsiblities translated to the context of the child's right to biomedical identity?

2. State Responsibilities and the Child's Right to Biomedical Identity: A Dual Model

The child's right to biomedical identity could be analyzed in view of these state responsibilities. Specifically, two parallel paths of investigation that should be evaluated against one another. First, as the health implications of bodily practices are often what raises the gravest concerns, the examination would have to be in combination with states' responsibilities with regards to the child's right to the "highest attainable standard of health."[200] Accordingly, bodily practices that *in themselves* cause death or long-term health implications would naturally be excluded. This exclusion also fits one of the key rights in the Children's Convention, that is, the child's right to life, survival, and development. Practices that revolve around issues of safety or appearance, on the other hand, would be permitted. Upholding states' responsibilities to provide a variety of functioning public facilities, goods, and services that are accessible, available (both physically and affordable), culturally acceptable, and of good quality[201] would ensure that the distinction between harmful biomedical practices and the means by which they are carried out is sustained. As has been recognized in the context of the right to health of indigenous peoples, states' responsibilities should also include the provision of resources for the various minority groups to design, deliver, and control such services.[202] Indeed, while the note of the committee monitoring the ICESCR that "the health of the individual is often linked to the health of the society as a whole and has a collective dimension" was aimed at indigenous peoples,[203] as has been shown throughout this study, there is no reason to assume that it applies only to them.

Such recognition logically leads to the second path that is centered on the issue of identity claims. Even if children's participation may be in the conventional form of claiming, blaming, negotiating, and the like at a young age, ultimately, children's participation has to be conceived also in terms of their web of relations and hence identity. With regard to the child's right to identity, then, the states' obligations to respect would require that they refrain from interfering with biomedical practices associated with the child's

---

[199] Committee on the Rights of the Child, *General Measures of Implementation of the Convention on the Rights of the Child (General Comment No. 5)*, paragraph 12, 34th Sess., U.N. Doc. CRC/GC/2003/5 (2003).

[200] Article 24 of the Children's Convention; Article 14 of the African Charter. Note, that the wording of the African Charter is somewhat different, stipulating the child's "right to enjoy the best attainable state of physical, mental and spiritual health."

[201] These also constitute, according to the Committee on Economic, Social and Cultural Rights, the "core content" of the right to health. *General Comment No. 14 (Health)*, paragraphs 12, 43–44; *General Comment No. 4 (Adolescent Health)*, paragraph 41.

[202] *General Comment No. 14 (Health)*, paragraph 27.

[203] Ibid.

development of cultural identity. The obligation to protect would require that states also protect individuals and communities from interference by third parties in the free enjoyment of the biomedical practices that aim at inscribing identity.[204] This would ensure, for instance, that bodily practices of one cultural group would not harm the cultural identity of other communities. Biomedical practices that revolve around issues of appearance and the mere removal of some (healthy otherwise) tissues would thus be permitted, granted that they hold substantial significance for the cultural identity of the child (and his or her cultural milieu). That would include, for instance, the case of male circumcision. It would also include scarification of children among groups who carry out the practice for inscribing cultural identity onto the child. As much of the rationale to eradicate the practice is that it is not within mainstream medical culture, calls to eradicate it should be rejected.

The obligation to fulfill would mean that states have a duty to take the appropriate legislative, administrative, budgetary, judicial, and other measures that are necessary for individuals and communities to develop and enjoy their cultural identity. This would also entail requiring that identity claims are substantially taken into account in judicial and other administrative discussions on biomedical conflicts. That is, the rights discourse develops the ability to incorporate and give appropriate weight to identity-related claims of both individuals and groups, as such.[205]

Eisenberg proposes an appealing model to do so.[206] Drawing on the liberal concept of accommodating differences, she suggests the "difference approach," which aims at providing a way of assessing conflicts in a manner that treats identity claims in the public sphere fairly.[207] She advances her approach in three steps, requiring understanding of the role a practice or value plays in constituting the identities of the parties involved in the conflict, considering and assessing evidence in relation to the interests that are at stake, and, finally, considering the claims in public debate, with the possibility of accepting such claims "as valid reasons to resolve conflicts one way rather than another."[208]

---

[204] The Human Rights Committee under the ICCPR emphasized in this context states' duties to adopt positive measures that are "necessary to protect the identity of minority and the rights of its members to enjoy and develop their own culture and language and to practice their religion, in community with the other members of the group." *General Comment No. 22 (Religious Freedom)*, paragraph 6.2.

[205] Eisenberg, 250.

[206] Eisenberg discusses the issue in the context of conflicts that involve minorities within minorities, though her approach is important and relevant to this discussion as well since all children are members of minority/indigenous groups. See Section D.3.

[207] Eisenberg, 250–51.

[208] Ibid., 259. Eisenberg's three-step discourse resembles Parekh's "dialogical consensus" in its effort to resolve multicultural conflicts (see the discussion in Chapter 4). Similar to Parekh, she also makes no particular reference to children's own voice in the process, and so the criticism of Parekh's model applies to her's as well. The key difference between Parekh and Eisenberg lies in the weight they give to identity-related claims, *as such.* While Parekh acknowledges the importance of identity (Bhikhu Parekh, *Rethinking Multiculturalism: Cultural Diversity and Political Theory* (Cambridge, MA: Harvard University Press, 2000), 162), his endeavor to circumscribe the multicultural clash into the legal category of equality and

The important element enshrined throughout this process, however, is that the contrasting political and legal burdens and benefits that those with particular identity-related characteristics have are compared to and weighed against each other as a means of determining whether the resolution is fair.[209] Among the elements to be factored in are, for example, whether a custom that is defended as essential to a community's identity is indeed controversial, whether the customs associated with the identity claim are central or only marginal to it, whether the custom infringes upon another's fundamental interest or only imposes a mild inconvenience, and what the implications are for the identity of those involved in accepting or rejecting a particular ritual.[210]

Eisenberg's model is appealing for a few reasons, particularly, the dialogical approach, the recognition of pluralism, and the formal recognition of identity claims. The model's suggestion to avoid the conventional effort of translating identity interests into legal rights and its requirement that identity claims are assessed at face value rather than adjudicated, ultimately, according to courts' own preferences of rights,[211] gives it additional force. It thus advances the discourse on children's bioethics insofar as it steps aside from the traditional legal categories of claiming and blaming and integrates the social and lived experiences into the legal debate. Still, there are three main difficulties in this context that need addressing.

One revolves around the question whether biomedical identity claims that are based on religious or on cultural rationales merit different protection from or give rise to different state obligations. Eisenberg does not make any such differentiation in her discussion, though the question is important because cultural rights under the ICCPR and those under the ICESCR seem to lay down separate state duties. Article 2(1) of the ICESCR stipulates the principle of progressive realization that conditions a state's implementation of its responsibilities under the convention by its availability of resources. Civil and political rights under the ICCPR, including those with cultural aspects (the right to religious freedom, linguistic rights, etc.), in contrast, do not.

This difference led to the well-known debate whether civil and political rights (the so-called first generation of rights) are leveled higher in the hierarchy of rights in comparison to cultural rights (as well as to economic and social rights that are considered as a "second generation of rights") and enjoy higher protection. This controversy is pertinent also in the discourse on children's bioethics, as although the Children's Convention includes both generations of rights, it replicates this distinction. Article 4 of the Convention stipulates that, "With regard to economic, social and cultural rights, States Parties shall undertake such measures to the maximum extent of their available resources

---

nondiscrimination is inapt in resolving such conflicts for reasons that were discussed in Chapter 4. The "difference approach," in contrast, intrinsically incorporates both individuals and groups' identity-related interests that need to be taken into account (Eisenberg, 259, 261).

[209] Ibid., 258.

[210] Ibid., 261, 267.

[211] Ibid., 262.

and, where needed, within the framework of international co-operation."[212] Thus, theoretically, if biomedical practices are included within the scope of religious freedom under the ICCPR, they enjoy a greater guarantee of protection.

There are two reasons however, why the discussion of children's bioethics as reflected in the child's right to identity appears to overcome this difference. First, Article 8 of the Children's Convention does not assign the child's right to preserve his or her identity to either generation of rights. As it is not stipulated in the other treaties, it is also impossible to assign it to either by drawing on these other instruments. Considering the centrality of identity to the child's exercise of all other rights and freedoms, however, its implementation should take, as a matter of public policy of human rights, the higher standard of protection. The terminology of Article 8(2) further strengthens this approach, as it requires states, in cases of illegal deprivation of the child's identity, "[to] provide appropriate assistance and protection, with a view to re-establishing [it] *speedily*,"[213] without conditioning it with availability of resources.

Second, the "generational division" has not been translated into a formal hierarchy among the rights granted under the international human rights treaties or provided any criteria for doing so. In fact, the trend has been the opposite. Numerous international declarations that were adopted over the years proclaimed the equal footing of the two generations of rights.[214] Furthermore, efforts have been made to narrow the gap of implementation between the various treaties. The Limburg Principles (1986), for instance, instruct that while the full realization of the relevant rights may be achieved progressively, states have the obligation to begin immediately taking certain steps toward that goal.[215] This principle is echoed in the general comment on "*The Nature of States Parties' Obligations*" adopted by the Committee on Economic, Social and Cultural Rights in 1990, and also later on, in its specific address of the "right to the highest attainable health."[216]

Another difficulty revolves around the substance and content of biomedical cultural identity claims. Scholars warn that as identity claims are subjective, they are difficult to challenge even if they appear as insincere or opportunistic.[217] The collective dimension of identity may further subject individuals to harm and to

[212] Interestingly, although the African Charter also includes both "generations or rights," it does not stipulate this limitation.

[213] Emphasis added. See also in this regard that the Children's Committee has classified Article 8 under the theme of "civil rights and freedoms" (paragraph 15(b) of the General Guidelines).

[214] The most cited proclamation in this context is paragraph 1 of the Vienna Declaration and Programme of Action (1993), reprinted in 32 I.L.M. 1661 (1993), 14 H.R.K.J. 352 (1993); Nieć, 177.

[215] Principles 8, 21 of the Limburg Principles on the Implementation of the International Covenant on Economic, Social and Cultural Rights, annex, U.N. Doc. E/CN.4/1987/17, reprinted in *Human Rights Quarterly* 9, no. (1987): 122–35.

[216] *General Comment No. 3 (States' Obligations)*, paragraph 2; *General Comment No. 14 (Health)*, paragraph 30.

[217] Eisenberg, 262.

discriminatory practices on behalf of the collective. Worse still, there is a risk that it would be utilized in internal power struggles even if these practices have little to do with the identity per se.[218] These arguments are raised also in the general discourse on the right to culture and to cultural rights, and the responses to them follow a similar vein.[219] Specifically, creating a forum in which identity claims may be raised does not guarantee that they will be accepted. Parties will have to prove their case by showing, for instance, the origin of the practice and its constitutive power to the individual and to the group's identity.[220] This is so also with regard to infants and very young children who are not able to express their views and preferences. The rationales for carrying out the customs will have to include serious consideration of the child's identity as well as that of his or her family and of the community to which the child belongs.

Some fear that acknowledging formally the collective's interests in the preservation of the children's cultural identity would sanction an approach toward children as a means to an end rather than as an end in and of itself. They warn that it would thus result in slipping back to the notion of children as property.[221] Both arguments, however, are somewhat pretentious. The child is never an end in itself when a decision to have it is made—even if for the mere fact that the child still does not exist.[222] As for identity preservation, cultural identity claims cannot be separated from the group, whether it is for the majority or minority, religious or secular. Just as individuals' identities are shaped in relation to others and go beyond mere individual choice, all collective identities need a community and the continuing commitment of its members for their creation, existence, and preservation.[223] In the end, the debate is about relationships, attachments, and detachments of individuals with their communities. Refusing to consider that formally merely ignores the reality and hence misses the point.

Finally, Eisenberg's model is limited in that it ultimately appears to change only the types of claims that are to be evaluated against each other, without observing the whole picture. The approach in this book differs in that it suggests that biomedical claims comprise two parallel paths—medical/health implications and culture/identity—and that they should be evaluated against one another. The combination of these paths seriously takes issue with the spirit of the Children's Convention, observing children as *beings* (rather than as *becomings*) in a comprehensive manner. It incorporates both physical and spiritual development in their various levels, bearing in mind the context in which children live. It thus gives a more inclusive and truthful content to the concept of the child's best interests.

The dual paths also mitigate, to an extent, cultural differences in the conceptualization of harm, addressing the complexities both Parekh and

[218] Donders, 100–102.
[219] See Section A.
[220] Eisenberg, 265.
[221] Archard, "Children, Multiculturalism and Education," 146–48.
[222] Davis, 12.
[223] Bilsky, 145.

Renteln's assessment of it raise.[224] Because many of the biomedical (and other cultural) conflicts are based on identity claims, dismissing a minority's assertion of the right to follow its biomedical practices if the majority is not persuaded otherwise (as suggested by Parekh) only ignores the real roots of the debate. If pluralism is the very nature of societal reality, and as the nature of identity is only contextually relevant, a legally based medical decision that intrinsically dictates also which identity is more desirable cannot stand.[225]

Similarly, not all biomedical practices that lead to a permanent body change (following Renteln's principle of irreparable harm) would be prohibited. While it is agreed that biomedical practices that cause death should be prohibited, before excluding other bodily practices, the extent to which the discontent with the practice has to do with appearance of others and the extent to which the practice is central to the identities of the individual and groups must be considered. Thus, in contrast to the international bodies, male circumcision,[226] scarification, or the practice of elongation of the neck would not be categorized as harmful under Article 24(3) of the Children's Convention. Male circumcision may have substantial implications on the child's entire membership in the community if not carried out. These may thus outweigh the potential medical implications if taken from a child-centered perspective on his sense of belonging. With scarification, even if followed for healing purposes rather than pure identity ones, the main issue seems to be a matter of beautification or what is presumed to be normal appearance. Similarly, neck elongation among the Padaung girls is grounded in their communal and national identities, which its contestation, as is evident from the expression of the girls themselves, has much more to do with difficulties others have in accepting their physical difference rather than from the girls' own Western feminist perspective of inconvenience.

By contrast, the practice of milk teeth extraction would be prohibited because it is not generally a core element of the identity of either the child or the group, but it is carried out mainly for medical reasons and may entail long-term medical implications (a point that needs further investigation).[227] As such, the provision of appropriate medical facilities, goods, and services along with health-related education and access to information may suffice to convince the group to discard this custom.[228] This is particularly so considering that teething has indeed traditionally been linked with symptoms such as sore and swollen gums, fever, and diarrhea, and children who are teething often become cranky, irritated, and have difficulty sleeping and eating.[229] While the link between teething and these symptoms has recently been more controversial, their presumed side effects can

---

[224] See Chapter 4, Section B.1.

[225] Oommen, 40.

[226] In light of the critique of Parekh, in Chapter 4, it can also be argued that female genital cutting in its lesser form should not necessarily be categorized as a "harmful traditional practice."

[227] See discussion in Chapter 3.

[228] *General Comment No. 14 (Health)*, paragraphs 11–12.

[229] Melissa Wake, Kylie Hesketh, and James Lucas, "Teething and Tooth Eruption in Infants: A Cohort Study," *Pediatrics* 106 no. 6(2000): 1374–79; Bradley Barlow, Michael J. Kanellis, and Rebecca Slayton, "Tooth Eruption Symptoms: A Survey of Parents and Health Professionals," *Journal of Dentistry for Children* 69, no. 2 (2002): 148–50(3).

be interpreted as illness if one is not educated about the relationship between the two. In this light, the practice of milk teeth extraction may be seen as a primordial but genuine effort to prevent these symptoms from occurring. Education about the causal relationship between the teething and the health symptoms may thus be enough.

Another argument for prohibiting the practice of milk teeth extraction is that evolvement of the practice into a link with identity (as has been argued, for instance, in the context of Angola),[230] does not contain constitutive benefits for the child's identity, but only for the mother who is negotiating her place within her community.[231] While such internal politics surely reflect on the children's identity as well, the mothers' endorsements of this element of identity is rooted in their lack of power within the community. Focusing on their equality and elimination of discrimination within the families and communities would thus yield a better result. It is also consonant with the child's right to nondiscrimination that, as with all other rights, needs to be understood relationally.[232]

F. CONCLUSION

The advanced argument is that biomedical practices carried out on children must be analyzed through the lens of their (right to) cultural identity. This argument is built on children's rights to culture and to cultural rights, on biomedical practices *as* culture, and on the status of children, particularly in infancy, as individuals who are universally dependent and who lack the conventional autonomous capacity to make biomedical decisions on their own. Both the will/power and the interest approaches to children's rights fail to grasp the life experiences of children as present subjects who are in the process of developing their autonomy. The feminist relational approach, or the ethic of care, offers a viable alternative, as it conceptualizes children's rights as a question of relations and context. As such, it also allows one to step away from conventional dichotomies such as adult/child that prevent theorists and policy makers from granting the appropriate space for children's voices and active participation. The conceptualization of children's autonomy in terms of identity fills this gap, as it seems to better reflect children's autonomy with others as a necessary means to the exercise of their rights.

The analysis of the child's right to cultural identity on the international level, however, was found rather lacking. With the exception of children belonging to minority and particularly indigenous groups, the Children's Committee associated the right to identity only with purely formal requirements such as name, nationality, and family relations as recognized by law. Such an approach

---

[230] Landau, 276.

[231] Henne O. Mogensen, "False Teeth and Real Suffering: the Social Course of "Germectomy" in Eastern Uganda," *Culture, Medicine & Psychiatry* 24 (2000): 345, 347.

[232] This path does not preclude identity claims from the discourse, but rather it weighs the identities of the mother and the child against one another, taking into account the reasons for carrying out the biomedical practice and the results of it. Some view such an approach as negative recognition of cultural identity, advocating for the elimination of discrimination and humiliation rather than for an explicit confirmation of identity. See Donders, 44.

is limited, as it reinforces prejudicial concepts of children's identity as an attribute of only exotic cultures that are generally fixed. It is also not faithful to the Children's Convention's drafters' intent and to the great interest and controversy that have arisen in identity issues over the past few decades.

Finally, this chapter outlined some of the state responsibilities that arise to ensure the child's right to biomedical identity. Following the tripartite approach to state obligations under international human rights framework, these responsibilities should be examined at the juncture between the child's cultural rights and right to health, and should establish an official forum in which identity claims can be heard. While following a dual process of medical/health implications and cultural identity claims do not resolve easily all biomedical conflicts that arise, they nevertheless provide a more realistic approach. They closely follow the four core principles of the Children's Convention, giving a space for children's unique voices through the recognition of their identity. Indeed, as identity issues are inherent and integral to many of these conflicts, particularly in the context of children, these should not be ignored.

Chapter 7

Broadening the Lens: Genetic Manipulation

This book has so far focused on the so-called traditional bodily practices, commonly understood as "longstanding, resisting to change, and embedded within the cultural fabric of a community."[1] This concentration followed the address the Monitoring Committee under the Children's Convention (Children's Committee or Committee) and the other international bodies gave to harmful traditional practices particularly under Article 24(3) of the International Convention on the Rights of the Child (Children's Convention or Convention).[2] It has been argued that this analysis is lacking, as biomedical practices are not carried out only on children belonging to long-established minority groups. Alternatively, considering the indisputable role the family and the community play in the construction of children's views and autonomy, as well as the mutual sense of belonging, connectedness, and, ultimately, identity, a child-centered approach has to view all children as belonging to minority, and particularly, indigenous groups.[3]

In this chapter, "invented traditions" in the genomic era are considered. The focus is on disability-related practices, specifically, genetic manipulations that are carried out in fetuses *in utero* and on preconception zygotes with the goal of bringing them to full maturation as human subjects.[4] Although there has been ample literature on the moral, legal, and other challenges that the genetic revolution has created, there has been strikingly scant work on the (future and present) children *as* the subjects of observation. The goal of this discussion is to fill in some of the gap by formally bringing to the international surface these children's interests, rights, and voices. It should be stated from the outset, however, that bearing in mind the limited information in this particular aspect of bioethics, the chapter is mostly speculative. Working within the framework of analysis proposed in Chapter 6 to examine children's bioethics, this chapter builds on the literature that exists in various disciplines, particularly disability studies, to highlight some of the main dilemmas and to suggest possible future paths for investigation.

This chapter begins with a brief introduction to the new scientific technologies in the context of genetic manipulation and explains the relevance of

[1] Corinne A. A. Packer, *Using Human Rights to Change Tradition: Traditional Practices Harmful to Women's Reproductive Health in Sub-Saharan Africa* (Oxford: Antwerpen Intersentia, 2002), 3.

[2] Convention on the Rights of the Child, G.A. Res. 44/25, annex, 44th Sess., 61st plenary meeting. U.N. GAOR Supp. (No. 49), at 167, U.N. Doc. A/44/49 (1989), entered into force September 2, 1990, reprinted in 28 I.L.M. 1448 (1989).

[3] Regarding the conceptualization of children as a minority and as an indigenous group, see Chapter 6.

[4] Discussion on research using tissues from aborted fetuses is beyond the scope of this study.

disability-related practices to the study. This is followed by an examination of the right to procreative freedom and family autonomy that have been the leading arguments raised in this context, and some critiques are provided. The rest of the chapter refocuses the discussion on children's bioethics. Different from research that has been conducted so far, here scientific developments from the point of view of the (future) children that are involved and in view of the children's right to identity are examined. In this context the status of fetuses under international law is explored, and the question whether the scientific developments gave rise to the child's "right to a sound mind and body" is explored. Finally, the chapter draws conclusions and proposes some paths for future inquiries.

A. GENETIC MANIPULATIONS

Progress in the study of human genetics occurred at a remarkable rate over the course of the past decade. The completion of the Human Genome Project, particularly the international effort to map and sequence the entire human genome in 2003, has played a central role in this development. It led to increased scientific endeavors to devise effective interventions to treat or cure some disabling conditions, both before and after birth.[5] An array of gene carriers for major disorders (such as cystic fibrosis and Tay Sachs) as well as the genetic propensity of developing major disorders later in life (such as heart disease, cancer, and Alzheimer's Disease) can now be identified both before and after birth. The newly developed technologies of assisted reproductive methods made it possible for scientists to determine the sex of a fetus post- and preconception, either *in vivo* (in the body) or *in vitro* (out of the body).[6] It also opened the door for future enhancement efforts in the form of improving genetic endowment and cloning. Thus, while the genome era has been applauded by some as proffering significant potential remedies, it has also posed substantial challenges to the moral, legal, political, and social understanding of human's lives.

The scientific revolution clearly bears a significant impact on children in an array of biomedical fields. This includes medicalization, research with children, children as organ and tissue donors, and others.[7] This chapter discusses one of these fields: prenatal genetic manipulations,[8] referring to interventions aimed at the avoidance of specific disability-related conditions.[9]

---

[5] Adrienne Asch, Lawrence O. Gostin, and Diann M. Johnson, "Respecting Persons with Disabilities and Preventing Disabilities: Is There a Conflict?" in *The Human Rights of Persons with Intellectual Disabilities: Different But Equal,* ed. Stanley S. Herr, Lawrence O. Gostin, and Harold Hongju Koh (Oxford: Oxford University Press, 2003), 326.

[6] Owen D. Jones, "Sex Selection: Regulating Technology Enabling the Predetermination of a Child's Gender," *Harvard Journal Law and Technology* 6 (1992–93): 7–8.

[7] See, for example, Lynn Hagger and Simon Woods, "Children and Research: A Risk of Double Jeopardy?" *International Journal of Children's Rights* 13, no. 1–2 (2005): 51–72 (discussing children and research); John Breeding and Fred Baughman, "Informed Consent and the Psychiatric Drugging of Children," *Journal of Humanistic psychology* 43, no. 2 (2003): 50–64 (medicalization).

[8] The terms genetic manipulation, genetic procedures, and genetic interventions are used intermittingly throughout the chapter, all referring to the general practice of genetic manipulation.

[9] The literature often makes a distinction in this context between a few types of genetic

B. WHY DISABILITY-RELATED PRACTICES?

There are a few reasons why the concentration on prenatal disability-related scientific practices is relevant to this study. First, scientific developments in the context of disabilities share a great deal of similarities with the concerns raised in the context of traditional bodily practices. They raise the questions that are associated with informed consent, including capacity versus incapacity, whose capacity, and what is the right biomedical decision that, in return, elucidates the necessity of autonomy in relations for one's exercise of rights. They touch upon the very thin line between harm and abuse versus benefit, reinforcing the necessity in contextualization. They are also often performed in the private sphere, even if under the auspices of a public institution or if funded by the government. They hence give rise to the concern of individuals' vulnerability to abuse if not regulated. Furthermore, if with traditional bodily practices, the presumption is that they are "resistant to change,"[10] the equivalent argument is that as far as scientific developments are concerned, ultimately, "science cannot be stopped." Indeed, it is for these reasons that both experimentation with and medicalization of children were explicitly raised during the drafting of the Children's Convention in one breadth with harmful traditional practices.[11] Although these proposals were eventually omitted, the recent European Convention on Human Rights and Biomedicine (Oviedo Convention) and the convention's additional protocols (collectively referred to as the Conventions on Biomedicine)[12] brought them back, formally, to the stage. Thus, prenatal

---

manipulations. *Genetic prevention* refers to such technological procedures aiming at the avoidance of specific conditions such as disease and disability (for example, cystic fibrosis). *Genetic enhancement* refers to such technological procedures aiming at improving one's characteristics for no particular health-related rationales (such as improving intelligence). A third type is *genetic treatment or intervention,* which refers to technological procedures that are carried out on genes, yet not necessarily for either health or nonhealth rationales as far as the future child is concerned. These include, for example, in vitro fertilization (IVF) treatment, sex selection, and others. The distinction between these three types of procedures is clearly somewhat arbitrary and contingent on one's particular outlook. Whereas sex selection, for example, may fall within within the category of genetic treatment if conducted for no serious hereditary sex-related disease, others may classify it as genetic prevention, as it aims at preventing an undesired sex. Similarly, selecting for a child's deafness may qualify under the rubric of either genetic treatment or of genetic enhancement. These categories are discussed jointly, while pointing out discrepancies and dilemmas throughout, where relevant. See discussion in Peter Wenz, "Engineering Genetic Injustice," *Bioethics* 19, no. 1 (2005): 5–11, and in John A. Robertson, "Procreative Liberty in the Era of Genomics," *American Journal of Law & Medicine* 29 (2003): 455–80.

[10] Packer, 3.

[11] See Chapter 2.

[12] Convention for the Protection of Human Rights and Dignity of the Human Being with Regard to the Application of Biology and Medicine: Convention on Human Rights and Biomedicine (the Oviedo Convention) (ETS No. 164), entered into force December 1, 1999; Additional Protocol to the Convention for the Protection of Human Rights and Dignity of the Human Being with regard to the Application of Biology and Medicine, on the Prohibition of Cloning Human Beings (ETS No. 168), opened for signature on January 1, 1998, entered into force March 1, 2001; Additional Protocol to the Convention on Human Rights and Biomedicine, on Transplantation of Organs and Tissues of Human Origin (ETS No. 186), opened for signature on January 24, 2002, entered into force May 1, 2006; Additional Protocol to the Convention on Human Rights and Biomedicine, concerning Biomedical Research, (ETS No. 195), entered into force September 1, 2007 (hereafter the Convention on Human

genetic interventions are both intuitively and practically within the scope of this study.

Second, the case of disability is particularly illuminating as, while it epitomizes the connection between body/culture and biomedical practices, it challenges the Western body/mind dichotomy by which the mind is presumed to be superior over the body. This assumption has dominated much of the conventional discourse in this field and has been a cornerstone in the scientific revolution. Indeed, the scientific revolution has been often characterized as Western pursuit of medical knowledge in the effort to improve the understanding of the human body and as a means to conquer it.[13] The assumption has been that it would provide solutions for the body's dysfunctions followed by a universally applicable standard about the good life.[14] These have also played a role in the demarcation of traditional bodily practices versus scientific progress, assuming that the latter reflects the power of reason over passions and emotions.[15] The context of disabilities, however, raises significant questions about the extent to which this is really so.

Third, there is perhaps no better context than disability to elucidate the fallacy of the common conceptualization of harmful traditional bodily practices pertinent only to minority groups. In fact, there are more than 600 million persons around the world who are currently categorized as having a disability, constituting about 10 percent of the world's population.[16] About a quarter of them, according to the United Nations Children's Fund's (UNICEF's) estimations, are children.[17] With respect to law, there is also no doubt that, as a group, persons with disabilities have universally suffered from discrimination and exclusion. Throughout history, states and societies have adopted a variety of segregation policies, attempting to exclude persons with disabilities from public view.[18] Simultaneously, persons with disabilities were sold and bought as objects for exhibition, reinforcing the notion of disability as "the ultimate deviance."[19] And oddly, also in societies where disability is viewed positively,

---

Rights and Biomedicine or the Oviedo Convention, interchangeably; Additional Protocol on the Prohibition of Cloning, the Additional Protocol on Transplantation of Organs and Tissues; and Additional Protocol on Biomedical Research, respectively. The term "Conventions on Biomedicine" will be used to refer to this set of conventions together).

[13] Deborah Lupton, *Medicine as Culture* (London: Sage Publications, 2003), 88.

[14] Stephan E. Lemmes, "The Marginalization of Religious Voices in Bioethics," in *Religion and Medical Ethics*, ed. Allen Verhey (Grand Rapids, MI: W. B. Eerdmans Publishing, 1996), 24, 35.

[15] Cynthia B. Cohen, Sondra E. Wheeler, and David A. Scott, "Walking on a Fine Line," *Hastings Center Report* 31, no. 5 (2001): 32–33.

[16] Theresia Degener, "Disability as a Subject of International Human Rights Law and Comparative Discrimination Law," in *The Human Rights of Persons with Intellectual Disabilities: Different But Equal*, ed. Stanley S. Herr, Lawrence O. Gostin, and Harold Hongju Koh (Oxford: Oxford University Press, 2003), 158; for global statistics, see *GeoHive: Global Statistics*, http://www.geohive.com/.

[17] UNICEF, *FactSheet: Discrimination*, http://www.unicef.org/protection/files/discrimination.pdf.

[18] Marc C. Weber, "Opening the Golden Door: Disability and the Law of Immigration," *Journal of Gender, Race & Justice* 8 (2004): 158–59; Harlan Hahn, "The Political Implications of Disability: Definition and Data," in *The Psychological and Social Impact of Disability*, ed. Robert P. Marinelli and Arthur E. Dell Orto (New York: Springer Publishing, 1999), 8.

[19] David L. Braddock and Susan L. Parish, "Social Policy Toward Intellectual Disabilities

persons with disabilities are nonetheless situated in a subordinated position.[20] For these reasons, persons with disabilities are commonly considered as one of the largest and most vulnerable minorities worldwide.[21]

Observing disability through the anthropological, sociological, and cultural prisms, however, illuminates the error in the conceptualization of biomedical practices as only a minority issue. Disability is a universal phenomenon and exists in one form or another in all societies across space and time. It is estimated that most people will face some sort of disability throughout their lifetime, either as a result of injurious events such as armed conflict, accidents, environmental haphazard, etc., or by disease, aging, and the like. Furthermore, in a Western-dominated world that is preoccupied with classifications, personal achievements, and presumed calculations of benefits and risks, additional categories of disability are constantly added to the list. This is particularly evident in the context of mental illnesses and other behavioral impairments where, although the objective criteria of diagnosis and treatment have been acutely criticized, children's disabilities are more likely to subside.[22] Thus, the discussion about disabilities cannot address persons and children with disabilities as a mere "other," as is often the case with minority groups, but requires its consideration under the understanding of the "I," "we," and "us."

Indeed, it is also these coupled aspects of disability that played a mobilizing force in the efforts of the international disability movement in the past few decades to draft a new convention that pertains to the rights of persons with disabilities. The efforts ultimately culminated in the recently adopted Convention on the Rights of Persons with Disabilities (Disability Rights Convention), stipulating as its purpose "to promote, protect and ensure the full and equal enjoyment of all human rights and fundamental freedoms by all persons with disabilities, and to promote respect for their inherent dignity."[23] Moreover, it also instructs, among its general principles, and for the first time in a core human rights treaty, "respect for difference and acceptance of persons with disabilities as part of human diversity and humanity."[24]

---

in the Nineteenth and Twentieth Centuries," in *The Human Rights of Persons with Intellectual Disabilities: Different But Equal,* ed. Stanley S. Herr, Lawrence O. Gostin, and Harold Hongju Koh (Oxford: Oxford University Press, 2003), 90.

[20] Alison D. Renteln, "Cross-Cultural Perceptions of Disability: Policy Implications of Divergent Views," in *The Human Rights of Persons with Intellectual Disabilities: Different But Equal,* ed. Stanley S. Herr, Lawrence O. Gostin, and Harold Hongju Koh (Oxford: Oxford University Press, 2003), 72, fn. 5.

[21] Theresia Degener, "Disabled Persons and Human Rights: the Legal Framework," in *Human Rights and Disabled Persons,* ed. Theresia Degener and Yolan Koster-Dreese (Dordrecht: Martinus Nijhoff, 1995), 11–12.

[22] "Mental disability" includes, as a category, the array of conditions such as schizophrenia, depression, but also autism, intellectual disabilities and others. Breeding and Baughman, 52–53.

[23] Article 1 of the Convention on the Rights of Persons with Disabilities (Disability Rights Convention), G.A. Res. A/61/611 (2006). For an overview of the international efforts to promote the rights of persons with disabilities, see http://www.un.org/esa/socdev/enable/rights/.

[24] Article 3(d) of the Disability Rights Convention.

Finally, the issue of disability is intertwined, and increasingly so, with identity dilemmas. How disability is constructed and what is the role biomedical practices play in addressing or inscribing it are central to the discourse. As illnesses and disabilities are increasingly acknowledged as sociocultural constructs, the efforts to eradicate specific physical/mental conditions are perceived by some as an intentional effort to impose what is assumed to be a normal body and normal identity at the cost of unique cultural groups and cultural diversity. Indeed, the reference in the Disability Rights Convention to the entitlement of persons with disabilities to "recognition and support of their specific cultural and linguistic identity"[25] is illuminative in this regard. It is also in this vein that the goal of protecting the "dignity and identity of all human beings" in biomedical practices, as stipulated in Article 1 of the Conventions on Biomedicine, is most interesting. Still, although (future) children are clearly the targets of such genetic interventions, children's identity politics in this context has only rarely been addressed. The vast literature (also within disability studies) has commonly focused on the mounting social expectation of aborting fetuses with a prospect of disability and on the implications in terms of human rights of persons with disabilities that the genetic screening yields. This chapter, which concentrates on genetic procedures that are carried out with the aim of bringing the fetus into maturity as a future human being, in view of the child's right to identity, thus filling in some of the gap.

C. GENETIC SELECTION OF CHILDREN'S CHARACTERISTICS: A PART OF PARENTAL REPRODUCTIVE FREEDOM?

Scholars dealing with the question of genetic selection of offsprings' characteristics have commonly tackled it on two related grounds. The first examines the issue within the scope of parental freedom of procreation and choice. The right has been recognized among the most fundamental rights under international law, conceptualized as a powerful manifestation of the right to self-determination, autonomy, and privacy in personal matters.[26] As the argument thus goes, if one has the general right to choose whether to reproduce, the freedom should extend also to choose which child he or she will have.[27] Such choice has been indeed at the heart of parental consent to avoid particular genetic characteristics, and it provides the grounds for parents' positive choice of which other particular genetic characteristics the child they bear will have.[28]

---

[25] Article 30(c)(4) of the Disability Rights Convention, dealing with the rights of persons with disabilities to take part in cultural life.

[26] Sonia Harris-Short, "An 'Identity Crisis' in the International Law of Human Rights? The Challenge of Reproductive Cloning," *International Journal of Children's Rights* 11 (2004): 335. For the international provisions, see Article 23(2) of the International Covenant on Civil and Political Rights (hereafter ICCPR), opened for signature December 16, 1966, G.A. Res. 2200A (XXI), 21st Sess., U.N. GAOR Supp. (No. 16), U.N. Doc. A/6316 (1966), reprinted in 999 U.N.T.S. 171, entered into force March 23, 1976; Article 16 of the Convention on the Elimination of Discrimination against Women, G.A. Res. 34/180, 34 U.N. GAOR Supp. (No. 46), at 193, U.N. Doc. A/34/46, entered into force September 3, 1981 (hereafter CEDAW).

[27] John A. Robertson, "Genetic Selection of Offspring Characteristics," *Boston University Law Review* 76 (1996): 422–49.

[28] Ibid., 427; John A. Robertson, "Procreative Liberty in the Era of Genomics," *American Journal of Law & Medicine* 29 (2003): 447–48.

Others base this parental prerogative on family autonomy in child rearing and on the parental primary responsibility toward the future child.[29] Both interests have also been widely recognized within leading international human rights instruments and have been particularly emphasized in the children-specific ones.[30] Considering the financial, social, emotional, and other burdens that raising a child entail, it is thus argued, parents ought to have the freedom to decide the sort of commitment they want and can undertake.[31] As Richard J. Hull insists, the discussion on genetic manipulation, particularly in the context of children with disabilities, needs to factor in also how the parental choices and decisions affect and reflect the life of others who are relevant to the choice, as otherwise the consideration is incomplete.[32]

In practice, these arguments have often configured into the doctrine of parental informed consent, particularly the mother. Within the conventional discourse, this of course makes sense considering the context of biomedical decision making and with the delegation of power to the parents over their child. Thus, although commentators increasingly question the validity of such consent under the circumstances,[33] it has nevertheless been fully ingrained within these two arenas.

The extent to which reproductive freedom extends to parental selection of their child's genetic characteristics has been debated, however. Opponents of this proposition raise various liberal-based objections including the status of the child as a subject and his or her inherent moral value as a human being. Dena Davis, for instance, reasons that such a parental prerogative refers to the child merely a means rather than as end. While she acknowledges that a decision to have a child is never an end in itself, she argues that morally, he or she has to be held as such.[34] Others also stress that it restores parental property rights in

---

[29] Richard J. Hull, "Cheap Listening?—Reflections on the Concept of Wrongful Disability," *Bioethics* 20, no. 2 (2006): 59; Robertson, "Genetic Selection," 424, 432.

[30] Articles 5 and 18 of the Children's Convention; Articles 18-20 of the African Charter on the Rights and Welfare of the Child, OAU Doc. CAB/LEG/24.9/49 (1990), entered into force November 29, 1999 (hereafter African Charter); Article 18(4) of the ICCPR. This argument also resonates with a few of the provisions on reproductive health in international law. Article 16(1)(e) of CEDAW states that women's equality in family matters extends also to "the same rights to decide *freely and responsibly* on the number and spacing of their children and to have access to the information, education and means to enable them to exercise these rights [emphasis added]." The committee under the ICESCR also interpreted "reproductive health" as including "the freedom to decide if and when to reproduce and the right to be informed and to have access to safe, *effective, affordable and acceptable methods of family planning of their choice* [emphasis added]" (see note 12 of the Committee on Economic, Social and Cultural Rights, *The Right to the Highest Attainable Standard of Health (General Coment No. 14)*, 22nd Sess., Agenda Item 3, U.N. Doc. E/C.12/2000/4 (2000), reprinted in *Compilation of General Comments and General Recommendations Adopted by Human Rights Treaty Bodies*, U.N. Doc. HRI/GEN/1/Rev.6, paragraph 27, at 85 (2003) (hereafter *General Comment No. 14 (Health)*).

[31] Robertson, "Genetic Selection," 451; Hull, 61.

[32] Hull, 61.

[33] Asch, Gostin, and Johnson, 330–34. Scholars point to the lack of sufficient information, the sense of authoritativeness of the medical professionals as the ones who have the knowledge, and to the social pressure.

[34] Dena S. Davis, "Genetic Dilemmas and the Child's Right to an Open Future," *Hastings Center Report* 27, no. 2 (1997): 12.

the child. Although both parental responsibility towards the child and their sense of identification with their offspring are undeniable, neither, it is argued, justifies translating it into such parental control.[35]

Still others challenge such an extended parental reproductive freedom on legal grounds as have developed within the international instruments themselves. Sonia Harris-Short, for example, examined the work of the international bodies addressing reproductive liberty as a part of the right to found a family.[36] Analyzing the general comments and proclaimed positions, she concludes that all interpreted the right to reproductive freedom distinctly conservatively.[37] Under the work of Committee on the Convention on the Elimination of All Forms of Discrimination against Women (CEDAW) the right to reproductive choice has been essentially equated with women's right to have an equal say in the decision on the number and spacing of their children and in the field of health care, including health care services such as those related to family planning.[38] The analysis of the Human Rights Committee, she points out, has been all the more limited. The committee referenced the right to found a family merely as implying "in principle, the possibility to procreate and live together," without suggesting any positive duties on states to provide assistance to those who want to bring this possibility into realization.[39] Harris-Short thus concludes that interpreting the right to reproductive freedom as including "a guaranteed right to conceive a child, whether by natural or artificial means," and even more so, the right to genetic design, "goes well beyond" the wording and authoritative guidance given to the provisions.[40]

Court cases on the European level seem to support this conclusion. It appears that in the two cases so far in which the question of the right to found a family in view of the scientific developments was raised, the European Court of Human Rights (ECHR) declined from taking a stance. In the case of *X, Y and Z v. the UK* (1997), the Court denied the joint request of a social family, comprised of a biological mother, a female-to-male transgender father, and an anonymous-donor in vitro fertilization (IVF) child, that the transgendered man be registered as the father of the child.[41] Although both the father's sex

---

[35] David Archard, "Children, Multiculturalism and Education," in *The Moral and Political Status of Children*, ed. David Archard and Colin M. Macleod (Oxford: Oxford University Press, 2002), 146–48.

[36] Harris-Short discusses Article 16(1) of CEDAW on the right to marriage and family relations and Article 23(2) of the ICCPR on the right to marry and to found a family. See Harris-Short, note 26.

[37] Harris-Short also draws on cases revolving around adoption that were delivered by the European Court of Human Rights (ECHR) to derive a similar conclusion, that is, that the right to found a family has not been interpreted on the European Union's level to include parental freedom to choose the genetic characteristics of the child. Neither of the cases, however, dealt with the questions of scientific techniques, reproduction and the right to found a family.

[38] Harris-Short, 337, 338–39.

[39] Ibid., 339.

[40] Ibid., 338, 340.

[41] The case of *X, Y and Z v. the UK* (Application no. 21830/93, European Court of Human Rights, Judgment of April 22, 1997). In this case, the couple met after the father had a reassignment surgery and cohabited over ten years at the time of the petition. The father had his own identity documentation changed, and there was no doubt that he acted as the

reassignment surgery and the IVF procedures were funded by the state, and the IVF procedures took place, according to the national law, with the father's formal legal acknowledgment of the child, the majority of the Court (13:7) granted the state a "wide margin of appreciation." The Court dismissed the claimants' concern that the lack of legal recognition would have an affect on the child's sense of personal identity and security, noting that the transgendered man is not prevented from acting as the social father.[42] The Court pointed out that, "although the technology of medically assisted procreation has been available in Europe for several decades, many of the issues to which it gives rise, particularly with regard to the question of filiation, remain the subject of debate."[43]

In the more tragic case of *Evans v. the UK* (2006), the majority of the ECHR dismissed the request of a woman to proceed with the implantation of her joint embryos with her separated husband, which were conceived through IVF, once he withdrew his consent.[44] Although the Court observed that the issue of assisted reproductive technologies clearly falls within the scope of one's right to

---

father in every sense of the term except his original physical birth (paragraphs 37 and 50 of the decision).

[42] Paragraph 50 of the judgment in the case of *X, Y and Z v.the UK.* Ironically, the Court also comments in this regard that the new man could apply for a joint residence order in respect of the child, which according to the English law, "would automatically confer on them full parental responsibility for her" (paragraph 50). The Court did not resolve the dual legal status that this state of affairs creates.

[43] Paragraph 44 of the case of *X, Y and Z v. the UK.* The Court reasoned that in view of the disagreements among the member dtates with regard to both granting parental rights to transgendered individuals and to the legal recognition of the social relationship between a child conceived by artificial insemination by the donor and the person who acts as the father, the state should enjoy a wide margin of appreciation. See, in contrast, the various dissenting opinions, emphasizing that legal solutions must follow medical, social, and moral developments by which transgendered individuals receive recognition, both legally and socially (especially as has been also in the circumstances of this case).

[44] *Evans v. the UK,* Application no. 6339/05, European Court of Human Rights, Judgment of March 7, 2006. In this case, a thirty-five-year-old woman was diagnosed during fertilization treatment with serious precancerous tumors in both ovaries. Before having the ovaries removed, the couple was advised that it would be possible to first extract some eggs for in vitro fertilization (IVF). She raised the possibility of freezing her unfertilized eggs, but this option was not available at the clinic. After the husband's reassurance, the couple went ahead with the treatment. Both signed the necessary consent forms and following the IVF procedure, six embryos were created and consigned to storage. Shortly after, the applicant had her ovaries removed. She was told to wait a couple of years before attempting to implant any of the embryos in her uterus, but six months later the relationship broke up, the husband withdrew his consent, and the clinic refused to continue the implantation of the embryos. The applicant filed the case in the ECHR arguing predominantly a violation of her right to privacy and family autonomy, nondiscrimination, and the fetuses' rights to life under Articles 8, 14, and 2, respectively, of the European Convention for the Protection of Human Rights and Fundamental Freedoms, 213 U.N.T.S. 222, entered into force September 3, 1953, as amended by Protocols Nos. 3, 5, 8, and 11, which entered into force on September 21, 1970, December 20, 1971, January 1, 1990, and November 1, 1998, respectively. The majority of the Court dismissed the main petition on the basis of the state's margin of appreciation. Both arguments under Articles 2 and 14 were dismissed in a unanimous vote. The first was dismissed citing previous decisions on a state's margin of appreciation with regard to the fetuses' rights to life; the second was dismissed on the basis of its conjunction with Article 8. See paragraphs 45, 70, 72–75 of the judgment.

respect of private life and the right to found a family,"[45] it refrained from settling the direct challenge as to what sort of state's positive and negative duties this right would entail.[46] The Court remarked that "the use of IVF treatment gives rise to sensitive moral and ethical issues against a background of fast-moving medical and scientific developments" in which there is disagreement among the member states.[47] It emphasized that there are strong policy considerations underlying the legislature's favor to stipulate "a clear or 'bright-line' rule which would serve both to produce legal certainty and to maintain public confidence in the law in a highly sensitive field."[48] Thus, although the Court recognized that it was the applicant's last chance of becoming a biological mother, it found the absolute ban on proceeding with the implantation of the embryos once a party to the IVF contract withdraws the consent not to be "such as to upset the fair balance required by Article 8 [dealing with the right to privacy and family life]," and dismissed the claim.[49]

Whereas these decisions may support Harris-Short's conclusion that procreation liberty does not extend today to genetic selection of one's offspring's characteristics, at least as far as they are contingent on such techniques,[50] both rulings seem socially and morally wrong. A part of the problem is the Court's effort to circumscribe the conflicts into the conventional form of liberty rights in which there are two parties standing in opposition to one another. In the case of *X, Y and Z v. the UK*, the Court framed the conflict in terms of the transgendered man's right to privacy and his freedom from the state's intervention in his family life versus the child's best interests. It is not clear, according to the Court, that the legal recognition would *necessarily* serve the latter, emphasizing the state's interest in maintaining a coherent system of family law.[51] The child's *possible* future interest in obtaining information about her biological father was a strong consideration as well.[52] Framed in this way, the Court opted to protect the more vulnerable side and dismissed the social father's request. In the case of *Evans v. the UK*, the Court framed the debate as a question of equal freedom of both the applicant and the husband to choose whether to become or not to become a parent, emphasizing the state's interest in "a bright-line rule."[53] Framed in such a way, the Court decided in favor of the husband whose imposed parenthood appeared to hold greater force.

---

[45] Paragraphs 57 of the judgment, in the case of *Evans v. the UK.*

[46] It is the first case that challenges directly state's positive duty in the context of assisted reproductive techniques. The Court poses the question in paragraph 57 of the judgment: "whether there exists a positive obligation on the State to ensure that a woman who has embarked on treatment for the specific purpose of giving birth to a genetically related child should be permitted to proceed to implantation of the embryo notwithstanding the withdrawal of consent by her former partner, the male gamete provider."

[47] Paragraphs 57, 62 of the judgment, in the case of *Evans v. the UK.*

[48] Paragraph 65 of the judgment, in the case of *Evans v. the UK.*

[49] Paragraph 67 of the judgment, in the case of *Evans v. the UK.*

[50] Although Harris-Short's conclusion is stated in rather broad terminology, her discussion essentially focuses on cloning.

[51] Paragraphs 44, 47 and 51 of the judgment in the case of *X, Y and Z v. the UK.*

[52] Paragraph 44 of the judgment in the case of *X, Y and Z v. the UK.* See also the particular adamant position in this context of Judge Pettiti (Separate Concurring Opinion).

[53] Paragraphs 57 and 65 of the judgment in the case of *Evans v. the UK.*

In both cases, however, the Court did not seem to take seriously the relationships involved and the particular context. In the instance of the *X, Y, and Z v. the UK*, the man acknowledged his parental role prior to the IVF procedure, and he also undeniably functioned as such. Furthermore, the legal recognition of parents/child relations is not normally conditioned by its prior approval that it would "necessarily" serve the child's best interests. Newborns and young children have no choice as to the family into which they are born and grow up, and only if the familial ties fail, is the parental legal recognition taken away. As most legal systems also allow for a legal social fiction of parenthood in one form or another,[54] if the family ties that are the most important to the child were in front of the Court, it appears rather clearly that the Court had to rule otherwise. Similarly, in the case of *Evans v. the UK*, the Court's insistence on the rigid contract bright-line rule ignored the circumstances of the case, including the specific social and psychological aspects that are involved.[55] By sticking to the legal frame yet not taking into account these critical social facts, the Court's assertion that a "fair balance" is sought thus comes across as somewhat misleading. Indeed, its legalist framing of the conflicts was such that it could only lead to a zero-sum result.

Moreover, it seems, that the Court failed to make use of the options the scientific advances offer in such cases in reaching more just rulings. To recall, Article 15 of the International Covenant on Economic, Social and Cultural Rights (ICESCR)[56] explicitly stipulates state's recognition of the "right of everyone . . . (b) To enjoy the benefits of scientific progress and its applications." This study argues that biomedical practices are a part of one's cultural rights and integral to his or her identity. Thus, were the claimants arguing their case under the rubric of their cultural rights, the Court could have provided a more socially appropriate result. Following this path, once the fertilization by scientific techniques has taken place, the issue is practically removed from the adversarial confrontation between the parties as the act of procreation has already occurred. What thus remains is the need to examine the social relations that are (or have been) in place. Accordingly, the legal recognition of family relations would not be dependent on the original biological gender of the father nor on the whim of the donor who made a commitment under very concrete circumstances. It would rather be determined by what actually constitutes the web of relations of the child (and the future child). This also brings the discussion to the examination of genetic manipulation in the context of children's rights and their right to identity.

D. SCIENTIFIC PROGRESS AND CHILDREN

Whether assisted reproductive techniques are to be recognized or not as parental reproduction, autonomy, or cultural rights, there is still a need to examine, where the child falls in the discourse. There is no doubt that the

---

[54] At least in the context of adoption or IVF from anonymous donors.

[55] Paragraphs 1, 3 and 4 of the Dissenting Opinion by Judges Traja and Mijovic, in the case of *Evans v. the UK*.

[56] International Covenant on Economic, Social and Cultural Rights, adopted Dec. 16, 1966, G.A. Res. 2200A (XXI), 21 Sess., U.N. GAOR Supp. (No. 16), at 49, U.N. Doc. A/6316 (1966), reprinted in 993 U.N.T.S. 3, entered into force January 3, 1976.

embryo/future child is the target of the practice, with three possible scenarios. If an IVF procedure is used, the child would not have been otherwise conceived (and exist). If any genetic manipulation were carried out, a very different child could have been born. The third scenario is that following a diagnosis of a prospective disability, the child would have been aborted—a scenario that is beyond the scope of this study. The most pertinent question is, then, in view of the scientific revolution, what sort of bioethical rights, if any, does the (future) child have? While parents and the medical profession clearly hold a decision-making power, it is crucial that it does not obscure the very relevant discussion on the children as targets and their rights. Two subsequent questions then follow. First, considering that prenatal scientific developments are carried out on embryos rather than on a born child, to what extent do fetuses have a status under international human rights law? The second question addresses the rights of the child who was born as a result of or in conjunction (or its lack) with genetic manipulations. For such a child, the scientific advancements (or their lack) are inherently a part of who he or she is. It is a part of the child's life story within a culture that prizes scientific capabilities. How does it correspond with the child's rights, particularly in light of his or her right to cultural identity?

1. Status of the Fetus under International Law

As pointed out in Chapter 2, the question whether fetuses are subjects under the Children's Convention was among the most contentious issues. It was raised in various contexts, including the definition of the child, and the right to life, survival, and development.[57] Most relevant to the present study is its discussion in connection with proposals made to prohibit experimentation with and medicalization of children as a part of state considerations of harmful traditional practices and of the child's health.[58] One of the proposals on experimentations also included a list of prohibited practices such as cloning, sex selection by genetic manipulation, and research and experimentation on living embryos.[59] Eventually, the drafters opted for a compromise by which references to the fetus as a separate subject were omitted from the operative part of the Convention, and the explicit reference to the child "before and after birth" remained only in the Preamble.[60] The legal implications of this compromise has been debated for some time but never fully settled.[61] The only

---

[57] Articles 1 and 6 of the Children's Convention.

[58] Article 24 of the Children's Convention.

[59] Other prohibited practices on the list were the creation of embryos using sperm from other individuals, ectogenesis, fusion of embryos or any other operation likely to result in monstrous/abnormal forms, creation of children from persons of the same sex, creation of identical twins, experimentation on living embryos whether viable or not. The proposal was submitted during the second reading of the working group but not discussed. See *Legislative History* on Article 1 (Definition), 18.

[60] Paragraph 9 of the Preamble of the Children's Convention reads:

> *Bearing in mind* that, as indicated in the Declaration of the Rights of the Child, adopted by the General Assembly of the United Nations on 20 November 1959, "the child, by reason of his physical and mental immaturity, needs special safeguards and care, including appropriate legal protection, *before as well as after birth* [emphasis added].

[61] Philip Alston, "The Unborn Child and Abortion under the Draft Convention of the Rights of the Child," *Human Rights Quarterly* 12 (1990): 156–78. Alston suggests three main

consensus has been that the Convention leaves an open door for state policies with regard to abortion, a stance that all other human rights bodies have also taken on the issue so far.[62]

In light of the adoption of the European Convention on Human Rights and Biomedicine, the issue of the status of the fetus under international law must be revisited. Specifically, there are a few provisions in this treaty that may give rise to the argument that the status of fetuses under international law has changed. Both Articles 1 and 2 of the Oviedo Convention (on purpose and primacy of human beings) guarantee the protection to "all human beings." Neither defines, however, what the term means, hence opening the possibility for the inclusion of fetuses. Article 12 of the Oviedo Convention on "predictive genetic tests" includes, according to the explanatory report, the right to carry out diagnosis interventions at the embryonic stage to find out whether an embryo carries hereditary traits that will lead to serious diseases in the future child.[63] Article 13 allows for genetic interventions if "undertaken for preventive,

---

reasons, supported by both treaties and case law, why the right to life under Article 6 of the Children's Convention does not extend to fetuses: the nature of treaties' preambles as an expression of general policy concerns, lacking in themselves legally binding force (pages 168–69, 177); the lack of support in the *travaux prepartoires* of the Children's Convention to such an agreed intention; and public policy considerations, among them, the debate whether life begins from the moment of conception or fertilization and the right of a woman to life, mental and physical health, and privacy that should prevail. He also examines in this context the American Convention on Human Rights, which contains within its statement of the right to life also "and in general, from the moment of conception." Reviewing the qualifying phrase "in general" as has been interpreted by the Inter-American Commission on Human Rights, he concludes, that there is no support to the inclusion of fetuses under the right to life within the Children's Convention (page 178).

62 So far, the European Court delivered a few decisions revolving around nonmedical abortion; yet, it has generally refrained from explicit consideration whether the right to life under Article 2 of the European Convention for the Protection of Human Rights and Fundamental Freedoms actually applies to the fetus on its own. The Court maintained this position also when the fetus's right to life was raised in the context of abortion following a mistaken medical treatment (rather than pro-life/pro-choice debate). In the case of *Vo. v. France* (Application no. 53924/00, European Court of Human Rights, Judgment of July 8, 2004), a pregnant woman had to abort her fetus after a medical treatment that was made in error (the attending doctor confused her with another patient with a similar name). The Cour de Cassation, the French court of last instance, acquitted the doctor of involuntary homicide on the grounds that a fetus is not a person within the meaning of the French Criminal Code. The applicant appealed to the European Court of Human Rights claiming a violation of the fetus's right to life under Article 2 of the European Convention for the Protection of Human Rights and Freedoms. The majority of the Court rejected her claim, pointing out that all the case law on the question of abortion so far has taken the stance that the unborn child is not regarded as a "person" directly protected by Article 2 of the European Convention and that if the unborn child does have a "right" to "life," it is implicitly limited by the mother's rights and interests (paragraph 80 of the judgment). See also, in this regard, the the case of *Tysiac v. Poland* (Application no. 5410/03, European Court of Human Rights, Judgment of March 20, 2007), where the European Court of Human Rights ruled that once a state provides an option for abortion, if only under special circumstances, the state has positive obligations to uphold in this regard, that is, to provide appropriate means of exercising such an option. Failure to do so, the Court resolved, amounts to a violation of the woman's right to her "effective respect" for her private life as guaranteed under Article 8 of the European Convention for the Protection of Human Rights and Freedoms.

63 Paragraph 83 of the Explanatory Report for Convention on Human Rights and Bio-

diagnostic or therapeutic purposes and only if its aim is not to introduce any modification in the genome of any descendents." The explanatory report further emphasizes that "interventions aimed at modifying genetic characteristics not related to a disease or to an ailment are prohibited."[64]

Additionally, the European Convention on Human Rights and Biomedicine contains a few provisions dealing specifically with fetuses. Article 14 requires gender equality in the usage of assisted reproduction techniques by prohibiting sex selection, "except when serious heredity sex-related disease is to be avoided." Article 18, entitled "Research on embryos *in vitro*," states that, "Where the law allows research on embryos *in vitro*, it shall ensure adequate protection of the embryo."[65] Article 18(2) also prohibits the creation of human embryos for research purposes. Cloning is also explicitly prohibited in a separate additional protocol.[66] Thus, different from the question of the fetus's right to life under the abortion debate, these operative provisions suggest that a fetus enjoys explicitly recognized protection under international law. Furthermore, there is a growing sense that it is all the more relevant now, as the ECHR expressed, "in light of the scientific progress and the potential consequences of research into genetic engineering, medically assisted procreation or embryo experimentation."[67] Such protection, the Court emphasized, may be required in the name of human dignity and, as a common ground between states, that the embryo/fetus belongs to the human race.[68] Indeed, it is in this vein that the ECHR has made a particular note in the case of *Vo v. France* that it may be requested, under Article 29 of the Convention on Human Rights and Biomedicine, to give an advisory opinion on the interpretation of this instrument.[69] In other words, it seems likely that it would not be too long before the international bodies are called to intervene, as the moral and ethical issues that arise would ultimately need to be resolved.[70] The question is then, what sort of protection do fetuses

---

medicine, http://conventions.coe.int/Treaty/en/Reports/Html/164.htm.

[64] Paragraph 90 of the Explanatory Report for Convention on Human Rights and Biomedicine.

[65] Article 18 of the Convention on Human Rights and Biomedicine is the only provision dealing directly with research on embryos in vitro. The scope of the Additional Protocol on Research, in contrast, is limited to research with embryos in vivo and explicitly excludes research on embryos in vitro. According to Article 19 of the Explanatory Report on the Additional Protocol on Research (http://conventions.coe.int/Treaty/EN/Reports/Html/195.htm), this category of research will be addressed in another separate treaty in the future.

[66] Additional Protocol on the Prohibition of Cloning Human Beings.

[67] Paragraph 84 of the judgment in the case of *Vo v. France.*

[68] Ibid.

[69] Ibid.

[70] The questions of the status of embryo under international law as well as genetic manipulations in the context of disability were also highly debated during the drafting of the Disability Rights Convention. Ultimately, however, the convention does not include reference to these issues. Although the conventional requirement under international human rights law of informed consent for medical and scientific experimentation exists, there is no mention of genetic manipulations. Similarly, although Article 25 of the Disability Rights Convention includes, for the first time in a legally binding international treaty, a reference to state obligations with regard to health services to provide "sexual and reproductive health," it was agreed during the drafting process that the convention does not aim at intervening in family planning policies in national states nor to constitute recognition of any new international law obligations or human rights, such as a right to abortion. That said, the same article requires

have or should have in the context of scientific practices? As future children, how would these correspond with the discourse on children's rights?

E. THE CHILD'S "RIGHT TO A SOUND MIND AND BODY"?

Before the scientific revolution, the question whether a child had a right to a sound mind and body was translated within the legal discourse into the so-called wrongful life claims. Such claims are normally brought up by parents on behalf of their child (often with his or her as a claimant as well), arguing that considering the child's (severe) disabilities, he or she would have been better off if not born at all. The medical professional is charged under such claims with negligence in carrying out his or her duty of care for which the child acquired the disabilities. For the most part, courts around the world were reluctant to accept publicly such cases. The assumption has been that the child's life always triumphs over nonexistence. And in any case, courts were reluctant to make a judgment on the question of at what level one's suffering or quality of life ceases being worth living and on how to quantify one's appropriate compensation.[71]

The scientific revolution gave rise to a new set of claims. In view of the technological capabilities of screening fetuses for disabilities and, to an extent, providing treatment before birth, the argument is that a child born with a disability was wrongly disabled. This claim is built on an extension of the bioethical duty of the medical professional to beneficence and nonmaleficence, and it now has been raised as a part of the parental duty of care toward the child. Jeffrey P. Kahn, for instance, suggests that the parental duty arises out of the general principle of "do no harm." He argues that parents have the obligation to prevent harmful conditions in their child, including a predisposition to genetic diseases that would bring about the child's suffering either at birth or later on in life.[72]

---

in paragraph 2 that states shall "Provide those health services needed by persons with disabilities specifically because of their disabilities, *including early identification and intervention as appropriate, and services designed to minimize and prevent further disabilities, including among children and older persons* [emphasis added]." Thus, while both the lack of agreement with regard to the status of fetuses (as a children) under the international human rights system, as well as the status quo with regard to the question of abortion remains, the issue will surely reemerge. For the discussions on these accounts, see the reports of the UN Ad Hoc Committee on a Comprehensive and Integral International Convention on the Protection and Promotion of the Rights and Dignity of Persons with Disabilities, available at http://www.un.org/esa/socdev/enable/rights/adhoccom.htm.

[71] In 1986, the Israeli Supreme Court accepted a "wrongful life" suit (Noam J. Zohar, "Prospects for "Genetic Therapy"—Can a Person Benefit from Being Altered?" *Bioethics* 5, no. 4 (1991): 278. In contrast, the Californian Supreme Court dismissed such a claim in the case of *Turpin v. Sortini* (31 Cal. 3d 220, 643 P.2d 954, 182 Cal. Rptr. 337(1982)). In this case, a deaf child sought damages for being "deprived of the fundamental right of a child to be born as a whole, functional human being without total deafness." The Californian Supreme Court rejected a claim of wrongful life action, referring to the difficulty in determining whether living life as a disabled person (even in cases that involve complex disabilities) is worse than no life at all and on the difficulty of estimating an appropriate sum as a general compensation. However, the court upheld the child and her family's right to "extraordinary and special" compensation.

[72] Jeffrey P. Kahn, "Genetic Harm: Bitten by the Body that Keeps You?" *Bioethics* 5, no. 4 (1991): 303–06.

Some aim to establish a moral duty based on the type of decision making that is involved. Scholars distinguish in this context between "same person" and "same number" choices.[73] Same person choices are those that, regardless of the alternative the decision maker chooses to take, the same person exists. As Noam J. Zohar and others point out, this type of choice may be difficult to apply to the context of genetic manipulations that are carried out on fetuses (and young children), as such procedures intrinsically mean changes to the "original" person who is involved.[74] Same number choices, in contrast, are those that, regardless of the alternative the decision makers takes, the same number of persons exist (even if the identities of the original persons changed).[75] According to this "principle of avoidability by substitution," whenever parents can choose a child without a disability, they have a moral duty to do so. If aborting a child with a disability, in contrast, would result in no child at all, they do not.[76] Others extend the parental duty beyond the particular child. Philip G. Peters, for example, argues in light of the substitutive principle that parents also have a duty to prevent disability even if not for the particular child, but out of their moral obligation to children as a general group.[77]

Although this discourse is of course pertinent, it is limited, as it ultimately focuses on the medical professional and on the parents as patients. As such, it endorses the traditional adult-centered will/power approach to rights, questioning what sort of "imperfect obligations" the various responsible adults have toward the child.[78] Considering the evolving recognition of children's rights, however, it is crucial to examine what sort of interests or rights the (future) children have as subjects on their own.

Chapter 6 delineated a proposal for the evaluation of biomedical practices carried out on children. Specifically, it called for the examination of the biomedical conflicts on two simultaneous medical/health implications and cultural/identity paths. The balance between the two venues will be a determinative factor in the classification of the harmfulness of the practice. As has been argued, the crux of the issue in the context of children's bioethics cannot focus on the medical implications and its derivative of informed consent. The conventional focus on the physical aspect is insufficient as it ignores the spiritual and mental aspects that are also ingrained in one's construction of the self. Similarly, while the doctrine of informed consent is presumably the ultimate moral-translated-into-legal/procedural requirement, it fails to capture the web of relations and the context in which biomedical decisions are made. Its focus on individualized autonomy and on decision-making capacity also does not correspond with the multiple medical cultures that coexist, nor is it capable of properly granting a place for children's own experiences and voice.

---

[73] Hull, 58.

[74] Jeffrey P. Kahn, "Commentary on Zohar's "Prospect for 'Genetic Therapy'—Can a Person Benefit from Being Altered?," *Bioethics* 5, no. 4 (1991): 314; Zohar, 285.

[75] Hull, 57–58.

[76] Hull, 59.

[77] Philip G. Peters, "Harming Future Persons: Obligations to the Children of Reproductive Technology," *Southern California Interdisciplinary Law Journal* 8 (1998–89): 399.

[78] See the discussion in Chapter 6.

As a complementary alternative, it is suggested that the notion of autonomy as a means to exercise rights, at least as children are concerned, be reconsidered in two subsequent steps. Primarily, it has to be understood as "autonomy in relations" or "autonomy with others" as has been advocated by the feminists' relational approach. The second step requires envisioning autonomy as falling on a scale in which identity and the traditional form of autonomy, as freedom from others are its two extremes. Such a conceptualization makes sense as it acknowledges that a person is not merely an individual in the abstract, but rather, the "entire fabric around [one's] knot, woven from the fabric of the real . . . [It includes] "one's parents, children, friends, foes, ancestors and successors . . . [It is in one's] ideas . . . feelings and [sense of] belonging."[79] This is intrinsically one's cultural identity that, particularly for children, plays a paramount role in both the formation of who they are and in their exercise of any given interests or rights. Under this identity path, the motivations for and the impact of any given biomedical practice will be evaluated and balanced, taking into account the familial, communal, and other webs of relations that surround the child. In the remainder of this chapter this framework for analysis is followed in order to examine genetic interventions in light of children's rights.

1. Are Genetic Interventions for Disability-Related Reasons Medically Justified?

Perhaps the most intuitive answer to the question whether genetic intervention to treat, prevent, or preserve disability is "right" is that it is medically justified. The inseparable bond with the medical professional, couched in terms of duty of care and the obligation of avoidance of harm, seems to reinforce this response. Indeed, the Oviedo Convention explicitly allows only for genetic interventions aimed at *preventive, diagnostic, or therapeutic disease-related purposes* to be carried out.[80] In reality, however, the issue is far more complex. First, on the philosophical level, it is seemingly impossible to determine harm in this context. This is so not only because of it being a cultural construct,[81] but also because harm requires comparison to a previous, better off, state that cannot be evaluated in the context of fetuses or newborns.[82] One alternative, as Kahn suggests, is to endorse instead a concept of wronging, which requires an interference with others' interests and rights.[83] This, however, goes only so far, as it goes back to either the discourse on parental rights or to questioning what are the (future) child's interests and rights that need examination.

Second, there seems to be a great misconception about the relationship between disability and health. Whereas in specific cases, such as Huntington's disease, Tay Sachs, cystic fibrosis, and others, the genetic carrier intrinsically

---

[79] Raimundo Panikar, "Is the Notion of Human Rights a Western Concept?" *Diogenes* 120 (1982): 90–91. Panikkar distinguishes between the "individual," who is only "an abstraction, i.e., a selection of a few aspects of the person for practical purposes," and "person," as defined above.

[80] Articles 12 and 13 of the Convention on Human Rights and Biomedicine and paragraph 90 of its accompanying Explanatory Report for Convention on Human Rights and Biomedicine, emphasize the need of "disease or ailment" for the purpose of genetic intervention.

[81] See the discussion in Chapter 5.

[82] Kahn, "Genetic Harm," 294.

[83] Ibid.

involves significant health implications and deterioration up to death, in many and most other types of disabilities, no such disease-related connection can be made. For the most part, persons with disabilities lead a completely healthy life except for the limitation that the physical impairment may cause. Relying on the health and disease-related rationales as a general justification for such genetic interventions is thus incorrect.

Third, the underlying assumption of this medical approach is that life with a disability is equated with a life of suffering, which raises the moral duty to act by avoiding the disability.[84] This presumption, however, is a sweeping generalization, which also has no support in the views expressed by many persons with disabilities themselves. The determination of what is suffering or intolerable suffering is only relative, and particularly in the context of disabilities, it has also been prone to change over time.[85] For most persons with disabilities, the impairment becomes a part of everyday life, and while recognizing the difference, "it is, ontologically, unimportant."[86] The equation between disability and suffering thus seems to conflate between the collective experience of persons with disabilities as an oppressed group (hence disabled) and the individuals' experiences of their own impairments.[87] As Hull points out correctly, "it ascribes too much weight to impairment in accounting for disability in society."[88]

Finally, a central supposition in this approach is that disability is an objective medical condition that is well known and agreed upon. In reality, the concept of disability itself is a relative term. It is defined by the norms of normalcy and the expected roles and tasks within each given cultural group, and no cross-cultural definition of disability can be discerned.[89] The question is thus not only where the line between disability and ability should be drawn, but also which types of disabilities ultimately give rise to one's (parents and others) moral duty to avoid. Many of the aforementioned scholars acknowledge that there is a need to establish criteria to distinguish between easy and severe cases of disability that would mitigate the appropriate parental and others' biomedical duties and response. Such a determination, however, is inherently biased and is

---

[84] Hull, 59, pointing out, with regard to the principle of avoidability by substitution, that "the idea . . . is that, if we can make suffering and limited opportunity (due to the disability) 'avoidable by substitution'," we should do so.

[85] Jo Bridgeman, "Caring for Children with Severe Disabilities: Boundaried Relational Rights," *International Journal of Children's Rights* 13, no. 1–2 (2005): 101 (discussing the changes in the conceptualization of Down Syndrome from a "so intolerable" condition that occurred in the past three decades).

[86] Nick Watson, "Well, I Know This is Going to Sound Very Strange to You, but I Don't See Myself as a Disabled Person: Identity and Disability," *Disability & Society* 17, no. 5 (2002): 518, 524. This is not to deny the pluralism of views expressed by persons with disabilities about the question of suffering, but only to emphasize that the essentialist medical approach is inapt. See, for example, that also among the persons with disabilities under Watson's research, a small number of women described their experiences profoundly negatively. See Watson, 522.

[87] Donna Reeve, "Negotiating Psycho-Emotional Dimensions of Disability and Their Influence on Identity Constructions," *Disability & Society* 17, no. 5 (2002): 495, 504.

[88] Hull, 56.

[89] Renteln, 59.

subject to a considerable disagreement both among and within groups (either of persons with disabilities or not). Whether one accepts or rejects claims of members of the Deaf community, for example, that "deafness" is not a disability that needs eradication, but rather a quality to cherish,[90] or if one approves or not of the concern of members of the Little People of America that prenatal testing would destroy their community,[91] goes a long way in elucidating this point. Ultimately, then, it is impossible to derive a moral duty for genetic intervention only within the vacuum of the medico-legal discourse.

The discussion now turns to the identity path.

2. "Disabled Identity"?

The second path of consideration requires examination of the implications of such biomedical practices on the identity of the (future) child. This path is particularly interesting in the context of genetic manipulation not only because identity ultimately reflects children's autonomy in their exercise of rights, but also because the European Conventions on Biomedicine make explicit reference to state duties to protect the "dignity and identity of all human beings." Although the European Court refrained from determining that fetuses fall within the scope of person or human being in the context of the right to life, it made it a point, in light of the European Conventions on Biomedicine, that this does not mean that the fetus's status could not be interpreted as such for purposes other than the abortion debate.[92] This raises the following questions: At what stage does the development of one's identity start? What is the interrelationship between the fetus's (and the future child's) identity and the prenatal genetic manipulations in the context of disability? How is or should the child's identity be protected and preserved under Article 8 of the Children's Convention?[93]

At the heart of these questions is the extent to which one's identity formation is dependent on his or her genetic makeup. Under the traditional "natural" or "biological essentialism" approach, identities stem from innate biological causes.[94] The assumption is that identities have an essential, natural, and intrinsic origin that is presocial and unchangeable.[95] Accordingly, once

---

[90] National Association of the Deaf. "NAD Position Statement on Cochlear Implants," http://www.nad.org/infocenter/newsroom/positions/CochlearImplants.htm; Diane Granat, "To Hear Again," *Washingotnian* 29 (1994): 64–76, http://www.hwwilson.com/Databases/omnifile.htm.

[91] Erik Parens and Adreine Asch, "The Disability Rights Critique of Prenatal Genetic Testing," *Hastings Center Report* 29, no. 5 (Special Suppl. 1999): 12.

[92] Paragraphs 85–86 of the judgment in the case *of Vo v. the France.*

[93] Article 3(h) of the Disability Rights Convention restates this right as one of the convention's general principles.

[94] Rose Galvin, "The Paradox of Disability Culture: the Need to Combine versus the Imperative to Let Go," *Disability & Society* 18, no. 5: 678; Watson, 509. There is a distinction between an animalist versus a naturalist approach to identity. The first essentially applies to animals; the latter assumes that human beings are potential conscious creatures. For further discussion, see Carol Rovane, "Genetics and Personal Identity," in *A Companion to Genethics,* ed. Justine Burley and John Harris (Malden, MA: Blackwell Publishing, 2002).

[95] Galvin, 678; Watson, 509.

conception takes place, whether it is sex, ethnic, racial, or disabled biological characteristics (or a combination thereof) one's identity is already established. Under a social or "humanist" approach, in contrast, identities are constructed through multiple factors that can be traced historically through one's kinship and other relationships.[96] The process of identity formation is assumed to take place within various power relations, building on the idea that identities exist only in opposites.[97] From this view, although biological characteristics play a part, the future child's identity is generally constructed only after birth (some argue also only beyond the age of infancy),[98] as it necessarily depends on his or her social interactions.[99]

Whether one endorses the natural or the humanist approach, the context of prenatal genetic interventions is unique, as no fetus has such a historical track. The only identity the fetus has is the functional or physical one, hence necessitating the conclusion that any prenatal genetic intervention inherently impacts the fetus's identity. It is here, then, where the complexity of the intersection between genetic manipulation, fetus/(future) children's rights in international law, and the child's right to preserve his or her identity seems to be in a confrontational clash. If one takes the view that fetuses fall within the scope of person and human being under the European Conventions on Biomedicine, then, as genetic alteration changes the personal identity of the targeted fetus, no such genetic procedure should be allowed. This, however, goes against the explicit provisions in the international instruments that allow disease-related genetic interventions to take place. It also gives rise to the question whether *every* genetic alteration leads to such an identity change that the original individual indeed ceases to exist.[100] This may be the case with regard to severe disease-related biological characteristics, as such conditions diminish the very existence of the person at stake. It is not at all clear, however, that it is so with regard to less severe cases. Accepting the proposition that minor impairments have a negative impact on the (future) child's identity implies that one's genetic makeup poses, in itself, harm.[101] Furthermore, if the protection of the (future) child is at stake, there is still a point to inquire whether the genetic alteration is indeed necessarily benefiting the personal identity of the altered embryo who, following the intervention, developed into a mature child.

The main assumption underlying the aforementioned questions is that one's physical impairment necessarily leads to the formation of a (fixed) disabled identity and that it is an essentialist one that triumphs all.[102] It also implies that disabled identity is substantially different from an "abled identity" and for the worse. Indeed, much of the existing literature on the identity of persons with disabilities has taken this line of thought. Studies traditionally

---

96 Galvin, 680.

97 Galvin, 678; Watson, 509.

98 Jeffrey P. Kahn, "Commentary on Zohar's "Prospect for 'Genetic Therapy'," 313–14.

99 Ingmar Persson, "Genetic Therapy, Identity and the person-Regarding Reasons," *Bioethics* 9, no. 1 (1995): 22.

100 Zohar, 285; Kahn, "Commentary on Zohar's "Prospect for 'Genetic Therapy'," 314.

101 Kahn, "Commentary on Zohar's "Prospect for 'Genetic Therapy'," 289.

102 Watson, 513.

focused on the issue of adaptation, assuming that starting from childhood, persons with disabilities pass through stages of adjustment in which they come to terms with their physical impairment in order to achieve the ultimate goal of normalization.[103] Others emphasized the various manifestations of the psycho-emotional dimensions of disability, particularly the feelings of loss, anger, and frustration and what some observed as "internalized oppression."[104] While recognizing that these reactions are affected by social stigma, they were nevertheless often perceived as an inherent characteristic of one's impairment.[105] Ironically, the vocal assertion of identity pride among some groups with impairments such as the Deaf community and Little People of America further reinforced these perceptions. As a result, also within disability studies, much of the discourse presented the issue of disabled identity as something collective, fixed, and based on a shared experience of subordination.[106]

If these perceptions of disabled identity are correct, then it may indeed be said that children have an interest/right to be born with an abled (presumably positive) identity. Parents in such scenario would have a parallel (moral) duty, whenever possible, to act upon. For this reason, a request by members of the Deaf community, for example, to have a Deaf child should also be rejected on the spot. As human beings are social creatures who are dependent on their web of relations, if one's disabled identity stands in the way, it is a harm that children have the interest and parents have the duty to avoid.

The question of disabled identity has attracted increasing attention. The literature is still limited, however, and it is particularly so in the context of children.[107] Most of the research that exists has been carried out on white children in Western states, focusing on physical impairments. Only recently have scholars started addressing children with mental (rather than physical) disabilities such as autism, learning and intellectual disabilities, and others.[108] It is also important to note that the issue is highly contentious both within and among various types of disability groups. Still, as persons with disabilities

---

[103] Rosalyn B. Darling, "Toward a Model of Changing Disability Identities: a Proposed Typology and Research Agenda," *Disability & Society* 18, no. 7 (2003): 882.

[104] Reeve, 495; Watson, 512.

[105] David Pfeiffer, "Eugenics and Disability Discrimination," in *The Psychological and Social Impact of Disability*, ed. Robert P. Marinelli and Arthur E. Dell Orto (New York: Springer Publishing, 1999), 19.

[106] Watson, 513.

[107] Most of the literature on children with disabilities has focused on how children with disabilities and their identities are viewed by others, such as the medical professional, parents, siblings. It is only recently that the perspectives of children with disabilities themselves are starting to be sought. This chapter focuses on the latter, as it takes children as subjects rather than passive objects of observations.

[108] Berni Kelly, "'Chocolate . . . Makes You Autism': Impairment, Disability and Childhood Identities," *Disability & Society* 20, no. 3 (2005): 261–75 (discussing children with learning disabilities); Rosalind Ekamn Ladd, "Rights of the Autistic Child," *International Journal of Children's Rights* 13, no. 1–2 (2005): 87–98 (discussing children with autism); Bridgeman, note 84 (children with severe disabilities); see also Melinda Jones, "Adolescent Gender Identity and the Courts," *International Journal of Children's Rights* 13, no. 1–2 (2005):121–48 (discussing adolescent gender identity).

are commonly the targeted group for genetic elimination, it may be useful to examine some of the findings on the process of identity formation within this group to highlight some of the complexities involved.

Perhaps the most intense challenge in the literature has been with regard to the image of "universal essentialist disabled identity." Rosalyn B. Darling, for example, found a range of responses individuals have toward their disability, including, alongside the traditional forms of identification such as normalization and resignation, also "new" ones such as affirmation, situational identification, and others.[109] She also points out that there are identity changes from one type of identification to another over time, depending on new and old interactions, encounters, and experiences.[110] Nick Watson's study further calls into question the conventional description of disabled identity as one that is constructed through the opposite of normalcy. Working with persons with disabilities, he emphasizes that they do not claim an identity that is based on their impairment, but rather feel normal despite it.[111] This latter point is particularly interesting in the context of children. Although both children with and without disabilities construct their identity inward, by comparing others to themselves, neither viewed disability per se as different or abnormal.[112] Also when they observed differences, they did not attribute them the same negative connotations as adults.[113]

The literature also increasingly notes the important role ethnic, religious, age, sex, and other factors play in the process of identity formation of persons with disabilities.[114] In contrast to the common Western perception of members of the Deaf community as a linguistic minority group, for example, children who are deaf belonging to Hispanic communities in the United States define deafness in terms of disability and tend to attribute it to religious sources.[115] In many African cultures, such as in Ghana and Zimbabwe, disability is attributed also to religious sources, witchcraft, curses of deities, and punishment.[116] Other cultural communities recognize as disability only psychological conditions but not physical ones.[117] Considering the impact these various conceptualizations have on the attitudes toward persons and children with disabilities within every

---

109 Darling, 885–89.

110 Ibid., 890.

111 Watson, 524–25.

112 Kirsten Stalker and Clare Connors, "Children's Perceptions of Their Disabled Siblings: 'She's Different but It's Normal for Us'," *Children & Society* 18, no. 3 (2004): 224.

113 Ibid., 225; Mark Deal, "Disabled People's Attitudes toward Other Impairment Groups: A Hierarchy of Impairment," *Disability & Society* 18, no. 7 (2003): 899.

114 This point has also been emphasized as one of the difficulties in obtaining further information on the issue as there are different conceptualizations of what counts as disability. Renteln, 62–65; Reeve, 504; Watson, 525; Monica Werngren-Elgstrom, Ove Dehlin, and Susanne Iwarsson, "A Swedish Prevalence Study of Deaf People Using Sign Language: A Prerequisite for Deaf Studies," *Disability & Society* 18, no. 3 (2003): 321; Deal, 900.

115 Annie G. Steinberg and others, "A Little Sign and a Lot of Love": Attitudes, Perception, and Beliefs of Hispanic Families with Deaf Children," *Qualitative Health Research* 7, no.2 (1997): 204–05, 209.

116 Amwutor Avoke, "Models of Disability in the Labeling and Attitudinal Discourse in Ghana," *Disability & Society* 17, no. 7 (2002): 771.

117 Renteln, 64.

particular group, it is thus only reasonable to assume that the disabled identities that evolve would also be significantly different. It is further worth noting in this context that children with disabilities who belong to minority groups actually attributed the fact that they were treated differently to ethnicity rather than to their physical impairment.[118]

The extent to which the identity politics of persons with disabilities is translated into a collective identity one has been also open for debate. While Susan Peters states enthusiastically that it exists as "a cross-cultural phenomenon that knows no national boundaries, and in particular, [it] is not limited to Martha's Vineyard and American Deaf people,"[119] Watson, Darling, and others did not find much support for this claim. Although they all concede that identity politics has played a significant role in the disability movement, they doubt whether it actually goes beyond the mere sense of empathy persons with disabilities have towards their fellow members and, in any case, whether it is substantial enough to be claimed as establishing a collective identity.[120] As Mark Deal remarks, groups with impairments have recognized that, aside from the impairments, they may have little in common with other groups with impairments and, moreover, that it may also be the case with other individuals with similar impairments as theirs.[121]

The complexity of disabled identities is further illustrated with reports that document a hierarchy of impairment among groups of persons with disabilities.[122] Deal surveyed an array of such studies in the United Kingdom showing that persons with traditional disabilities such as cerebral palsy doubt the authenticity of the newer impairments such as dyslexia or Asperger's syndrome.[123] In-group members of one group of persons with disabilities (such as athletes with disabilities) also tended to make downward comparison with other groups of persons with disabilities on the basis of their higher functioning.[124] Scholars observed that people who are deaf, blind, and dwarves denounced eugenic practices of their own disability but not of others[125] and, moreover, that there are noticeable preferences also *within* each subtype disability.[126] The literature

---

[118] Zoebia Ali and others, "Disability, Ethnicity and Childhood: A Critical Review of Research," *Disability & Society* 16, no. 7 (2001): 961.

[119] Susan Peters, "Is There a Disability Culture? A Syncretisation of Three Possible World Views," *Disability & Society* 15, no. 4 (2000): 584.

[120] Darling, 889; Watson, 525.

[121] Deal, 902.

[122] Susan B. Wetstein-Kroft and James W. Vargo, "Children's Attitudes Towards Disability: A Review and Analysis of the Literature," *International Journal of Advancement of Counselling* 7 (1984): 184.

[123] Deal, 903, 905.

[124] Ibid., 905.

[125] Gregor Wolbring, "Where Do We Draw the Line? Surviving Eugenics in a Technological World," in *Disability and the Life Course: Global Perspective,* ed. Mark Priestley (Cambridge: Cambridge Universtiy Press, 2001), 46, quoted in Deal, 907.

[126] Parens and Asch (page 12), for example, observed that some members of the Little People of America community showed preference for their own particular strand of dwarfism over other strands of dwarfism. Werngren-Elgstrom and others also point out that, "deaf people with intellectual impairment do not frequently identify and participate in Deaf culture" (314).

also indicates that persons with disabilities attribute greater suffering to other subgroups of disabilities and that their general assessment of the various groups resembles the hierarchy suggested by nondisabled people.[127]

These patterns of hierarchy have also been observed among children with disabilities, particularly in the context of special education. Scholars remark that children with disabilities differentiated themselves from other children with disabilities by labeling one another, often using similar criteria of functional capacities as adults.[128] Children with visual impairment leveled themselves higher than those with learning or other academic incapacity,[129] and they also expressed preference for their own disability as being better off.[130]

What comes out of these studies is not only that there is a clear pluralism in the formation of identity among children with disabilities, but that, in fact, it resembles the process that takes place among nondisabled individuals. Both build on physical and mental inclusion and exclusion, attribute suffering, incapacity, and homogeneity to the other, and create hierarchies of impairment by comparing others to themselves. The problem does not lie, then, in the impairment and its by-product of disabled identity, but rather in the negative sociocultural interaction that forms it. In other words, it is emotions rather than reason that play the paramount role in the increasing scientific efforts to have a disability-free child. Thus, both the genetic selection for or against disability should be treated as a having a similar moral worth.

3. Purposeful Parental Selection for and against Disability—A Valid Comparison?

Part of the concern that the new genetic technologies have brought up is the fear that some parents would purposefully select a child with a disability. Much of the debate in this context revolved around the Deaf community.[131] It received particular attention since 2002, when the efforts of a Deaf couple in the United States to conceive a Deaf child through artificial insemination became public.[132] The effort did not succeed on the scientific level, as congenital deafness precludes potential sperm donors from the pool.[133] In view of the discussion on the medical and identity-related justifications for genetic manipulations, however, there is perhaps a place to reconsider whether such a selection is, from the child's perspective, indeed, wrong. It is also in place to reevaluate whether it is substantially different from other traditional bodily practices aimed at inscribing a cultural identity to justify a different response.

---

[127] Deal, 903.

[128] J. M. Davis and N. Watson, "Where Are the Children's Experiences? Analysing Social and Cultural Exclusion in 'Special' and 'Mainstream' Schools," *Disability & Society* 16, no. 5 (2001): 682.

[129] Davis and Watson, 682.

[130] Deal, 905.

[131] The focus on the Deaf community is both because of the public "identity pride" of the group and as it may have genetic link. Philosophically, however, the discussion is not limited to this type of impairment. There are other impairments that have genetic links, such as muscular dystrophy, dwarfism, and some types of blindness.

[132] M. Spriggs, "Lesbian Couple Create a Child Who Is Deaf Like Them," *Journal of Medical Ethics* 28, no. 5 (2002): 283.

[133] Ibid.

Philosophically, at least as far as non–disease-related claims are involved, there is not much difference between genetic selection for and against disabilities. Nor is there much difference between male circumcision and scarification, for example, and genetic selection for deafness. Within Western literature, particularly disability studies, the Deaf community is often described as "a vibrant culture with its own folklore, visual humor, publications and associations, as well as its own primary, sign language."[134] Members of the Deaf community also tend to socialize and to marry other members within the Deaf community, hence resembling any other religio-cultural and linguistic minority group.[135] To an extent, these characteristics have also received international recognition, materializing in the Disability Rights Convention. With regard to the rights to education and to participation in cultural life, there are provisions referring to the cultural and linguistic identity of persons with disabilities, including explicit mention of (only) sign languages and Deaf culture.[136] The existence of disagreements within the Deaf community on the matter is irrelevant in this context, as pluralism exists in all minority and majority cultures. It may also be said that the Deaf community has higher moral grounds to justify such an intervention, as unlike the Western individualist and alienating culture, it provides a strong sociocultural web or security and support to the child.[137] Arguments that such a request equates with an effort to pass on a victim identity following years of subordination are problematic, as they essentialize the identity into one factor that, in reality, does not hold. Moreover, as ostensibly all cultural groups have experienced discrimination at some point, it appears that all have "victimhood" factors that need to be taken into account. Thus, theoretically, there is no substantial difference between purposeful genetic selection for and against disability nor between selection for deafness and other identity-related traditional bodily practices.

Opponents of this comparison advance two key arguments. One is that genetic selection can be morally acceptable only as long as it does not impede the (future) child's autonomy, what Joel Feinberg coined as "the child's right to an open future."[138] The idea is that individuals have and should have the capacity to form, revise, and preserve their lifestyles in an informed rational

[134] Susan Burch, "Transcending Revolutions: the Tsars, the Soviet and Deaf Culture," *Journal of Social History* 34, no. 2 (2000): 393.

[135] Ibid.; K. W. Anstey, "Are Attempts to Have Impaired Children Justifiable?." *Journal of Medical Ethics* 28 (2005): 286.

[136] Articles 24(3)(b) and 30(c)(4) of the Disability Rights Convention.

[137] See also Lane's discussion on the construction of the deaf child by medical professionals and other "mainstream" institutions. While the medical efforts to "correct" the child's hearing theoretically aim at including him or her within the "mainstream" (abled) culture, in practice it always retains the child as an outsider. Harlan Lane, "Constructions of Deafness," *Disability & Society* 10 (1995): 177.

[138] Joel Feinberg, 'The Child's Right to an Open Future,' in *Whose Child? Children's Rights, Parental Authority, and State Power*, ed. Will Aiken and Hugh La Falleete (Totowa, N.J.: Littlefield, Adams, 1980), 126. Matthew Clayton, "Individual Autonomy and Genetic Choice," in *A Companion to Genethics*, ed. Justine Burley and John Harris (Malden, MA: Blackwell Publishing, 2002), 200; Davis, "Child's Right to an Open Future," 9; Archard, "Children, Multiculturalism and Education," 155–56.

manner[139] and that legitimate genetic selection should be determined in this light. In the context of the Deaf community, scholars cite the lower income and educational level of people who are deaf as well as the communication difficulties with the larger society that substantially limit "the child's right to an open future."[140] Conversely, even if deafness is a linguistic culture and not a disability, "it is an exceedingly narrow one."[141]

The other argument is as members of the larger society, Deaf people have a reciprocal social responsibility to it. Considering the burden that is associated with providing appropriate accommodation, including translators, special education, and so forth, people who are deaf have the duty, as much as possible, to reduce the costs.[142] Even in a culture in which one's authenticity is expensive,[143] there are social, cultural, and economic limits to society's responsibility to respect one's right to be different. It is here that the Deaf community also differs from other religio-cultural groups. Unlike other traditional bodily practices that, once carried out, require no additional medical provision,[144] deafness requires an ongoing accommodation.

The intuitive, disability and human rights response to such objections is that they follow too closely the medical approach to disability yet ignore the picture as a whole. They also elucidate the double standard in the discourse. On the particular level, if appropriate public policies were installed, it would raise the public's awareness and create a more inclusive society. This, in return, would equalize both economic and educational grounds without obliterating the unique linguistic cultural community.[145] Disability activists also emphasize that the long-term cost-effective calculations do not support the high estimations of financial costs, particularly considering the limited number of requests for deafness that cannot really be regarded as threatening the socioeconomic resources. Furthermore, the mainstreaming of various genetic screenings, prevention, and treatment are, by far, more costly.[146]

---

139 See discussion in Chapter 6, Section D.

140 Davis, "Child's Right to an Open Future," 12; N. Levy, "Deafness, Culture and Choice," *Journal of Medical Ethics* 28 (2005): 284.

141 Davis, "Child's Right to an Open Future," 13.

142 Bonnie P. Tucker, "Deaf Culture, Cochlear Implants, and Elective Disability," *Hastings Center Report* 28, no. 4 (1998): 10.

143 Erik Parens, "Authenticity and Ambivalence: Toward Understanding the Enhancement Debate," *Hastings Center Report* 35, no. 3 (2005): 34–36.

144 See the discussion in Chapter 6, in which practices that entail long-term health implications were excluded.

145 One of the main achievements of the Disability Rights Convention is what has been termed: "a paradigm shift," meaning that the medical approach to disability gave way to a more social approach to the issue of disability rights. Accordingly, the Disability Rights Convention comprehensively addresses the necessary measures states should take to ensure that persons with disabilities are full, equal, and active participants in society. Among the requirements are the provision of "reasonable accommodation," raising awareness to foster respect for the rights and dignity of persons with disabilities, to combat negative stereotypes and prejudice, and to promote accessibility, personal mobility, an inclusive working environment, and others.

146 Within the general debate on genetic prevention and treatment, scholars also charge that it is in fact the mere availability of such procedures that widens the socioeconomic gap. It

While these counterarguments are valid, the extent to which they undercut the basis for objection is limited. Ultimately, whether it is members of the Deaf community, who want to preserve deafness as cultural identity through the use of genetic treatment, or the effort to create a disability-free society that preserves the supremacy of the scientific culture, both focus on an essentialist notion of the impairment as the determinative factor. Although they seem to clash on the question whether it is the medical or social model of disability that should apply, they both subside within the medical one. Both rely on the medical profession to achieve their goals, yet whereas members of the Deaf community essentialize deafness as a personal (and collective) quality to cherish and embrace, members of the nondisabled culture essentialize hearing as such a trait.[147] Selection for deafness thus only replicates the very same practice of exclusion by enhancement that, when carried out by members of the nondisabled society, members of the Deaf community oppose. Indeed, the notion of respect for physical (and mental) difference as part of human diversity and humanity has been so ingrained within the disability rights movement that it is also explicitly stipulated among the general principles of the Disability Rights Convention.[148] Thus, even if only for the reason that the request is based on a similar attitude of discrimination, its rejection is in place.

There is still another reason to support this conclusion. As discussed earlier,[149] all children are born into the nonvoluntary association of the family of which they generally have no say. They internalize the cultural characteristics of the groups and the family unconsciously, and even before the cognitive process of understanding the culture takes place. This also resonates with the consistent scholastic finding that children up to the age of eight to ten hold more positive perceptions of disability than adults, a positivism that is reduced later.[150]

This is so also in the context of the Deaf community. A Deaf child who is born to Deaf parents who are members of the Deaf community is not much different from any child who is born to parents belonging to a minority group and by extension to all other children. Efforts to extract social pressure on such parents to alter the genetic factor before birth are thus, from the child's perspective, unjustified.[151] For the most part, this is not the case, however, as 90

---

strengthens the power of the "haves" over the "have-nots" who are less likely to have physical and fiscal accessibility to such procedures. Feminists are also particularly concerned with the burden on women that such technological advancements create. See Immaculada De Melo Martin, "On Our Obligation to Select the Best Children: A Reply to Savulescu," *Bioethics* 18, no. 1 (2004): 75–78, 79–80.

[147] Anstey, 287.

[148] Article 3(d) of the Disability Rights Convention.

[149] See discussion in Chapter 4.

[150] Deal, 899; Stalker and Connors, 223–24.

[151] See, in this regard, also Articles 3(h), 8(1)(b) and 30(4) of the Disability Rights Convention. The first stipulates among the convention's general principles "respect for the right of children with disabilities to preserve their identities," which may include also Deaf identity, particularly in light of Article 30(4) on cultural life, which explicitly references to "cultural and linguistic identity, including sign languages and deaf culture." The second, stipulated as part of the article on awareness-raising, requires states "to adopt immediate, effective and

percent of children who are deaf are born to hearing parents, hence lacking the "genetic heritage."[152] On the other hand, the "rules of acceptance" of the Deaf community are generally flexible. The literature suggests that there are three key conditions for one to become a member of the Deaf community: fluency in sign language; sense of cultural collectivity and belonging to the group; and self-identification as being nondisabled.[153] The genetic link, however, is not a perquisite, nor does it guarantee one's enculturation, inclusion, or desire to belong to the group.[154] While some people who are deaf use sign language, others do not. Hearing people may just as well acquire fluency in sign language and practically become members of the community.[155] Moreover, any child, whether hearing or deaf, would naturally pick up the language if exposed to it and identify with the culture as it is what provides him or her the social sources of support. Thus, while the cultural difference and the disability pride should be valued, rather than duplicating negative paths of identity formation, these bilingual children are ultimately the bridge to finding a more constructive response.

F. CONCLUSION

Biomedical practices, whether traditional or invented are ultimately motivated by similar emotional and identity-related rationales. Yet, while the traditional ones have received an international condemnation, the invented ones often escape a similar approach. The assumption is that the latter are for medical causes in which the scientific developments endeavor to triumph. In reality, the general support of genetic selection against disabilities and the antagonism to those in favor of it are often based on misconceptions about the nature of disability and about its connection with health and disease. In general, there seems to be a confusion between the impairment and the social disabling, creating an anxiety and hence, presumably, the exclusionary response.

Much of the discussion on genetic modification has focused on the parental right to select their offspring's characteristics and on the biomedical and moral justifications that are involved. While the international bodies refrained so far from explicitly espousing the scientific advancements within the human rights framework, in view of the European Conventions on Biomedicine and the Disability Rights Convention, the moral, social, and cultural dilemmas will ultimately need to be resolved. They will also have to face the question, mostly absent so far, of where the child is in the discourse. What are his or her rights and interests? And are prenatal genetic manipulations really carried out for the child's benefit?

---

appropriate measures . . . to combat . . . harmful traditional practices relating to persons with disabilities." Whether this would include altering genetic factors before birth with regard to disabilities such as deafness is yet to be seen.

[152] Jim G. Kyle and Gloria Pullen, "Cultures in Contact: Deaf and Hearing People," *Disability, Handicap & Society* 3, no.1 (1988): 57.

[153] Peters, "Is There a Disability Culture?" 584; Deal, 904.

[154] Levy, 285; Peters, "Is There a Disability Culture?" 592.

[155] Anna-Miria Muhlke, "The Right to Language and Linguistic Development: Deafness from a Human Rights Perspective," *Virgina Journal of International Law* 40 (2000): 738.

Where no long-term health implications are involved, allowing for genetic manipulation for and against disability has to be viewed through the child's right to preserve his or her identity. The literature on the issue of disabled identity is only in its inception. It is overwhelmingly Western, white, and prone to focus on physical impairments alone. Children's own voices (rather than other's perceptions of and on children with disabilities) are seemingly lacking. Still, it does give some basic idea about the complexities within the notion of the disabled identities that are involved and leaves one to wonder to what extent "normal" and "abnormal" actually diverge.

The scientific revolution and its power of genetic selection of children's characteristics thus necessitate reevaluation. There seems to be a great deal of fear about parental selection for disability. It is exacerbated by the growing sense of identity pride among some subtypes of disability, among which the claim of the Deaf community to recognition as a linguistic minority group is most known. This also highlights the point that the more sociocultural approach to disability one takes, the harder it is to condemn a genetic intervention as morally wrong. Ultimately, however, it also needs to be acknowledged that selection against disabilities is motivated by similar grounds. Thus, rather than debating the moral justifications to reject or to endorse one type of genetic selection over another, both proponents and opponents should consider how to change the dynamic for the benefit of all.

CHAPTER 8
CONCLUSION

The Convention on the Rights of the Child (Children's Convention or Convention)[1] envisioned a new world order for children. On the one hand, it provides children with an array of special protection rights. These include both traditional rights, such as one's freedom from torture, inhumane, and degrading treatment, as well as more innovative ones, which originated from the basis of children's difference from adults, such as the provision on abuse and neglect. On the other hand, the Children's Convention stipulates an array of rights aimed at positioning children on one level with adults, such as self-determination, religious freedom, and others. The Convention presumably establishes a direct link between children and both states and the international community. States are now bestowed with a greater share of the traditional parental responsibility of raising and caring for the child and hence have greater say about their future (full) citizens-to-be.

The discussion about children and traditional biomedical practices, however, comes across as alienated from both strands of rights. The most prevalent path taken by many scholars and human rights activists addressing the issue has been the protective approach. As shown throughout the study, however, this approach is an inappropriate vehicle to tackle it. The applications of the provisions on child abuse and neglect, on violence against children, and the extension of one's freedom from torture, cruel, inhuman, and degrading treatment clearly aim at securing children from being victims of harmful practices that seem to infringe on their interests and rights. Yet traditional biomedical practices do not fall comfortably within either of these. They are not clearly within the scope of child-rearing practices. What is harm is culturally contingent, and the Western emphasis on physical harm and on scientific orientation is not universally shared. Traditional biomedical practices also cannot be merely assumed to reflect a sick society. Male circumcision and scarification of children were and are still carried out in some of the wealthiest states. Furthermore, even with respect to practices that originated under circumstances of social and political ills, the serious questions are how children themselves perceive them and why they persist.

The examination of children and biomedical practices through the lens of autonomous subjects and bearers of rights hardly advances the discourse.

[1] Convention on the Rights of the Child, G.A. Res. 44/25, annex, 44th Sess., 61st plenary meeting. U.N. GAOR Supp. (No. 49), at 167, U.N. Doc. A/44/49 (1989), entered into force September 2, 1990, reprinted in 28 I.L.M. 1448 (1989).

Most relevant to the present context are the right to self-determination and the related principles of religious freedom and of decision making with regard to body modifications. In practice, however, the discussion tends to be inconclusive. Particularly when traditional bodily practices are carried out at a very early age and even in infancy, children are subjected to the substitutive decision making of others. They cannot be provided with the relevant information to enable them to give informed consent as far as traditional bodily practices are concerned. Nor can they decide autonomously that *their* religious freedom mandates them to follow one traditional bodily practice or another. The child's exercise of his or her right of religious freedom is intrinsically intertwined with and largely dependent on others' interests, rights, and duties. The issue remains unresolved, then, as it ultimately only returns the dilemma back to adults, whether the parents, the community or the state, whose determination is, to a great extent, simply a matter of preference.

It is perhaps also for these reasons that children remain, by far, out of the discourse on group/minority rights and on the extent of state accommodation of multicultural claims. The scholarly work has focused on participatory rights in the public sphere as the key for activating Charles Taylor's "politics of difference."[2] Be it Chandran Kukathas's autonomous decision making to exercise one's "right to exit," or James Tully, Bhikhu Parekh, and others' alternative of active participation for mollifying identity/cultural-based encounters,[3] the general emphasis has been on the public, rather than private, domain. At the same time, when one considers the private realm, children are generally simply invisible and addressed only through the lens of protection from the group. Conceptualized as such, there is very little room for a substantial discussion to take place on children belonging to conventional minority groups and, perhaps all the more so, to children in general belonging to "familial" groups. Indeed, this ongoing discussion on multiculturalism seems to have been possible only by excluding children from the discourse in its entirety.

The discourse on children and traditional bodily practices on the international level fails to resolve the issue. In contrast to the worldwide controversy over the practice of female circumcision (as well as other traditional practices performed on girls, even if to a lesser extent), there has been no general discussion about children and traditional biomedical practices; there has been silence.

Theoretically, Jack Donnelly's grid of internal/external moral judgment offers some sort of criteria for discussion. Taking a universal approach to human rights, he calls for the international community to press ahead with a negative moral judgment when the practices are externally very important. He suggests doing so regardless of the moral importance that is attributed to the practice from within. There is, or should be, however, a substantial difference between negating a practice of the other that does not have a significant internal

[2] Charles Taylor, "The Politics of Recognition," in *Multiculturalism*, ed. Amy Gutman (Princeton, NJ: Princeton University Press, 1994), 42.

[3] See the discussion in Chapter 4.

importance and one that does. Yet the criteria as they stand are too vague to discern. This lack of clear guidelines thus ultimately leads to an outright ethnocentric approach.[4] It also comes across as a retrospective measure, one to return to for justification *after* the negative judgment has already been made.

The international bodies provide little information to elucidate the considerations that led to their negative judgment. All the practices under consideration in this study (male circumcision, scarification, milk teeth extraction and the Padaung girls' elongation of the neck) were raised, at least in some cases, as harmful either by the Monitoring Committee under the Children's Convention (Children's Committee or Committee) or by other international bodies (mainly, Special Rapporteurs). With regard to the work of the Children's Committee, all were addressed under the auspice of Article 24(3) of the Children's Convention. Both the Special Rapporteurs on Harmful Traditional Practices Affecting the Health of Women and Children and on Violence against Women commented on the harmfulness of these practices, and scarification and extraction of milk teeth have been on the list of harmful traditional practices at least since 1996.[5] The classification of male circumcision as harmful has been more complex. Even though the Special Rapporteur on Harmful Traditional Practices declined to examine male circumcision,[6] the practice has been nevertheless increasingly in the international spotlight. Concurrently, although the Children's Committee has only rarely commented on the practice in its address of reports from countries where it is carried out regularly for religious rationales,[7] the Committee has expressed its concerns with regard to the practice on a few occasions revolving minority groups (e.g., South Africa, Finland, Lesotho, Zambia, and others).[8] There is also a growing scholarly literature on the issue

---

[4] Ibid.

[5] Commission on Human Rights, Subcommission on Prevention of Discrimination and Protection of Minorities, *Final Report of the Special Rapporteur on Traditional Practices Affecting the Health of Women and Children*, 48th Sess., Item 4, paragraph 37, U.N. Doc. E/CN.4/Sub.2/1996/6 (June 14, 1996).

[6] The Special Rapporteur rejected the request to address male circumcision, making the point that, "the circumcision of male children did not concern the United Nations as only female circumcision was deemed harmful practice to be eradicated. Consequently, it would seem inappropriate to consider under one head both female circumcision which is harmful to health and male circumcision which has no undesirable effect and it even considered to be beneficial." Commission on Human Rights, Sub-Commission on Prevention of Discrimination and Protection of Minorities, *Follow-up Report of the Special Rapporteur on Traditional Practices Affecting the Health of Women and Children*, 49th Sess., Item 5(a), paragraph 18, U.N. Doc. E/CN.4/Sub.2/1997/10 (June 25, 1997).

[7] See in this regard also Marie Fox and Michael Thomson, "Short Changed? The Law and Ethics of Male Circumcision," *International Journal of Children's Rights* 13, no. 1–2 (2005): 161–81, arguing that the discourse on male circumcision within the Anglo-American societies downplays the physical medical risks and implications that are involved. They also challenge the conventional comparison between male circumcision and female circumcision as one of the main reasons for the insufficient address of male circumcision.

[8] Committee on the Rights of the Child, *Concluding Observations: Lesotho*, paragraph 43, U.N. Doc. CRC/C/15/Add.147 (February 21, 2001); Committee on the Rights of the Child, *Summary Record: Sweden*, paragraph 12, U.N. Doc. CRC/C/SR.522 (January 28, 1999); Committee on the Rights of the Child, *Concluding Observations: Myanmar*, paragraph 58, U.N. Doc. CRC/C/15/Add.237 (June 30, 2004); Committee on the Rights of the Child, *Concluding*

calling for its abolishment. Amnesty International and some other human rights organizations have even launched a lobbying plan, confident that their success in mobilizing the international community against female circumcision will replicate itself.[9]

Yet, although describing the practices as "detrimental to the health of the child," a discussion on the factors that have been calculated within "health" is largely missing. The emphasis essentially remains on the physical level alone, building on mainstream perceptions of what the normal (Western and liberal) body should look like. The protocols of the Committee's sessions with state delegates on their reports show no substantial discussion of the cultural bias. State delegates tend to merely excuse themselves with the backwardness of their respective populations, and the Committee assumes to express its concerns about the cultural and social impediments.[10] The negative judgment expressed later in the Committee's concluding observations simply appears to translate the medicalized (Western) perceptions into general knowledge.

This sense is further exacerbated as the international bodies seem to conflate under the cloak of health between the practices themselves and the means by which they are performed, although these are two quite different concerns.[11] The lack of discussion about the internal social and cultural fabric in which the practices take place, yet nevertheless referring to the harmfulness of the various traditional bodily practices under Article 24(3) of the Children's Convention thus, ultimately, suggests an attempt to avoid the difficult questions. Combined with the occasional analysis of some of these practices under the auspices of the international agencies dealing with discrimination against women and girls gives an illusion that these practices are gender based, further hampering the possibility of advancing the mainstreaming of the discourse.[12]

Observations: Ethiopia, Committee on the Rights of the Child, paragraphs 64–65, U.N. Doc. CRC/C/15/Add.144 (February 21, 2001).; Committee on the Rights of the Child, *Concluding Observations: Zambia,* paragraphs 46–47, U.N. Doc. CRC/C/15/Add.206 (July 2, 2003).

[9] Amnesty International USA, "A Bill to End Male Genital Mutilation in the U.S.," http://www.mgmbill.org/ai.htm. The draft resolution was voted down in November 2005.

[10] Sonia Harris-Short, "International Human Rights law: Imperialism, Inept and Ineffective? Cultural Relativism and the UN Convention on the Rights of the Child," *Human Rights Quarterly* 25, no. 1 (2003): 146–50.

[11] The only explicit reference to the harmful manner in which the practices are performed (rather than the practices themselves) is in the context of male circumcision. See, for example, *Concluding Observations: Zambia,* paragraphs 46–47; *Concluding Observations: Lesotho,* paragraph 43.

[12] The Special Rapporteur herself, when refusing to discuss male circumcision, provides only a general argument about the difference between male and female circumcision, which deems the comparison, according to her, "inappropriate." She does not make any distinction for this purpose between the various forms of female circumcision nor question, for example, to what extent male circumcision may be comparable to the more lenient form of female circumcision. She also does not clarify the sources from which she concludes that male circumcision "has no undesirable effect and it [is] even considered to be beneficial." She thus strengthens the conception that these two practices are significantly different, although she presents no substantial reasons for that. See *Follow-up Report of the Special Rapporteur on Traditional Practices Affecting the Health of Women and Children,* paragraph 18.

Certainly, not all traditional bodily practices should be accepted. The social and cultural collective importance that is attributed to a given practice does not and should not always supersede other considerations, such as the objections of the person to experience the procedure. However, considering the unquestionable impact traditions have on one's (and groups') identity as well as on his or her exercise of rights, these issues have to be discussed. The particular complexity in the examination of children's bioethics from the perspective of children as rights holders does not justify the neglect. In fact, it should indicate that, notwithstanding the difficulties associated with medical cultures and cultural identities, the very essence of rights has to be reexamined.[13]

Scholars theorizing on children's rights endeavored to do so by interpreting the meaning and function of rights in the special context of children. Power/will theorists suggest a framework that conceptualizes children's rights as a matrix of fundamental obligations.[14] The argument they advance is that as (particularly young) children are universally, unavoidably, and naturally dependent on those who care for them,[15] the only practical way to secure their interests is by establishing a set of (adults') obligations towards them.[16] Interest theories, in contrast, emphasize the moral aspect of rights in furthering one's interests, which constitutes a primary source for the normative inclusion of children as bearers of rights.[17]

As explained in Chapter 6, however, at least in the context of children's bioethics, the debate between the power/will and the interests approach to children's rights is somewhat moot. The effort to read into the traditional notion of rights as also including children's rights (as interests theorists do), or to draft a parallel system of obligations that is embedded within this traditional understanding of rights (as power/will theorists do), does not get to the heart of the question: to what extent does it reflect children's own interests and voice? It is particularly significant, as neither approach questions in any substantial way the factors that ascertain the scope and content of the morality, the very factor that gives rise to the particular corresponding duty, interest, and hence protection. The assumption seems to be that the moral obligation toward children is (only) adults' common knowledge. Conceived as such, they seemingly approach children merely as future citizens or as vulnerable others (whether or not conceptualized as a legally acceptable minority group), both stances that ultimately do not follow the spirit of the Children's Convention.

To give substance to the concept of children's rights, bioethical rights

---

[13] See the discussion in Chapter 6.

[14] Onora O'Neill, "Children's Rights and Children's Lives," in *Children, Rights and the Law,* ed. Philip Alston, Stephen Parker, and John Seymour (New York: Oxford University Press, 1995), 25–27.

[15] Ibid., 38–39.

[16] Ibid., 25–27.

[17] Tom D. Campbell, "The Rights of the Minor: As Person, as Child, as Juvenile, as Future Adult," in *Children, Rights and the Law,* ed. Philip Alston, Stephen Parker, and John Seymour (New York: Oxford University Press, 1995), 5.

included, one has to step aside from the conventional presumption of independent, separate individuals who are capable, autonomously, of exercising their rights. Recognizing the web of relations as the precondition to one's exercising of rights, as advanced by the feminist approach of the ethic of care, is a first step. There is no doubt that it is these multiple semilegal sociocultural orders that play a prominent role in children's lives. Yet for children, as argued, the mere recognition that the exercise of rights is contingent on their relationships with others would not be enough.

One of the underlying assumptions about relationships as mediums of rights is that there is some leverage of choice. This has been raised particularly in the context of minority groups, assuming that adult members of any community inherently have at least the potential capacity to negotiate their equal status or to exit.[18] As was discussed in Chapters 4 and 6, however, the extent to which this presumption exists in the context of children is questionable. Although there is no doubt that children influence adults and others around them,[19] children are not commonly assumed to have this option. Children do not choose their family, their community, their place of residence, and so forth. These decisions are generally made on their behalf, and they are given a say, essentially, only when the family unit fails—a situation that is neither the common nor the aspired way to enjoy family life.[20] This is so regardless of the question of whether the particular child belongs to a minority group. In other words, the basic idea of some sort of equilibrium of relationships for the purpose of exercising rights cannot be simply extended to children—unless they are viewed, once more, only as future adults. Yet again, as has been stressed throughout this work, such an approach overlooks children as *present* subjects, *beings* rather than merely *becomings*, which overlooks the innovative facet of the Children's Convention.

The way forward thus necessitates reconceptualization of children's bioethical (and other) rights in terms of their cultural identity. Accordingly, a dual path of investigation for the resolution of biomedical conflicts is suggested: a medical/health implications and a cultural/identity one, by which the balance between them will play a determinative role. The rationales for this are built on the following framework. First, the conventional focus on the physical aspect is insufficient, as it ignores the inseparable connection between the body, mind, and culture. The calculation of physical risks and benefits also fails to grasp the spiritual risks and benefits that are associated with the various biomedical

---

[18] Much of the debate in this regard focused on women belonging to minority groups. For various opinions on the issue, see the collection of essays in Susan M. Okin, ed., *Is Multiculturalism Bad for Women?* (Princeton, NJ: Princeton University Press, 1999). See also Rainer Baubock, "Cultural Minority Rights for Immigrants," *International Migration Review* 30, no. 1 (1996): 203–50.

[19] James J. Dilon, "The Role of the Child in Adult Development," *Journal of Adult Development* 9, no. 4 (2002): 270. Dilon discusses children's direct and indirect agency. He suggests that such agency exists from infancy, individually and indirectly (such as by the power to cry and eye contact), but agency also exists on a broader level, having impact on the political values, views of life, and general development of the adults around them.

[20] See the discussion in Chapter 5, Section D.1, about "Children's Religious Freedom as an Autonomous Right," particularly in the context of spiritual custody cases.

practices that, ultimately, construct the person one is. Similarly, the dominant weight given to the doctrine of informed consent, including the evaluation of children's capacity in doing so, is inapt as it assesses children by the criterion of what they lack: adulthood. It thus measures children only as like-adults or as future agents, rather than focusing on children as present beings.

Secondly, autonomy, capacity, and exercise of rights can be understood only relationally. They all take place within one's web of relations, and they are inherently contextual. Incorporating these two previous presumptions into children's relational experiences and voice necessitates translating children's rights into an identity-autonomy continuum in which children are generally located closer to the identity edge. Such a conceptualization takes children not merely as individuals in the abstract, but as a present and integral part of the entire communal fabric to which they belong. It hence gives an explicit space to the only intrinsic right a child holds.

There is still a need to examine what considerations must be taken into account within each of these nexuses. This is a complicated task, particularly in light of the very limited cross-cultural scholarly work on the issue. The set of policy considerations and guidelines proposed in the next section should thus be viewed as a preliminary one, which should be adjusted, expanded, and reexamined according to the particular factors of any given case, and as the body of literature on children's bioethics develops.

A. CONSIDERATIONS UNDER THE PHYSICAL PATH

The most prevalent argument raised against traditional bodily practices is that the practices are physically harmful, intrusive, or unnecessary. Hence, they are in violation of the child's rights. As elaborated on in Chapter 5, these are three very different rationales, and their analysis needs to be handled separately. Harm is culturally constructed; not all physical interferences are exceedingly intrusive (for instance, vaccinations); and the physical modification following any given practice, regardless of its perceived necessity, is not inevitably, in itself, wrong.

From the outset, it has been emphasized that the book's focus is on biomedical practices that are culturally empowering at least from the *emic* perspective of the particular group.[21] Bodily practices that in themselves cause death were excluded as, by definition, they prevent individuals from becoming members in the communities to which they belong. Death provides the ultimate objective criterion for no life[22] and undermines the very basic aspiration of any cultural group to survive. This exclusion also fits the child's right to life, survival, and development, under Article 6 of the Children's Convention. Such cases are also the easier ones to handle, so it seems, as most bodily practices do not aim at bringing about the child's death or at putting his or her life at risk; hence, numerically, there are likely to be only a few.

Traditional bodily practices that cause long-term health implications, including such practices in which the pain, suffering, and medical outcomes

---

[21] See Chapter 3, Section A, on "Case Selection."

[22] The question whether there is life after death is beyond the scope of this work.

exceed a reasonable time for recuperation and inconvenience that are normally involved, should be excluded as well. While harm, pain, and suffering are, to a great extent, cultural constructs, it does not entirely preclude some scientifically proven measures, such as the contraction of HIV/AIDS and hepatitis, which are incurable diseases. In this context, it is important to distinguish between traditional bodily practices, which in themselves cause long-term health consequences and suffering, and practices in which such implications occur incidentally as a result of an unsterilized environment and techniques. Such a distinction would ensure that biomedical practices are not wrongly classified as harmful just because of the means by which they are carried out.

If a traditional bodily practice falls within the scope of the first instance (for example, female circumcision in its severe forms),[23] it should be excluded for all the reasons mentioned above. Conversely, in cases where the safety of the procedure is at stake, as has been raised in the context of both male circumcision and scarification,[24] it would be preferable to enforce state obligations under the human rights conventions rather than prohibit the practices.[25] As was discussed in Chapter 6, states have the duty to "respect, protect and fulfill" individuals' rights, *inter alia*, the right to the highest attainable standard of health. It includes state responsibilities to provide a variety of functioning public facilities, goods, and services that are accessible, available (both physically and affordably), culturally acceptable, and of good quality. Bearing in mind that health also has a collective dimension, and that the health of the individual is linked to the health of the society as a whole, state responsibilities should also include providing resources for the various minority groups to design, deliver, and control such services.

Traditional bodily practices that only lead to some body modification, in contrast, should be generally allowed. The extent to which a practice is indeed merely a body modification rather than a physically harmful one should be determined by scientifically and culturally accepted standards. For that,

---

[23] Female circumcision is generally classified into four different types of procedures: mere wash or prick of the clitoris or prepuce without removal of any tissues, the removal of the clitoral prepuce ("*sunna* circumcision"), full clitoridectomies ("excision" or "intermediate"), and infibulation or pharaonic circumcision. For further discussion on this issue, see Ellen Gruenbaum, *The Female Circumcision Controversy: An Anthropological Perspective* (Philadelphia: University of Pennsylvania Press, 2001), 2–3. See also the entries for each type of circumcision.

[24] See Chapter 3.

[25] In New Zealand, for example, the national prohibition of scarification among members of the Maori group has been lifted since the employment of sterilized, technological machines to carry out the *Ta Moko* (see Chapter 3). According to the second report submitted by New Zealand to the Committee on the Rights of the Child, children from the age of sixteen can consult a doctor and give an informed consent for "any medical, surgical or dental procedure," if carried out for the child's benefit and by a person who is qualified to do so. Under the age of sixteen, the general view is that the doctrine of the "mature child" would apply, following the decision of the House of Lords in *Gillick v. West Norfolk and Wisbech Area Health Authority* [1985] 3 All E.R. 402. So far, however, the application of the doctrine has not been tested in New Zealand's courts, and it is also not clear whether it would include children's decision to be scarified. Committee on the Rights of the Child, *Second Periodic Report: New Zealand*, paragraphs 630–635, U.N. Doc. CRC/C/93/Add.4 (March 12, 2003).

anthropological and sociological studies as well as medical research would be required to carry out an appropriate assessment of the practice before it is approved or prohibited. For instance, as was pointed out in Chapter 3, there is not much information available on the medical implications of milk teeth extraction and of neck elongation. With regard to the practice of milk teeth extraction, it may also be biased, considering the means and the settings in which the information was collected, as well as the general negative and derogatory approach expressed by the researchers.[26] Thus, although, at first glance, it appears as harmful, further research is needed to evaluate the extent to which it is so. Similarly, despite the Children's Committee's observation, it is not at all clear that neck elongation should be classified as a harmful practice. Aside from the general disagreement on the medical implications and their possible reversal, neither of the potential hazards is probable, also by the Committee's remark, unless the rings are removed. There are no other justifications provided, though, as to *why* they should be removed. The condemnation of the practice thus appears as "putting the carriage before the horse," giving the sense that it was simply made to defend a predetermined decision.

Theoretically, when a traditional bodily practice leaves its marks in a hidden place (such as male circumcision) and not visible (as facial scarification and neck elongation), it may be easier to accept its performance. In essence, however, both should be approached in a similar manner. First, the question of appearance does not in itself merit the prohibition of a practice. Physical diversity is an integral and natural part of life. Any other conclusion would also require, for example, that all persons with visible disabilities would be left out of sight, as they seem to threaten what is perceived as the normal body.[27] Yet it is exactly this point that persons with disabilities and disability rights advocates have challenged, and justly so. They have called, instead, for the inclusion of persons with disabilities in their respective communities, regardless of, and despite, the physical difference.[28]

Some may argue that the comparison between the physical diversity exhibited by persons with disabilities and other traditional bodily modifications is mistaken because, in the first case, the bodily difference is natural, whereas the latter one is human made. The argument is unconvincing, however, as not all disabilities are neonatal or genetically based, but they may also be the outcome of accidents, wars, one's negligence, or other risky behaviors that led to the

---

[26] See Chapter 3.

[27] Hahn terms the traditional exclusion of persons with (physical) disabilities as "aesthetic anxiety." Harlan Hahn, "The Political Implications of Disability: Definition and Data," in *The Psychological and Social Impact of Disability*, ed. Robert P. Marinelli and Arthur E. Dell Orto (New York: Springer Publishing, 1999), 8–9; Tom Shakespear, "Cultural Representation of Disabled People: Dustbins for Disavowal?" *Disability & Society*, 9, no. 3 (1994): 296–97.

[28] Hahn, 7–8; Theresia Degener, "Disabled Persons and Human Rights: the Legal Framework," in *Human Rights and Disabled Persons*, ed. Theresia Degener and Yolan Koster-Dreese (Dordrecht: Martinus Nijhoff, 1995) 11–20; See also Article 3(d) of Convention on the Rights of Persons with Disabilities (Disability Rights Convention), G.A. Res. A/61/611 (2006), stipulating the general principle of "respect for difference and acceptance of persons with disabilities as part of human diversity and humanity."

result. It is, nevertheless, inconceivable that the cause of the disability would influence the determination of one's physical acceptance into or rejection from the community.

Second, the call for a prohibition of a traditional bodily practice is most likely to arise in cases where it is not endorsed by the majority, but rather carried out by minority groups. But if the majority's rejection of other's practices is always taken as the determinative factor, it practically grants it the power of a tyranny.[29] Furthermore, as shown in the discussion on genetic selection and disabilities, the process of inclusion and exclusion is not limited to majority and minority conflicts.[30] Apparently, within every group, there are minorities and a majority at stake, and scapegoating[31] is not restricted to particular biomedical practices or appearances. It rather evolves and changes, depending on the given space and time.[32] If endorsing cultural diversity has any meaning, it thus seems that, instead of submitting cultural minority's biomedical practices to extinction, raising public awareness of pluralist appearances should be advanced.

The case of genetic selection and particularly, deafness by choice, poses a significant challenge in this context. As pointed out in Chapter 7, many disabilities are not connected with health. They do not involve any threat to life nor do they cause any significant health implications to the individual except for the limitation of the impairment itself. This is the case with regard to deafness. For the most part, then, genetic selection for or against disability prevention is not justified any more than other elective biomedical practices under the medical path. The issue is further complex, however, for three reasons.

First, the scenario of genetic selection commonly refers to a fetus rather than to an existing child. The status of the fetus under international law has been controversial, and the European Convention on Human Rights and Biomedicine (Oviedo Convention) and the convention's additional protocols (collectively referred to as the Conventions on Biomedicine)[33] perpetuate the uncertainty.

---

[29] See, in this context, the criticism expressed on Parekh's model in Chapter 4.

[30] See Chapter 7.

[31] "Scapegoating" refers to the psychological and social processes in which other groups are devalued or seen as an ideological enemy. Ervin Staub discusses the phenomenon in the context of genocide and mass killing. Ervin Staub, "Individual and Group Identities in Genocide and Mass Killing," in *Social Identity, Intergroup Conflict and Conflict Reduction*, ed. Richard D. Ashmore, Lee Jussim, and David Wilder (Oxford: Oxford University Press, 2001), 161–65; Shakespear makes the explict application of the term also with regard to persons with disabilities. Shakespear, 298.

[32] Jo Bridgeman, "Caring for Children with Severe Disabilities: Boundaried Relational Rights." *International Journal of Children's Rights* 13, no. 1–2 (2005): 101 (discussing the changes in the past three decades in the conceptualization of Down syndrome, from a "so intolerable" condition to one that allows leading independent and productive lives).

[33] Convention for the Protection of Human Rights and Dignity of the Human Being with Regard to the Application of Biology and Medicine: Convention on Human Rights and Biomedicine (the Oviedo Convention) (ETS No. 164), entered into force December 1, 1999; Additional Protocol to the Convention for the Protection of Human Rights and Dignity of the Human Being with regard to the Application of Biology and Medicine, on the Prohibition of Cloning Human Beings (ETS No. 168), opened for signature on January 1, 1998, entered into force March 1, 2001; Additional Protocol to the Convention on Human Rights and

Because of the connection between the status of the fetus and the pro-life/pro-choice debate, the European Court of Human Rights has refrained, so far, from accepting "right to life" claims on behalf of fetuses. However, it has granted them some protection rights and left the door open for future developments. Thus, while the practice of genetic selection in the instance of the abortion of a fetus with prospects for disability, for example, cannot be classified itself as harmful on legal grounds, it may change if ultimately found as prejudicial and harmful to the realization of rights of persons with disabilities.[34]

Second, the innovative nature of scientific progress is such that the precise physical, mental, and other implications of much of the new biomedical procedures are still not fully known. Consequently, the distinction between genetic practices that are harmful in themselves and others, in which long-term implications may occur only incidentally, is blurred. The question of harmfulness thus essentially relies on speculations of risks, of which its results may become known only *post factum.*

Finally, scientific progress and biomedical advancements are inherently intertwined with one's right to scientific development under Article 15 of the International Covenant on Economic, Social and Cultural Rights (ICESCR).[35] While, as suggested, it may be a useful alternative social route to resolve legal disputes in the context of parental reproductive choice, in the long run, it may also give rise to wrongful disability claims. Thus, the harmfulness or the benevolence of this invented traditional bodily practice is tied up with an array of other policy considerations that, at some point, will have to be resolved.

In any case, in order to give a voice to the child, and similar to other bodily practices, allowing such a biomedical practice to occur should also be examined in light of the identity path. The more complex policy considerations that arise with regard to the child's identity are thus examined in the next section.

B. CONSIDERATIONS UNDER THE IDENTITY PATH

The analysis of a given bodily practice under the identity path comes into play only after the practices that are harmful (see Section A) are excluded.

Biomedicine, on Transplantation of Organs and Tissues of Human Origin (ETS No. 186), opened for signature on January 24, 2002, entered into force May 1, 2006; Additional Protocol to the Convention on Human Rights and Biomedicine, concerning Biomedical Research, (ETS No. 195), entered into force September 1, 2007 (hereafter the Convention on Human Rights and Biomedicine or the Oviedo Convention, interchangeably; Additional Protocol on the Prohibition of Cloning, the Additional Protocol on Transplantation of Organs and Tissues; and Additional Protocol on Biomedical Research, respectively).

[34] Article 8(1)b) of the Disability Rights Convention requires states "to adopt immediate, effective and appropriate measures . . . (b) To combat stereotypes, prejudices and harmful practices relating to persons with disabilities, including those based on sex and age, in all areas of life." The provision is included within state obligations with regard to "awareness-raising," however, and whether the committee under the Disability Rights Convention (or any other international body) will take such an approach is yet to be seen.

[35] International Covenant on Economic, Social and Cultural Rights, adopted Dec. 16, 1966, G.A. Res. 2200A (XXI), 21 Sess., U.N. GAOR Supp. (No. 16), at 49, U.N. Doc. A/6316 (1966), reprinted in 993 U.N.T.S. 3, entered into force January 3, 1976.

The focus is thus on practices that lead to some body modification, carried out by either majority or minority groups. The central question under this path is which actors play a significant role in the child's development of a sense of belonging and identity. The best criterion to do so is to establish what constitutes the child's center of sociocultural life. This concept essentially identifies the webs of relations that influence and are influenced by the child. Particularly, the child's center of life includes the following sociocultural circles that have to be considered: the family (nuclear and extended); religious, ethnic, linguistic, and other culturally based communities; the community at large (that is, the nation); and the child's group of peers.[36]

With the exception of the child's group of peers, all these sources of identification have been stipulated in the Children's Convention, and they are granted a formal place in the child's life. The family is perhaps the most instant and immediate circle of reference, with the Convention's Preamble recognizing that for the full and harmonious development of the child's personality, he or she should grow up in a family environment.[37] In Western culture, it is oftentimes translated into the nuclear family alone, giving the paramount power to the parents. Article 18 of the Children's Convention follows this line of thought, stating that both parents have common and primary responsibilities for the upbringing and development of the child. However, the Convention also contains references to the "extended family,"[38] "members of the family,"[39] "family relations,"[40] and "family environment."[41] While the Convention does not define the range of relationships that are encompassed in those terms, it clearly goes beyond the parent-child relationship. Other provisions further clarify the link between the community, the child's development, and his or her cultural identity. The latter explicitly includes ethnic, linguistic, and religious communities that the child looks to as a source of reference, as well as to the child's broader community of the nation.[42] They are thus all primary and essential sociocultural webs for the child's identity.

Although the Children's Convention does not contain any specific provision on the child's peer group, it does include a number of references to the child's

---

[36] The question of the relative weight of these sociocultural circles is discussed in Section C.

[37] Paragraphs 5–6 of the Preamble to the Children's Convention.

[38] Article 5 of the Children's Convention.

[39] Articles 9(4), 10(1) and 22(2) of the Children's Convention.

[40] Articles 8(1) of the Children's Convention.

[41] Articles 20(1), 22(2) of the Children's Convention.

[42] Article 30 of the Children's Convention deals specifically with children belonging to ethnic, linguistic, and religious communities. The child's right to nationality is stipulated in Articles 7 and 8 of the Convention, and it is also linked to various protection and provisional rights that the child in entitled to, such as social security (Article 26), standard of living (Article 27), and national values (Article 29). Article 29(1)(c) of the Convention further ties the family, community, nation, and the child's cultural identity, by directing the child's education to "the development of respect for the child's parents, his or her own cultural identity, language and values, for the national values of the country in which the child is living, the country from which he or she may originate, and for civilizations different from his or her own."

social well-being, social development, integration, and health.[43] Given that the peer group has been attributed a substantial role in the child's development and in his or her formation of the sociocultural self, these provisions must inherently include also those who stand on an equal basis with the child. Anthropological studies observed, for example, that children's construction of childhood, development, and gender relations is highly dependent on the acceptable social practices that they absorb through their interaction with their peers.[44] Scholarly work further emphasizes the unique manner in which the child's sense of belonging and self-identification are made through his or her circle of friends. Unlike adults, children construct their identity inward, by comparing their peers and others to themselves, and they are usually not too judgmental while doing so.[45] Thus, for instance, research with children has consistently shown that they do not view disability, per se, as different or as abnormal. Also when they observe differences, they generally do not attribute to it the negative connotation that adults do.[46] Of further interest in this context are the reactions and opinions recorded among children who are siblings of children with disabilities. They tend not only to ascribe a great deal of their sibling's difference to adults' attitudes towards them (such as teachers, neighbors, and so forth), but their attitudes toward disability also reflect those of their parents.[47] As young people's views on disability are influenced by the perspectives of the adults who care for them, and in light of the impact of children's interaction on the child's development, the peer circle should be an integral part of the consideration.

Procedurally, biomedical conflicts would require that identity-related claims are formally incorporated into the legal discourse. As discussed in Chapter 6, such an approach acknowledges the sociocultural dimension of law rather than pretends that it does not exist. Integration of such identity-related claims would necessitate examination of the practice and its value to the identities of the parties involved. It would also entail a comparison and a proper assessment of the evidence submitted in relation to the child's identity interests that are at stake. Among the factors to be considered are: the centrality of a bodily practice to the community's identity and to the child; the extent to which it is controversial among the members of the community; the identity implications the acceptance or rejection of a particular bodily practice would have on the child; the positive and negative affect the performance or the avoidance of the practice would have on the child's relationships with the familial, communal, national, and peer group; and the extent to which these various circles

---

[43] Articles 17, 19, 23, 27, 32, 33 and 39 of the Children's Convention.

[44] Helga Kelle, "The Discourse of "Development": How 9-to-12-year-old Children Construct 'Childish' and 'Further Developed' Identities within Their Peer Culture," *Childhood* 8, no. 1 (2001): 108–11.

[45] Kirsten Stalker, Kirsten Clare Connors, "Children's Perceptions of Their Disabled Siblings: 'She's Different but It's Normal for Us'," *Children & Society* 18, no. 3 (2004): 224.

[46] This finding has been noticed in research with both children with and without disabilities. Stalker and Connors, 224–25; Mark Deal, "Disabled People's Attitudes toward Other Impairment Groups: A Hierarchy of Impairment," *Disability & Society* 18, no. 7 (2003): 899.

[47] Stalker and Connors, 220, 223.

provide the child with a sufficient sense of security and belonging. Finally, and in accordance with Article 12 of the Children's Convention, it would also necessitate providing a space for a child, who is capable of making his or her views, to express these views throughout the process.

C. RESOLUTION OF BIOMEDICAL CONFLICTS

One of the main difficulties identity claims conflicts raise is how to determine the relative weight of each sociocultural web. Another problem is that, theoretically, any type of upbringing can be rejected by the child as he or she grows up. This may be particularly so if the practices are carried out by minority groups, as the children may have a preference over time to assimilate into the broader society.[48] Such an option is more complicated in the context of religio-cultural biomedical practices. It may be impossible to reverse the bodily modification, hence making appearance resemblance unattainable.[49] However, it seems that one's decision to opt out of his or her group of reference is tied up with two other issues. One is the extent to which the various sociocultural webs provide for the child, in practice, a significant source of identification. It seems probable that if the child's relational circles are sufficiently strong and positive, the child is more likely to embrace the identity that is conferred upon him or her, and less prone to reject it. The second point has to do with the relationships between individuals and groups and the extent to which the principle of cultural diversity is actually endorsed. If greater tolerance and acceptance of bodily differences were to exist within society at large, much of the need to assimilate by resemblance would be eliminated on its own.

In any case, the primary assumption here is that there is no one bright line rule that could apply to all cases. Each biomedical/identity conflict has its own particularities that need to be examined, and a case-to-case approach is the only way in which such dilemmas can be resolved. For this reason, it is also impossible to come up with a rigid formula that prioritizes any of the child's sociocultural circles. Whereas in Western thought, the parents are presumed to rank higher than the cultural community, the national identity, and the peer group, this preference may differ among societies and cultures. Focusing on the case studies in the book, the following subsections discuss some of the biomedical conflicts that may arise, their complexities, and their resolutions. It should be emphasized, that this is not in any way an attempt to cover all the possible scenarios, but rather just an attempt to illuminate some of the considerations involved.

The argument advanced is that biomedical practices are integral to the child's cultural rights—broadly defined—which, if taken from a child-centered approach, need to be conceptualized in terms of his or her identity. The degree

---

[48] Alison D. Renteln, *The Cultural Defense* (Oxford: Oxford University Press, 2004), 214.

[49] See, however, that, with the exception of male circumcision, the other practices under consideration may be reversible, at least to an extent. Tattoos and scarification can be removed by laser procedures; the extraction of milk teeth may be treated like other dental deformities, and, according to some, a neck that has been elongated can be rehabilitated (see Chapter 3).

of physical harm certainly should be included in the international determination of which traditional bodily practices are "prejudicial to the child's health," and hence can be eliminated. But taking into account the mental imagery of the body *as* culture and *as* sociocultural context is also critical because the body is used for the child's development of identity and, consequently, for his or her exercise of all other rights. Understanding children's bioethics relationally and through the lens of identity is also more consistent with the spirit of the Children's Convention, as it takes seriously children of all ages as subjects. Thus, while the legal discourse on the child's rights can provide a framework, the multiple social, cultural interrelational factors, and, particularly, their accompanying identity claims should be clearly and explicitly incorporated into the discourse. Failure to take this multifaceted, contextual approach will lead to incomplete ethnocentric interpretations of a child's rights and overlook the child's own voice.

1. Majority's Biomedical Practices

The simplest case that enables the determination of whether following a traditional bodily custom should be allowed is when the practice is carried out by a majority of the population in all the sociocultural circles of the child. Male circumcision in Israel is one such example, as the religious (Jewish and Muslim) population of the country follows the practice. Also secular people (Jews and Muslims) perform it as a matter of tradition,[50] and, overall, an estimated 99 percent of the male population is circumcised. In such cases, circumcising the child is inherently part of the familial, communal, national, and peer identity levels in which the child grows, and hence it is most likely to reflect the identity of the child.

The main complexity in such a situation arises in a case where parents are opposed to the practice (although it is overwhelmingly carried out). In liberal democracies, such refusal is commonly presumed to be beyond the state's or the community's reach. It would seem inconceivable to insist that the parents be compelled to follow the practice despite their opposition.[51] Such a demand may also appear to contradict the respect and tolerance advocated here for biomedical practices that are carried out within other minority groups. Taking it from the child's perspective, however, requires refocusing the dilemma on the child rather than on the parental choice. The question that needs answering is whether the dissident minority provides the child an alternative sense of community that overrides his or her commitment to other circles of identification that support the practice.

---

[50] Ilan Katz, "Is Male Circumcision Morally Defensible?" in *Moral Agendas for Children's Welfare*, ed. Michael King (New York: Routledge, 1999), 103. This would also apply in Muslim countries where male circumcision is carried out for religio-cultural reasons. See the discussion in Chapter 3.

[51] Parental refusal to consent to a medical treatment for their child in life-threatening situations on the basis on their religio-cultural beliefs is beyond the scope of this study, as it is not likely to pass the "medical" path (see Chapter 6, Section E.2). The study's focus, in contrast, is on parental refusal to follow elective biomedical practices to inscribe identity.

At first glance, such a scenario appears to be a reversal of a demand by a minority group that its particular biomedical practice would be allowed, despite the majority's divergent view. Both minorities' appeals call attention to the centrality of the biomedical practice to the community's identity and also to the important role it plays in the child's life or, conversely, in the case of dissident parents, to their lack thereof. The analogy is not complete, however, as the broader social fabric in these two cases differs. Immigrant communities usually establish a communal network that is based on family and common place of origin, and, typically, it also provides material and personal support to its members.[52] Dissident parents and their children, in contrast, may be overwhelmingly alone in their dissent. While there should be reluctance to allow intervention in the family's private sphere, one should consider whether the parental refusal, against all the other sources of the child's identification, is indeed aimed at benefiting the child or if it is merely an imposition of the parents' own personal beliefs. Since physically harmful practices are already excluded under the medical path, on the one hand, and the child may suffer a sense of alienation and ridicule if certain practices are excluded, on the other hand, then one must consider whether the practice would be mandated if the child's own voice was heard.

The result may be different, however, if the practice, although widely performed, does not, in fact, constitute the main source of identification of the child (and his or her close web of relations). As was argued earlier,[53] a child does not have an innate preference to be born into a particular religio-cultural community nor to the performance of the bodily practices associated with it. Thus, if other important socio-cultural systems of support that surround the child, including, in particular, the family and other cultural affiliations, accept or at least tolerate the difference, there is no reason to assume that the child's own voice would have chosen otherwise.

2. Minority's Biomedical Practices

A more complicated case is one in which traditional bodily practices are carried out within minority groups, but not in the larger national circle of identification, and not necessarily within the child's group of peers. In such cases, the child's physical difference may stand out and may even be ridiculed. Yet, as has been argued throughout the study, different appearance does not merit in itself the rejection of a given custom. Furthermore, as the comparison between the "us" and the "other" always exists, a decision whether to allow or to ban a biomedical practice cannot be grounded only on the extent to which the child is ridiculed. Rather, in order to determine whether the practice is in sync with the child's voice, it necessitates an examination of whether the other sociocultural circles of the child have the paramount impact on the development of his or her identity. The answer, it seems, depends on the extent

---

[52] Stephen Castles, "International Migration at the Beginning of the Twenty-First Century: Global Trends and Issues," *International Social Science Journal* 52, no. 165 (2000): 272.

[53] See the discussion in Chapter 5, particularly with regard to the child's right to religious freedom and to self-determination as reflected in the doctrine of informed consent.

to which it is performed in supportive and nourishing (cultural) families and communities. This requires distinguishing between two different scenarios.

First, if the child's surrounding includes other immediate sociocultural sources of reference that are connected with the practice (such as religious observation, geographic residence, and so forth), carrying it out should be allowed. In such cases, even if the child may be somewhat ridiculed for his or her physical difference by the larger society, the value he or she may be receiving from the immediate sociocultural communities of reference (family and cultural group) may exceed the sense of assault and also provide the measures to cope with it. For example, when the practice of neck elongation is carried out among the Padaung tribe in Myanmar or in Northern Thailand, the immediate circles of reference include the girls' family, the tribe, the national inspiration of the Karen group to which they belong, and the girls' peer group both from the tribe and from Thai society. On the one hand, the girls generally enjoy supportive communal lives, surrounded by family members, a cultural community, and their cultural peer group who uphold the practice and are proud of it. The fact that the custom benefits the family financially should not detract from the positive value that girls gain from belonging to this environment, even if contributing to family income at such a young age is not common in other (Western) cultures.[54] On the other hand, in light of their political persecution, their sense of reference to the Karen group may seem negative to some, and the girls may also be ridiculed among Thai society (peer group).[55] Yet, neither of these latter considerations provide a sufficient basis for banning the practice. Both are merely the result of society's intolerance of differences rather than "ill community" in itself. Thus, promoting respect for and acceptance of bodily differences would be a more qualified way forward.

In the second scenario, the practice is carried out without any other context of the particular religio-cultural community. Performing the practice may perplex the child and alienate him or her from the general society, with no secured alternative of belonging. It thus may be better to prohibit it. For example, if one family of the Paduang tribe (rather than a community) resettles permanently in a state in which the practice of neck longation is not performed, continuing the practice without having the girl's views heard should not be accepted. Although the circles of the immediate (presumably supportive) family and of the (scorning) national and peer circles remain constant, the girls do not enjoy the other benefits of communal belonging. Allowing the practice may thus put the girls in a lose-lose situation. In such a case, it appears that, ultimately, the paramount reason for performing the

[54] Much of the debate with regard to girls' participation in the community's working force revolved around the abuse of the practice by tourists and around the impact it would have on their education (as guaranteed under Articles 23, 28–19 of the Children's Convention). There is no inherent contradiction between the two, however, as long as the child's right to education is not denied and his or her right, as every other individual, not to be exploited is upheld. See The Nation, "Kayan Girls Want to Be More than Just Tourist Attractions," *New Frontiers 9*, no. 6 (2003): part 4 (Thailand), http://www.twnside.org.sg/title/nf96.doc.

[55] Ibid.

practice is not the child's interests, but rather the *parental* desire for cultural preservation. Tradition, however, does not have any value on its own, as it is not so much the particular practice itself but the sociocultural associations one has with it.[56] Thus, while parental and communal desire for cultural preservation is important, it should not trump the child's own voice and identity.

It is interesting to note in this context the British court's decision in the case of *R. v. Adelsanya* (1974).[57] In this case, a Yoruba woman from Nigeria who cut her nine- and fourteen-year-old sons' faces in accordance with the custom of ritual scarification was charged with assault occasioning bodily harm. The practice was carried out as an attempt to ensure the maintenance of the Yoruba identity of the children. She was found guilty but was absolutely discharged on the grounds that she, as apparently also other members of the Nigerian community in England, did not realize it was in contravention of the law.[58] For purposes of this study, the question is, if the case was being tried today, should the court have decided differently?

While the limited information that is available on the case curtails the ability to fully ascertain the verdict, the resolution could have been procedurally, and potentially, substantially, different. Considering that the cuttings were not significant and with no health implications,[59] a conviction on these grounds is unjustified under the medical path. A more qualified approach would have been to examine the various sociocultural circles of the boys and determine the relative weight of these sources of identification. It is not clear why the children were being raised in a foster home and not by the mother and if it was only a temporary measure or one with a goal of future adoption. One also does not know whether the children were involved with the Nigerian community (except through the mother's membership in it) or if other children within the community were scarified as well. At first glance, it thus appears that the only unambiguous sources of the children's identification were their foster parents and the British society at large, both circles that reject the practice.[60] However, for a decision from the boys' perspective to take place, the gaps in information would have had to be questioned and filled in. Thus, for example, if the mother-children relationship was strong, if the children were involved with the Nigerian community, and if the practice was common among children

[56] Chandran Kukathas, "Are There Any Cultural Rights," *Political Theory* 20, no. 1 (1992): 111–12. Kukathas rejects any constitutive or fundamental element in culture itself. He contends that the collective matters only because, and as long as, it is essential for the well-being of the individual.

[57] *R. v. Adesenya* [1975] 24 I.C.L.G. 136 (noted).

[58] For a discussion on the case in the context of cultural defense, see Renteln, *The Cultural Defense*, 49–51.

[59] Ibid., 50; Peter Lloyd, "The Case of Mrs. Adesnya," *RAIN: Royal Anthropological Institute News* 4 (1979): 2.

[60] It was the first time the court was confronted with such a practice, and it was brought to the officials' attention by the foster parents of the boys. On the other hand, the court did make a general warning to other immigrant members who may consider following the practice (cited in Renteln *The Cultural Defense*, 50). This may imply that it was more prevalent, particularly considering the expert opinion that others in the community were not aware of its illegality, although no other charges against others members of the community were made.

within it, there is no substantial reason why the practice should be prohibited (although the safety of the means in which it is carried out can, and should, be regulated). This is especially so, given that the children were said to be willing participants, and it is mostly so with regard to the elder son, who arrived in England when he was already eleven years old. He was thus perhaps also accustomed to the "origin community" and had embraced, at least to an extent, its cultural identity.[61]

There are a few clear difficulties with this approach. Perhaps the most important one is that examining the parental and the child's ties with the sociocultural community and with its traditional bodily customs seems to require a considerable degree of state surveillance in the minority's family sphere. It is particularly worrisome in light of the mutual "yuck" response and the natural tendency to reject others' biomedical practices in favor of one's own.[62] Such an evaluation is thus also prone to be subjective and difficult to prove. In addition, it is arguably further discriminatory against children who do not belong to minority groups, yet who may nevertheless still need the state's protection. Furthermore, it seems to require greater judicial activism, as courts will have to ensure that all the relevant information is available to them before delivering their verdict. Such activism, however, is not endorsed by many judicial systems.

Neither of these problems can be entirely resolved on the theoretical level, and concerns in this regard were expressed earlier in the study.[63] In reality, however, it is not possible for any given state to follow each individual child and family. As with other cases of parental medical (and other) negligence, states are oftentimes more likely to discover the performance of the practice only *post factum*, after it has already taken place.[64] Clearly, this does not mean that the incapacity of states to provide adequate protection to its young citizens should be upheld or encouraged. On the contrary, this failure is highly disheartening and needs to be addressed. However, it also indicates that the conventional focus on children belonging to minority groups is inapt in promoting children's rights on its own, and, moreover, there is an urgent need to reevaluate the order of priorities and of policies when biomedical decisions are made. Particularly in cases involving family issues, there may be a necessity to adjust some of the rigid judicial regulations in favor of a more just solution. For instance, if judicial activism per se is not desired, as may be the case in adversarial legal systems, courts may list questions that still require addressing for the parties, and, similar to other legal cases, the decision would be made on the basis of the evidence

---

[61] Renteln, *The Cultural Defense,* 50; Lloyd, 2.

[62] See Chapter 1; Richard Shweder, "What About FGM?" And Why Understanding Culture Matters in the First Place?" in *Engaging Cultural Difference: The Multicultural Challenge in Liberal Democracies,* ed. Richard A. Shweder, Martha Minow, and Hazel Rose Markus (New York: Russell Sage Foundation, 2002), 222.

[63] See the discussion in Chapter 1.

[64] For a discussion on medical negligence cases, see Renteln, *The Cultural Defense,* 61–67; Alison D. Renteln, "Is the Cultural Defense Detrimental to the Health of Children?" in *Law and Anthropology: International Yearbook for Legal Anthropology,* ed. René Kupper and Richard Potz (Dordrecht: Martinus Nijhoff, 1994), 41–53.

the parties provide. While this approach does not resolve the cultural bias of many decisions, one can hope that the legal requirement that the identity/cultural information is taken into account would sensitize the judiciary and the public over time. Thus, instead of giving a green light to states' (excessive) intervention in the private sphere of minority groups, advancing preventive measures within society at large would be preferable. By assessing the extent to which the conflict is rooted in identity considerations rather than medical ones, on the one hand, and raising public awareness to the child's voice as a separate subject under the law, on the other hand, states' valuable time and resources would be devoted to those cases where intervention is clearly required, as in the case of children who have life-threatening conditions.

3. Mixed Minority/Majority Biomedical Practices

Another complicated case may arise when parents who belong to different religio-cultural communities disagree about the performance of a particular bodily practice on their child. In such a case, the factors to be examined in order to determine the child's webs of relationships include whether the parents live together, if one of them has full custody of the child, and whether the child's general environment (the extended family, sociocultural and national communities, as well as peers) supports the practice.

There is one such court case involving a parental disagreement on whether to circumcise their five-year-old son. In the case of *Re J (A Minor)* (1999), a nonpracticing Muslim father requested a court order "that in order to fulfill his parental duty to J within Islam, J be circumcised thereby confirming J's personal and religious identity and hence his upbringing."[65] The mother refused. She was a nonpracticing Christian, who had primary custody of the child since the parent's separation when he was two and a half years old. The court correctly dismissed the father's request on three main grounds. First is the fact that J was to be brought up in England, in a completely secular environment. Neither parent attended the church or the mosque, respectively, or had a religious lifestyle. The second reason is that, essentially, J's only contact with Islam was through the father. Neither parent had Muslim friends or mixed in Muslim circles. Furthermore, as the father's extended Muslim family resides in Turkey, J has had (and was likely to have) relatively little contact with them. Finally, the court took into account J's group of peers as another important factor that needs to be calculated in its decision making. If circumcised, the court observed, he is likely to be in a small minority among his peers. He may be "picked on or teased" for his difference, without having the reassurance, as Turkish boys have when a ritual circumcision takes place, that it is a shared religio-cultural experience.[66]

---

[65] *In Re J. (A Minor),* [1999] 2 F.C.R. 345, [1999] 2 F.L.R. 678 (F.D.), http://www.cirp.org/library/legal/Re_J/. The father submitted an application for two separate court orders. The first was "(i) that J [the child] be brought up in the Muslim religion," and the second revolved around the circumcision as stated above. Both requests were dismissed as well as an appeal on the decision. See *In Re J. (A Minor)* [2000] 1 F.C.R. 307 (C.A.).

[66] J. attended a local state primary school, and there was no evidence submitted

Such cases are clearly not easy to resolve. It is further complicated when religio-cultural practices are mandatory for their followers but clash with the child's interests as a separate subject of rights. In the case of *Re J. (A Minor),* for example, under Islamic law, the decision about the circumcision of the son is left in the father's hands as a part of his religious duty, and Islam does not consider the child as having any role in the decision making in this regard. Simply rejecting the father's argument would be culturally insensitive and, considering the interdependency of individuals in the exercise of rights, also misleading.[67] Likewise, it is not possible to outright simply dismiss the father's perception in this case that the circumcision is "fundamental and essential part . . . of his identity and J's identity" nor his beliefs that the physical similarity between the father and son would "demonstrate and reinforce" the relationship.[68] However, a discussion on children's biomedical rights needs to step away from the conventional concentration on the parents' (one or both) interests. Although they are certainly important, it is not enough. While community members, parents, and children surely share some elements of identity, identities are not fixed, nor can they be assumed to be identical between parents and children. In this sense, the father's interests are not substantially different from a mother's effort to promote *her* rights in the community by extracting her child's milk teeth,[69] or from parental desire to preserve *their* cultural background, yet without providing any other sociocultural context to their child. Rather, to incorporate the child's own voice in the discourse, the focal point has to be by balancing the various and multiple relationships (family, community, peers) in which the child grows and develops his or her sociocultural identity.

4. Genetic Manipulation, Disability, and Deafness by Choice

As was demonstrated in Chapter 7, the question of genetic selection for and against disability under the identity path is complicated for a couple of reasons. First, it does not fit into the conventional understanding of minority and majority's interrelationships that is commonly characterized by numerical and cultural differences. Although, both numerically and legally, persons with disabilities are often conceptualized as members of a minority group, in reality, disability is a universal phenomenon. It is an open minority group that new members continuously join. No one is immune from it, both directly and by proxy, that is, having a dear one with some sort of a disability. Furthermore, one's entrance into the disability group is rather arbitrary, cutting across ethnic, religious, gender, and all other forms of identification. The traditional understanding of minority-majority divides is thus completely blurred.

Second, the practice of genetic selection for disability prevention does not entirely resemble the goal of inclusion that characterizes the other religio-

---

whether there were any other Muslim children in his school. In *Re J. (A Minor),* Conclusion, paragraph (e).

[67] See the discussion in Chapters 5 and 6.

[68] In *Re J. (A Minor),* Conclusion, paragraph (e).

[69] See the discussion in Chapter 3 where the historical background of the practice is described, as well as Chapter 6, where the reasons for prohibiting it were expressed.

cultural biomedical practices under consideration. Although theoretically it aims at the inclusion of (present and future) children in the nondisabled society, the reality is that it does not preclude the acquisition of some other disability throughout one's lifespan. The accessibility and the costs associated with genetic interventions are also not equally available to everyone. As a result, the practice has been argued to further exacerbate the internal stratification between the "haves" and the "have-nots." The goal of creating a disability-free society is thus not only practically impossible, but also, and different from other religio-cultural biomedical practices, it is inherently exclusionary.

It is also for these reasons why the case of "deafness by choice" is so provocative.[70] Unlike the general group of persons with disabilities, where their classification as a minority group is culturally (rather than legally) somewhat artificial, the Deaf community arguably qualifies physically, legally, and culturally (linguistically) as a minority group. In terms of communal goals, the Deaf community is also not substantially different from other religio-cultural biomedical communities that aim at inscribing a cultural identity in the child. Similar to other minority groups, the other immediate circles of relationships of a Deaf child would include the immediate (Deaf) family, the Deaf community, and Deaf peers. Thus, on the face of it, Deaf parents who request having a Deaf child are not morally different from other parents who want to have a say in the genetic combination of their child or from other minority's identification practices. Some may even argue that in liberal democracies, and unless other justifications exist, such a minority-by-definition also requires extra protection, as it is the most vulnerable to the majority's tyranny. Indeed, the closer one gets to the understanding of disability through a sociocultural lens (rather than medical ones), the harder it is to reject such a minority conceptualization, including parental decisions to conceive, purposefully, a child who is deaf. The question is thus whether such "other justifications" exist, and as this study indicates, the answer is in the affirmative.[71]

To begin with, accepting parental reproductive requests for deafness by choice reduces the child's identity into one single genetic factor. Unlike other ethnic, linguistic, religious, and cultural communities, there are generally no other shared characteristics such as skin color, origin, place of residence, and name that constitute the community.[72] The Deaf community is considered to be a transnational one,[73] and unlike other minorities, Deaf members of the community do not have the potential of being in a majority, by say, returning to their original hometowns. By upholding the community merely by the

---

[70] As pointed out in Chapter 7, theoretically, the conceptualization of a subgroup of persons with disabilities as a minority group may extend beyond the Deaf community. Whereas it has been suggested, for example, with regard to the "Little Persons of America," over time, it may also go beyond that.

[71] For further discussion on the Deaf community as a linguistic minority, see Maya Sabatello, "Disability, Cultural Minorities, and International Law: Reconsidering the Case of the Deaf Community," *Whittier Law Review* 26, no. 4 (2005): 1025–50.

[72] Muhlke, 738

[73] Ibid.

shared Deaf culture, it ignores the diverse and multiple factors that influence one's sociocultural identity. Thus, although there is no doubt that the Deaf community is a supportive social artifact for its members, it is closer, so it seems, to other social groups that lead a particular lifestyle. This, however, does not merit the protection of the Deaf culture on its own.

The second reason is that it provides for the child a rather limited sociocultural community to associate with. Although deafness itself does not pose a threat to one's life or health implications, it does lead to another long-term deficiency: the inability to fully communicate with the general environment.[74] Bridging the linguistic barrier is also not always possible. Different from other minority groups, it is not merely a question of *potential* acquisition of another language. It is rather a parental choice to cut off the child's most intrinsic feature for his or her interaction with others, with no way of return.[75] It is thus seemingly merely a parental statement about *their* culture of preference, in this case, the Deaf culture. This is especially evident considering that membership in the Deaf community is not contingent on one's deafness in itself. As the scholastic work illuminates, hearing people with sign language fluency may become members of the community just as well.[76] Children are particularly predestined to pick up the language if exposed to it, and hearing children will have no problem in becoming bilingual. Both hearing and deaf children are also likely to identify with the culture, as it is what provides their social sources of support.[77] Thus, and notwithstanding the importance of cultural diversity, deafness by parental selection should be prohibited, at least, on the identity path.[78]

D. CHILDREN'S BIOETHICS: A REEVALUATION

The question of which traditional biomedical practices that are carried out on children are harmful, and hence should be prohibited, has been highly contentious. According to Western perceptions, it is often assumed that the decisions are made objectively and on the basis of scientifically proven methods.

---

[74] Linguistic development (of whatever sort, and including sign language) is considered to be a predominant means of communication, a social tool that shapes one's relationship, experiences, values, and morals. Yet, while lack of linguistic communication cannot be automatically equated with intelligence and cognitive abilities, research has established that the two are connected to one another. See Johannes Borgstein, "*A Sense of Language*," *Lancet* 357, no. 9261 (2001): 1036–37; Muhlke, 710.

[75] Dena Davis, *Genetic Dilemmas: Reproductive Technology, Parental Choices, and Children's Future: Reproductive Technology, Parental Choices, and Children's Future* (New York: Routledge Publishing, 2001), 64.

[76] Muhlke, 738; N. Levy, "Deafness, Culture and Choice," *Journal of Medical Ethics* 28 (2005): 285; Susan Peters, "Is There a Disability Culture? A Syncretisation of Three Possible World Views," *Disability & Society* 15, no. 4 (2000): 592.

[77] Sabatello, 1042–43, 1046–49 (discussing the Deaf community and the question of cochlear implants).

[78] Communication incapacity in the context of the Deaf community may be regarded as falling under either the medical or the identity paths. My inclination is to the latter, since sign language provides an alterative means of communication. In any case, the words "at least" aim to cover the first option as well.

The accompanying condemnation of some practices thus resonates with what is presumed to be the individual child's best interests and choice.

These conceptualizations, however, are oftentimes only a pretext in an effort to conceal the identity clashes that may appear. In practice, the medical path contains great uncertainty, and decisions are often made only on minimal information, if it is available at all. Despite the universal minority-like status of children, the focus has often been merely on children belonging to minority groups. At the same time, the communal aspects of the child, as reflected in his or her sociocultural identity, are often overlooked. Children's rights are simply portrayed as a norm possessed by solitary atoms in the sociocultural world. The result is thus biased, alienating, and, moreover, inattentive to the child's own interests and voice.

Before any decision making is made, the international and national bodies have to inquire into the anthropological and sociological explanations for the biomedical practice that is at stake. They have to examine carefully the accuracy of these accounts and what breadth of implications they would entail. Only when a given practice risks the life of the child, or involves significant long-term health implications, should it be prohibited. Bodily modifications alone do not provide sufficient justification for banning them, as diversity (whether physical, cultural, or other), is integral to and at the heart of not only the ideology of liberal democracies, but, more importantly, of humanity itself.

For children's biomedical (and other) rights to have meaning, the appropriate space for children's voices to be heard must be provided. This can only be done by taking into consideration the child's center of life, including the family, the community, the national, and the peer sociocultural webs. Individuals do not live in isolation nor do they exercise their rights in solitude. Relationships and sociocultural identities play a significant and inseparable role in human development. While this is not limited to children, their particular status of dependency on others is most indicative in its representation of individuals' interaction. Thus, rather than dismissing identity claims as irrelevant or pretending that they do not exist, they should be fully incorporated into the discourse on children's bioethical (and other) rights.

BIBLIOGRAPHY

COURT CASES

D. v. Ireland, Application no. 26499/02, European Court of Human Rights, Judgment of June 27, 2006.

Evans v. the UK, Application no. 6339/05, European Court of Human Rights, Judgment of March 7, 2006.

In Re. J. (A Minor), [1999] 2 F.C.R. 345, [1999] 2 F.L.R. 678 (F.D.), http://www.cirp.org/library/legal/Re_J/.

R. v. Adesenya [1975] 24 I.C.L.G. 136 (noted).

S. T. v. the Netherlands, Communication no. 175/2000, Committee against Torture, 27th Sess., U.N. Doc. CAT/C/27/D/175/2000, adopted November 23, 2001.

Tysiac v. Poland, Application no. 5410/03, European Court of Human Rights, Judgment of March 20, 2007.

V. v. Canada, Communication no. 47/1996, Committee against Torture, 20th Sess., U.N. Doc. CAT/C/20/D/47/1996, adopted May 19, 1998.

Vo v. France, Application no. 53924/00, European Court of Human Rights, Judgment of July 8, 2004.

X, Y and Z v. UK, Application no. 21830/93, European Court of Human Rights, Judgment of April 22, 1997.

INTERNATIONAL DOCUMENTS

[**Author's Note:** International Treaties and Declarations are available on the UN Web site, http://www.un.org as well as the University of Minnesota Human Rights Library, http://www1.umn.edu/humanrts/.]

Beijing Declaration and Platform of Action of the Fourth World Conference on Women, Beijing, China, 4–15 September 4–15. 1995, U.N. Doc. A/CONF.177/20 (1995) and A/CONF.177/20/Add.1 (1995), annexes 1–2, U.N. Sales No. E.96.IV.13 (reprinted in 35 I.L.M. 401, 407 (the Declaration), 409 (the Platform)).

Canadian Commission for UNESCO, *A Working Definition of Culture for the Canadian Commission for UNESCO* (1977).

Commission on Human Rights, Sub-Commission on Prevention of Discrimination and Protection of Minorities, *Final Report of the Special Rapporteur on Traditional Practices Affecting the Health of Women and Children*, Commission on Human Rights, Sub-Commission on Prevention of Discrimination and Protection of Minorities, 48th Sess., Item 4, U.N. Doc. E/CN.4/Sub.2/1996/6 (June 14, 1996).

Commission on Human Rights, Subcommission on Prevention of Discrimination and Protection of Minorities, *Follow-up Report of the Special Rapporteur on Traditional Practices Affecting the Health of Women and Children,* Commission on Human Rights, Sub-Commission on Prevention of Discrimination and Protection of Minorities, 49th Sess., Item 5(a), U.N. Doc. E/CN.4/Sub.2/1997/10 (June 25, 1997).

Committee on Economic, Social and Cultural Rights, *The Nature of States Parties' Obligations (General Comment No.3),* Committee on Economic, Social and Cultural Rights, 5th Sess., U.N. Doc. E/1991/23, annex III, at 86 (1991), reprinted in *Compilation of General Comments and General Recommendations Adopted by Human Rights Treaty Bodies,* U.N. Doc. HRI/GEN/1/Rev.6, at 14 (2003).

Committee on Economic, Social and Cultural Rights, *The Right to the Highest Attainable Standard of Health (General Comment No. 14),* Committee on Economic, Social and Cultural Rights, 22nd Sess., Agenda Item 3, U.N. Doc. E/C.12/2000/4 (2000), reprinted in *Compilation of General Comments and General Recommendations Adopted by Human Rights Treaty Bodies,* U.N. Doc. HRI/GEN/1/Rev.6, at 85 (2003).

Committee on Economic, Social and Cultural Rights, *The Right of Everyone to Benefit from the Protection of the Moral and Material Interests Resulting from Any Scientific, Literary or Artistic Production of which He or She Is the Author (General Comment No. 17),* 35th Sess., U.N. Doc. E/C.12/GC/17 (2006).

Committee on the Elimination of Discrimination against Women, *Violence Against Women (General Recommendation 19),* Committee on the Elimination of Discrimination against Women, 11th Sess. (1992), U.N. Doc. A/47/38, at 1 (1993), reprinted in *Compilation of General Comments and General Recommendations Adopted by Human Rights Treaty Bodies,* U.N. Doc. HRI/GEN/1/Rev.6, at 243 (2003).

Committee on the Elimination of Racial Discrimination, *Documents Submitted in Compliance with a Special Edition of the Committee: Bosnia and Herzegovina (Additional Info from State Party),* Committee on the Elimination of Racial Discrimination, U.N. Doc. CERD/C/247/Add.1 (April 11, 1995).

Committee on the Rights of the Child, *Adolescent Health and Development in the Context of the Convention on the Rights of the Child* (*General Comment No. 4*), Committee on the Rights of the Child, 33rd Sess., U.N. Doc. CRC/GC/2003/4 (2003).

Committee on the Rights of the Child, *Concluding Observations: Brazil,* Committee on the Rights of the Child, U.N. Doc. CRC/C/15/Add.241 (November 3, 2004).

Committee on the Rights of the Child, *Concluding Observations: Denmark,* Committee on the Rights of the Child, U.N. Doc. CRC/C/15/Add.33 (February 15, 1995).

Committee on the Rights of the Child, *Concluding Observations: Ethiopia,* Committee on the Rights of the Child, U.N. Doc. CRC/C/15/Add.144 (February 21, 2001).

Committee on the Rights of the Child, *Concluding Observations: Finland,* Committee on the Rights of the Child, U.N. Doc. CRC/C/15/Add.132 (October 16, 2000).

Committee on the Rights of the Child, *Concluding Observations: Finland,* Committee on the Rights of the Child, U.N. Doc. UN Doc.U.N. Doc. CRC/C/15/Add.272 (October 20, 2005).

Committee on the Rights of the Child, *Concluding Observations: France,* Committee on the Rights of the Child, U.N. Doc. CRC/C/15/Add.20 (April 25, 1994).

Committee on the Rights of the Child, *Concluding Observations: Kyrgyzstan,* Committee on the Rights of the Child, U.N. Doc. CRC/C/15/Add.127 (August 9, 2000).

Committee on the Rights of the Child, *Concluding Observations: Lesotho* Committee on the Rights of the Child, U.N. Doc. CRC/C/15/Add.147 (February 21, 2001).

Committee on the Rights of the Child, *Concluding Observations: Lesotho.* Committee on the Rights of the Child, U.N. Doc., CRC/C/15/Add.147 (February 21, 2001).

Committee on the Rights of the Child, *Concluding Observations: Malawi,* Committee on the Rights of the Child, U.N. Doc. CRC/C/15/Add.174 (April 2, 2002).

Committee on the Rights of the Child, *Concluding Observations: Monaco,* Committee on the Rights of the Child, U.N. Doc. CRC/C/15/Add.158 (June 8, 2001).

Committee on the Rights of the Child, *Concluding Observations: Myanmar,* Committee on the Rights of the Child, U.N. Doc. CRC/C/15/Add.237 (June 30, 2004).

Committee on the Rights of the Child, *Concluding Observations: Nigeria,* Committee on the Rights of the Child, U.N. Doc. CRC/C/15/Add.257 (April 13, 2005).

Committee on the Rights of the Child, *Concluding Observations: Norway,* Committee on the Rights of the Child, U.N. Doc. CRC/C/15/Add.23 (April 25, 1994).

Committee on the Rights of the Child, *Concluding Observations: South Africa,* Committee on the Rights of the Child, U.N. Doc. CRC/C/15/Add.122 (February 23, 2000).

Committee on the Rights of the Child, *Concluding Observations: Sweden,* Committee on the Rights of the Child, U.N. Doc. CRC/C/15/Add.2 (February 18, 1993).

Committee on the Rights of the Child, *Concluding Observations: Switzerland,* Committee on the Rights of the Child, U.N. Doc. CRC/C/15/Add.182 (June 7, 2002).

Committee on the Rights of the Child, *Concluding Observations: the* Netherlands, Committee on the Rights of the Child, U.N. Doc. CRC/C/15/Add.186 (June 7, 2002).

Committee on the Rights of the Child, *Concluding Observations: Togo,* Committee on the Rights of the Child, U.N. Doc. CRC/C/15/Add.255 (March 31, 2005).

Committee on the Rights of the Child, *Concluding Observations: Togo,* Committee on the Rights of the Child, U.N. Doc. CRC/C/15/Add.83 (October 10, 1997).

Committee on the Rights of the Child, *Concluding Observations: Togo,* Committee on the Rights of the Child, U.N. Doc. CRC/C/15/Add.83 (October 10, 1997).

Committee on the Rights of the Child, *Concluding Observations: Ukraine,* Committee on the Rights of the Child, U.N. Doc. CRC/C/15/Add.42 (November 27, 1995).

Committee on the Rights of the Child, *Concluding Observations: Ukraine,* Committee on the Rights of the Child, U.N. Doc. CRC/C/15/Add.42 (November 27, 1995).

Committee on the Rights of the Child, *Concluding Observations: Ukraine,* Committee on the Rights of the Child, U.N. Doc. CRC/C/15/Add.191 (October 9, 2002).

Committee on the Rights of the Child, *Concluding Observations: Zambia,* Committee on the Rights of the Child, U.N. Doc. CRC/C/15/Add.206 (July 2, 2003).

Committee on the Rights of the Child, *Concluding Observations: Zambia,* Committee on the Rights of the Child, U.N. Doc. CRC/C/15/Add.206 (July 2, 2002).

Committee on the Rights of the Child, *Day of Discussion: Indigenous Groups,* Committee on the Rights of the Child, U.N. Doc. CRC/C/SR.899 (September 26, 2003).

Committee on the Rights of the Child, *General Guidelines Regarding the Form and Contents of Periodic Reports to be Submitted by States Parties under Article 44, paragraph 1(b) of the Convention,* Committee on the Rights of the Child, U.N. Doc. CRC/C/58, 20 November (November 20, 1996).

Committee on the Rights of the Child, *General Measures of Implementation of the Convention on the Rights of the Child (General Comment No. 5),* Committee on the Rights of the Child, 34th Sess., U.N. Doc. CRC/GC/2003/5 (2003).

Committee on the Rights of the Child, *HIV/AIDS and the Rights of the Child (General Comment No. 3),* Committee on the Rights of the Child, U.N. Doc. CRC/GC/2003/3 (2003).

Committee on the Rights of the Child, *Implementing Child Rights in Early Childhood (General Comment No. 7),* Committee on the Rights of the Child, 41st Sess., U.N. Doc. CRC/C/GC/7 (2005).

Committee on the Rights of the Child, *Initial State Report: Albania,* Committee on the Rights of the Child, U.N. Doc. CRC/C/11/Add.27 (July 5, 2004).

Committee on the Rights of the Child, *Initial State Report: Sweden,* Committee on the Rights of the Child, U.N. Doc. CRC/C/3/Add.1 (September 23, 1992).

Committee on the Rights of the Child, *Initial State Report: Togo,* Committee on the Rights of the Child, U.N. Doc. CRC/C/3/Add.42 (February 27, 1996).

Committee on the Rights of the Child, *List of issuesIssues: Argentina,* Committee on the Rights of the Child, U.N. Doc. CRC/C.6/WP.1 (February 17, 1994).

Committee on the Rights of the Child, *List of issuesIssues: Croatia.,* Committee on the Rights of the Child, U.N. Doc. CRC/C.11/WP.1 (November, 27, 1995).

Committee on the Rights of the Child, *List of Issues: Finland,* Committee on the Rights of the Child, U.N. Doc. CRC/C/Q/FIN/2 (June 26, 2000).

Committee on the Rights of the Child, *List of issuesIssues: Ukraine,* Committee on the Rights of the Child, U.N. Doc. CRC/C/Q/UKR/2 (June 14, 2002).

Committee on the Rights of the Child, *Overview of the Reporting Procedures*, Committee on the Rights of the Child, 7th Sess., U.N. Doc. CRC/C/33 (October 24, 1994).

Committee on the Rights of the Child, *Second Periodic Report: New Zealand*, Committee on the Rights of the Child, U.N. Doc. CRC/C/93/Add.4 (March 12, 2003).

Committee on the Rights of the Child, *Second Periodic Report: Nigeria*, Committee on the Rights of the Child, U.N. Doc. CRC/C/70/Add.24 (September, 17, 2004).

Committee on the Rights of the Child, *Summary Record: Sweden*, Committee on the Rights of the Child, U.N. Doc. CRC/C/SR.522 (January 28, 1999).

Committee on the Rights of the Child, *Summary Record: Ukraine*, Committee on the Rights of the Child, U.N. Doc. UN. Doc. CRC/C/SR.240 (November 7, 1995).

Committee on the Rights of the Child, *Summary Record: Ukraine*, Committee on the Rights of the Child, U.N. Doc. CRC/C/SR.821 (October 1, 2002).

Committee on the Rights of the Child, *The Rights of Children with Disabilities (General Comment No. 9)*, Committee on the Rights of the Child, U.N. Doc. CRC/C/GC/9 (2007).

Committee on the Rights of the Child, *Third Periodic Report: Finland*, Committee on the Rights of the Child, U.N. Doc. CRC/C/129/Add.5 (January 5, 2005).

Evaluation Report: Participatory Qualitative Evaluation of Life Skills and HIV/ /AIDS Training for Youth and Women. UNICEF/ /Myanmar: Population Council (Thailand) Inc., June 1998.

Fact Sheet No. 23: Harmful Traditional Practices Affecting the Health of Women and Girls, United Nations' Office of the High Commissioner for Human Rights, http://www.unhchr.ch/html/menu6/2/fs23.htm.

Federal Democratic Republic of Ethiopia, "Response to the Questionnaire on Violence Against Children Submitted to the UN Secretary General's Independent Expert on the Study on Violence Against Children," paragraph 8 (May 2005), http://www2.ohchr.org/english/bodies/CRC/docs/study/responses/Ethiopia.pdf.

Human Rights Committee, *Nature of the General Legal Obligation on States Parties to the Covenant (General Comment No. 31)*, Human Rights Committee, U.N. Doc. CCPR/C/21/Rev.1/Add.13 (2004).

Human Rights Committee, *Prohibition of Torture and Cruel Treatment or Punishment (General Comment No. 20)*, Human Rights Committee, 44th Sess. (1992), reprinted in *Compilation of General Comments and General Recommendations Adopted by Human Rights Treaty Bodies*, U.N. Doc. HRI/GEN/1/Rev.1, at 30 (1994).

Human Rights Committee, *The Right to Freedom of Thought, Conscience and Religion (General Comment No. 22)*, Human Rights Committee, 48th Sess. (1993), reprinted in *Compilation of General Comments and General Recommendations Adopted by Human Rights Treaty Bodies*, U.N. Doc. HRI\GEN\1\Rev.1, at 35 (1994).

Human Rights Committee, *The Right to Life (General Comment No. 6)*, Human Rights Committee, 6th Sess. (1982), reprinted in *Compilation of General*

Comments and General Recommendations Adopted by Human Rights Treaty Bodies, U.N. Doc. HRI\GEN\1\Rev.1, at 6 (1994).

Human Rights Committee, *The Rights of Minorities (General Comment No. 23),* Human Rights Committee, 5th Sess. (1994), reprinted in *Compilation of General Comments and General Recommendations Adopted by Human Rights Treaty Bodies,* U.N. Doc. HRI\GEN\1\Rev.1, at 38 (1994).

Human Rights Committee, *The Rights of the Child (General Comment No. 17),* Human Rights Committee, 35th Sess. (1989), reprinted in *Compilation of General Comments and General Recommendations Adopted by Human Rights Treaty Bodies,* U.N. Doc. HRI\GEN\1\Rev.1, at 23 (1994).

Revised General Guidelines Regarding the Form and Contents of Reports to be Submitted by States Parties under Articles 16 and 17 of the International Covenant on Economic, Social and Cultural Rights, U.N. Doc. E/C.12/1991/1 (June 17, 1991), Annex.

Statement by Mr. Paulo Sérgio Pinheiro, Independent Expert for the United Nations Secretary-General's Study on Violence against Children, U.N. General Assembly, 62nd Sess., http://www.violencestudy.org/IMG/pdf/62_UNGA_statement.pdf.

U.N. Commission on Human Rights, *Report of the Working Group on Traditional Practices Affecting the Health of Women and Children,* U.N. Commission on Human Rights, 42nd Sess., Item 19, U.N. Doc. E/CN.4/1986/42 (February 4, 1986).

U.N. Economic and Social Council, *Report of the 1980 Working Group on the Draft Declaration on the Elimination of All Forms of Intolerance and of Discrimination based on Religion or Belief,* U.N. Economic and Social Council, 36th Sess., Supp. no. 3, U.N. Doc. E/1980/ /13, E/CN.4.1408 (February 4–March 14, 1980).

U.N. Economic and Social Council, *Report of the 1980 Working Group to the Commission on Human Rights,* Economic and Social Council, U.N. Doc. E/CN.4/L.1542 (1980)

U.N. Economic and Social Council, *Report of the 1981 Working Group on the Draft Declaration on the Elimination of All Forms of Intolerance and of Discrimination based on Religion or Belief,* U.N. Economic and Social Council, 36th Sess., Supp. no. 3, UN Doc.U.N. Doc. E/1982/25; E/CN.4/1475 (February 2–March 13, 1981).

U.N. Economic and Social Council, *Report of the 1985 Working Group on a Draft Convention on the Rights of the Child,* U.N. Economic and Social Council, 41st Sess., Agenda Item 13, U.N. Doc. E/CN.4/1985/64 (April 3, 1985).

U.N. Economic and Social Council, *Report of the 1986 Working Group on a Draft Convention on the Rights of the Child,* U.N. Economic and Social Council, 42st Sess., Agenda Item 13, U.N. Doc. E/CN.4/1986/39 (March 13, 1986).

U.N. Economic and Social Council, *Report of the 1987 Working Group on a Draft Convention on the Rights of the Child,* U.N. Economic and Social Council, 43rd Sess., Agenda Item 13, UN Doc.U.N. Doc. E/CN.4/1987/25 (March 3, 1987).

U.N. Economic and Social Council, *Report of the 1989 Working Group on a Draft Convention on the Rights of the Child,* U.N. Economic and Social Council, 45h Sess., Agenda Item 13, U.N. Doc. E/CN.4/1989/48 (March 2, 1989).

U.N. Economic and Social Council, *Report of the Special Rapporteur on Violence Against Women, Integration of the Human Rights of Women and the Gender Perspective: Violence Against Women,* Economic and Social Council, 59th Sess., Item 12(a), Commission on Human Rights, U.N. Doc. E/CN.4/22003/75/ Add.1 (February 27, 2003).

U.N. Economic and Social Council, *Technical Review of the Text of the Draft Convention on the Rights of the Child,* U.N Economic and Social Council, 45th Sess., U.N. Doc. E/CN.4/1989/WG.1/CRP.1 (October 15, 1988).

U.N. General Assembly, *Report of the Independent Expert for the United Nations Study on Violence against Children,* 60th Sess., U.N. Doc. A/60/282 (August 19, 2005).

U.N. General Assembly, *Report of the Independent Expert for the United Nations Study on Violence against Children,* U.N. General Assembly, 61st Sess., U.N. Doc. A/61/299 (August 29, 2006).

U.N. Press Release, *Sub-Ccommission Completes Debate on Obstacles to Development,* U.N. Press Release, U.N. Doc. HR/SC/98/14 (13 AugustAugust 13, 1998).

SOURCES

Abu-Sahlieh, S.A. Aldeeb. "Muslims' Genitalia in the Hands of the Clergy Religious Arguments about Male and Female Circumcision." In *Male and Female Circumcision—Medical, Legal and Ethical Considerations in Pediatric Practice,* edited by George C. Denniston, Frederick Mansfield Hodges, and Marilyn Fayre Milos, 131–71. New York: Kluwer Academic/Plenum Publishers, 1999.

Accorsi, Sandro and others. "The Burden of Traditional Practices, Ebbino and Tea-Tea on Child Health in Northern Uganda." *Social Sciences & Medicine* 57 (2003): 2183–91.

Ackroyd, Judith, and Andrew Pilkington. "Childhood and the Construction of Ethnic Identities in a Global Age." *Childhood* 6, no. 4 (1999): 443–54.

Addis, Adeno. "Individualism, Communitariarism, and the Rights of Ethnic Minorities." *Notre Dame Law Review* 67 (1992): 615–76.

Ahdar, Rex J. "Children's Religious Freedom, Devout Parents and the State. "In *Law and Religion in Contemporary Society: Communities, Individualism and the State,* edited by Peter W. Edge and Graham Harvey, 93–114. Aldershot, UK: Ashgate Publishing, 2000.

Ahdar, Rex J. "The Right of the Child to a Godly Future." *International Journal of Children's Rights* 10, no. 1 (2002): 89–107.

Agence France Press. "Thai "Longneck" Ethnic Group Losing Identity: Governor." October 11, 2002, International News. http://www.lexisnexis.com.

Airhihenbuwa, Collins O. *Health and Culture: Beyond the Western Paradigm.* London: Sage Publications, 1995.

Akunga, Alice, and others. *The Impact of HIV/AIDS on Education in Kenya and the Potential for Using Education to the Widest Sense for the Prevention and Control of HIV/AIDS: Final Report."* Government of Kenya & UNICEF Kenya Country Office publications, 2000. http://www.kanco.org/ktmlstandard/files/uploads/HIVaids%20and%20education%20in%20Kenya.pdf.

Alderson, Priscilla. *Children's Consent to Surgery*. Buckingham, UK: Open University Press, 1993.

Alderson, Priscilla, and Christopher Goodey. "Research with Disabled Children: How Useful Is Child-Centred Ethics?" *Children & Society* 10 (1996): 106–16.

Alderson, Priscilla, Joanna Hawthorne, and Margaret Killen. "The Participation Rights of Premature Babies." *International Journal of Children's Rights* 13, no. 1–2 (2005): 3–50.

Al-Hibri, Azizah Y. "Is Western Patriarchal Feminism Good for Third World/ Minority Women?" In *Is Multiculturalism Bad for Women?* edited by Susan M. Okin, 41–46. Princeton, NJ: Princeton University Press, 1999.

Ali, Zoebia, and others. "Disability, Ethnicity and Childhood: A Critical Review of Research." *Disability & Society* 16, no. 7 (2001): 949–68.

Alston, Philip. "The Unborn Child and Abortion under the Draft Convention of the Rights of the Child." *Human Rights Quarterly* 12 (1990): 156–78.

Alston, Philip. "The Best Interests Principle: Towards a Reconciliation of Culture and Human Rights." In *The Best Interests of the Child: Reconciliation of Culture and Human Rights,* edited by Philip Alston, 1–25. New York: Oxford University Press, 1994.

Amand, Metthew G. St. "Public Committee against Torture in Israel v. The State of Israel et al.: Landmark Human Rights Decision by the Israeli High Court of Justice or Status Quo Maintained?" *North Carolina Journal of International Law & Commercial Regulation* 25 (2000): 655–84.

Amnesty International USA. "A Bill to End Male Genital Mutilation in the U.S." http://www.mgmbill.org/ai.htm.

Anderson, Benedict. *Imagined Communities,* rev. ed. London: Verso, 1990.

Anstey, K. W. "Are Attempts to Have Impaired Children Justifiable?" *Journal of Medical Ethics* 28 (2005): 286–88.

Appiah, Kwame A. "Identity, Authenticity, Survival: Multicultural Societies and Social Reproduction." In *Multiculturalism,* edited by Amy Gutman, 149–64. Princeton, New Jersey: Princeton University Press, 1994.

Archard, David. *Children: Rights and Childhood.* London: Routledge, 1993.

Archard, David. "Can Child Abuse Be Defined?" In *Moral Agendas for Children's Welfare,* edited by Michael King, 74–89. New York: Routledge, 1999.

Archard, David. "Children, Multiculturalism and Education." In *The Moral and Political Status of Children,* edited by David Archard and Colin M. Macleod, 142–59. Oxford: Oxford University Press, 2002.

Armstrong, Alice, Matrine Chuulu, Chuma Himonga, and Puleng Letuka. "Towards a Cultural Understanding of the Interplay between Children's and Women's Rights: An Eastern and Southern African Perspective." *International Journal of Children's Rights* 3 (1995): 333–68.

Arneil, Barbara. "Becoming Versus Being: A Critical Analysis of the Child In Liberal Theory." In *The Moral and Political Status of Children,* edited by David Archard and Colin M. Macleod, 71–93. Oxford: Oxford University Press, 2002.

Asch, Adrienne, Lawrence O. Gostin, and Diann M. Johnson. "Respecting Persons with Disabilities and Preventing Disabilities: Is There a Conflict?" In *The Human Rights of Persons with Intellectual Disabilities: Different But Equal,* edited by Stanley S. Herr, Lawrence O. Gostin, and Harold Hongju Koh, 324–27. Oxford: Oxford University Press, 2003.

Asefa, Makonnen, Jenny Hewison, and Robert Drewett. "Traditional Nutritional and Surgical Practices and Their Effects on the Growth of Infants in Southwest Ethiopia." *Paediatric & Perinatal Epidemiology* 12 (1998): 182–98.

Avoke, Amwutor. "Models of Disability in the Labeling and Attitudinal Discourse in Ghana." *Disability & Society* 17, no. 7 (2002): 769–77.

Ayeni, Olubimpe. "Observations on Medical and Social Aspects of Scarification in Sub-Saharan Africa." http://www.med.uottawa.ca/medweb/hetenyi/ayeni.htm.

Bailey, Robert C., and Daniel T. Halperin. "Male Circumcision and HIV Infection." *Lancet* 355, no. 9207 (2000): 927.

Barlow, Bradley, Michael J. Kanellis, and Rebecca Slayton. "Tooth Eruption Symptoms: A Survey of Parents and Health Professionals." *Journal of Dentistry for Children* 69, no. 2 (2002): 148–50(3).

Bassiouni M. Cherif, and others. "Rape and Sexual Assault: Final report of the United Nations Commission of Experts established pursuant to Security Council Resolution 780 (1992)." United Nations Security Council, S/1994/ 674/ Add.2, Vol. V (1994): Annex IX. http://www.ess.uwe.ac.uk/comexpert/ANX/IX.htm.

Baskind, Roy, and Gretchen Birbeck. "Epilepsy Care in Zambia: A Study of Traditional Healers." *Epilepsia* 46, no. 7 (2005): 1121–26.

Bates, Don G. "Why Not Call Modern Medicine 'Alternative'?" *Perspective in Biology & Medicine* 43, no. 4 (2000): 502–18.

Baubock, Rainer. "Cultural Minority Rights for Immigrants." *International Migration Review* 30, no. 1 (1996): 203–50.

Beaman, Lori G. "Religion and Rights: the Illusion of Freedom and the Reality of Control." *Culture and Religion* 6, no. 1 (2005): 17–29.

Bell, Shannon. "Tattooed: A Participant Observer's Exploration of Meaning." *Journal of American Culture* 22, no. 2 (1999): 53–58.

Bellon, Christina M. "The Promise of Rights for Children: Best Interests and Evolving Capacities. " In *Children as Equals: Exploring the Rights of the Child,* edited by Kathleen Alaimo and Brian Klug, 103–26. Lanham, MD: University Press of America, 2002.

Bennett, Walter H. "A Critique of the Emerging Children's Convention." *Cornell International Law Journal* 20, no. 1 (1987): 1–47.

Benson, Kaaron. "Management of the Jehovah's Witness Oncology Patient: Perspective of the Transfusion Service." *Cancer Control Journal* 2, no. 6 (1995). https://www.moffitt.usf.edu/pubs/ccj/v2n6/article13.html.

Bentley, Kristine A. "Can There Be Any Universal Children's Rights?" *International Journal Human of Rights* 9, no. 1 (2005): 107–23.

Benzaquen, Adrian S. "Childhood, History and the Science of Childhood." In *Multiple Lenses, Multiple Images,* edited by Hillel Goelman, Sheila K. Marshall, and Sally Ross, 14–37. Toronto: University of Toronto Press, 2004.

Ben-Zion, Garty. "Garlic Burns." *Pediatrics* 91 (1993): 658–59.

Berger, Leslie. "Learning to Tell Custom from Abuse." *Los Angeles Times,* August 24, 1994, A16.

Bernard, Suzanne M. "An Eye for an Eye: The Current Status of International Law on the Humane Treatment of Prisoners." *Rutgers Law Journal* 25 (1994): 759–98.

Beauchamp, Tom L., and James F. Childress. *Principles of Biomedical Ethics.* New York: Oxford University Press, 2001.

Bilsky, Leora. "Child-Parent-State: the Absence of Community in the Courts' Approach to Education." In *Children's Rights and Traditional Values,* edited by Gillian Douglas and Leslie Sebba, 134–59. Burlington, VT: Ashgate Publishing, 1998.

Blackhall, Leslie J., and others. "Ethnicity and Attitudes Toward Patient Autonomy." *Journal of the American Medical Association* 274, no. 10 (1995): 820–25.

Bohannan, Laura. *The Tiv of Central Nigeria.* London: International African Institute, 1953. http://www.yale.edu/hraf/collections.htm (eHRAF Collection of Ethnography).

Bonner, Charles A., and Michael J. Kinane. "Circumcision: the Legal and Constitutional Issues." In *2nd International Symposium on Circumcision,* San Francisco, California, April, 30–May 3, 1991. http://www.nocirc.org/legal/bonner2.php.

Boroffice, O. B. "Women's Attitudes to Men's Sexual Behaviour." *Health Transition Review* 5 (1995): 67–79. http://htc.anu.edu.au/pdfs/Boroffi1.pdf.

Borrell J. "Last of the Long Necks." *Herald Sun,* May 29, 1992, Travel (Suppl.), 37. http://www.lexisnexis.com.

Bossuyt, Marc J. *Guide to the "Travaux Preparatoires" of the International Covenant on Civil and Political Rights.* Dordrecht: Martinus Nijhoff, 1987.

Braddock, David L., and Susan L. Parish. "Social Policy Toward Intellectual Disabilities in the Nineteenth and Twentieth Centuries." In *The Human Rights of Persons with Intellectual Disabilities: Different But Equal,* edited by Stanley S. Herr, Lawrence O. Gostin, and Harold Hongju Koh, 83–114. Oxford: Oxford University Press, 2003.

Branford, Victor V. "Science and Citizenship." *The American Journal of Sociology* 11, no. 6 (1906): 721–62.

Breeding, John, and Fred Baughman. "Informed Consent and the Psychiatric Drugging of Children." *Journal of Humanistic Psychology* 43, no. 2 (2003): 50–64.

Brennan, Samantha. "Children's Choices or Children's Interests: Which Do Their Rights Protect?" In *The Moral and Political Status of Children,* edited by David Archard and Colin M. Macleod, 53–68. Oxford: Oxford University Press, 2002.

Bridgeman, Jo. "Caring for Children with Severe Disabilities: Boundaried Relational Rights." *International Journal of Children's Rights* 13, no. 1–2 (2005): 99–119.

Brighouse, Harry. "What Rights (If Any) Do Children Have?" In *The Moral & Political Status of Children,* edited by David Archard and Colin M. Macleod, 31–52. Oxford: Oxford UniversityPress, 2002.

Brigman, William. "Circumcision as Child Abuse: the Legal and Constitutional Issues." *Journal of Family Law,* 23 no. 3 (1984–85). Library of Circumcision Information and Resource Pages. http://www.cirp.org/library/legal/brigman/.

British Medical Association. *Circumcision of Male Infants: Guidance for Doctors.* London, 1996. Library of Circumcision Information and Resource Pages. http://www.cirp.org/library/statements/bma/.

Brown, Gillian. *The Consent of the Governed: The Lockean Legacy in Early American Culture.* Cambridge, MA: Harvard University Press, 2001.

Bunting, Annie. "Elijah and Ishmael: Assessing Cultural Identity in Canadian Child Custody Decisions." *Family Court Review* 42, no. 3 (2004): 471–84.

Burch, Susan. "Transcending Revolutions: the Tsars, the Soviet and Deaf Culture." *Journal of Social History* 34, no. 2 (2000): 393–401.

Burr, Rachel. "Global and Local Approaches to Children's Rights in Vietnam." *Childhood* 9, no. 1 (2002): 49–61.

Callan, Eamonn. "Autonomy, Child-Rearing, and Good Lives." In *The Moral and Political Status of Children,* edited by David Archard and Colin M. Macleod, 118–41. Oxford: Oxford University Press, 2002.

Campbell, Tom D. "The Rights of the Minor: As Person, as Child, as Juvenile, as Future Adult." In *Children, Rights and the Law,* edited by Philip Alston, Stephen Parker, and John Seymour, 1–23. New York: Oxford University Press, 1995.

Campbell, Tom D. "Really Equal Rights? Some Philosophical Comments on 'Why Children Shouldn't Have Equal Rights' by Laura M. Purdy." *International Journal of Children's Rights* 2 (1994): 259–63.

Capps, Lisa L. "Change and Continuity in the Medical Culture of the Hmong in Kansas City." *Medical Anthropology Quarterly* 8, no. 2 (1994): 161–77.

Capps, Lisa L. "Fright Illness in Hmong Children." *Pediatric Nursing* 25, no. 4 (1999): 378–83.

Capron, Alexander. M. "The Authority of Others to Decide About Biomedical Intervention with Incompetent." In *Who Speaks for the Child—the Problems of Proxy Consent,* edited by Willard Gaylin and Ruth Macklin, 115–152. New York: Plenum Press, 1982.

Casper, Monica J., and Barbara A. Koenig. "Reconfiguring Nature and Culture: Intersections of Medical Anthropology and Technoscience Studies." *Medical Anthropology Quarterly* 10, no. 4 (1996): 523–36.

Cavet, Judith, and Patricia Sloper. "Participation of Disabled Children in Individual Decisions about Their Lives and in Public Decisions about Service Development." *Children & Society* 18, no. 4 (2004): 278–90.

Chafel, Judith A., and Carin Neitzel. "Young Children's Ideas about the Nature, Causes, Justification, and Alleviation of Poverty." *Early Childhood Research Quarterly* 20 (2005): 433–50.

Cheewin, Satha. "Rights: Governor Denies Karens Exploited." *Bangkok Post,* December 11, 1997, 3. http://lexisnexis.com.

Cheng-tek Tai, Michael, and Chung Seng Lin. "Developing a Culturally Bioethics for Asian People." *Journal of Medical Ethics* 27, no. 1 (2001): 51–54.

Chessler, Abbie J. "Justifying the Unjustifiable: Rite v. Wrong." *Buffalo Law Review* 45 (1997): 555–613. http://www.cirp.org/library/legal/chessler.

Christensen, Pia, and Alan Prout. "Working with Ethical Asymmetry in Social Research with Children." *Childhood* 9, no. 4 (2002): 477–97.

Christensen, Pia Handrup. "Children's Participation in Ethnographic Research: Issues of Power and Representation." *Children & Society* 18 (2004): 165–76.

Clark, Stephanie. "Male Circumcision Could Help Protect Against HIV Infection." *Lancet* 356, no. 9225 (2000): 225.

Clayton, Matthew. "Individual Autonomy and Genetic Choice." In *A Companion to Genethics*, edited by Justine Burley and John Harris, 191–205. Malden, MA: Blackwell Publishing, 2002.

Cockburn, Tom. "Children and the Feminist Ethic of Care." *Childhood* 12, no. 1 (2005): 71–89.

Cohen, Cynthia B., Sondra E. Wheeler, and David A. Scott. "Walking on a Fine Line." *Hastings Center Report* 31, no. 5 (2001): 29–39.

Cohen, Cynthia P. "The United Nations Children's Convention: Involvement of NGOs." In *The Legitimacy of the United Nations: Towards an Enhanced Legal Status of Non-State Actors*, edited by Theo C. van Boven, Cees Flinterman, Fred Grunfeld, and Rita Hut, 169–89. Utrecht, the Netherlands: SIM, 1997. http://www.uu.nl/content/14Price.pdf.

Cohen, Cynthia P., and Susan Kilbourne. "The Jurisprudence of the Committee on the Rights of the Child: A Guide for Research and Analysis." *Michigan Journal of International Law* 19, no. 3 (1998): 633–728.

Cohen, Lawrence. "The Other Kidney: Biopolitics Beyond Recognition." *Body & Society* 7, no. 2–3 (2001): 9–29.

Cohen, Ronald. *The Structure of Kanuri Society*. Ann Arbor, Michigan: University Microfilms, 1960. http://www.yale.edu/hraf/ (eHRAF Collection of Ethnography).

Conrad, Peter, and Joseph W. Schneider. *Deviance and Medicalization: From Badness toSickness*. St. Louis: Mosby Publishing, 1980.

Conrad, Peter. "Medicalization and Social Control." *Annual Review of Sociology* 18 (1992): 209–32.

Cook, Rebecca J. "International Human Rights and Women's Reproductive Health." *Studies in Family Planning* 24, no. 2 (1993): 73–86.

Cowen, Perle Slavik. "Child Neglect: Injuries of Omission." *Pediatric Nursing* 25, no. 4 (1999): 401–18.

Craig, Anita P. "Cultural and the Individual." *Theory & Psychology* 13, no. 5 (2003): 629–50.

Cranston, Maurice. "Are There Any Human Rights?" *Daedalus* 112, no. 4 (1984): 1–18.

Crossley, Nick. "Embodiment and Social Structure: A Response to Howson and Inglis." *Sociological Review* 49, no. 3 (2001): 318–26.

Crouch, Robert A. "Letting the Deaf Be Deaf: Reconsidering the Use of Cochlear Implants in Prelingually Deaf Children." *Hastings Center Report* 27 (1997): 14–21.

Darling, Rosalyn B. "Toward a Model of Changing Disability Identities: a Proposed Typology and Research Agenda." *Disability & Society* 18, no. 7 (2003): 881–95.

Das, Veena. "Public Good, Ethics, and Everyday Life: Beyond the Boundaries of Bioethics." *Bioethics & Beyond (Daedalus)* 128, no. 4 (1999): 99–134.

Davis, Dena S. "Genetic Dilemmas and the Child's Right to an Open Future." *Hastings Center Report* 27, no.2 (1997): 7–15.

Davis, Dena. *Genetic Dilemmas: Reproductive Technology, Parental Choices, and Children's Future: Reproductive Technology, Parental Choices, and Children's Future.* New York: Routledge Publishing, 2001.

Davis, J. M., and N Watson. "Where Are the Children's Experiences? Analysing Social and Cultural Exclusion in 'Special' and 'Mainstream' Schools." *Disability & Society* 16, no. 5 (2001): 671–87.

Davis, Kathy. "A Dubious Equality: Men, Women and Cosmetic Surgery." *Body & Society* 8, no. 1 (2002): 49–65.

De Melo-Martin, Immaculada. "On Our Obligation to Select the Best Children: A Reply to Savulescu." *Bioethics* 18, no. 1 (2004): 72–83.

Deal, Mark. "Disabled People's Attitudes toward Other Impairment Groups: A Hierarchy of Impairment." *Disability & Society* 18, no. 7 (2003): 897–910.

Degener, Theresia. "Disabled Persons and Human Rights: the Legal Framework." In *Human Rights and Disabled Persons,* edited by Theresia Degener and Yolan Koster-Dreese, 9–39. Dordrecht: Martinus Nijhoff, 1995.

Degener, Theresia. "Disability as a Subject of International Human Rights Law and Comparative Discrimination Law." In *The Human Rights of Persons with Intellectual Disabilities: Different But Equal,* edited by Stanley S. Herr, Lawrence O. Gostin, and Harold Hongju Koh, 151–84. Oxford: Oxford University Press, 2003.

DeMello, Margo. "'Not Just for Bikers Anymore': Popular Representations of American Tattooing." *Journal of Popular Culture* 29, no. 3 (1995): 37–52.

Detrick, Sharon. *A Commentary on the United Nations Convention on the Rights of the Child.* Dordrecht: Martinus Nijhoff, 1999.

Detrick, Sharon, ed. *The United Nations Children's Convention: A Guide to the "Travaux Preparatoires."* Dordrecht: Martinus Nijhoff, 1992.

Dewhurst, S. N., and C. Mason. "Traditional Tooth Bud Gouging in a Uganda Family: A Report Involving Three Sisters." *International Journal of Paediatric Dentistry* 11, no. 4 (2001): 292–97.

Dilon, James J. "The Role of the Child in Adult Development." *Journal of Adult Development* 9, no. 4 (2002): 267–75.

Donchin, Anne. "Understanding Autonomy Relationally: Towards a Reconfiguration of Bioethical Principles." *Journal of Medicine & Philosophy* 26, no. 4 (2001): 365–86.

Donders, Yvonne M. *Towards a Right to Cultural Identity?* Oxford: Antwerpen Intersentia, 2002.

Donnelly, Jack. "Human Rights and Human Dignity: An Analytic Critique of Non-Western Conceptions of Human Rights." *American Political Science Review* 76 (1982): 303–16.

Donnelly, Jack. "Human Rights, Individual Rights and Collective Rights." In *Human Rights in a Pluralist World,* edited by J. Berting and others, 39–62. Westport, CT: Meckler, 1999.

Donnelly, Jack. *Universal Human Rights in Theory and Practice.* 2nd ed. Ithaca, NY: Cornell University Press, 2003.

Durkheim, Emile. *The Elementary Forms of Religious Life.* Translated by Josepf Ward Swain. New York: Free Press, 1965.

Dworkin, Gerlard. "Consent, Representation and Proxy Consent." In *Who Speaks for the Child—The Problems of Proxy Consent,* edited by Willard Gaylin and Ruth Macklin, 191–208. New York: Plenum Press, 1982.

Dwyer, James G. "Parents' Religion and Children's Welfare: Debuking the Doctrine of Parents' Rights." *California Law Review* 82 (1994): 1371–1446.

Dyer, Clare. *Doctors, Patients and the Law.* Oxford: Blackwell Scientific Publishing, 1992.

Eisenberg, Avigail. "Identity and Liberal Politics: the Problem of Minorities within Minorities." In *Minorities within Minorities: Equality, Rights and Diversity,* edited by Avigail Eisenberg and Jeff Spinner-Halev, 249–70. Cambridge: Cambridge University Press, 2005.

Eisenberg, Leon. "Cross-Cultural and Historical Perspectives on Child Abuse and Neglect." *Child Abuse & Neglect* 5 (1981): 299–308.

Eisenbruch, Maurice, and Lauren Handelman. "Cultural Consultation for Cancer: Astrocytoma in Cambodian Adolescent." *Social Science & Medicine* 31 (1990): 1296.

Ekamn Ladd, Rosalind. "Rights of the Autistic Child." *International Journal of Children's Rights* 13, no. 1–2 (2005): 87–98.

Ensalaco, Mark, and Linda Majka C. *Children's Human Rights: Progress and Challenges for Children Worldwide.* Oxford: Rowman and Littlefield Publishing, 2005.

Ertem, Ilgi O., and others. "Medical Neglect of a Child: Challenges for Pediatricians in Developing Countries." *Child Abuse & Neglect* 26 (2002): 751–61.

Falk, Ze'ev W. "Rights and Autonomy—Or the Best Interests of the Child?" In *Children's Rights and Traditional Values,* edited by Gillian Douglas and Leslie Sebba, 111–17. Burlington, VT: Ashgate Publishing, 1998.

Feldman, Kennth W. "Pseudoabusive Burns in Asia Refugees." *American Journal of Diseases of Children* (AJDC) 138 (1984): 768–69.

Feinberg, Joel. "The Child's Right to an Open Future." In *Whose Child? Children's Rights, Parental Authority, and State Power,* edited by Will Aiken and Hugh La Falleete, 124–53. Totowa, NJ: Littlefield, Adams, 1980.

Ferrari, Anne M. "The Impact of Culture upon Child Rearing Practices and Definitions of Maltreatment." *Child Abuse & Neglect* 26 (2002): 793–813.

Fidler, David P. "'Geographical Morality' Revisited: International Relations, International Law, and the Controversy over Placebo-Controlled HIV Clinical Trials in Developing Countries." *Harvard International Law Journal* 42, no. 2 (2001): 299–354.

Fletcher, Christopher R. "Circumcision in America in 1998—Attitudes, Beliefs, and Charges of American Physicians." In *Male and Female Circumcision—Medical, Legal and Ethical Considerations in Pediatric Practice,* edited by George C. Denniston, Frederick Mansfield Hodges, and Marilyn Fayre Milos, 259–71. New York: Kluwer Academic/Plenum Publishers, 1999.

Forjuoh, Samuel. "Pattern of Intentional Burns to Children in Ghana." *Child Abuse & Neglect* 19, no. 7 (1995): 837–41.

Foucault, Michel. *The History of Sexuality, Volume One: An Introduction.* London: Penguin, 1979.

Fox, Marie, and Michael Thomson. "Short Changed? The Law and Ethics of Male Circumcision." *International Journal of Children's Rights* 13, no. 1–2 (2005): 161–81.

Franklin, Sarah. "Science as Culture, Cultures of Science." *Annual Review of Anthropology* 24 (1995): 163–84.

Freeman, Michael. "Taking Children's Rights More Seriously." In *Children, Rights and the Law,* edited by Philip Alston, Stephen Parker, and John Seymour, 52–71. New York: Oxford University Press, 1995.

Freeman, Michael. "Children's Health and Children's Rights: An Introduction." *International Journal of Children's Rights* 13, no. 1–2 (2005): 1–10.

Frosh, Stephen. "Identity, Religious Fundamentalism and Children's Welfare." In *Moral Agendas for Children's Welfare,* edited by Michael King, 198–211. New York: Routledge, 1999.

Galik, Shimon M. "An Unlimited Autonomy of the Individual—Is It a Question of Culture?" *A Letter to A Friend (Michtav LaChaver)* 59, no. 3 (1997): 13–15 (Heb.)

Galvin, Rose. "The Paradox of Disability Culture: the Need to Combine Versus the Imperative to Let Go." *International Journal of Children's Rights* 18, no. 5 (2003): 675–90.

Gausset Quentin. "AIDS and Cultural Practices in Africa: the Case of the Tonga (Zambia)." *Social Sciences & Medicine* 52 (2001): 509–19.

Gelles, Richard J., and Claire P. Cornell. "International Perspectives on Child Abuse." *Child Abuse & Neglect* 7 (1983): 375–86.

Gengenbach, Heidi. "Boundaries of Beauty: Tattooed Secrets of Women's History in Magude District, Southern Mozambique." *Journal of Women's History* 14, no. 4 (2003): 106–41.

Gluckman, Ron. *Stretching One's Neck.* http://www.gluckman.com/LongNeck.html.

Golan, Ofra. "The Requirement of "Informed Consent" as an Expression of Human Dignity." *Shaarei Mishpat* 2, no. 2 (2000): 171–88 (Heb.).

Goodhart, Michael. "Origins and Universality in Human Rights Debates: Cultural Essentialism and the Challenge of Globalization." *Human Rights Quarterly* 25, no. 5 (2003): 935–64.

Gordon, Alysa. "Multiculturalism in Medical Decision-making: the Notion of Informed Waiver." *Fordham Urban Law Journal* 23, no. 3 (1995–96): 1321–62.

Granat, Diane. "To Hear Again." *Washintonian,* April 29 1994, 64–76. http://www.hwwilson.com/Databases/omnifile.htm.

Gray, Denis D. "Long-Necked Tourism: 'Human Zoo' or Boon to the Poor?" *Associated Press,* March 30, 1998, International News. http://lexisnexis.com.

Griffith, James. "Do Children Have Rights?" In *The Moral and Political Status of Children,* edited by David Archard and Colin M. Macleod, 19–30. Oxford: Oxford University Press, 2002.

Griffith, John. "What Is Legal Pluralism?" *Journal Legal Pluralism & Unofficial Law* 24 (1986): 1–55.

Grosz, Elizabeth. *Volatile Bodies: Toward a Corporeal Feminism,* 39–40. Bloomington: Indiana University Press, 1994.

Grove, Noel. "The many Faces of Thailand." *National Geographic Magazine* 189, February 1996, 82–105. http://www.hwwilson.com/Databases/omnifile.htm.

Gruenbaum, Ellen. *The Female Circumcision Controversy: An Anthropological Perspective.* Philadelphia: University of Pennsylvania Press, 2001.

Gunn, Jeremy T. "The Complexities of Religion and the Definition of "Religion" in International Law." *Harvard Human Rights Journal* 16 (2003): 189–215.

Gutman, Emy, ed. *Multiculturalism: Examining the Politics of Recognition.* Princeton, New Jersey: Princeton University Press, 1994.

Haberfield, Les. "Informed Consent and Infant Male Circumcision." *Australian Law Teachers Conference,* Sydney, New South Wales, Australia, October 3, 1997. Library of Circumcision Information and Resource Pages. http://www.cirp.org/library/legal/haberfield/.

Hagger, Lynn, and Simon Woods. "Children and Research: A Risk of Double Jeopardy?" *International Journal of Children's Rights* 13, no. 1–2 (2005): 51–72.

Hahn, Harlan. "The Political Implications of Disability: Definition and Data." In *The Psychological and Social Impact of Disability,* edited by Robert P. Marinelli and Arthur E. Dell Orto, 3–11. New York: Springer Publishing, 1999.

Halley, Janet E. "Culture Constrains." In *Is Multiculturalism Bad for Women?* edited by Susan M. Okin, 100–104. Princeton, NJ: Princeton University Press, 1999.

Halperin, Daniel T., and Robert C. Bailey. "Male Circumcision and HIV Infection: 10 Years and Counting." *Lancet* 354, no. 9191 (1999): 1814.

Hansen, Karen K. "Folk Remedies and Child Abuse: A Review with Emphasis on Caida De Mollera and Its Relationship to Shaken Baby Syndrome." *Child Abuse & Neglect* 22, no. 2 (1997): 117–27.

Harris-Short, Sonia. "Listening to "the Other"? The Convention on the Rights of the Child." *Melbourne Journal of International Law* 2 (2001): 304–50.

Harris-Short, Sonia. "International Human Rights law: Imperialism, Inept and Ineffective? Cultural Relativism and the UN Children's Convention." *Human Rights Quarterly* 25, no. 1 (2003): 130–81.

Harris-Short, Sonia. "An "Identity Crisis" in the International Law of Human Rights? The Challenge of Reproductive Cloning." *International Journal of Children's Rights* 11 (2004): 333–68.

Hefner, Philip. "The Spiritual Task of Religion in Culture: An Evolutionary Perspective." *Zygon* 33, no. 4 (1998): 535–44.

Hellsten, S. K. "Rationalizing Circumcision: From Tradition to Fashion, From Public Health to Individual Freedom—Critical Notes on Cultural Persistence of the Practice of Genital Mutilation." *Journal of Medical Ethics* 30, no. 3 (2004): 248–53.

Helman, Cecil G. *Culture, Health and Illness.* Oxford: Butterworth, 2000.

Hemingway, Sara. "Tourism and Women's Human Rights in South East Asia." *International Journal of Human Rights* 8, no. 3 (2004): 275–304.

Herodous, *The Histories,* Book III, part 38. Reproduced by Harmondsworth: Penguin Classics, 1954.

Hodgkin, Rachel, and Peter Newell. *Implementation Handbook for the Convention on the Rights of the Child.* New York: UNICEF, 1998.

Hodgson, Douglas. "The Child's Right to Life, Survival and Development." *International Journal of Children's Rights* 2, no. 2 (1994): 369–94.

Hong, George K., and Lawrence K. Hong. "Comparative Perspectives on Child neglect and Abuse: Chinese vs. Hispanics and Whites." *Child Welfare* 70, no. 4 (1991): 463–75.

Honig, Bonnie. "My Culture Made Me Do It." In *Is Multiculturalism Bad for Women?* edited by Susan M. Okin, 35–40. Princeton, NJ: Princeton University Press, 1999.

Howard, Rhoda E. "Dignity, Community and Human Rights." In *Human Rights in Cross-Cultural Perspectives: A Quest for Consensus,* edited by Abdullahi Ahmed An-Na'im, 81–104. Philadelphia: University Pennsylvania Press, 1992.

Hull, Richard J. "Cheap Listening?—Reflections on the Concept of Wrongful Disability." *Bioethics* 20, no. 2 (2006): 55–63.

Ireland, Lorrain, and Immy Holloway. "Qualitative Health Research with Children." *Children & Society* 10 (1996): 155–64.

Iriso Robert, and others. "Killer" Canines: The Morbidity and Mortality of *Ebino* in Northern Uganda." *Tropical Medicine & International Health* 5, no. 10 (2000): 706–10.

James, Allison, and Adrian L. James. *Constructing Childhood: Theory, Policy and Social Practice.* New York: Palgrave Macmillan Publishing, 2004.

Jans, Marc. "Children as Citizens: Towards A Contemporary Notion of Child Participation." *Childhood* 11, no. 1 (2004): 27–44.

Jeppsson, Andres, Mequanent Tesfu, and Lars-Ake Persson. "Health Care Providers' Perspectives on Harmful Traditional Health Practices in Ethiopia." *Ethiopian Journal of Health Development* 17, no. 1 (2003): 35–44. http://www.cih.uib.no/journals/EJHD/ejhdv17-no1/ejhdv17-n1-page33.pdf.

Jaramillo, Canela A. "Defining 'Comfort': Padaung Women in Thailand." *Standards* 7, no. 2 (2001). http://www.colorado.edu/journals/standards/V7N2/EDITORIAL/editorial.html.

Jegede, Ayodele, Samuel. "The Yoruba Cultural Construction of Health and Illness." *Nordic Journal of African Studies* 11 no. 3 (2002): 322–35.

Jenks, Chris. "Many Childhoods?" *Childhood* 11, no. 1 (2004): 5–8.

Jones, Melinda. "Adolescent Gender Identity and the Courts." *International Journal of Children's Rights* 13, no. 1–2 (2005): 121–48.

Jones, Owen D. "Sex Selection: Regulating Technology Enabling the Predetermination of a Child's Gender." *Harvard Journal Law and Technology* 6 (1992–93): 1–62.

Kahn, Jeffrey P. "Genetic Harm: Bitten by the Body that Keeps You?" *Bioethics* 5, no. 4 (1991): 289–308.

Kahn, Jeffrey P. "Commentary on Zohar's "Prospect for 'Genetic Therapy'—Can a Person Benefit from Being Altered?"." *Bioethics* 5, no. 4 (1991): 312–17.

Karpman, Anna. "Informed Consent: Does the First Amendment Protect a Patients' Right to Choose Alternative Treatment." *New York Law School Journal Human Rights*16 (2000): 933–57.

Katz, Ilan. "Is Male Circumcision Morally Defensible?" In *Moral Agendas for Children's Welfare,* edited by Michael King, 90–104, New York: Routledge, 1999.

Kelle, Helga. "The Discourse of "Development": How 9-to-12-year-ld Children Construct 'Childish' and 'Further Developed' Identities within Their Peer Culture." *Childhood* 8, no. 1 (2001): 95–114.

Kelly, Berni. 'Chocolate . . . Makes You Autism': Impairment, Disability and Childhood Identities." *Disability & Society* 20, no. 3 (2005): 261–75.

Kim, D. S., J. Y. Lee, and M. G. Pang. "Male Circumcision: A South Korean Perspective." *BJU International* 83, Supp. 1 (1999): 28–33.

King, Michael. "Images of Children and Morality." In *Moral Agendas for Children's Welfare*, edited by Michael King, 15–32. New York: Routledge, 1999.

King, Patricia. A. "Treatment and Minors: Issues Not Involving Lifesaving Treatment." *Journal of Family Law* 23 (1984–85): 241–65.

Kirkland, Anna. "Identity and the Properly Functioning Individual: Imagining the Confluence of Fat Rights and Disability law." USC Center for Law, History and Culture Workshop (2004): 1–47. http://law.usc.edu/academics/centers/clhc/archives/workshops/documents/kirkland_000.pdf.

Kluckhohn, Clyde, and William H. Kelly. "The Concept of Culture." In *The Science of Man in the World Crisis*, edited by Ralph Linton, 78–106. New York: Octagon Books, 1980.

Korbin, Jill E. "The Cross Cultural Context of Child Abuse and Neglect." In *The Battered Child*. 3rd ed., edited by Henry C. Kenpa and Ray Helfer, 21–35. Chicago: University of Chicago Press, 1980.

Korbin, Jill E. "A Cross-Cultural Perspective on the Role of the Community in Child Abuse and Neglect." *Child Abuse & Neglect* 3 (1979): 9–18.

Korbin, Jill E. "Child Maltreatment in Cross-Cultural Perspective: Vulnerable Children and Circumstances." In *Child Abuse and Neglect: Biosocial Dimensions*, edited by Richard J. Gelles and James B Lancester, 31–55. New York: Aldin De Gruyter, 1987.

Korbin, Jill E. "Children, Childhood, and Violence." *Annual Review Anthropology* 32 (2003): 431–46.

Kratz, Corinne A. "Circumcision Debates and Asylum Cases: Intersecting Arenas, Contested Values and Tangled Webs." In *Engaging Cultural Difference: The Multicultural Challenge in Liberal Democracies*, edited by Richard A. Shweder, Martha Minow, and Hazel Rose Markus, 309–43. New York: Russell Sage Foundation, 2002.

Kukathas, Chandran. "Are There Any Cultural Rights?" *Political Theory* 20, no. 1 (1992): 105–39.

Kukathas, Chandran. "Cultural Rights Again: A Rejoinder to Kymlicka." *Political Theory* 20, no. 4 (1992): 674–80.

Kuper, Jenny. "Reservations, Declarations and Objections to the 1989 Convention on the Rights of the Child." In *Human Rights as General Norms and a States' Right to Opt Out: Reservations and Objections to Human Rights Conventions*, edited by J. P. Gardner, 104–13. London: B.I.I.C.C. Publishing, 1997.

Kuwahara, Makiko. *Tattoo: An Anthropology*. Oxford: Berg Publishing, 2005.

Kyle, Jim G., and Gloria Pullen. "Cultures in Contact: Deaf and Hearing People." *Disability, Handicap & Society* 3, no.1 (1988): 49–61.

Kymlicka, Will. *Liberalism, Community & Culture*. Oxford: Clarendon Press, 1989.

Kymlicka, Will. "The Rights of Minority Cultures: Reply to Kukathas." *Political Theory* 20, no.1 (1992): 140–46.

Kymlicka, Will. Multicultural Citizenship: A Liberal Theory of Minority Rights. Oxford: Clarendon Press, 1995.

Lamparello, Adam. "Taking God Out of the Hospital: Requiring Parents to Seek Medical Care For Their Children Regardless of Religious Belief." *Texas Forum on Civil Liberties & Civil Rights* 6 (2001): 47–115.

Landau, Paul S. "Explaining Surgical Evangelism in Colonial Southern Africa: Teeth, Pain and Faith." *Journal on African History* 37 (1996): 261–81.

Lane, Harlan. "Constructions of Deafness." *Disability & Society* 10 (1995): 171–89.

Langman, Lauren. "Culture, Identity and Hegemony: the Body in a Global Age." *Current Sociology* 51, no. 3–4 (2003): 223–47.

Lannon, Carole M., and others. "Circumcision Policy Statement." *Pediatrics* 103, no. 3 (1999): 686–93.

Lansdown, Gerison. *Promoting Children's Participation in Democratic Decision-Making.* Florence, Italy: UNICEF & Innocenti Research Centre, 2001.

Lansdown, Gerison. *The Evolving Capacities of the Child.* Florence, Italy: UNICEF & Innocenti Research Centre, 2005.

Latukefu, Sione. "Noble Traditions and Christian Principles as Nations Ideology in Papua New Guinea: Do Their Philosophies Complement or Contradict Each Other?" *Pacific Studies* 11, no. 2 (1988): 83–96.

Lau, Joseph T. F., and Joseph L. Y. Liu. "Conceptualization, Reporting and Underreporting of Child Abuse in Hong Kong." *Child Abuse & Neglect* 23, no. 11 (1999): 1159–74.

Lauterbach-Goren, Ayala. "The Adaptability of Cancer Patients Who Turn to Complementary Medicnie in Addition to Conventional Medicine." Ph.D. diss. Haifa University, Israel, 1998.

Lemmes, Stephan E. "The Marginalization of Religious Voices in Bioethics." In *Religion and Medical Ethics,* edited by Allen Verhey, 19–43. Grand Rapids, MI: W. B. Eerdmans Publishing, 1996.

Leonard, Mary. "Making a Mark on the Culture: Body Piercing, Tattoos and Scarification Push the Cutting Edge." *Boston Globe,* February 15, 1998, Focus, Commentary, C1.

Lerner, Natan. *Religion, Beliefs, and International Human Rights*. Maryknoll, NY: Orbis Books, 2000.

Levy, N. "Deafness, Culture and Choice." *Journal of Medical Ethics* 28 (2005): 284–85.

Lightfoot, Jane, and Patricia Sloper. "Having a Say in Health: Involving Young People with a Chronic Illness of Physical Disability in Local Health Services Development." *Children & Society* 17, no. 4 (2003): 277–90.

Lingle, Elizabeth A. "Treating Children by Faith Colliding Constitutional Issues." *Journal of Legal Medicine* 17 (1996): 301–30.

Lloyd, Peter. "The Case of Mrs. Adesnya." *RAIN: Royal Anthropological Institute News* 4 (1979): 2.

Loustaunau, Martha O., and Elisa J. Sobo. *The Cultural Context of Health, Illness and Medicine.* London: Bergin & Garvey, 1997.

Lowy, Catherine. "Autonomy and the Appropriate Projects of Children: A Comment on Freeman." In *Children, Rights and the Law,* edited by Philip Alston, Stephen Parker, and John Seymour, 72–75. New York: Oxford University Press, 1995.

Lucker-Babel, Marie-Francoise. "The Right of the Child to Express Views and to Be Heard: An Attempt to Interpret Article 12 of the UN Convention on the Rights of the Child." *International Journal of Children's Rights* 3 (1995): 391–404.

Lupton, Deborah. *Medicine as Culture.* London: Sage Publications, 2003.

Marshall, Andrew. *The Trouser People.* Washington DC: Counterpoint, 2002.

Marshall, Harry Ignatius. *The Karen People of Burma.* Ohio: University of Columbus, 1922.

Martin, Emily. "Toward an Anthropology of Immunology: the Body as the Nation State." *Medical Anthropology Quarterly* 4, no. 4 (1990): 410–26.

Mary, Braid. "The Long Road to Freedom." *Independent,* November 7, 1998, Features, 26–3. http://www.lexisnexis.com/.

McCullough, Marie. "Medical Conditions Can Look Like Child Abuse." *Chicago Tribune,* May 30, 1995, Tempo, 3.

McDonald, Michael. "Should Communities Have Rights? Reflections on Liberal Individualism." In *Human Rights in Cross-Cultural Perspectives: A Quest for Consensus,* edited by Abdullahi Ahmed An-Na'im, 133–61. Philadelphia: University of Pennsylvania Press, 1992.

McGillivray, Anne. "Why Children Have Equal Rights: in Reply to Laura Purdy." *International Journal of Children's Rights* 2 (1994): 243–58.

McIntosh, Ian S. "State Sanctions Child Abuse in Thailand." *Cultural Survival Voices* 1, no. 1 (2001). http://209.200.101.189/publications/csv/csv-article.cfm?id=3&highlight=McIntosh.

Mercer, Kobena. "Welcome to the Jungle: Identity and Diversity in Postmodern Politics." In *Identity: Community, Culture, Difference,* edited by Jonathan Rutherford, 43–72. London: Lawrence & Wishart, 1990.

Milos, Marilyn F., and Donna Macris. "Circumcision: A Medical or A Human Rights Issue?" *Journal of Nurse-Midwifery* 37, no. 2 (Suppl.) (1992): 87S–96S. Library of Circumcision Information and Resource Pages. http://www.cirp.org/library/ethics/milos-macris/.

Miller, Geoffrey P. "Circumcision: Cultural—Legal Analysis." *Virginia Journal of Social Policy & Law* 9, no. 3 (2003): 497–585.

Minow, Martha. "Rights for the Next Generation: A Feminist Approach to Children's Rights." *Women's Law Journal* 9 (1986): 1–24.

Minow, Martha. "Putting Up and Putting Down: Tolerance Reconsidered." In *Comparative Constitutional Federalism: Europe and America,* edited by Mark Tushnet, 77–113. New York: Greenwood Press, 1990.

Minow, Martha. "What Ever Happened to Children's Rights?" *Minnesota Law Review* 80, no. 1 (1995): 267–98.

Minow, Martha. *Not Only For Myself: Identity, Politics, and the Law.* New York: New Press, 1997.

Minow, Martha. "About Women, About Culture: About Them, About Us." In *Engaging Cultural Difference: The Multicultural Challenge in Liberal Democracies,* edited by Richard A. Shweder, Martha Minow, and Hazel Rose Markus, 252–67. New York: Russell Sage Foundation, 2002.

Mogensen, Henne O. "False Teeth and Real Suffering: The Social Course of "Germectomy" in Eastern Uganda." *Culture, Medicine & Psychiatry* 24 (2000): 331–51.

Montagu, Ashley. "Mutilated Humanity." *Humanist* 55, no. 4 (1995): 12–15.

Morrow, Virginia, and Martin Richards. "The Ethics of Social Research with Children: An Overview." *Children & Society* 10 (1996): 90–105.

Muhlke, Anna-Miria. "The Right to Language and Linguistic Development: Deafness from a Human Rights Perspective." *Virgina Journal of International Law* 40 (2000): 705–61.

Muller, Jessica H. "Anthropology, Bioethics and Medicine: A Provocative Trilogy." *Medical Anthropology Quarterly* 8, no. 4 (1994): 448–67.

Murray, Rachel. *Human Rights in Africa: From the OAU to the African Union.* Cambridge: Cambridge University Press, 2004.

Mutua, Makau. "The Complexity of Universalism in Human Rights." In *10th Annual Conference on "the Individual vs. the State" Central European University*, Budapest, June 14–16, 2002. http://www.ceu.hu/legal/ind_vs_state/Mutua_paper_2002.htm.

Nation. "Kayan Girls Want to Be More than Just Tourist Attractions." *New Frontiers* 9, no. 6 (2003). http://www.twnside.org.sg/title/nf96.doc.

National Association of the Deaf. "NAD Position Statement on Cochlear Implants." http://www.nad.org/infocenter/newsroom/positions/CochlearImplants.htm.

Nedelsky, Jennifer. "Re-conceiving Autonomy: Sources, Thoughts and Possibilities." *Yale Journal of Law & Feminism* 1 (1989): 7–36.

Newell, Peter. *Children and Violence.* Florence, Italy: UNICEF ICDC, 1997.

Nguyen, Maj Duong. "Culture Shock: A Review of Vietnamese Culture and Its Concepts of Health and Disease." *Western Journal of Medicine* 142, no. 3 (1985): 409–12.

Nguyen, Nga, Phuoc H. (Frank) Nguyen, and Loc H. Nguyen. "*Coin Treatment in Vietnamese Families: Traditional Medical Practices vs. Child Abuse.*" Los Angeles: County of LA, Department of Children's Services, 1987.

Nieć, Halina. "Casting the Foundation for the Implementation of Cultural Rights." In *Cultural Rights and Wrongs*, edited by Halina Nieć, 176–90. Paris: UNESCO Publishing, 1998.

Nikora, Linda Waimarie, Mohi Rua, and Ngahuia Te Awekotuku. "In Your Face: Wearing Moko—Maori Facial Marking in Today's World." *Tatau/Tattoo: Embodied Art and Cultural Exchange Conference* 2003. http://psychology.waikato.ac.nz/mpru/pubs/confpapers/2004facesdraft7.pdf.

Nnko, Soori, Robert Washija, and J. Ties Boerma. "Dynamics of Male Circumcision Practices in Northwest Tanzania." *Sexually Transmitted Diseases* 28, no. 4 (2001): 214–18.

Noggle, Robert. "Special Agents: Children's Autonomy and Parental Authority." In *The Moral and Political Status of Children*, edited by David Archard and Colin M. Macleod, 97–117. Oxford: Oxford University Press, 2002.

"Notes: Children as Believers: Minor's Free Exercise Rights and the Psychology of Religious Development." *Harvard Law Review* 115 (2002): 2205–27.

Nugen, Maj Doung. "Cultural Shock—A Review of Vietnamese Culture and Its Concepts of Health and Disease." *Western Journal of Medicine* 142, no. 3 (1985): 409–12.

Nussbaum, Martha. "A Plea for Difficulty." In *Is Multiculturalism Bad for Women?* edited by Susan M. Okin, 105–14. Princeton, NJ: Princeton University Press, 1999.

O'Donnell, Clifford R. "The Right to a Family Environment in Pacific Island Cultures." *International Journal of Children's Rights* 3 (1995): 87–99.

O'Manique, John. *The Origins of Justice: the Evolution of Morality, Human Rights and Law.* Philadelphia: University of Pennsylvania Press, 2003.

O'Neill, Onora. "Children's Rights and Children's Lives." In *Children, Rights and the Law,* edited by Philip Alston, Stephen Parker, and John Seymour, 24–42. New York: Oxford University Press, 1995.

Obiechina, A. E., and A. O. Alutayo. "Attitudes to Facial Marks in South Western Nigeria." *Odonto-Stomatologie Tropicale* 23, no. 91 (2000): 23–26.

Okin, Susan M. "Is Multiculturalism Bad for Women?" In *Is Multiculturalism Bad for Women?* edited by Susan M. Okin, 7–20. Princeton, NJ: Princeton University Press, 1999.

Okin, Susan M., ed., *Is Multiculturalism Bad for Women?* Princeton, NJ: Princeton University Press, 1999.

Olsen, Frances. "Children's Rights: Some Feminist Approaches to the United Nations Convention on the Rights of the Child." *International Journal of Law & Family* 6 (1992): 192–220.

Oommen, Tharaileth K. *Pluralism, Equality and Identity: Comparative Studies.* New Delhi: Oxford University Press, 2002.

Osowole, Oladunni, and others. "A Survey of Treatment Practices for Febrile Illnesses among Traditional Healers in the Nigerian Middle Belt Zone." *African Journal of Traditional, Complementary and Alternative Medicines* 2, no. 3 (2005): 337–44.

Otto, Dianne. "Linking Health and Human Rights: A Critical Legal Perspective." *Health & Human Rights* 1, no. 3 (1995): 272–81.

Packer, Corinne A. A. *Using Human Rights to Change Tradition: Traditional Practices Harmful to Women's Reproductive Health in Sub-Saharan Africa.* Oxford: Antwerpen Intersentia, 2002.

"The Pa Dong Village of Nai Soi: A Visit to the Long Necked Women." *Sunbbaytours.* May 14, 2001. http://www.djparadisetour.com/MaeHongSon/ePadong.html.

Panikar, Raimundo. "Is the Notion of Human Rights a Western Concept?" *Diogenes* 120 (1982): 75–102.

Parekh, Bhikhu. *Rethinking Multiculturalism: Cultural Diversity and Political Theory.* Cambridge, MA: Harvard University Press, 2000.

Parens, Erik. "Authenticity and Ambivalence: Toward Understanding the Enhancement Debate." *Hastings Center Report* 35, no. 3 (2005): 34–41.

Parens, Erik, and Adreine Asch. "The Disability Rights Critique of Prenatal

Genetic Testing." *Hastings Center Report* 29, no. 5 (Special Suppl. 1999): S1–S22.

Pee, Daw. "It's a Curse to Be a Women," *Women in Action* 72, no. 1–2 (2000). http://www.isiswomen.org/wia/wia100/index.html.

Persson, Ingmar. "Genetic Therapy, Identity and the person-Regarding Reasons." *Bioethics* 9, no. 1 (1995): 16–31.

Peters, Philip G. "Harming Future Persons: Obligations to the Children of Reproductive Technology." *Southern California Interdisciplinary Law Journal* 8 (1998–99): 375–400.

Peters, Susan. "Is There a Disability Culture? A Syncretisation of Three Possible World Views." *Disability & Society* 15, no. 4 (2000): 583–601.

Pfeiffer, David. "Eugenics and Disability Discrimination." In *The Psychological and Social Impact of Disability*, edited by Robert P. Marinelli and Arthur E. Dell Orto, 12–31. New York: Springer Publishing, 1999.

Picone, Jack. "The Ring Cycle." *MATP (Australian Nationwide News)*, June 14, 2003, Magazine, 20. http://www.lexisnexis.com/.

Pierce, Lois, and Vivienne Bozalek. "Child Abuse in South Africa: An Examination of How Child Abuse and Neglect are Defined." *Child Abuse & Neglect* 28 (2004): 817–32.

Povenmire, Ross, "Do Parents Have the Legal Authority to Consent to the Surgical Amputation of Normal, Healthy Tissue from Their Infant Children?: The Practice of Circumcision in the United States." *Journal of Gender, Social Policy and the Law* 7 no.1 (1998–9): 87–123.

Price, Christopher. "Male Circumcision: An Ethical and Legal Affront." *Bulletin of Medical Ethics* 128 (1997): 13–19.

Primosch, Robert E., and Stephen Kent Young. "Pseudobattering of Vietnamese Children (Cao Gio)." *Journal of American Dental Assocication* 101 (1980): 47–48.

Prott, Lyndel. "Understanding One Another on Cultural Rights." In *Cultural Rights and Wrongs*, edited by Halina Niec , 161–75. Paris: UNESCO Publishing, 1998.

Purdy, Laura M. "Why Children Shouldn't Have Equal Rights?" *International Journal of Children's Rights* 2 (1994): 223–41.

Queensland Law Reform Commission. *Circumcision of Male Infants Research Paper.* Brisbane, 1993. Library of Circumcision Information and Resource Pages. http://www.cirp.org/library/legal/QLRC/.

Quigley, John. "International Limits on Use of Force to Elicit Confessions: A Critique of Israel's Policy on Interrogation." *Brooklyn Journal of International Law* 16, no. 3 (1988): 485–502.

Rabello De Castro, Lucia. "Otherness in Me, Otherness in Others: Children's and Youth's Constructions of Self and Other." *Childhood* 11, no. 4 (2004): 469–93.

Raz, Joseph. "How Perfect Should One Be? And Whose Culture Is?" In *Is Multiculturalism Bad for Women?* edited by Susan M. Okin, 95–99. Princeton, NJ: Princeton University Press, 1999.

Reeve, Donna. "Negotiating Psycho-Emotional Dimensions of Disability and

Their Influence on Identity Constructions." *Disability & Society* 17, no. 5 (2002): 493–508.

Reitman, Valerie. "With Less Blood Shed." *Los Angeles Times*, January 31, 2005, Health, F1 and F8.

Renteln, Alison D. "Is the Cultural Defense Detrimental to the Health of Children?" In *Law and Anthropology: International Yearbook for Legal Anthropology*, edited by René Kupper and Richard Potz, 27–106. Dordrecht: Martinus Nijhoff, 1994.

Renteln, Alison D. "Cross-Cultural Perceptions of Disability: Policy Implications of Divergent Views." In *The Human Rights of Persons with Intellectual Disabilities: Different But Equal*, edited by Stanley S. Herr, Lawrence O. Gostin, and Harold Hongju Koh, 59–82. Oxford: Oxford University Press, 2003.

Renteln, Alison D. *The Cultural Defense*. Oxford: Oxford University Press, 2004.

Richards, David. "Male Circumcision: Medical or Ritual?" *Journal of Law & Medicine* 3, no.4 (1996): 371–76.

Robertson, John A. "Genetic Selection of Offspring Characteristics." *Boston University Law Review* 76 (1996): 421–82.

Robertson, John A. "Procreative Liberty in the Era of Genomics." *American Journal of Law & Medicine* 29 (2003): 439–86.

Roche, Jeremy. "Children: Rights, Participation and Citizenship." *Childhood* 6, no. 4 (1999): 475–93.

Rodd, Helen D., and Lesley E. Davidson. ""Ilko Dacowo": Canine Enucleation and Dental Sequelae in Somali Children." *International Journal of Paediatric Dentistry* 10 (2000): 209–97.

Rojek, Chris, and Bryan Turner. "Decorative Sociology: Towards a Critique of the Cultural Turn." *The Sociology Review* 48, no. 4 (2000): 619–48.

Ronen, Ya'ir. "The Child's Right to Identity as a Right to Belong." *Tel Aviv University Law Review* 26, no. 3 (2003): 935–84.

Rose, Marcus. "Human Zoo: Neck-Ringing Refugees." *New Internationalists*, February 1995, 264, 4. http://www.lexisnexis.com.

Rosenblatt, Daniel. "The Antisocial Skin: Structure, Resistance, and "Modern Primitive" Adornment in the United States." *Cultural Anthropology* 12, no. 3 (1997): 287–334.

Rovane, Carol. "Genetics and Personal Identity." In *A Companion to Genethics*, edited by Justine Burley and John Harris, 245–52. Malden, MA: Blackwell Publishing, 2002.

Rua, Mohi. "Contemporary Attitudes to Traditional Facial Ta Moko." In *Maori and Psychology: Research and Practice—The Proceedings of a Symposium Sponsored by the Maori and Psychology Research Unit*, edited by N. Robertson, 1–7. Hamilton, New Zealand: Maori & Psychology Research Unit, 1999. http://wfass-trinity.fass.waikato.ac.nz/docushare/dsweb/Get/Document-999/rua.pdf.

Russell, Katherine E., Cheryl Coffin, and Margaret Kenna. "Cochlear Implants and the Deaf Child: A Nursing Perspective." *Pediatric Nursing* 25, no. 4 (1999): 396–401.

Rutenberg, Jim, and Andy Newman. "Mayor Balances Hasidic Ritual against Fears of Babies' Health." *New York Times*, January 6, 2006, A1. http://www.nytimes.com/2006/01/06/nyregion/06rite.html.

Rutherford, Jonathan. "A Place Called Home: Identity and the Cultural Politics of Difference." In *Identity: Community, Culture, Difference*, edited by Jonathan Rutherford, 9–27. London: Lawrence & Wishart, 1990.

Sabatello, Maya. "Disability, Cultural Minorities, and International Law: Reconsidering the Case of the Deaf Community." *Whittier Law Review* 26, no. 4 (2005): 1025–50.

Saetersdal, Tore. "Symbols of Cultural Identity: A Case Study from Tanzania." *African Archaeological Review* 16, no. 2 (1999): 121–35.

Sanders, Douglas. "Collective Rights." *Human Rights Quarterly* 13, no. 3 (1991): 368–86.

Sanghas, Richard J., and Laila Monaghan. "Signs of Their Times: Deaf Communities and the Culture of Language." *Annual Review of Anthropology* 31 (2002): 69–97.

Sarat, Austin, and Jonathan Simon. "Beyond Legal Realism?: Cultural Analysis, Cultural Studies and the Situation of Legal Scholarship." *Yale Journal of Law & Humanities* 13, no. 1 (2001): 3–34.

Schabas, William A. "Reservations to the Convention on the Elimination of All Forms of Discrimination against Women and the Convention on the Rights of the Child." *William and Mary Journal of Women and Law* 3 (1997): 79–112.

Scheper-Hughes, Nency. "Commodity Fetishism in Organs Trafficking." *Body & Society* 7, no. 2–3 (2001): 31–62.

Schildkrout, Erid. "Body Art as Visual Language." *AnthroNotes*, 22, no. 2 (2001). http://www.nmnh.si.edu/anthro/outreach/anthnote/Winter01/anthnote.html.

Schildkrout, Erid. "Inscribing the Body." *Annual Review of Anthropology* 33 (2004): 319–44.

Schoen, Edgar J., Thomas E Wiswell, and Stephen Moses. "New Policy on Circumcision—Cause for Concern." *Pediatrics* 105 (2000): 620–23.

Schroeder, Fred E. H. "Say Cheese! The Revolution in the Aesthetic of Smiles." *Journal of Popular Culture* 32, no. 2 (1998): 103–45.

Scott, Daniel G. "Spirituality in Child and Youth Care: Considering Spiritual Development and 'Relational Consciousness'." *Child & Youth Care Forum* 32, no. 2 (2003): 117–31.

Scott, James George. *Burma and Beyond*. London: Grayson & Grayson, 1932.

Serrano, Barbara A. "Cultures Clash in Rearing Children—State Acts When Abuse Is Feared—Parents Follow Custom in Laotian Boy's Case." *Seattle Times*, August 30, 1991, A1.

Shachar, Ayelet. "The Puzzle of Interlocking Power Hierarchies: Sharing the Pieces of Jurisdictional Authority." *Harvard Civil Rights & Civil Liberties Law Review* 35 (2000): 385–426.

Shachar, Ayelet. *Multicultural Jurisdiction: Cultural Differences and Women's Rights*. Cambridge: Cambridge University Press, 2001.

Shakespear, Tom. "Cultural Representation of Disabled People: Dustbins for Disavowal?" *Disability & Society*, 9, no. 3 (1994): 283–99.

Shapiro, Ian, and Will Kymlicka, eds. *Ethnicity and Groups Rights*. New York: New York University Press, 1997.

Sherwin, Susan, ed. *The Politics of Women's Health: Exploring Agency and Autonomy.* Philadelphia: Temple University Press, 1998.

Shestack, Jerome J. "The Philosophic Foundations of Human Rights." *Human Rights Quarterly* 20 (1998): 201–34.

Shilling, Chris "Embodiment, Experience and Theory: In Defense of the Sociological Tradition." *Sociological Review* 49, no. 3 (2001): 327–44.

Shisana, Olive, and others. *HIV Risk Exposure among Young Children—A Study of 2–9 Years Old.* Pretoria, South Africa: Human Sciences Research Council Press, 2005. http://www.hsrc.ac.za/media/2005/4/20050405_1Report.pdf.

Short, R. V. "Male Circumcision: A Scientific Perspective." *Journal of Medical Ethics* 30 (2004): 242–47.

Shweder, Richard. "What About FGM?" And Why Understanding Culture Matters in the First Place?" In *Engaging Cultural Difference: The Multicultural Challenge in Liberal Democracies,* edited by Richard A. Shweder, Martha Minow, and Hazel Rose Markus, 216–51. New York: Russell Sage Foundation, 2002.

Silverman, Eric K. "Anthropology and Circumcision." *Annual Review of Anthropology* 33 (2004): 419–45.

Smeeton, Winifred. "Tattooing Among the Arabs of Iraq." *American Anthropologists, New Series* 39 no. 1 (1937): 53–61.

Smith, Jacqueline. "Male Circumcision and the Rights of the Child." 1998, Library of Circumcision Information and Resource Pages. http://www.cirp.org/library/legal/smith/.

Smith, Joan M. "A Child-Centered Jurisprudence: Reconciling the Rights of Children and Parents within the Family." In *Children as Equals: Exploring the Rights of the Child,* edited by Kathleen Alaimo and Brian Klug, 145–64. Lanham, MD: University Press of America, 2002.

Smucker, Philip. "Burma: Longnecks in Exile Fight to Stay Alive." *IPS-Inter Press Service,* January 20, 1989. http://www.lexisnexis.com.

Snow, Loudell F. "Folk Medical Beliefs and Their Implications for Care Patients: A Review Based on Studies among Black Americans." *Annals of Internal Medicine* 81 (1974): 82–96.

Spicker, Stuart F. "Bioethic(s): One or Many?" *Journal of Medicine and Philosophy* 23, no. 4 (1998): 347–55.

Spinner, Jeff. *The Boundaries of Citizenship: Race, Ethnicity and Nationality in the Liberal State.* Baltimore: John Hopkins University Press, 1994.

Spriggs, M. "Lesbian Couple Create a Child Who Is Deaf Like Them." *Journal of Medical Ethics* 28, no. 5 (2002): 283.

Stalker, Kirsten, and Clare Connors. "Children's Perceptions of Their Disabled Siblings: 'She's Different but It's Normal for Us'." *Children & Society* 18, no. 3 (2004): 218–30.

Staub, Ervin. "Individual and Group Identities in Genocide and Mass Killing." In *Social Identity, Intergroup Conflict and Conflict Reduction,* edited by Richard D. Ashmore, Lee Jussim, and David Wilder, 159–86. Oxford: Oxford University Press, 2001.

Stauch, Marc. "Rationality and the Refusal of Medical Treatment: A Critique of the Recent Approach of the English Courts." *Journal of Medical Ethics* 21 (1995): 162–65.

Stavenhagen, Rodolfo. "Cultural Rights: A Social Science Perspective." In *Cultural Rights and Wrongs*, edited by Halina Niec , 1–20. Paris: UNESCO Publishing, 1998.

Steinberg, Annie G., and others. "'A Little Sign and a Lot of Love': Attitudes, Perception, and Beliefs of Hispanic Families With Deaf Children." *Qualitative Health Research* 7, no.2 (1997): 202–22.

Steiner, Henry J., and Philip Alston. *International Human Rights in Context: Law, Politics, Morals.* New York: Oxford University Press, 1996.

Steiner, Hillel. "Silver Spoons and Golden Genes: Talent Differntials and Distributive Justice." In *The Moral and Political Status of Children*, edited by David Archard and Colin M. Macleod, 183–94. Oxford: Oxford University Press, 2002.

Stephens, Sharon. "Introduction: Children and the Politics of Culture in 'Late Capitalism'." In *Children and the Politics of Culture*, edited by Sharon Stephens, 3–51. Princeton, NJ: Princeton University Press, 1995.

Stephens, Sharon. "The "Cultural Fallout" of Chernobyl Radiation in Norwegian Sami Regions: Implications for Children." In *Children and the Politics of Culture*, edited by Sharon Stephens, 292–318. Princeton, NJ: Princeton University Press, 1995.

Stephens, Sharon, ed. *Children and the Politics of Culture*, Princeton, NJ: Princeton University Press, 1995.

Stephenson, Paul. *Describe the "Rights" of the Child and the Christian Response to It.* http://www.viva.org/?page_id=267.

Stewart, George A. "Interpreting the Child's Right to Identity in the UN Convention on the Rights of the Child." *Family* Law *Quarterly* 26, no. 3 (1992): 221–33.

Such, Elizabeth, and Robert Walker. "Being Responsible and Responsible Beings: Children's Understanding of Responsibility." *Children & Society* 18 (2004): 231–42.

Sunstein, Cass R. "Should Sex Equality Law Apply to Religious Institutions?" In *Is Multiculturalism Bad for Women?* edited by Susan M. Okin, 85–94. Princeton, NJ: Princeton University Press, 1999.

Svoboda, Steven J. "Attaining International Acknowledgment of Male Genital Mutilation as a Human Rights Violation." In *Male and Female Circumcision—Medical, Legal and Ethical Considerations in Pediatric Practice*, edited by George C. Denniston, Frederick Mansfield Hodges, and Marilyn Fayre Milos, 455–69. New York: Kluwer Academic/Plenum Publishers, 1999.

Swartz, Martha. "The Patient Who Refuses Medical Treatment: A Dilemma for Hospitals and Physicians." *American Journal of Law & Medicine* 11 (1985): 147–94.

Taddio, Anna, and others. "Effect of Neonatal Circumcision on Pain Responses During Vaccination in Boys." *Lancet* 345, no. 8945 (1995): 291–92.

Tahzib, Bahiyyah G. *Freedom of Religion or Belief: Ensuring Effective International Legal Protection.* The Hague: Kluwer Law International, 1996.

Tamir, Yael. "Siding with the Underdogs." In *Is Multiculturalism Bad for Women?*, edited by Susan M. Okin, 47–52. Princeton, NJ: Princeton University Press, 1999.

Tangwa, Godfrey B. "Circumcision—An African Point of View." In *Male and Female Circumcision—Medical, Legal and Ethical Considerations in Pediatric Practice*, edited by George C. Denniston, Frederick Mansfield Hodges, and Marilyn Fayre Milos, 183–93. New York: Kluwer Academic/Plenum Publishers, 1999.

Tangwa, Godfrey B. "The Traditional African Perception of a Person: Some Implications for Bioethics." *Hastings Center Report* 30, no. 5 (2000): 39–43.

Tannenbaum, Nicola. "Tattoos: Invulnerability and Power in Shan Cosmology." *American Ethnologist* 14, no. 4 (1987): 693–711.

Taylor, Charles. "The Politics of Recognition." In *Multiculturalism*, ed. Amy Gutman, 25–74. Princeton, NJ: Princeton University Press, 1994.

Te Awekotuku, Ngahuia. "Ta Moko: Maori Tattoo." In *Goldie: the Art of Charles F. Goldie*, edited by Roger Blakely and David Bateman, 109–14. Auckland: David Bateman, 1997. http://psychology.waikato.ac.nz/mpru/pubs/articles/1997awekotuku.pdf.

Te Awekotuku, Ngahuia. "Ta Moko: Culture, Body Modification, and the Psychology of Identity." *The Proceedings of the National Maori Graduates of Psychology Symposium* (2002): 123–27. http://psychology.waikato.ac.nz/mpru/mad/Proc/NMGPS_Paper_Te_Awekotuku.pdf.

Tegade, Ayodale S. "The Yoruba Cultural Construction of Health and Illness." *Nordic Journal of African Studies* 11, no. 3 (2002): 322–35.

Thwe, Pascal Khoo. *From the Land of Green Ghosts: A Burmese Odyssey*. New York, Harper Collins, 2002.

Thomas, Nigel, and Claire O'Kane. "The Ethics of Participatory Research." *Children & Society* 12 (1998): 336–48.

Thomas, Nigel, and Claire O'Kane. "When Children's Wishes and Feelings Clash with Their 'Best Interests'." *The International Journal of Children's Rights* 6 (1998): 137–54.

Tirri, Kirsi, Mary K. Tallen Runnels, and Petri Nokelainen. "A Cross-Cultural Study of Pre-Adolescents' Moral, Religious and Spiritual Questions." *British Journal of Religious Education* 27, no. 3 (2005): 207–14.

Tomanović, Smiljka. "Negotiating Children's Participation and Autonomy within Families." *International Journal of Children's Rights*, 11 (2003): 51–71.

Tucker, Bonnie P. "Deaf Culture, Cochlear Implants, and Elective Disability." *Hastings Center Report* 28, no. 4 (1998): 6–14.

Tully, James. "The Challenges of Re-imagining Citizenship and Belonging in Multicultural and Multinational Societies. " In *The Postnational Self: Belonging and Identity* edited by Ulf Hedetoft and Mette Hjort, 152–77. Minneapolis: University of Minnesota Press, 2002.

Turner, Leigh G. "Bioethics in a Pluralistic World: Truth Telling, Informed Consent, and Euthanasia." Ph.D. diss., University of Southern California, 1996.

Underhill-Sem, Yvonne. "Marked Bodies in Marginalized Places: Understanding Rationalities in Global Discourses." *Society for International Development* 46, no. 2 (2003): 13–17.

United Nations Centre for Human Rights, ed. *Legislative History of the Convention on the Rights of the Child (1978–1989)*. U.N. Doc. HR/1996.Ser.1. Geneva, 1996.

UNICEF East Asia and Pacific Regional Office (EAPRO), *The Mekong Partnership and Beyond: Papua New Guinea.* http://www.unicef.org/eapro-hivaids/general/overview.htm.

Van Bueren, Geraldine. "Children's Rights: Balancing Traditional Values and Cultural Plurality." In *Children's Rights and Traditional Values,* edited by Gillian Douglas and Leslie Sebba, 15–30. Burlington, VT: Ashgate Publishing, 1998.

Van Howe, R. S., J. S. Svoboda, J. G. Dwyer, and C. P. Price, "Involuntary Circumcision: the Legal Issues," *BJU International* 83 (Suppl. 1 1999): 63–73. http://www.cirp.org/library/legal/vanhowe5/#n27.

Veermen, Philip, and Caroline Sand. "Religion and Children's Rights." *International Journal of Children's Rights* 7, no. 4 (1999): 385–93.

Wake, Melissa, Kylie Hesketh, and James Lucas. "Teething and Tooth Eruption in Infants: A Cohort Study." *Pediatrics* 106, no. 6 (2000): 1374–79.

Walshe, Karen. "What Do Young People Today Really Think About Jesus?" *British Journal of Religious Education* 27, no. 1 (2005): 65–78.

Watson, Nick. "Well, I Know This Is Going to Sound Very Strange to You, but I Don't See Myself as a Disabled Person: Identity and Disability." *Disability & Society* 17, no. 5 (2002): 509–27.

Weber, Marc C. "Opening the Golden Door: Disability and the Law of Immigration." *Journal of Gender, Race & Justice* 8 (2004): 153–76.

Wenz, Peter. "Engineering Genetic Injustice." *Bioethics* 19, no. 1 (2005): 1–11.

Werngren-Elgstrom, Monica, Ove Dehlin, and Susanne Iwarsson. "A Swedish Prevalence Study of Deaf People Using Sign Language: A Prerequisite for Deaf Studies." *Disability & Society* 18, no. 3 (2003): 311–23.

Wetstein-Kroft, Susan B., and James W. Vargo, "Children's Attitudes towards Disability: A Review and Analysis of the Literature," *International Journal Advancement of Counselling* 7 (1984): 181–95.

Witz, Ann, and Barbara L. Marshall. "The Quality of Manhood: Masculinity and Embodiment in the Sociological Tradition." *Sociological Review* 51, no. 3 (2003): 339–56.

Wolbring, Gregor. "Where Do We Draw the Line? Surviving Eugenics in a Technological World." In *Disability and the Life Course: Global Perspective,* edited by Mark Priestley, 46. Cambridge: Cambridge Universtiy Press, 2001.

Womenaid International. *Female Gential Mutilation: Governments Respond.* http://www.womenaid.org/press/info/fgm/fgmgov.htm.

Wood, James E. "*An Apologia for Religious Human Rights.*" In *Religious Human Rights in Global Perspective—Religious Perspective,* edited by Johan D. van der Vyver, and John Jr. Witte, 455–84. The Hague: Martinus Nijhoff, 1996.

Yectman, Gentry W. "Cao Gio (Coin Rubbing): Vietnamese Attitudes Toward Health Care." *Journal of the American Medical Association* 244, no. 24 1980: 2748–50.

Young, Katharine. "The Memory of the Flesh: The Family Body in Somatic Psychology." *Body & Society* 8, no. 3 (2002): 25–47.

Zohar, Noam J. (1991). "Commentary on Khan's 'Genetic Harm: Bitten by the Body that Keeps You'?" *Bioethics* 5, no. 4 (1991): 309–11.

Zohar, Noam J. "Prospects for "Genetic Therapy"—Can a Person Benefit from Being Altered?" *Bioethics* 5, no. 4 (1991): 275–88.

Zuberi, Farhana. *Assessment of Violence Against Children in the Eastern and Southern Africa Region—Results of an Initial Desk Review for the UN Secretary General's Study on Violence against Children.* UNICEF, 2005. http://www.unicef.org/southafrica/SAF_resources_vac_esarassessment.doc.

INDEX